VICTORIAN BOSTON

∾ TWE͟͟ ͟ ͟ ͟ ͟URS ∾

Edited, and with an Introduction, by
MARY MELVIN PETRONELLA

for the New England Chapter,
the Victorian Society in America

with a Foreword by Edward W. Gordon

Northeastern University Press
Boston

Northeastern University Press

DISCLAIMER AND LIMITATION OF LIABILITY

You are responsible for your own safety while taking these walking tours. The publisher, the Victorian Society in America, the VSA/NE, the editor, the cartographer, and the authors accept no liability and hereby disclaim any liability to any party for any loss, injury, or damage incurred as a consequence, directly or indirectly, howsoever caused so far as such can be excluded by law, of the use and application of any of the contents of this informational book. We assume no legal responsibility for the completeness or accuracy of its contents or any legal responsibility for the appreciation or depreciation of the value of any premise, commercial or otherwise, by reason of inclusion in or exclusion from this book. All contents contained in this book are provided in good faith and are based on information available at the time of compilation. Some maps are diagrammatic and may be selective of street inclusion.

Library of Congress Cataloging-in-Publication Data
Victorian Boston today : twelve walking tours / edited, with an introduction, by Mary Melvin Petronella for the New England Chapter of the Victorian Society in America.
p. cm
Includes bibliographical references and index.
ISBN 1-5553-605-0 (pbk. : alk. paper)
1. Boston (Mass.)—Tours. 2. Historic buildings—Massachusetts—Boston—Guidebooks. 3. Historic sites—Massachusetts—Boston—Guidebooks.
4. Walking—Massachusetts—Boston—Guidebooks. 5. Boston (Mass.)—Buildings, structures, etc. I. Petronella, Mary Melvin, 1942– II. Victorian Society in America. New England Chapter.
F73.18.V53 2004
917.44′6104—dc22   2004005762

Designed and composed in Minion by Joyce C. Weston

Maps by Charles Bahne

Printed and bound by Edwards Brothers, Inc., Lillington, North Carolina. The paper is EB Opaque, an acid-free stock.

MANUFACTURED IN THE UNITED STATES OF AMERICA
08 07 06 05 04   5 4 3 2 1

Victorian Boston Today
is dedicated to all who have seen and
who see the value of preserving the best of the past
in order to enrich the present.

IN MEMORIAM

Rosamond Gifford
dedicated preservationist of things Victorian;
VSA/NE member; board member
and president of Gibson Society,
the Gibson House Museum.

Margaret Henderson Floyd
a founder of the New England Chapter
of the Victorian Society in America
and long time friend to the chapter.

CONTENTS

PART II. FROM DOWNTOWN BOSTON TAKE THE T TO THESE TOURS

ACKNOWLEDGMENTS

Our reaching the completion of this edition is due in large part to the steadfast support and encouragement of Edward W. Gordon, president of the New England Chapter of the Victorian Society in America (VSA/NE) since 1991, and also to the kind support and generous participation of VSA/NE's board members, past and present, whose ideas, expertise, and devotion to Boston's history, institutions, architecture, culture, and urban spaces have been a constant source of inspiration.

We are indebted to the generosity of our contributors, each dedicated to the heritage of Victorian Boston and each willing to contribute time, energy, and tours to the VSA/NE "book project." The desire of the VSA/NE to create a series of reliable scholarly tours for the 2004 edition of *Victorian Boston Today* has required extra attention to detail; we are grateful for their flexibility and gracious response to comments and suggestions. We are fortunate to have with us the editors of our first edition, Pauline Chase-Harrell and Margaret Supplee Smith, and several of its contributors, Robert B. MacKay, Eugenia Kaledin, and Margaret Henderson Floyd. And we extend special gratitude to Margaret Supplee Smith and Eugenia Kaledin, who cordially welcomed a second author to join them "on tour." We are appreciative also of the valuable ideas and useful comments of the contributors to the evolution of this edition. We are deeply obliged to a faithful group of stalwart readers, in particular Edward W. Gordon, William Pear, Vincent F. Petronella, and Charles Bahne, for their erudition and astute suggestions and comments.

The VSA/NE and *Victorian Boston Today*'s contributors, in turn, wish to express their gratitude to Mary Melvin Petronella as editor for her readiness to undertake the guidebook project; creation of the guide's introduction, preface, and introductory directions; addition of cross references between and within tours; addition of Web sites, telephone numbers, and references to the locations of sibling Boston heritage and preservation groups; implementation of correspondence and permissions for the book's illustrations; creation and unification of the twelve tours' format; amplification of diverse between-site directions; provision of various pertinent illustrations; and copious suggestions, clarifications, and supplements.

VSA/NE, the contributors, and the editor would also like to express their special appreciation of the expertise of our reader-contributor-cartographer, Charles Bahne, whose interest in our project, comprehensive knowledge about Boston, map-making ability, germane observations, rare attention to detail, and generosity during the map-making process as he adjusted between-site walking directions (and at times even walked and developed them), were of invaluable assistance to the editor. His observations (beyond Tour 12) are included in four endnotes.

The editor and Robert MacKay are especially grateful for the able perseverance of Lewis Whitlock and Sally Bradshaw, members and former board members of the VSA/NE, for their helpful contribution of essential between-site walking directions for Tour 5 (Back Bay) and Tour 4 (Commercial District). Their knowledge of Boston was of enormous benefit when, after volunteering to be the first persons to walk these tours, they supplied the editor with crucial directions. Lewis Whitlock, moreover, answered a further call to clarify several progressions between elusive addresses, and Sally Bradshaw also created the first preliminary tour index to serve as a model for others.

We would like to thank numerous individuals and Boston-area institutions for their support. We express our profound gratitude to John Weingartner, longtime senior editor of Northeastern University Press, for his steadfast interest in, counsel about, and assistance with the publication of *Victorian Boston Today*, and to Robert J. Gormley, editor-in-chief of Northeastern University Press, for his adoption of our project with such cordial guidance and encouragement. We are also most grateful to Ann Twombly, production director, Northeastern University Press, for her expertise and assistance with a myriad of detailed questions about textual details, illustrations, and maps before and during the customary manuscript preparation, and our thanks to the copyeditor, David Estrin, for his skillful work with not only our copy but also our amendments. We are most appreciative as well of Joyce Weston for the attractive style and creativity of her book design. Our gratitude also to Jill Bahcall, associate director at NUP, for her knowledgeable help.

We are indebted to the former director of the Museum of Afro-American History, Sylvia Watts McKinney, the present director, Beverly Morgan-Welch, and in particular to the help of Amber Meisenzahl, manager of Museum Services and Collections, for her kind assistance with our request to include the "Black Heritage Trail®" (please see information about the staff of the Museum of Afro-American History in our "About the Contributors" section). Our appreciation goes as well to Bernard Kramer and the Honorable Byron Rushing for their early interest and efforts on our behalf.

We are particularly indebted to Renee Inomata, Esq., of Burns and Levinson LLP, for her special expertise, help, affability, and exceptional generosity. We express special appreciation also to Anne Emerson, former executive director of the Bostonian Society, for her interest and helpful comments about our project. We are most grateful to Roberta Canter, former senior vice president of Fisher College, for permission to hold early planning and organizational meetings at Fisher.

Special gratitude is extended to Dr. William J. Buchholz, professor of English,

Information Design and Corporate Communication chair, and former English Department chair, Bentley College, for his assistance in allowing us to create, compile, edit, index, and convert files with an English Department computer, and to Dr. Bruce I. Herzberg, professor of English and current English Department chair, for his assistance in helping upgrade the computer's program in order to deal with the many technical complexities of our text. We also would like to express our appreciation to the able staff of the Bentley College English Department, Cheryl K. Rendel, senior administrative assistant, Joan P. Oliveri, academic administrative assistant, and former academic administrative assistant Diane Ridgley, for making accessible, as a "special project," the valuable part-time assistance of two talented undergraduates serving in the Bentley College English Department as work-study students: Lindsey Montgomery, accounting major, Class of 2003 (during Spring 2000), and Jessie M. Jerry, Information Design and Corporate Communication major, Class of 2004 (Fall 2000–Spring 2003). To Lindsey, and to Jessie for her special longtime assistance, our deepest thanks for resourceful, skillful, and cheerful help. We are also grateful to William B. VanderClock, instructor/CIS lab coordinator, for his conversion of several incompatible computer files; and to Maria Krings, Help Desk coordinator, and Esther Bellott, Help Desk analyst, for their assistance with numerous computer "snags"; and also to James A. Zeitler, former senior research consultant at Bentley College, for his assistance with electronic scanning before the technology was widely available.

We are very much obliged to the Boston Athenæum; the Boston Landmarks Commission; the Department of Fine Arts, Boston Public Library; the Solomon Baker Library, Bentley College; the Mugar Memorial Library, Boston University; the Goldfarb/Faber Library, Brandeis University; Cary Memorial Library, Lexington; Charlestown Public Library; the State Library, Massachusetts State House; and the Clapp Library, Wellesley College.

The generosity of the Boston community and its cultural, historic, and preservationist institutions to our project is particularly noteworthy. Under ordinary circumstances the VSA/NE would have been able to include only a fraction of the illustrations presented here.

The exceptional goodwill of those who provided illustrations from private and public collections to enhance this edition deserves particular gratitude. We are especially indebted to Robert L. Beal; Bradley H. Clarke; David R. Hocker; William M. Fowler, director, and Nicholas Graham, reference librarian, Massachusetts Historical Society; the Trustees and Martha H. Holden, director, Peabody Institute Library; Robert A. M. Stern Architects (New York); Dorothea Hass, WalkBoston; Susan Lewis, library director, Boston Architectural Center Memorial Library; Philip E. McNulty, director, and Dan Hacker, Milton Public Library; and to contributors Charles Bahne, Richard O. Card, Robert B. MacKay, Patricia C. Morris, Mary M. Petronella, and Anthony M. Sammarco.

We are also extremely gratified by those who have made feasible the inclusion of a more extensive representation of images for *Victorian Boston Today*. We are indebted to Lorna Condon, librarian and archivist, Society for the Preservation of New England Antiquities; Kristin Parker, manager of the collection, and Mario Pereira, curatorial assistant and photographic services coordinator, Isabella Stewart Gardner Museum; Sally Pierce, curator of prints and photographs, Boston Athenæum; Nancy Richard, director of the Library and Special Collections, the Bostonian Society; and Karen L. Davis, executive director of the Cambridge Historical Society.

At times our illustrations were not easy to locate; we would like to thank those whose extra effort was of such great benefit. Again our special thanks to Sally Pierce for her interest, time, and careful, detailed assistance; to Lorna Condon for her extra searching through special archives; to Nancy Richard for her ready assistance; to Kathleen L. Rawlins, assistant director, Cambridge Historical Commission, for help in tracking an elusive illustration. We are also grateful in this regard to Allan Goodrich, chief archivist, John F. Kennedy Library; Sinclair Hitchings, keeper of prints, Print Department, Boston Public Library; Aaron Schmidt, Print Department Photograph Collection, Boston Public Library; Roberta Zonghi, keeper of rare books and manuscripts, and Barbara Davis, Boston Public Library. We express appreciation also to Anita Israel, archives specialist, Longfellow National Historic site; the Board and Edie Clifford, librarian, Milton Historical Society; and Steve Rosenthal, photographer.

We should also like to thank Charlotte Houtz, information specialist, Library of Congress, Geography and Map Division; Jennifer R. Robertson, Office of Rights and Reproductions, National Portrait Gallery, Smithsonian Institution; and Jean Williams, reference librarian, Cary Memorial Library, Lexington, for her assistance in tracking down several difficult sources.

We are very much obliged to the Boston Redevelopment Authority, in particular Gregory W. Perkins, AICP, research manager, Policy Development and Research; and Janet Abramowitz, Geographic Information Systems specialist, for helping us early on with information about the Boston neighborhood maps that she had created, and for her consenting to allow our consideration of them for possible adoption. And in this regard we are much obliged to Catherine Eisenmann for her efforts in the location of these maps for possible use in planning tour itineraries. We are also grateful to Marilyn Lanza, who graciously enabled us to visit Annie Fields's garden.

Our special appreciation to Elise Ciregna for typing our early directions and guidelines for contributors, several biographies, a tour's index, and the transcription of an entire tour. Particular gratitude is also due to Jack Grinold, who, as always, provided generous crucial assistance, and to Anthony M. Sammarco for his suggestions and for keeping track of finances. We would like to express our gratitude to Helen C. Hannon for her suggestions, solutions, help with pasting and photocopying, creating and typing indices, and coordinating board members Margaret Clarke, Laura D. Eisener, Mary Ethel Grady, Paul Kenworthy, Sally Ann Kydd, and Douglas S. McNeish in the creation of initial indices for tours. Our deep appreciation goes to each. We thank also Margaret Clarke, Sally Ann Kydd, Phebe Goodman, and John Neale for each reading a tour.

We express special gratitude to Vincent F. Petronella, an invaluable resource in the preparation of Tour 6, for taking time to review our manuscript, photographing an archival illustration, and working with the complexities of the illustrations. Thanks are also due to Richard Card and to Northeastern University Press for help with illustration scanning. We would like to thank Mark Vassar, resident fellow at the Cambridge Historical Society, for personally photographing the Kennedy Biscuit Box so that it might be included.

Our deep gratitude goes to the following VSA/NE board members and members past and present—Charles Bahne, John Burrows, Margaret Clarke, Rupert Davis, Laurie Estes, Rosamond Gifford, Ed Gordon, Jim Gorman, Mary Ethel Grady, Jack Grinold, Helen C. Hannon, Anne Harbour, Pauline Chase-Harrell, Karen Hilliard, Stephen Jerome, Diane L. Kuebler, Sally Ann Kydd, Constance W. McMillan, Ann Marie Moore, William H. Pear II, Lois G. Peters, Karen Peterson, Joseph A. Russo, Anthony M. Sammarco, Eileen ("Lolly") Sharpe, Kenneth Turino, Jan Turnquist, Janet R. Young, and William S. Young—who helped with initial planning; the location of useful remainder files and data from our 1975 edition; providing information about the creation of the original edition; making available needed space in which to hold meetings; providing library privileges; printing and photographic tips; identifying street addresses; supplying photocopying assistance; updating us about changes in the cityscape; making telephone calls; helping to keep costs down; suggesting relevant publications and contacts; and preparing for the book's arrival.

Finally, a heartfelt "thank-you" from the editor to VSA/NE board members and members—especially to Susan Ashbrook, Sally Bradshaw, Rupert Davis, Sheila Donahue, Catherine Eisenmann, Edward Gordon, Mary Ethel Grady, Gigi Grenier, Jack Grinold, Mabel-Marie Herweg, Annmarie Gionet Hubing, Sally Ann Kydd, Bill Pear, Vincent Petronella, Ken Turino, and Lewis Whitlock—whose words of encouragement were splendidly timed to lighten the endeavor.

THE NEW ENGLAND CHAPTER OF THE VICTORIAN SOCIETY IN AMERICA

The founding of the New England Chapter of the Victorian Society in America (VSA/NE), in 1972, helped to rally a constituency for the nascent local historic preservation movement in Boston and New England.

The New England Chapter is one of twenty that make up the national Victorian Society in America (VSA), a nonprofit organization based in Philadelphia (205 South Camac St., Philadelphia, PA 19107; www.victoriansociety.org (215)-545-8340). The VSA supports the education, preservation, and enjoyment of the Victorian heritage of the United States by sponsoring lectures, study tours, and symposia; providing summer school programs in Newport, Rhode Island, and London, England; publishing *Nineteenth Century Magazine* and the quarterly *Victorian Newsletter*; and holding annual meetings (featuring tours of private residences) to spotlight the Victoriana of select cities in the United States.

The VSA was founded in 1966. Six years later, the New England Chapter was organized and has had its headquarters at the Gibson House Museum, 137 Beacon St. in Boston's Back Bay, since 1974. The VSA/NE newsletter, *The Beacon*, features an article about Victorian New England, and keeps its membership informed about current neighborhood walks, lectures, special events, and upcoming trips.

The mission of the VSA/NE is twofold. First and foremost, the Society strives to educate the public about the myriad aspects of Victorian culture available in New England by sponsoring seasonal walking tours, primarily of Boston-area neighborhoods, as well as throughout the year offering lectures on subjects that include period architecture, fine and decorative arts, historic attire, interior design, personalities, gardens, music, photography, literature, and social customs, and leading group tours to Victorian sites farther afield.

In its mission to enlighten the public, the VSA/NE welcomes the opportunity to cosponsor educational programs with other cultural nonprofit organizations and has collaborated on special tours and talks with many Boston-area institutions, including the Society of Architectural Historians, the Bay State Historical League, the Boston Browning Society, Friends of the Julia Margaret Cameron Trust, the Boston Athenæum, the Elder Hostel at Bentley College, and the Gibson Society, Inc.

Second, the Society serves as an advocate for the preservation of Boston's and New England's nineteenth-century built environment. Society members testify at public hearings on behalf of endangered Victorian cultural resources and promote preservation awareness through the VSA/NE's popular annual Preservation Awards Program (see p. xix), which honors those who have saved historic properties from destruction and/or returned historic buildings, objects, and landscapes to their original glory.

Edward W. Gordon, President
New England Chapter, Victorian Society in America

New England Chapter, Victorian Society in America
Gibson House Museum
137 Beacon St.
Boston, MA 02116

To reach the Gibson House Museum and the VSA/NE: telephone (617)-267-6338.

NEW ENGLAND CHAPTER OF
THE VICTORIAN SOCIETY IN AMERICA (VSA/NE)
BOARD OF DIRECTORS, 2004

President
Edward W. Gordon

Vice Presidents
Rupert Davis, First Vice President
Jack Grinold, Second Vice President

Treasurer
Anthony Mitchell Sammarco

Secretary
Mary Ethel Grady

Preservation Awards Chairperson
Jack Grinold

The Beacon Editors
Mary Ethel Grady and Edward W. Gordon

Board Members

Richard O. Card	Sally Ann Kydd
Karen Chaney	Douglas McNeish
Elise M. Ciregna	Marilee Boyd Meyer
Margaret L. Clarke	Ann Marie Moore
Laura D. Eisener	William Pear II
Ghislaine Grenier	Lumona June Petroff
Mabel-Marie Herweg	Mary Melvin Petronella
Karen Hilliard	Brian Powell
Annemarie Gionet-Hubing	Barbara Pugliese
Paul Kenworthy	Jan Turnquist
Kiki Kneeland	Kenneth Turino
Diane L. Kuebler	Carolyn Wahto

TO HONOR THOSE WHO HAVE
ADVANCED THE CAUSE OF
VICTORIAN-ERA HERITAGE

A Selection of the New England Chapter of the Victorian Society in America Preservation, Commendation, and Lifetime Achievement Awards, 1973–2004

Jack Grinold, Preservation Awards Chairperson, 1991–

Preservation Awards are presented to projects that represent a noteworthy effort in the preservation of a significant aspect of New England's Victorian-era heritage. Projects are considered in the following three categories:

Victorian-Era Architecture and Building
Victorian-Era Public Spaces
Victorian-Era Cultural and Social History

Lifetime Achievement Awards are presented to an individual whose devotion and dedication to preservation has helped maintain New England's Victorian heritage. (Please note: many of our tours visit a variety of these award sites.)

2004 PRESERVATION AWARDS

Massachusetts Historical Society, for renovation and restoration
Historic New England (formerly SPNEA), Harrison Gray Otis House, for Victorian boardinghouse recreation
Strawbery Banke Museum, Portsmouth, New Hampshire, for restoration of the Goodwin Garden, "Tanglewood Grove," and Greenhouse
Lifetime Achievement Award: **Stanley Smith,** longtime Executive Director, Historic Boston, Inc. (HBI)

2003 PRESERVATION AWARDS

The Boston Athenaeum, for major renovation and acclimatization to preserve their collections, and for preservation of the fifth-floor Reading Room, the second-floor Long Room, and the Director's Room

Hildene, the estate of Robert Todd Lincoln, Manchester, Vermont, for restoration of its formal garden and the kitchen garden

The Longfellow National Historic Site, for restoration of the interior

Lifetime Achievement Award: **James Alexander,** for his work as a preservation architect

2002 PRESERVATION AWARDS

The Fenway Studios, Ipswich Street, for restoration of the Arts and Crafts brick facade (1905)

The Rye Driftwood Garden Club, Rye, New Hampshire, for the care and upkeep of Celia Thaxter's Garden on Appledore Island

The Massachusetts National Guard Military Museum and Archives, for restoration of the Worcester Armory (1891) and the preservation of the Massachusetts National Guard records (from 1636)

Lifetime Achievement Award: **Eric Parkman Smith,** longtime volunteer at Louisa May Alcott's Orchard House

2001 PRESERVATION AWARDS

Worcester Redevelopment Authority, for restoration of Union Station

The Ayer Mansion, Commonwealth Avenue, for restoration of the Tiffany interior

The Stonehurst Museum, Waltham, for restoration of the Frederick Law Olmsted Landscape (1886) surrounding the Robert Treat Paine Estate

Lifetime Achievement Award: **Judith Brew McDonough,** executive director, Boston Landmarks Commission and the Massachusetts Historical Commission

2000 PRESERVATION AWARDS

Memorial Hall, Harvard University, for restoration of the tower and returning it to the roof

Orchard House Museum, Concord, for restoration of Bronson Alcott's study

Beacon Hill Garden Club

Lifetime Achievement Award: **Jonathan Fairbanks,** longtime curator of American Decorative Arts at the Museum of Fine Arts and a founding member of the VSA/NE

1999 PRESERVATION AWARDS

New England College of Optometry, Commonwealth Avenue, for restoration

Lesley College, Cambridge, for building restoration

Hancock Shaker Village, Pittsfield

Lifetime Achievement Award: **Charles M. Sullivan,** longtime director of the Cambridge Historical Commission

1998 PRESERVATION AWARDS

The Brookline Music School, for restoration of the Hill-Kennard-Ogden House
Forest Hills Cemetery, for restoration
Saint-Gaudens National Historic Site, Cornish, New Hampshire
Lifetime Achievement Award: **Robert Neiley,** for long-term work as a preservation architect

1997 PRESERVATION AWARDS

Jordan Hall, the New England Conservatory
Mount Auburn Cemetery
Joan Severa, for *Dressed for the Photographer*
Lifetime Achievement Award: **Stella Trafford,** advocate for public parks—Commonwealth Avenue Mall and the Public Garden

1996 PRESERVATION AWARDS

Boston Public Library, for restoration
Walden Woods Project, Concord
Norlands, Livermore, Maine
Lifetime Achievement Award: **Antonia Pollak**, long-term executive director of the Boston Preservation Alliance

1995 PRESERVATION AWARDS

South Church, Andover, for restoration of the church steeple
The Arnold Arboretum
State House Flag Project, for restoration
Lifetime Achievement Award: **Henry Lee,** president of the Friends of Boston Public Gardens, for his dedication to the preservation of the Boston Public Garden

1994 PRESERVATION AWARDS

Flint Memorial Library, Reading
Boston University Dormitories, Bay State Road
Blackstone/Franklin Park Squares Neighborhood Association, South End
Northeastern University Press, for the publication of *From Jo March's Attic: Stories of Intrigue and Suspense*, Madeleine B. Stern and Daniel Shealy, editors

Lifetime Achievement Award: **Ann Beha,** for her work as a preservation architect

1992–93 PRESERVATION AWARDS

Church of the Covenant, Boston
Marlene D. Merrill, editor, *Growing Up in Boston's Gilded Age: The Journals of Alice Stone Blackwell*

Commendations

Jacob Wirth Restaurant, Boston
Larz Anderson Park, Brookline
Women's Educational and Industrial Union, editors, *Boston Cooks*

1991 PRESERVATION AWARDS

Lynn Heritage State Park
Saint-Gaudens's *Robert Gould Shaw and the 54th Regiment Memorial,* Boston Common, for restoration
Morse Libby Mansion, Portland, Maine

Commendations

Wilbur F. Haven House, Malden
Henderson Boat House, Northeastern University
South End Landmark District, for Historic Landmark Plaques

1990 PRESERVATION AWARDS

Carousel, Oak Bluffs, Martha's Vineyard
Hotel Barre, Barre
Commonwealth Vintage Dancers

1989 PRESERVATION AWARDS

The Berkeley Building, Boylston Street
The Public Garden, for reinstatement of ice skating
The Dimock Community Health Center, Roxbury
Office of the Senate President, for restoration, State House, Boston

1988 PRESERVATION AWARD

Museum of Afro-American History, Smith Court, Beacon Hill, for restoration

1987 PRESERVATION AWARD

Graham Gund, for Bulfinch Square, Cambridge

1986 PRESERVATION AWARDS

New Old South Church, Copley Square, for restoration, Dan Coolidge, architect
Municipal Building, Codman Square

1985 PRESERVATION AWARD

Historic Boston

1984 PRESERVATION AWARD

Abbot Lowell Cummings, architectural historian

1983 PRESERVATION AWARDS

Bedford Building, Boston
Hopkinton Supply Company, restoration of the Oakes Ames Memorial Hall, North
    Easton
Carol Zellie, for *Beyond the Neck*

1982 PRESERVATION AWARD

Worcester County's Mechanics Hall, restoration and revitalization as a concert hall

1981 PRESERVATION AWARDS

Hartford Architecture Conservatory, Connecticut
Victoria Society of Maine Women
John A. Sullivan
Hudson Historical Society, Hudson
Preservation Society of Newport County, Rhode Island
Vergennes Main Street Revitalization Committee, Vermont
Worcester County's Mechanics Hall, for restoration and revitalization as a concert hall

1980 PRESERVATION AWARDS

Richard Heath, Franklin Park Alliance
Alan Emmett, for *Cambridge, Massachusetts: The Changing of a Landscape*
Adams Nervine Asylum, Jamaica Plain, for restoration

Charles Sullivan, responsible for placement of Charles River Basin on the National Register

1978–79 PRESERVATION AWARDS

Commercial Street Elderly Housing, North End
Kathlyn Hatch, teacher
Ann Beha, architect
CDM, Inc., developer
Unihab/Renovate Inc., developer

1977 PRESERVATION AWARD

Swan Boats–the Paget Family, Boston Common, one hundredth anniversary of operations

1976 PRESERVATION AWARD

Currier Museum, Manchester, New Hampshire, for "A Sense of Place, A Way of Life" Exhibit

1975 PRESERVATION AWARDS

Dorchester Savings Bank, for supporting *Church Building in Boston 1720–1970,* by Douglass Shand-Tucci
Massachusetts Housing Finance Agency of Boston, for restoration

1974 PRESERVATION AWARDS

Alan Chesney, landscape architect, Mount Auburn Cemetery, Cambridge
Jonathan Fairbanks, for "Confident America" Exhibit, Museum of Fine Arts
Mr. and Mrs. Kenneth Sampson, for preservation of the Gardner Kingman House, Brockton

1973 PRESERVATION AWARD

Raymond Cattle Company, for restoration of the Ames-Webster House, Commonwealth Avenue

FOREWORD

It is with great pleasure that the New England Chapter of the Victorian Society in America (VSA/NE) presents the second edition of *Victorian Boston Today.* Our first edition, *Victorian Boston Today: Ten Walking Tours,* edited by Pauline Chase-Harrell and Margaret Supplee Smith, was privately printed in 1975 for the American Bicentennial. It fostered a new appreciation of Boston's Victorian architecture, civic art, and urban neighborhoods at a time when several Victorian landmarks were threatened by demolition or had recently succumbed to the wrecker's ball.

The first edition of *Victorian Boston Today* became a valuable resource for scholars and local residents, as well as visitors to the city. Still available in many public libraries in the Boston area, the first edition provided entrée to some of Boston's most fascinating quarters for those who wished to learn about the evolution of Boston neighborhoods, about the wide range of historic architectural styles represented within the tour areas, and about interesting anecdotes associated with Victorian landmarks and luminaries.

The second edition of the VSA/NE's guidebook, inspired by our first edition, is indebted to the invaluable volunteer efforts of the VSA/NE's board and chapter members, and of the members of Boston's academic and historic preservation communities. Above all, the guidebook's production is inextricably bound to the extraordinary efforts of its editor, Professor Mary Melvin Petronella of Bentley College. As a result of Mary's perseverance and talents as a scholar and editor, *Victorian Boston Today* will not only attract longtime students of Boston history and architecture but also lure visitors to Boston who are interested in American culture and urban history.

Most chapters in this knowledgeable guide identify the architects, construction dates, and noteworthy occupants of Victorian Boston's most interesting buildings and sites. It thus serves as an up-to-date reference book that reflects the rich inventory of Victorian cultural resources of today's Boston. Its publication is a fitting way for the New England Chapter of the Victorian Society in America to celebrate thirty-two years as a nonprofit cultural organization and to commemorate the one hundred third anniversary of the death of a remarkable era's namesake: Queen Victoria (1819–1901).

Edward W. Gordon, President
New England Chapter, Victorian Society in America

INTRODUCTION: DISCOVERING TODAY'S VICTORIAN BOSTON

Cities ... are certain to be in layers ... each representing either a long or rapid stage of growth and development, different from its predecessor, but unerringly growing out of and resting on it. ... Something of this kind has certainly taken place in Boston.

—Walt Whitman, *Specimen Days,* 1906

Growing out of and resting on the city's acclaimed Colonial and Federal substrata, Boston's impressive Victorian heritage provides us with a plethora of accessible, affordable, and inspiring delights. Our guidebook, a celebration of the attractions of Victorian Boston, presents twelve tours that provide the walker and the armchair traveler alike a personal discovery of the city's outstanding Victorian treasure trove.

Dr. Oliver Wendell Holmes, in the persona of "Little Boston," heralded the city as "the thinking centre of the continent, and therefore of the planet" (*Poet at the Breakfast Table* 83). With similiar city-chauvinism, we proclaim that Boston's collection of nineteenth-century properties, possessions, and resources, its substantial Victorian "layer" and evocative genius loci, make it the Victorian hub of New England. Accordingly, the purpose of the present edition is to supply both the native and the visitor with a vade mecum—a take-along guide—to the best of Victorian Boston today. Appropriate for a "thinking centre" such as Boston, our guide is also a scholarly resource for those interested in an illumination of the city's nineteenth-century urban history, architecture, literature, culture, and socioeconomic roots. In addition, our intimate "bookshelf-to-street-corner" exploration of Boston has a mission: to serve as inspiration for the ongoing preservation of the city's outstanding heritage.

The Victorian Era

The Victorian era falls between 1837, when Victoria (born 1819) was crowned queen of England, and 1901, the year of her death. Our primary interest lies between these years. However, because the tenor of "Victorian" life changed little in Boston during her son Edward VII's reign (1901–10), and the tone of the era lingered until the dramatic changes caused by World War I, our tours will, occasionally, include items from these later years. Hence, the scope of our exploration bridges antebellum, Civil War (1861–65), postbellum, fin-de-siècle, and early-twentieth-century Boston.

"Victorian" Boston

Boston is deeply associated in the American mind with the spirit of freedom, as exemplified by Ralph Waldo Emerson's poem "Boston":

> The cargo came! and who could blame
> If *Indians* seized the tea,
> And, chest by chest, let down the same,
> Into the laughing sea?
> For what avail the plough or sail,
> Or land or life, if freedom fail?

The Boston/freedom connection is probably the reason some question whether the term "Victorian" is an appropriate description of a city fundamental to the American Revolution. If Bostonians "lived in an atmosphere of the Stamp Act, the Tea Tax, and the Boston Massacre" (Adams, *Education* 41), is it fitting to describe the city with the name of an era so intimately linked to the British and the British monarchy?

For an informed answer we turn to Henry Adams (1838–1918), whose family members (great-grandfather, President John Adams; grandfather, President John Quincy Adams; and father, Charles Francis Adams) bridged the Colonial, Federal, and Victorian eras. In *The Education of Henry Adams* (1907), the author explains that in spite of Boston's former animosity toward and break with England, the city had a long-standing affinity with and veneration for English values. Adams makes clear that "the tone of nineteenth-century Boston society was Colonial" (22)—still English in spirit.

This revelation allows us to appreciate how fitting the designation "Victorian" is for Boston of the 1800s. Adams goes on to describe the era by saying that "the true Bostonian always knelt in self-abasement before the majesty of English standards" (*Education* 22); and then he specifies that British influence "ruled [Boston] society long after" the mid-nineteenth century. In a similar vein, the New England historian Van Wyck Brooks points out that "the more the center of gravity of the nation shifted toward the West, the more the Boston mind, thrown back on itself, resumed its old colonial allegiance" (*Flowering* 91).

Although "nationalism was a typical feature of American Victorianism" (D. W. Howe 7) and the creation of a national literature was an important endeavor of nineteenth-century American writers, English influence had remained astonishingly potent in Boston in spite of the Tea Party. In addition, the intensity of

Queen Victoria (1867), by the London artist F. A. Tilt, watercolor on enamel with gold frame (and detail of surrounding maroon velvet and gold fretwork frame). This portrait was commissioned by Queen Victoria to serve as her personal gift to the merchant, banker, and philanthropist George Peabody (1795–1869). It was, in turn, his gift to the town that now bears his name, Peabody, Mass. *(Courtesy of Peabody, Mass., Collection of Peabody Institute Library.)*

Queen Victoria's March 28, 1866, letter from Windsor Castle reads: "[Be] assured by herself how deeply she appreciates the noble act of more than princely munificence, by which he has sought to relieve the wants of her poorer subjects residing in London [Peabody Sq., Islington]" (Hanaford 143). For the portrait sitting Queen Victoria is dressed in "demi-robes of state," a rare event occurring so "soon" after the 1861 death of Prince Albert. The queen, who lived in seclusion until 1866, did not resume her customary life until the late 1870s. She wears the Garter, the Koh-i-noor diamond, and a jeweled cross, which were presented to her by Prince Albert.

Boston's interest in Queen Victoria and her royal activities should not be underestimated. Bostonians had enjoyed entertaining His Royal Highness Albert Edward, prince of Wales,[1] in 1860, and in 1870 the queen's favorite son, Prince Arthur, duke of Connaught, whose presence had paid tribute to the return of the embalmed body of the financier-philanthropist George Peabody[2] to the United States. Peabody,[3] who had not accepted knighthood or the Grand Cross of the Order of Bath from the queen in appreciation of his benevolence to London's poor, gratefully received instead an individually commissioned portrait[4] of Her Royal Highness and her personal note[5] of gratitude.

Queen Victoria and the royal family were in the news as well as on the lips and in the imagination of Bostonians. In fact, the stated objective in the Constitution of Boston's "Victorian Club" was the dissemination of information about the British Empire (*Constitution* 5). Literary Boston, of course, was aware that Longfellow had created a singular stir at court when he had met Queen Victoria, and that Oliver Wendell Holmes also had been invited to meet the queen. It is possible that Isabella Stewart Gardner (1840–1924), who wore her hair during her adolescence in the same style as young Queen Victoria, and whose friends addressed her at times as "Queen" (Lingner)—sometimes even as "Queen of the Holy Back Bay" (Tharp 156)—had Queen Victoria's royal staircase in Buckingham Palace in mind when

Isabella Stewart Gardner (1888), by John Singer Sargent. *(Courtesy of the Isabella Stewart Gardner Museum, Boston.)* "On the landing at the top of the horse-shoe staircase stood Mrs. Gardner, dressed in black, her diamond antennae waving above her head; up the stairs the representatives of Boston's proudest families climbed to greet their hostess . . . some of them inwardly fuming, but most of them amused at the homage Mrs. Gardner had exacted of them." Morris Carter, *Isabella Stewart Gardner and Fenway Court,* Houghton Mifflin, 1925.

she created a similarly shaped horse-shoe staircase in the white Music Room (no longer extant) in her museum. Certainly, Gardner did not hesitate to play the "royal role" when she greeted her guests at the top of the staircase during the opening (1903) of Fenway Court. The name Gardner and her friends used for her museum-home had a contemporary connotation far beyond the central courtyard of the Isabella Stewart Gardner Museum.

Mrs. Gardner's longtime friend Henry Adams [6] illuminates another significant "Victorian" aspect of nineteenth-century Boston: its English "social standards"—that is, Boston society's almost impregnable social hierarchy, something the young Mrs. John Lowell Gardner, an "outsider" from New York City, had been herself subjected to. Adams illustrates this unyielding attitude when he describes, in direct contrast to the conventional Brahmin, the unusual nature of his father, Charles Francis Adams (Lincoln's minister to England during the Civil War): "Almost alone among his Boston contemporaries, he was not English in feelings or in sympathies. . . . [He was] indifferent to social distinction. Never once in forty years of intimacy did his son notice in him a trace of snobbishness" (*Education* 29).

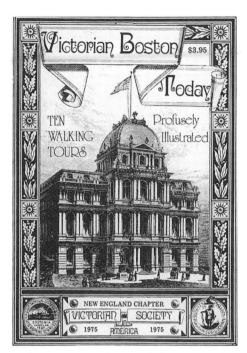

The engraving on the cover[8] of the VSA/NE's *Victorian Boston Today* (1975) heralded an important icon of post–Civil War Boston, its new City Hall (1861–65) by Bryant and Gilman, and at the same time affirmed the recent hard-fought but victorious drive for the adaptive preservation of Boston's "Old" City Hall.

Boston's well-known "English" social impenetrability—sometimes referred to as "Cold Roast Boston," sometimes spoken of gently as the tradition of "the American gentry"—was as extensive as it was excessive. In fact, the city's social traditions are a dominant theme in William Dean Howells's classic novel, *The Rise of Silas Lapham* (1885), in which the destruction by fire of Lapham's extravagant new Beacon Street town house, built on landfill in the fashionable Back Bay, comes to symbolize a vain effort by the Laphams to "rise" in Boston Society.

Victorian Boston Today

Pauline Chase-Harrell and Margaret Supplee Smith, when editing our first, privately printed edition (1975), faced the predicament of having to do justice to the innumerable luminaries and the myriad of outstanding Victorian sites offered in Boston. They addressed this quandary by asking a daunting series of questions:

Whom should we omit? Oliver Wendell Holmes,[7] the Autocrat of the Breakfast Table, or his friend James [T.] Fields, who made Boston the publishing center of the United States? Charles Bulfinch, who shaped Boston at the beginning of the century, or Henry Hobson Richardson, who recreated much of it in his own image toward the end of the century? Elizabeth Palmer Peabody, proprietress of its intellectual center and educator of its children? Wendell Phillips or Theodore Parker, leaders of the abolition movement and keepers of Boston's conscience? Amos A. Lawrence, who dealt in textiles and industrial cities? Or Isabella Stewart Gardner and Henry Lee Higginson, who created art museums and symphony orchestras?

And even if we could choose among the well-known names, what about the Immigrant, both foreign and rural, who swelled the city, creating the need for new residential areas? The Engineer, who built the vast transportation system and indeed the very land to be built on? The Builder, who fashioned red brick Boston and the Victorian suburbs? (Harrell and Smith iii).

In creating the present edition we faced the same task of dealing with the astounding variety of Victorian resources in today's Boston. Actually, the approach of both editions may be described as replicating Lytton Strachey's method of selection among a tantalizing number of nineteenth-century personalities for his *Eminent Victorians* (1918). Using Strachey's analogy to describe our modus operandi,

A section of the masthead engraving of *Ballou's Pictorial Magazine* for 1857.
(Boston Public Library/Rare Print Department; courtesy of the Trustees.)
Boston Harbor provides an appropriate image for the analogy of a vast repository within which one may discover revelations about Victorian Boston. Here the dome of the State House dominates a picturesque antebellum skyline. From left to center along the old waterfront, we see the columns and original dome of the Custom House, the front pediment of Faneuil Hall, topped by its cupola, and the front pediment and facade of Quincy Market (1825–26), which abutted the harbor before landfill made it landlocked. The lineup of prosperous clipper ships affords a view of Boston's famous "forest of masts," with a sign of major change, the new side-wheel steamship, entering the scene.

we have examined Boston's "obscure recesses hitherto undivined, [by] row[ing] out over . . . [its] great ocean of material, and lower[ing] down, here and there, a little bucket, which will bring up to the light of day some characteristic specimen" (v)—a feature of Victorian Boston. In fact, each of the twelve tours in *Victorian Boston Today* may be thought of as a singular specimen bucket, drawn from a vast repository within which one discovers remarkable reflections and curious revelations about facets of Victorian Boston. Viewed as a whole, the series of tours offers a brimming collection of Boston Victoriana.

OUR COLLECTION OF TOURS

Boston's Nineteenth-Century Waterfront

Pauline Chase-Harrell provides us with a sophisticated look at Boston's waterfront. As we savor the salt flavor of the romantic clipper-ship era and witness the consequence of the waterfront's "wharfing out," we encounter the site of T Wharf, from which the 54th Massachusetts Regiment departed during the Civil War, as well as a Boston Landmark "street pattern"—which recognizes the historic "crooked and narrow" streets of old Boston. A sweeping view of Boston Harbor, including the scene that first appeared to most of Boston's nineteenth-century immigrants, is just one of the diversions of this tour, where architectural styles change before us while we view the evolution of the waterfront's expansion and observe the latest modification caused by Boston's Big Dig, the Central Artery/tunnel project.

Boston's South End: Mid-Nineteenth-Century Urban Planning and Architecture

We tour the largest Victorian brick row-house district in the United States in the company of Margaret Supplee Smith and Richard O. Card. Smith's original tour, used as an admirable model for the new contributors to this edition, has been enhanced for today's walkers by Richard O. Card, founder of the South End Historical Society. While we view the South End's signature residential squares, the evolution of its fashionable St. James Hotel (Franklin Square House), and the setting of Childe Hassam's *Rainy Day, Boston*, we realize that even classic architecture must be adapted for different uses if it is to survive in a central urban setting.

Ethnic Diversity in the Victorian North End

We are glad to feature Boston's nineteenth-century immigrant history with Will Holton's adroit exploration of the North End. Holton sheds light on the reluctance of many Bostonians to deal with the hodgepodge nature of the Victorian North End in spite of its famous American Revolutionary sites. The complexity and plight of the populace in this evolving immigrant quarter on the edge of the waterfront, who grappled with poverty, frequent intergroup conflict, substandard hous-

ing, and itinerant sailors "on leave," moved the renowned "Father" Taylor, a prototype for Herman Melville's preacher Father Mapple in *Moby-Dick* (1851), and
Pauline Agassiz Shaw to organize benevolent societies, which have provided assistance to generations of seamen and immigrants to this day.

The Commercial District

Robert B. MacKay's tour, a dream come true for architecture buffs, is an elucida-
tion of the splendid variety of Victorian architectural styles that are the positive
consequence of the central business and financial district's devastation by the
Great Fire of 1872. His exploration of the architectural and commercial renaissance
that took place during the following decade recognizes the expertise, confidence,
and exuberance of nineteenth-century Boston business. MacKay's longtime interest in the Charles Street Jail, whose cruciform design was a new concept in prison
reform (and widely acclaimed far beyond Boston), provides energetic walkers with
an alternative starting point for touring the Commercial District.

Touring through Time to the Heart of Back Bay

Margaret Henderson Floyd's reworking of her explication of Back Bay architecture
and the decorative arts from the first edition is a lively "tour-critique" of twentieth-
century Back Bay architecture juxtaposed with the grandeur of its Victorian
Franco-Anglo inheritance. In an adept commentary on the scale and presence of
twentieth-century buildings in the milieu of the Back Bay, Floyd commends the
Hancock Tower, I. M. Pei's "elegant accent for Boston's skyline," and praises 222
Berkeley Street, Robert A. M. Stern's welcome alleviation of what had begun as a
disproportionate alteration to Boylston Street's ambiance. While affirming worthy
new architectural and restoration champions—and being frank about twentieth-
century raw spots—Floyd also provides us an intimate visit within five Victorian
magna opera in the heart of Back Bay.

Floyd's interior descriptions of Arlington, Trinity, and New Old South churches,
the Boston Public Library, and the Frederick L. Ames House include the artwork of
mural painters, stained glass designers, woodworkers, and sculptors—those nineteenth-century collaborators in decorative arts who enhanced the Back Bay's mas-
terworks of architecture.

Floyd, a founding member of the VSA/NE, is fondly remembered by our members and Bostonians at large for her substantial scholarly contribution to the city's
cultural history.

Boston's Victorian Authors: Thinkers in the Center of the Planet

It has been a delight for me, while editing this edition, to join Eugenia Kaledin "on
tour" to present "Boston's Victorian Authors: Thinkers in the Center of the Planet,"
whose title is a lighthearted parody of Oliver Wendell Holmes's city conceit. Walk-

ing in the company of a host of Boston's nineteenth-century authors, we peruse the homes, buildings, and topography with which they were familiar, including the streetscape Henry James described in *The American Scene* as "the happiest street scene in the country" (243)—Beacon Hill's Mt. Vernon Street. As literary enthusiasts, we explore the exceptional role played by Boston's Victorian authors in determining currents of American thought and fiction and offer the walker and reader a bountiful series of entrées for a literary feast.

Black Heritage Trail®

Eager to draw attention to the diversity of nineteenth-century Boston, we are particularly pleased to highlight the vital role played by African-American Victorians in the center of Boston as recorded in "Black Heritage Trail®" (published here with the kind permission of the Museum of Afro-American History).

Along the Trail we encounter the Phillips Street address of an Underground Railroad station on Beacon Hill, which was the home of Lewis and Harriet Hayden, who successfully provided refuge for fugitive slaves. We also see the Pinckney Street home of John J. Smith, whose barber shop, often frequented by Senator Charles Sumner, was a Boston rendezvous point for fugitive slaves. We hear about Joshua B. Smith, the former fugitive slave and employee of the Shaw family, who became a state representative from Cambridge and established a fund to erect the *Robert Gould Shaw and 54th Regiment Memorial*. Don't miss the lovely old African Meeting House on Smith Ct., where William Lloyd Garrison founded the New England Anti-Slavery Society. Of interest also are the notable people who were responsible for the evolving creation of "Black Heritage Trail,®" Susan Bailey Thurman, J. Marcus Mitchell, Gaunzetta L. Mitchell, the Honorable Byron Rushing, and the staff of the Museum of Afro-American History.

Walking with Women in Victorian Boston

We are pleased to renew our emphasis on the contributions of nineteenth-century women with the longtime Boston women's history advocate Patricia C. Morris. Beyond highlighting important women—some of whose names we are familiar with, many of whose names we seldom encounter (Ellen Swallow Richards, Maria W. Stewart, Harriet Clisby)—Morris connects their names with Boston sites such as the interior of the Bulfinch State House as well as the streets and parks with which each was intimate. Such personal linking of Boston's historic buildings and neighborhoods with yesterday's women weaves a web of familiarity and provides confirmation of their important gifts to both their society and ours.

Charlestown in the Victorian Era

We are pleased to be able to include two tours written by Edward W. Gordon, president of VSA/NE, and a dedicated advocate of the historic, cultural, and architectural milieu of Boston. Gordon's tour de force, "Charlestown in the Victorian Era," recognizes prominent nineteenth-century Charlestown residents, evokes picturesque civic vignettes, and reveals the absorbing and often overlooked Victorian heritage of a community usually associated with Boston's Revolutionary roots.

Victorian Boston's Chocolate Village

It will be difficult to resist sampling Boston aficionado Anthony Mitchell Sammarco's "Victorian Boston's Chocolate Village." Sammarco, a sought-after lecturer about the history of Victorian Boston and author of numerous volumes of Boston-area pictorial histories, explores the architectural highlights, industrial development, and history of an unusual nineteenth-century mill village, whose aroma whetted Bostonian's craving for delicacies made from imported cacao beans. When we encounter the very mill that extracted the nascent chocolate from the bean, we begin to appreciate the creative business and marketing techniques of the Baker Chocolate Company—a classic nineteenth-century Boston business success. Don't forget to "BYO" (bring your own) chocolate!

Victorian Jamaica Plain: Monument Sq. and Sumner Hill

If you happen to be looking for commentary by a connoisseur of Victorian neighborhoods and would enjoy seeing a splendid variety of vintage houses noteworthy for their ornamentation and prominent Victorian owners, a vantage point—accompanied by a lyrical description of its scene and followed by a firsthand look at its sites—all with a sprinkling of ecclesiastical architecture in a leafy suburban setting, then Gordon's "Victorian Jamaica Plain" is for you.

A Victorian Boulevard Preserved: Cambridge's Brattle Street

Cambridge and Boston enthusiast Charles Bahne, who designed the fine maps for our edition, provides us a breath of bucolic fresh air along Brattle Street, one of the outstanding Victorian streetscapes in the United States. This "museum of American domestic architecture" includes the Vassall-Craigie-Longfellow House, whose interior is worth a tour in itself; examples of early architecture by Ralph Adams Cram; the residence of John Bartlett, of "familiar quotations" fame; stories about eminent Brattle Street Cantabrigians, and the most picturesque explanation you're likely to encounter of "pudding stone"—a building material whose name is derived from English pudding embedded with fruits and nuts!

It may be surprising to some to find a tour about Victorian Cambridge in *Victorian Boston Today*. Although technically not part of the City of Boston, Cambridge enjoyed a reciprocal relationship with the city before, during, and after the Victorian era. It provides us today with an ideal entry point for an exploration of

Boston's Victorian sites, with its direct T Red Line transportation to the two central T intersections in downtown Boston.

"When preservation is at stake."
—Henry James, *The American Scene,* 1907

Boston aficionados will take pleasure in reviewing, at the beginning of our edition, the listing of Preservation Awards, Commendations, and Lifetime Achievement Awards given by the New England Chapter of the Victorian Society in America between 1973 and 2004 to scores of dedicated, resourceful, and forward-thinking Boston– and New England–area preservationists. In view of the unending nature of preservation needs, the VSA/NE renews its congratulations to each recipient.

The City of Boston and the Victorian Society in America Have English Roots

The inspiration for the founding of the Victorian Society in America (1966) was England's Victorian Society (1958), whose early mission was to preserve the best of England's Victorian and Edwardian architecture, promote the history of the era, and encourage an appreciation of all facets of the Victorian arts. Today, with its original goals still at the forefront, the Victorian Society (1 Priory Gardens, Bedford Park, London W4 1TT, England; telephone [from U.S.A.]: 011-44-208-994-1019; http://www.victorian-society.org.uk) publishes *The Victorian,* continues its struggle to save England's threatened architecture, and organizes educational activities,[9] including walks, publications, and lectures, toward this end. Information about the Victorian Society in America and our New England Chapter precedes Edward W. Gordon's Foreword.

FEATURES OF THIS EDITION

Most of our walking tours average one to two hours. We provide directions between tour sites in addition to a map designed for each tour. Our Downtown Boston Key Map shows the location of each downtown tour and the T route to the specific neighborhood. The Greater Boston Key Map indicates the location of nearby tours in relation to the downtown area. Additional features include telephone numbers and Web sites for tour sites open to the public. Endnotes contain pertinent information and addresses, and include our sibling Boston heritage and preservation organizations (see note 4, T6). There are numerous cross-references to sites both within and between tours that furnish contextual framework, plentiful descriptive captions for period illustrations, as well as a section "About the Contributors" and an extensive index. Conscious of the enduring power of Bostonian hearsay and legend, we provide substantial scholarly depth to our tours and a comprehensive bibliography.

"The ages coming back/And the ages coming forward"
—Edwin Arlington Robinson[10]

During your journeys with us, Victorian Boston will "come back" while tomorrow's Boston presses forward. Boston exists in a continual state of flux; however, we hope you will agree that our attempt to encompass the "great ocean" of Victorian materials still available in Boston proves a valiant one. So rich in Victoriana is Boston that our contributors are quick to recite enticing lists of favorite Victorian heritage sites, gems whose locations lie frustratingly beyond the scope of a manageable walking tour. One of my favorites—a must for an understanding of the extraordinary beauty that bloomed in Victorian Boston in spite of its "cold-roast" temperament—is the Isabella Stewart Gardner Museum (http://www.gardnermuseum.org; (617)-566–1401; 280 The Fenway, Boston. For directions see note 6, T8). The quantity and quality of these favorites show that there is a great deal of Victorian Boston to visit and portend other jam-packed volumes will act as companions to the present one.

"Interest in all the nooks and crannies"

In *A Modern Instance* (1882), William Dean Howells emphasizes the sleazy and impatient character of Bartley Hubbard by describing his thoughtless, unenthusiastic, and severely abridged tour of Boston. Sightseeing abruptly ends with a hasty gesture toward four of the city's major attractions: "'The State House . . . Beacon Street; Public Garden; Back Bay'" (153).

If you choose instead to journey with our guides as narrators, whose inquisitiveness may be compared with Nathaniel Hawthorne's "interest in all the nooks and crannies and every development" of Boston (479), you will find you have chosen the right company. Once equipped with our discoveries, you will go on to make your own. Together we shall prove Emerson's words: "Of great cities you cannot compute the influences" (187).

Tomorrow's Victorian Boston is in your hands. We, as advocates of the city's outstanding nineteenth-century heritage, are vitally interested in its preservation. It is our hope that you will be as eager to safeguard the city's Victorian layer as we, and that *Victorian Boston Today* will inspire you to continue to encourage the active preservation of Boston's distinctive and delightful Victorian inheritance.

Mary Melvin Petronella
Bentley College

TOUR DIRECTIONS: WALKING AND USING TRANSPORTATION IN TODAY'S BOSTON

Walking in Boston

One of the real charms of Boston today is the ambiance of its Victorian neighborhoods. It is still a manageable, "walkably" pleasant city made the more pleasant by the survival of neighborhoods where solid collections of extraordinarily attractive Victorian streetscapes and human-scale architectural classics provide ornament and alleviate the canyon effect of the central city. However, in spite of Boston's attractive Victorian atmosphere, it is necessary to be "street smart"—that is, you need to be aware of your immediate surroundings in the same way that you must be in any urban area. Unfortunately, crime, accidents, and traffic accidents occur here, as well as elsewhere, without warning or logical reason.

Some streets, intersections, and localities are more pedestrian-friendly than others (sidewalk and street conditions vary significantly), and some vicinities, depending on the hour, the day, the week, and the month, project a friendlier environment than at other times. It is important that the walker, who may be distracted by the scene, or reading directions/descriptions, not slip into a "tourist's trance"— the walker should remain vigilant of both immediate surroundings and nearby company. Plan your walks during daylight hours, avoid streets and places that are too lonely, and be aware of traffic conditions. Please exercise the same caution in Boston that you would in any city.

At a Glance: Using Our Tour Maps

Judging Distances: To help you judge short walking distances with our tour maps' frequently used $1/10$ of a mile scale, the following handy conversions use the "standard" calculation: a football field = 100 yards (in other words, the field without the two 10-yard endzones).

About a $1/6$ mile = 1 football field (100 yards)
$1/10$ mile = about 1¾ football fields
¼ mile = about 4½ football fields
⅓ mile = about 5¾ football fields
½ mile = (5/10) mile about 8¾ football fields
1 mile = about 17½ football fields

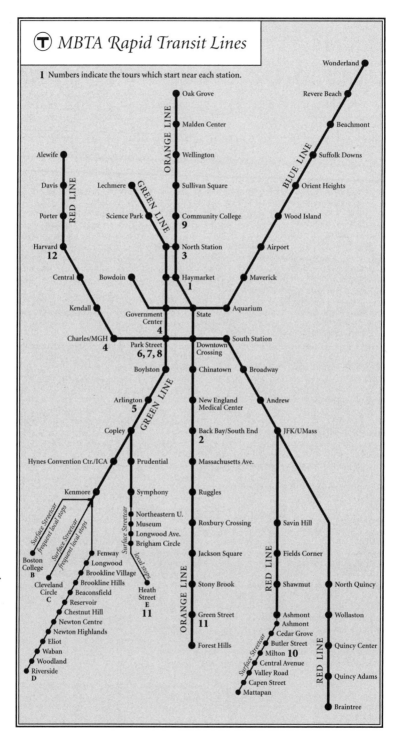

MBTA Rapid Transit Lines

1 Numbers indicate the tours which start near each station.

Oak Grove

Wonderland

Revere Beach

Malden Center

ORANGE LINE

Beachmont

Wellington

Alewife

BLUE LINE

Suffolk Downs

Davis

Lechmere

RED LINE

GREEN LINE

Sullivan Square

Orient Heights

Porter

Science Park

Community College
9

Wood Island

Harvard
12

North Station
3

Airport

Central

Bowdoin

Haymarket
1

Maverick

Kendall

Government
Center
4

State

Aquarium

Charles/MGH
4

Park Street
6, 7, 8

Downtown
Crossing

South Station

Boylston

Chinatown

Broadway

Arlington
5

New England
Medical Center

Andrew

GREEN LINE

Copley

Back Bay/South End
2

JFK/UMass

Hynes Convention Ctr./ICA

Prudential

Massachusetts Ave.

Kenmore

Symphony

Ruggles

*Surface Streetcar
frequent local stops*

*Surface Streetcar
frequent local stops*

*Surface Streetcar
frequent local stops*

*Surface Streetcar
local stops*

Northeastern U.

Museum

Roxbury Crossing

Savin Hill

Longwood Ave.

Brigham Circle

Fenway

Jackson Square

RED LINE

Fields Corner

Boston
College
B

Longwood

Brookline Village

Cleveland
Circle
C

Brookline Hills

Beaconsfield

ORANGE LINE

Stony Brook

Shawmut

North Quincy

Reservoir

Heath
Street
E
11

Chestnut Hill

Green Street
11

Wollaston

Newton Centre

Ashmont

Newton Highlands

Eliot

Forest Hills

Cedar Grove

RED LINE

Quincy Center

Waban

Butler Street

Milton **10**

Woodland

Central Avenue

Riverside
D

Valley Road

Quincy Adams

Capen Street

Mattapan

Braintree

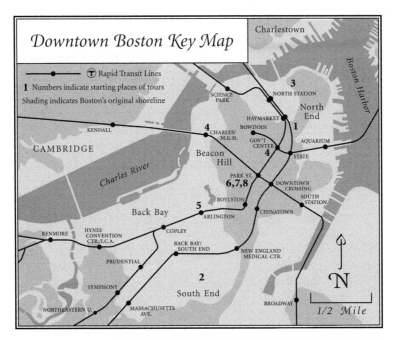

Downtown Boston Key Map

Charlestown

● ──── Ⓣ Rapid Transit Lines
1 Numbers indicate starting places of tours
Shading indicates Boston's original shoreline

SCIENCE PARK

3

NORTH STATION

North End

Boston Harbor

KENDALL

CAMBRIDGE

HAYMARKET
BOWDOIN
1
4
CHARLES/ M.G.H.
GOV'T CENTER
4
STATE
AQUARIUM

Charles River

Beacon Hill

PARK ST.
6,7,8

DOWNTOWN CROSSING
SOUTH STATION

Back Bay

BOYLSTON
5
ARLINGTON
CHINATOWN

KENMORE
HYNES CONVENTION CTR./I.C.A.
COPLEY

BACK BAY/ SOUTH END
NEW ENGLAND MEDICAL CTR.

PRUDENTIAL

SYMPHONY

2
South End

NORTHEASTERN U.
MASSACHUSETTS AVE.
BROADWAY

N

1/2 Mile

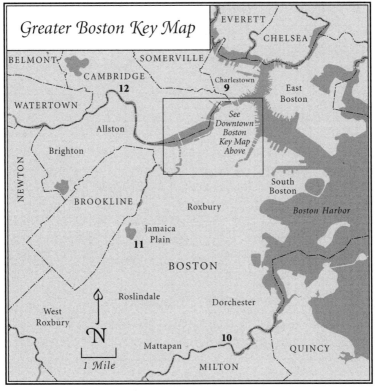

Greater Boston Key Map

EVERETT
CHELSEA

BELMONT
SOMERVILLE

CAMBRIDGE
12
Charlestown
9
East Boston

WATERTOWN

Allston

See Downtown Boston Key Map Above

Brighton

NEWTON

BROOKLINE

Roxbury

South Boston

Boston Harbor

Jamaica Plain
11

BOSTON

West Roxbury

Roslindale

Dorchester

N

1 Mile

Mattapan

10

QUINCY

MILTON

Transportation on the T

Each tour starts and ends near a T stop. A "T" (MBTA) diagram is on page xl. Tour numbers below the name of T stops show where tours start.

"Park St." and "Downtown Crossing" are Boston's two central downtown T line intersections. The Massachusetts Bay Transportation Authority (MBTA) operates both the subway and the buses in Boston and its suburbs. T Stations are indicated by a large capital "T" inside a circle. "Visitor Passports" are available. For the MBTA "Information Line" call (617)-222–3200. Press "0" to speak personally to an MBTA Travel Information Agent. Or visit http://www.mbta.com.

Downtown Key Map with T Stops and Greater Boston Key Map

The Downtown Boston Key Map, page xli, shows where each downtown tour is located, and rapid transit routes to the specific neighborhoods we explore.

The Greater Boston Key Map, page xli, shows the location of each tour not in the downtown area by its tour number.

Using Your Own Transportation

Boston's irregular one-way streets can, at times, make rush-hour travel a matter of waiting in gridlock, and even "in-between" rush hour traffic is often very heavy. If you decide to use private transportation and you plan extra time to get there, using your own car is generally feasible, and there are often paid parking garages or lots nearby, although they are sometimes full. Using public transportation to reach the starting point for each tour is a great help.

About Tour Sites

Many of our tour sites are private homes, and several commercial buildings are no longer open to the public. With increased security concerns, owners have been instructed to be alert. However, there are numerous sites that are open and will welcome visitors. Because current open-hour/day and fee schedules are often posted nearby (these schedules change often, even radically, depending on the season), and some sites close for renovation, we have listed telephone numbers and Web sites for your convenience. We suggest that you either check pertinent Web site listings, pack a cellphone, or, even better, call before leaving (sometimes Web site listings are not current). Please respect the privacy and private property of the residents and owners of all of our tour sites.

About Tour Symbols

{🦋 = leafy suburban setting} Two of our tours visit leafy suburban settings. When choosing these tours, you may need to consider the lack of nearby restaurants, stores, rain shelter, and restroom facilities after leaving the conveniences near the

T Station area. As always, we suggest comfortable shoes and appropriate gear when walking distances under variable weather conditions.

{ ◢ = incline} Some of our tours include slopes and inclines that are: gentle { ◢ }, moderate { ◢ ◢ }, or steep { ◢ ◢ ◢ }. To manage steep inclines, see "Tweaking Tours to Taste" below.

{(T5) = Tour 5} Cross-references to relevant information in other tours are indicated with tour-number abbreviations.

{(p. 120) = see illustration on page 120}

Tweaking Tours to Your Taste

Our independent, peripatetic tours offer several advantages—self-determined time, freedom of pace, and the possibility of skipping to sites that interest you most. Therefore, steep and moderate inclines should not prevent your enjoying a tempting tour. For example, after the first few sites in the North End (T3), the tour continues on level ground. It is also possible to skip the steeper streets among Beacon Hill sites, walk diagonally across the Common, and rejoin the Authors' tour (T6) and the Women's tour (T8) on Charles St. Likewise, there are wonderful sites on the Charlestown tour (T9) that are accessible below the moderate slope to the Bunker Hill monument. Look over initial and between-site directions beforehand, and adjust your tour to suit your own inclinations. Choosing a well-known starting site should make it easier to get verbal directions to an address within a tour. The location of T stations on our maps should also help you with tweaking your tour to your taste.

PREFACE: TOURING BOSTON'S TOPOGRAPHY—
THE BIG FILL AND THE BIG DIG

Mary Melvin Petronella

And twice each day the flowing sea
Took Boston in its arms.
—Ralph Waldo Emerson, "Boston"

If we joined the tourists, in 1837, in the lantern atop the dome of the Bulfinch State House crowning Beacon Hill, to enjoy the spectacular 360-degree bird's-eye view of Boston's surroundings, our prospect (except from the south window, where Shawmut peninsula's widening "Boston Neck" was visible) would be a city surrounded by salt water.

From the east window over the city toward Massachusetts Bay and the Atlantic Ocean, the vista at the city's edge included waterfront wharves and ships; the harbor, its inlets, and its islands; and the ocean—to the horizon.

From the north window, to the left, the view encompassed the ocean's water spreading into the inner harbor, wrapping in between Charlestown and the North End, and swelling amid wharves and ships. The view from the west window revealed the sea encircling the city's "back," streaming into the current of the Charles River beside the Mill Dam, and mixing with freshwater in the expansive Back Bay estuary.

From the lantern's lookout windows it was obvious that the Boston harbor waterfront played a spectacular role in city affairs. The nineteenth-century waterfront, fringed with its substantial wharves, facilitated worldwide travel, commerce, and immigration, and Civil War activity to come. However, the entire shoreline, the uneven sea margins around and in back of the city, along with the harbor waterfront, offered a fundamental potential to Boston that, at the inception of the Victorian era, may well have been overlooked by sightseers enjoying the view: namely, the possibility of continuing to expand city limits by escalation of the landfill at the water's edge.

Bostonians, however, since the city was established had definitely had their sights fixed on the advantages of adding more fill, and their appetite for more land was

The State House, dome (first gilded 1874) and original cupola (replaced with reproduction in 1897). *(From Hezekiah Butterworth,* Young Folks History of Boston, *Boston: D. Lothrop, 1881, facing p. 324.)*
"The State House is built upon the summit of a hill, which rises gradually at first, and afterwards by a steep ascent, almost from the water's edge.... The site is beautiful: and from the top there is a charming panoramic view of the whole town and neighborhood."
Charles Dickens, *American Notes* (1842).

seemingly insatiable. They not only had added substantial landfill along the harbor's waterfront (see T1), at the water's edge and in the Mill Pond in the North End (see T3), and northwest in the Charles St. area (see T6, T7, T8), but were also in the very process of adding fill during the 1830s in the Neck lands (see T2). The unremitting pressure to expand land area continued as population increased, augmented by the enormous influx of immigrants, a consequence, mainly, of the Irish famine (1845–50). Finally, just before the Civil War, Bostonians undertook the ultimate landfill project—a feat that only Boston's Big Dig has rivaled in scope—covering miles of shoreline and the entire saltwater tide flats and marshes of the Back Bay.

Old Boston Water Front about 1840
(Drawing [ca. 1915] by Malcom Fraser, from William S. Rossiter, ed., Days and Ways in Old Boston, *Boston: R. H. Sterns, 1915, facing p. 47.)*
"The streets were all narrow, and most of them crooked ... but at the end of one the spars of a vessel [were visible].... Trucks heavily straggl[ed] toward the wharf with their long string teams.... The cobble-stones ... were worn with the dint of ponderous wheels and ... here and there, in wandering streaks over its surface, was the gray stain of the salt water."
William Dean Howells, *The Rise of Silas Lapham* (1885).

Boston's Seascape Becomes Its Landscape

By the end of the nineteenth century the Back Bay had literally become city landscape. "Whole forests from the State of Maine, vast quarries of granite, and hills of country gravel, [had] been put to service in fringing water-margins, constructing ... causeways, redeeming the flats, and furnishing pilings and solid foundations" (*Encylcopædia Britannica* 74). The Back Bay was the pride of Boston, a fashionable, level place of residence, and a prime setting for the emerging multiplicity of its cultural milieu (see T5, T8).

The illustration "Old and New Boston" (1903) allows us to see the impact of city's phenomenal growth and its new seascape-to-landscape transformation. Old Boston's substrata, the Shawmut peninsula,[1] is shown in black, surrounded by New Boston's sprawling landfill in gray. More fill continued to be added throughout the nineteenth century (see T1), and by 1903 the city had annexed neighboring towns and cities (see Charlestown T9, Dorchester T10), but it was the city's skillful transformation of its water boundaries that is the emphasis of this illustration. (See the following page for areas that downtown Boston tours traverse on the Shawmut Peninsula and over landfill.)

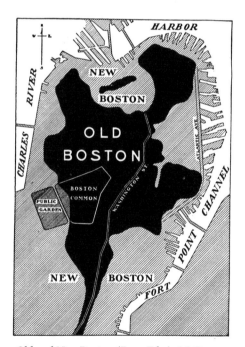

Old and New Boston *(From Edwin M. Bacon,* Boston: A Guide Book, *Boston: Ginn, 1903, p. 2.)* We will tour over Shawmut Peninsula (black) and Boston's landfill (gray)

Adding New Acres to Boston: "Then and Now"

In the nineteenth century new acres added to Boston grew horizontally, alongside older land. However, in spite of the city's growth, by the end of the century traffic congestion downtown called for tunneling underground for new space (see nation's first subway, 1897, T4, T6, T8). The city continued to add surface space during the twentieth century, but for the most part it changed direction and grew vertically. Additional subterranean space was needed for transportation, and acres of critical space were claimed above ground for elevated transportation corridors and for layers upon layers of air-space as the city surged upward with growing crowds of skyscrapers (see T5). As the twenty-first century approached, serious traffic problems demanded once again the use of the city's substrata—hence the Big Dig. A huge benefit of moving through-traffic underground is the liberation of a corridor of surface land near the waterfront. The demolition of the entire elevated expressway (Boston's Central Artery I-93), whose dark underbelly had artificially divided the waterfront from the city proper for a half century (see T1), allows recovery of acres of land surface, Boston's twenty-first-century windfall—a new "pocket frontier."

We will be exploring the environs of the Big Dig when we visit the waterfront, where intense throngs of traffic, thanks to the Big Dig, today speed underground. As Boston loses the gloomy ribbon of land under the Central Artery, secures the potential of coveted parcels of parkland, and unveils a vital new intra-Boston surface corridor adjacent to downtown neighborhoods, a light-filled alliance with the city's waterfront will play an integral role in restoring to Boston its Victorian unity.

Touring Shawmut Peninsula and Boston's Landfill

The key locations listed below identify areas[2] where downtown Boston tours are on the Shawmut Peninsula and where they are on the city's landfill (see Downtown Boston Key Map, page xli, for overall orientation; individual tour maps for specific streets; and the illustration on p. xlvi for clarification).

The following tours are on the Shawmut Peninsula when they are in these locations:
Boston Common (T6) Authors; (T7) Black Heritage Trail®; (T8) Women
Beacon Hill (T6) Authors; (T7) Black Heritage Trail®; (T8) Women
Between Washington St. and the Common (T4) Commercial District; (T6) Authors; (T8) Women
West and east of Washington St. (T4) Commercial District (on Shawmut with the exception of Sites 1 and 5)
Along Washington St. north from "Boston Neck" (T2) South End; (T4) Commercial District; (T6) Authors
East of North Margin St. (T3) North End

The following tours are on Boston landfill when they are in these locations:
Charles St. (T6) Authors; (T7) Black Heritage Trail®; (T8) Women
Public Garden (T6) Authors; (T5) Back Bay, Arlington St. side; (T8) Women
Copley Square and west of the Public Garden (the "big" Back Bay fill) (T5) Back Bay; (T8) Women
Beside "Boston Neck," east and west (T2) South End
Clarendon, Dartmouth, and Tremont Sts. to Union Park and adjacent streets; Columbus Avenue (T2) South End
West and east of Atlantic Avenue (T1) Waterfront (on fill with exception of first two sites)
West and northwest of North Margin St. (Mill Pond) (T3) North End

· P A R T ·

I

TOURS THAT BEGIN IN DOWNTOWN BOSTON

I remember the black wharves and the slips,
    And the sea-tides tossing free;
And Spanish sailors with bearded lips,
And the beauty and mystery of the ships;
    And the magic of the sea.
                    —Henry Wadsworth Longfellow,
                        In My Lost Youth (1855)

· T O U R · 1

BOSTON'S NINETEENTH-CENTURY WATERFRONT

by Pauline Chase-Harrell

Tour Location: See Downtown Key Map for the location of the Tour and its T stop, page xli.

About Walking the Tour: The tour on level ground begins at the Blackstone Block, near the Congress St. exit of the Orange Line's Haymarket T stop, and ends near the Red Line's T stop at South Station. Between those points, it crisscrosses Boston's Central Artery corridor, territory of the Big Dig. After more than twenty years of planning and construction, the highway that loomed over the waterfront for fifty years has been placed underground, and the state, the city, and its citizens have embarked on planning and constructing the new face of the area above it. This process will undoubtedly be ongoing in some form whenever you take this tour, changing yet again the surroundings but not the sites. The tour provides ubiquitous opportunities for refreshment, including the vintage establishments at Site 2, the Union Oyster House (1713–17), established in 1826, and, within Site 4, Durgin Park (1827).

Thumbnail Sketch of Sights: See Introduction, page xxxiii.

Approximate Walking Time: 1 hour

T Stop: Haymarket T Station, Green and Orange lines

Begin at: The Blackstone Block, bounded by Hanover, Union, North, and Blackstone Sts. (From the Haymarket T Station, walk south along Congress St., and turn left on Hanover to the Blackstone Block.)

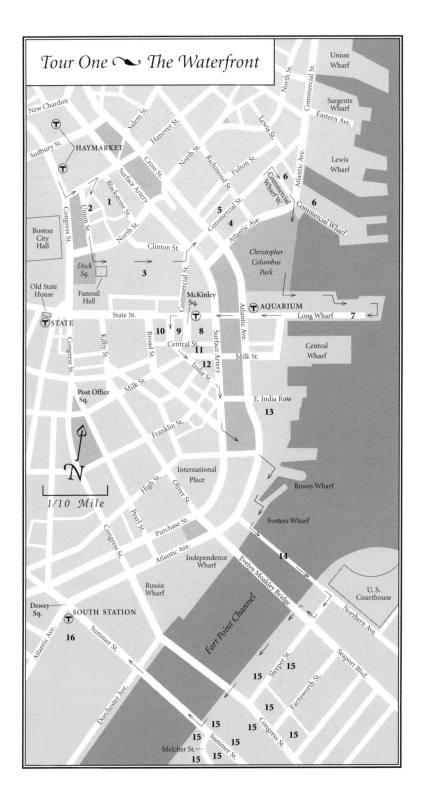

Tour One ∾ The Waterfront

INTRODUCTION

The nineteenth century, apogee of Boston's maritime fortunes, was also the period of the most dramatic growth of its waterfront. From its beginnings in Dock Sq. to today's container facilities upriver at Moran Terminal and out on Castle Island, Boston's waterfront has undergone continuous evolution for more than 350 years. Indeed, nearly all of the landforms we know today as "the waterfront" were creations of the process known as "wharfing out," which reached its zenith in the nineteenth century. Wharves that had been built jutting into the water silted in with the natural action of currents, the water becoming shallower even as larger ships required deeper berths; so the shallow areas were filled and built on, and new, longer wharves were built in a continuous process. This process had started with the first settlement, but the nineteenth century improved on it, creating whole new streets and districts with ambitious landfill projects, and the waterfront moved seaward in great strides.

Today much of the historic waterfront has been destroyed by highway construction and urban renewal. Nevertheless, much of it has also been preserved, and if we look at the surviving examples from each generation, it is possible to get a feeling for the way the waterfront evolved from the beginning to the end of the nineteenth century. This is the theme and structure of our tour.

At the beginning of the nineteenth century, the waterfront's character had changed little since Long Wharf had been built early in the previous century. Larger and more prosperous, it still retained the "higgledy-piggledy" look of crooked streets and alleys crowded with a mix of mast-ringed wharves, sheds, shops, and houses for artisans and merchants, blending almost imperceptibly into the rest of the town. By the end of the century, steam had replaced sail, and a massively scaled, regularized waterfront designed for easy rail access had become a distinct district, separated from the rest of the city by railroads and industrial facilities.

We will not see all the great nineteenth-century waterfront buildings, but rather trace the development of the nineteenth-century waterfront through examples of each period. Indeed, we cannot hope to cover all of Boston's remaining waterfront in one sixty-minute tour; this itinerary, for example, leaves out scenes of major nineteenth-century activity in Charlestown and East Boston, focusing on what today comprises the downtown waterfront. Within this area, which represents several different generations of waterfront development, we will be moving, for the most part, from the older to the newer, although the happenstance nature of preservation makes a direct progression impossible. Most of the buildings we will see are no longer used for maritime purposes, and some have suffered some alterations in the name of adaptive reuse, but they stand as reminders of one of Boston's proudest achievements: the prosperity brought to the city by her maritime prowess.

Beginning at the Haymarket T Station, walk south along Congress St. and turn left on Hanover to

1. **The Blackstone Block,** bounded by Hanover, Union, North, and Blackstone Sts.

The Blackstone Block derives its present name from urban renewal days, when it stood isolated amid the massive demolitions for the Central Artery and Government Center projects. The street pattern here is a designated Boston Landmark, the most extensive survival of the original "crooked and narrow streets" of old Boston. The buildings date from the eighteenth, nineteenth, and even twentieth centuries, but the tiny streets and alleys were the main streets of the old waterfront when Creek Sq. was actually a creek and Scottow's dock occupied what is now the center of the block. Walking these lanes—first **Salt Ln.,** then **Marsh Ln., Marshall St.,** and **Creek Sq.**—gives us an idea of what the Boston waterfront was like at the beginning of the nineteenth century. If you look carefully, you can see evidence of how, as the century progressed, many of the older buildings were reoriented with new fronts to face other, widened streets, and the old lanes became back alleys.

Walk up Hanover St. and take a sharp right turn back onto Marshall St. to discover the alleys in the interior of the block. Then continue to the end of Marshall St. and turn left onto Union St. You are in front of

2. **The Union Oyster House,** 41–43 Union St. (1713–17), oyster house (1826) {still serves Bostonians as a restaurant}

Although not a nineteenth-century building, the Union Oyster House is a rare survival of a nineteenth-century institution. In this, one of the oldest buildings in Boston,

built between 1713 and 1717, an oyster house has been in continuous operation since 1826, and its ground floor remains virtually unchanged. The avid talkers devouring oysters in Richard Caton Woodville's painting *Politics in the Oyster House* (1848) would feel at home here.

Continue south on Union St. Cross North St., and walk past the flower shop, then turn left.

3. **Faneuil Hall Markets** (1824–26), by Alexander Parris

In the 1820s, Boston gave up its town meeting form of government and became a city. Its second mayor, Josiah Quincy (mayor 1823–28),[1] had a bold vision of replacing the gin mills, brothels, and sailors' boardinghouses that occupied the old waterfront buildings along Ann and North Sts. (see Ann and North Sts. T3) with a modern market facility grand enough to match Boston's new status. In the resulting undertaking, which might be characterized as the first urban renewal project in the United States, the City of Boston acquired the land, razed the buildings, filled in the old docks, and built new streets.

Alexander Parris, an architect from Portland, Maine, who was also designing buildings at the Charlestown Navy Yard, designed the handsome domed Grecian Doric Quincy Market building and flanking North and South Markets in the newest style—Greek Revival—and the newest material—granite—of the day. This project, along with the building of the Bunker Hill Monument, initiated a new building technology and style that would change the character of Boston's waterfront and commercial district in the Victorian era: the Granite School (see Quincy Market, p.xxxii, Introduction; Boston Granite School T4, Parris T6, T9; Bunker Hill Monument T9).

Plentiful in the region, granite had been little used in the Colonial period because of its great expense: it was hard to work and heavy to transport. New quarrying technologies in the nineteenth century, together with the new railroads for hauling, made granite a feasible building material. It lent itself especially well to the plain, massive Greek Revival style, which enjoyed so much popularity in the new republic because of its associations with democracy, and which so appealed to Boston's austere sense of style. The burgeoning waterfront was soon lined with handsome granite structures in the Greek style.

The granite was brought from Quincy, on the South Shore, utilizing the first commercial railroad built in the United States. Railroad pioneer Gridley Bryant constructed this horse-drawn railroad to haul the heavy blocks from the quarry down to the ships, which then unloaded them at docks near the building sites. After this, although "red brick Boston" continued to hold sway in residential areas, granite would dominate the Victorian downtown and waterfront (see G. Bryant T9).

The Markets opened with great fanfare in August 1826. Exactly 150 years later, rescued from dereliction, abandonment, and potential demolition and rehabilitated for a late-twentieth-century "urban marketplace," they reopened with similar fanfare as Faneuil Hall Marketplace. Lovers of Victorian architecture mourned the loss of Victorian accretions—elaborate oriel windows, cast-iron storefronts, and such, which had altered the original design over the years—that resulted from the decision to restore the buildings to their 1826 appearance. But the restored buildings are as vital a part of Boston today as they were in the nineteenth century, when carters jostled their heavy drays through the streets

and fed their hefty appetites at Durgin Park (1827, still serving in the North Market building), and Boston merchants and housewives picked their way through the stalls, buying meat, fish, and produce for dinner. Josiah Quincy decorously refused to have the markets named after himself, but generations of Bostonians, beginning with the Victorians, have steadfastly called them "Quincy Market"—and they still do.

Walk along North Market St., then turn left on Commercial St.—a pedestrian walkway at this point—and cross the Central Artery corridor to the

4. **Mercantile Wharf Building** (1857), 73-117 **Commercial St.**, by Gridley J. F. Bryant

Son of the railroad builder Gridley Bryant, Gridley James Fox Bryant was the most successful commercial architect in mid-nineteenth-century Boston. In the Great Fire of 1872, 152 buildings, or almost 20 percent of the buildings destroyed, had been designed by Bryant (see G. J. F. Bryant T2, T4; Great Fire T4). After the fire, he was commissioned to rebuild 111 of these. Mercantile Wharf, in a section far from the fire, has survived as an example of Bryant's pre-fire work, although it was truncated by highway builders in the twentieth century. In the Italianate style, with rough-faced granite piers highlighted by smoothly finished stringcourses, it represents the mid-century development of the Granite School of Boston architecture.

As fashion moved on to favor the more elaborate Italianate and Second Empire styles over Greek Revival, granite buildings followed the trend, as in this example.

In the 1970s, the massiveness of Mercantile Wharf made it an especially difficult building to rehabilitate for apartments and shops. The problem was eventually solved by creating a large skylit atrium to admit light to the center of the building. The atrium is accessible through the shops and allows a view of the internal structure of these massive buildings.

Continue up Commercial St. On the left, opposite Mercantile Wharf, is

5. 70–120 Commercial St. (before 1867)

This row of four-story Greek Revival commercial buildings was typical of many streets along the Boston waterfront in the mid-nineteenth century, when many less important buildings continued to be built in the simple Greek Revival style, even as more important buildings adopted newer styles. Although many of these buildings have undergone modernization at the first-floor level, the original trabeated (post and lintel) granite construction has been retained and restored in most places. The strength of these trabeated granite first floors, flat three-bay fronts, and simple dentilated cornices and gable roofs has enabled them to retain much of their original feeling.

Follow Commercial St., past Richmond St., until you see "Commercial Wharf West" on the right. Turn right here and look across Atlantic Ave. to

6. Commercial Wharf (1832), 81–85 Atlantic Ave., by Isaiah Rogers

In this massive granite Greek Revival warehouse, we can see two generations of nineteenth-century waterfront development: the proud new wharf construction of the 1830s through 1850s, the clipper-ship era, and the modernization of the waterfront by the creation of Atlantic Ave. in 1868–70, which literally cut through the middle of Commercial Wharf and several other earlier wharves.

Senator Henry Cabot Lodge, in his *Early Memories,* described Commercial Wharf in its heyday:

> Father was a China merchant, and, after the fashion of the merchants in those days, had his office in the granite block that stretched down to the end of Commercial Wharf. His counting-room was at the very end in the last division of the block, and from the windows I could look out on the ships lying alongside the wharf. They were beautiful vessels, American clipper ships in the days when our ships of this type were famous throughout the world for their speed and staunchness. I wandered about over the docks, making friends with the captains, the seamen, and the shop-keepers, and taking a most absorbing interest in everything connected with them. They brought me from China admirable firecrackers and strange fireworks, fascinating in appearance, but which I could not "make go" at all. From them, too, came bronzes and porcelains and pictures and carved ivories, which I was wont to look at wonderingly, and ginger and sweetmeats and lychee-nuts (then almost unknown here), of which I used to partake with keen delight. For the teas and silks which filled the holds I cared nothing, but the history and adventures of the ships interested me greatly. (257)

After the Civil War, steam rapidly replaced sail, and ships grew larger to carry bulk cargoes of grain, wool, and other raw materials and the ever-growing industrial output of New England's mills. Efficient connections between wharves and railroads became paramount, and the waterfront created by Mayor Quincy and the architects Charles Bulfinch, Isaiah Rogers, Alexander Parris, and Gridley J. F. Bryant was overwhelmed by traffic jams of toiling teamsters, horses, and drays. In 1868 the city again acquired property, filled in old docks, and tore down buildings (and parts of buildings) to create a broad, straight avenue the length of the waterfront to provide rapid access for bulky loads. Cut in two by the project, Commercial Wharf received two new facades facing both sides of Atlantic Ave.

A third generation of waterfront development is also visible here: the conversion of the old maritime structures to housing in the 1960s and 1970s. Commercial Wharf was one of the first wharves to be converted, when artists and others discovered the charms of both the waterside area and the old buildings whose massive wood beams and large spaces made interesting apartments. When the movement caught on and residential redevelopment became official policy in the 1970s, Atlantic Ave. was relocated to curve around the new waterfront park.

Turn right and walk along the water's edge, through the park, stopping just before you come to the Marriott Long Wharf Hotel.

7. Long Wharf (1710–21)

Built by subscription by the merchants in 1710-21, Long Wharf permanently shaped the downtown waterfront by creating its major axis, State St. (then called King St.). Extending half a mile into the harbor, it was the major wharf in town and led directly to the Custom House and the seat of royal government in the Old State House at the head of the street. Long Wharf retained a central role well into the nineteenth century and fostered the growth of many banks and insurance companies nearby. Landfill gradually took over most

T Wharf, looking toward Commercial Wharf (1880s), photographed by Baldwin Coolidge. *(Courtesy of the Society for the Preservation of New England Antiquities.)* By the 1880s, the post–Civil War transportation revolution of steam and rail had made the sailing packet in the foreground nearly obsolete. T and Commercial Wharves, which in the 1850s and 1860s had been crowded with such packets serving the coastal, river, and Cape Cod communities, were now dominated by fishermen.

of the length of the wharf. The financial institutions built grandiose buildings where warehouses and chandleries had once stood, and State St. became the heart of Boston's financial district, the greatest financial center in the United States until it was eclipsed by New York's in the 1890s.

Walk partway down the wharf to the

Custom House Block (1848)

The beginning of the waterside boardwalk in front of the Custom House Block marks the site where T Wharf branched off to the left. This was the wharf from which the 54th Regiment, the Civil War's first black regiment, embarked for the front in South Carolina (see 54th Regiment T6, T7). After the war, this area became the center of Boston's fishing industry in the 1880s, and a new wooden building was constructed along T Wharf to accommodate the fishermen.

Don't miss the end of Long Wharf, which affords a sweeping view of Boston's nineteenth-century waterfront. To the north are Commercial Wharf (1832), and beyond that, Lewis Wharf (1836–38), Union Wharf (1846–47), the U.S. Coast Guard Wharf, and, just this side of the Tobin Bridge, the Charlestown Navy Yard (active 1800–1974; see map T9). Directly across the harbor is East Boston, where Donald McKay's yards turned out the world's fastest clipper ships in the 1840s and 1850s, and where the Cunard Lines docked and most of Boston's immigrants arrived before immigration was centralized at New York's Ellis Island at the end of the century. And to the south is the turn-of-the-century industrial waterfront development of South Boston.

Walk back along the opposite (south) side of the wharf beside the granite facade of the Custom House Block. Continue straight up State St., across the Central Artery corridor, to

8. State Street Block, McKinley Sq.
(1856–57), by Gridley J. F. Bryant

With its heavily rusticated piers, deeply projecting stringcourses, bracketed cornice, and pedimented projecting pavilion facing the Custom House, the State Street Block, by Gridley J. F. Bryant (Site 4), demonstrates the degree of elaboration attained in Granite School buildings of the Italianate style in the 1850s. (From McKinley Sq. it is possible to compare three generations of granite treatments: the State Street Block, the Custom House (1830s) across the square, and the ornate spires and crockets of the Grain Exchange Building (1890s) above the red-brick Central Wharf to the south.) Nearly three-quarters of the original twenty-two-bay building on the seaward end was amputated for construction of the Central Artery in the 1950s, and the roofline of the

remainder has been destroyed, but enough remains to convey a sense of the Boston waterfront at its apogee in the clipper-ship era. The Long and Central Wharf Corporation, which owned the recently filled land, sold each bay to individual owners, requiring that "the granite to be used for the sidewalk & facade of each bay must be purchased from the Corporation & erected according to the architect's plan" (Boston Landmarks Inventory File).

Next to the State Street Block is

9. Custom House (1837–47), McKinley Sq., by Ammi Burnham Young; tower (1913–15) by Peabody and Stearns

This monumental structure, which, in its original form, combined a Doric-order facade with a low Roman dome, was the most impressive Greek Revival building of its day. Its history encapsulates the development of this part of the waterfront in the nineteenth century. When construction began in 1837, Young's design was hailed as forward-looking; when it was completed a decade later, the design was criticized as old-fashioned (M. S. Smith 99–105). When construction began, the site was on the water at the head of the dock between Long and Central Wharves; within a decade of its completion, that dock had been filled, and the State Street Block landlocked the new Custom House. By 1912, the federal government needed more space and commissioned the well-known Boston architectural firm of Peabody and Stearns to design the unique addition. It is a solution that, as a Boston Landmarks Commissioner once noted, "no review board in its right mind would allow today, but we all love it!" (see Peabody and Stearns T3, T4, T5).

The tall brick building just beyond the Custom House is the

Long Wharf (left) and **Central Wharf** (1870s)
(Courtesy of The Bostonian Society/Old State House.)
In the 1870s, Boston's harbor was filled with a mix of sailing and steam vessels. This view shows the new Atlantic Ave. cutting through Central Wharf in the right foreground. (The portion of Central Wharf that remains standing today is out of this picture to the right; the portion visible in the lower right corner was lopped off for the Central Artery.)

10. **Board of Trade Building** (1901), across from Custom House on India St., by Winslow and Bigelow

This early steel-frame skyscraper marks the transition of the old waterfront area to business other than maritime trade. Formed in 1854 to advance the interests of the port, the Board of Trade had by the end of the century reconstituted itself to promote "the general interests of Boston." This building housed not only the board and trade-related businesses, such as merchandise brokers, but interests as far flung as the management of the Boston-owned Atchison, Topeka, and Santa Fe Railroad (see Winslow and Bigelow T10).

Turn left on India St., between the Custom House and the Board of Trade Building. Look on your left for

11. **Central Wharf** (1816), 146–176 **Milk St.**, by Charles Bulfinch

This row of eight redbrick buildings is all that remains, after depredations first by the construction of Atlantic Ave. and then by the Central Artery, of the fifty-four that once stretched the length of Central Wharf

all the way to where the New England Aquarium now stands. Central Wharf was the final segment of Charles Bulfinch's plan to redevelop Boston's waterfront area in the 1800s by filling and laying out Broad St. and the surrounding areas. Shubael Bell wrote in 1817 that "the completion of this undertaking, unparalleled in commercial History, is a proof of the enterprize, the wealth, and persevering industry of Bostonians" (quoted in Whitehill, *Boston: A Topographical History*, 2d ed. 86); this wharf and the related improvements laid the foundations for the great developments of the Victorian age.

The end building facing McKinley Sq., although altered by a later storefront, retains its original roofline and much of its original form and detailing, giving a good idea of what the pre-Victorian, Bulfinch-era waterfront was like. The street pattern he laid out remains largely unchanged in the immediate vicinity, and several smaller Bulfinch buildings are scattered throughout the area.

Continue up India St. On the left, just beyond Central Wharf, is the

The Grain and Flour Exchange/Chamber of Commerce Building (1890s), lithograph. *(Restored and owned by the Beal Companies, LLP. Image courtesy of the Beal Companies, LLP.)*

12. Grain and Flour Exchange/Chamber of Commerce Building (1890–92), 177 Milk St., by Shepley, Rutan and Coolidge

Directly across from the Central Wharf buildings, the Grain and Flour Exchange building represents the development of the Boston waterfront at the end of the nineteenth century. Asymmetrically designed to fit the odd-shaped lot, the rounded, elaborately detailed, rock-faced granite facade of the Grain and Flour Exchange is one of the most picturesque in Boston. It was designed in the Richardsonian Romanesque style by H. H. Richardson's successor firm (see Shepley, Rutan, and Coolidge Site 16, T4, T5, T12). The three-story arches reflect the interior volume of the trading floor. The Chamber of Commerce, founded in 1885, was the third such body in Boston's history, the first two having been short-lived. It was formed by the merger of two corporate

trade bodies, the Corn Exchange and the Produce Exchange. At the end of the nineteenth century, Boston was the largest exporter of grain in the United States, a fact appropriately symbolized by this grandiloquent building.

Walk to the end of India St. and look seaward to the

13. Site of **India Wharf**

From the India St. corner of the Grain and Flour Exchange, the site of Charles Bulfinch's great pedimented brick India Wharf of 1805, which inaugurated the Federal-era development of the area and was perhaps its handsomest achievement, is visible directly across the Central Artery corridor. "At this wharf," Shubael Bell noted, "the Amorys, the Perkins, the Higginsons, and other respectable Merchants transact business" (quoted in Whitehill, *Boston: A Topographical History,* 2d ed. 86). In its heyday, before the Civil War, India Wharf was home to the East Indian and West Indian trades and the New Orleans cotton trade. But after the war, like the other early nineteenth-century wharves, it

India Wharf (1860s) *(Courtesy of The Bostonian Society/Old State House.)*
Soon after this picture was taken, Atlantic Ave. cut a wide swath through the middle of the building, taking out the central arch section.

had become obsolete, its docks too narrow and too isolated from the newly dominant railroads. Bisected by Atlantic Ave. in 1868 and truncated by the Central Artery in the 1950s, India Wharf languished until the last remnant was demolished for urban renewal and replaced by Harbor Towers in 1962. Looking at India Wharf in its prime, one can sympathize with Colonel Frank Forbes's lament, "In the sixties, when Atlantic Ave. was constructed, then and forever departed the traditional glory of the old Boston wharves" (quoted in W. H. Bunting 26).

Walk beyond the end of Broad St., and cross the Central Artery corridor. Go through the huge arch at Rowe's Wharf.

The commuter and excursion boats are a pale shadow of the many ferries that plied the harbor in the nineteenth century, but they may be credited for beginning the rejuvenation of the harbor's activity.

Turn right, walk along the water's edge to Northern Ave., and cross the bridge over

14. Fort Point Channel

At the end of the nineteenth century, Boston's waterfront development moved south to what had been the tidal flats of South Boston, beyond the channel that mariners had long known as "the point" where the seventeenth century fort had stood. What is today referred to as the Fort Point Channel area, including the channel itself, the bridges that cross it, and the wharves, warehouses, and transportation facilities on either side, constitutes a record of the complex transportation developments that accompanied Boston's rapid industrial expansion in the late nineteenth and early twentieth centuries.

A century later, another generation of complex transportation developments—the Big Dig, the Central Artery/Tunnel project, and the new Silver Line T connec-

tion to the South Boston piers area—has brought massive construction to this area. Federal, state, and local preservation laws have ensured that extraordinary care is taken to protect this historic record.

As the wharves along the old peninsula stretched ever farther toward the sea and extended southward into the South Bay, and the South Boston flats were filled, the water around the Fort Point Channel shrank. However, passage for ships through the channel was necessary to service the South Bay wharves that lay farther south along Albany St., where piano factories and other industries needed mahogany and other raw materials and shipping facilities for their products (see pianoforte; mahogany T2). This access was ensured by construction of granite bulkheads to terminate the fill along a line drawn by the U.S. Harbor Commission in 1890, thus permanently defining the channel.

Rail and vehicular access between the downtown and the growing industrial area in South Boston was provided by bridges, which of course had to open for ships. The result was a series of bridges with technologically advanced draw systems, considered to be one of the outstanding collections of late-nineteenth- and early-twentieth-century drawbridges in the country. The great rolling bascule railroad bridge, which dominated the head of the channel, has fallen victim to the Big Dig, but several others remain. As uses of the channel changed, opening was no longer required, and most are no longer operable, but efforts have been made to retain their mechanisms as a historic record.

One of these, the Old Northern Avenue Bridge, constructed in 1908, is a pivotal lift swing bridge (the center section lifts and pivots to allow vessels to pass). No longer viable, it has been replaced but retained as a

History Belongs
To Those Who Save It.

The Old Northern Avenue Bridge   BOSTON, 1919

WalkBoston's postcard for the coalition to Save the
Northern Avenue Bridge shows the bridge and the
downtown waterfront in 1919. *(Courtesy of WalkBoston.
Postcard produced by WalkBoston for the Save the Old
Northern Avenue Bridge coalition. Artwork by Joe
Heroun; concept by Paul Farrell, architect.)* ·

historic feature in the channel. As this
guidebook goes to press, a prolonged battle
to determine whether the preservation laws
will work to preserve this bridge appears
likely to succeed. Its outcome will decide
whether you cross the channel on a restored
Old Northern Avenue Bridge or on a pallid
modern substitute.

The South Boston side of the bridge
runs into the former Commonwealth Flats,
which, at the turn of the century, became
the last part of the central Boston area to be
filled. (Landfill continued in other areas—
East Boston, farther out in South Boston,
and in the South Bay and Roxbury Canal
areas—until the 1960s.) Development of
the Commonwealth Flats culminated in the
building of **Commonwealth Pier** (1914)
(now the World Trade Center) and the Fish
Pier farther out on Northern Ave. Both
were state-of-the-art (for the time) facilities
built by the Commonwealth in what turned
out to be an unsuccessful attempt to stem
the decline of the port of Boston. At the
turn of this century, a booming economy

has once again fueled intensive
development on the Commonwealth Flats, now redubbed the
"Seaport District."

*Turn to the right at Sleeper St.,
then turn right and go down the
stairs, taking the boardwalk under
the modern Evelyn Moakley Bridge.
(If you crossed the channel on the
Moakley Bridge, there are stairs
down from the right sidewalk to the
boardwalk. If the boardwalk is
closed, you can follow a path along
nearby Sleeper St. instead.) Stay on
the boardwalk until you come to the
Children's Museum, in one of the*

15. Boston Wharf Company Buildings

Between 1880 and 1930, the Boston
Wharf Company, which had filled the land
and developed the area, built block after
block of huge brick warehouses to meet the
need of Boston industries for warehousing
accessible to both rail and sea. These were
soon filled, primarily with wool for the textile industry. The Boston and Albany, Old
Colony, and New York and New England
Railroads built lines into the area as the
land was filled, and each warehouse had its
own spur.

Boston Wharf Company Warehouse (1889), Congress St. at Fort Point Channel, by M. D. Safford

The building now known as Museum
Wharf, occupied by the Children's
Museum, typifies Boston Wharf Company
construction, although it has been somewhat altered for museum use. The rail spur
ran alongside, between the building and the
channel. In recent years, this area has
undergone a renaissance as an in-town
community of residences, offices, and
artists' lofts. Many of the buildings have

bronze medallions indicating their construction dates.

Just beyond this building is the **Congress Street Bridge.** Built in 1930 to replace an earlier structure, the Congress St. Bridge represents the final period of development of the channel and the warehouse district. It is a single-leaf bascule bridge. The heavy concrete bascule acts as a counterweight to raise the draw section.

Cross Congress St. and continue along the walkway beside the channel—under the arcade of a modern office building—to Summer St. Look to your left along Summer St. and across to Melcher St. to see another view of the Boston Wharf Company's buildings.

Built in 1898, the Summer St. Bridge was a retractable bridge, in which the two center sections move aside horizontally on rails, a design developed in Boston. In the 1990s the bridge was entirely rebuilt as a modern fixed bridge, although many elements of the old bridge were retained. As you cross the bridge, the diagonal rails on which the original bridge once rolled back to let boats pass are visible over the railing.

Walk across it and along Summer St. to

16. **South Station,** 620–690 Atlantic Ave., head house (1898), by Shepley, Rutan and Coolidge

When the Grand Union Station, or South Station, was built in 1898, it consolidated terminals for five separate railroads that had connected Boston to the south and west since the 1850s, and heralded the consolidation of those lines. This consolidation, controlled by New York owners who would use freight rate differentials to place Boston shippers at a disadvantage to New York shippers, would ultimately deal a major blow to the port of Boston. In the short run, however, the building of South Station spurred the development of the

South Boston industrial waterfront and the modernization of transportation facilities in the area.

South Station was the prototype of the "double-decker" system of train terminals, designed with twenty-eight tracks for trains arriving on two floors—the upper (or main) floor at ground level for long-distance travel and a loop track arrangement below grade for subway and suburban electric service, although the latter was never used. The thirteen-acre train shed, demolished in the 1930s and recently replaced with a more modern "multimodal transportation facility," was the largest in the world at the time. A 1901 Y.M.C.A. guidebook ticked off its impressive statistics:

> The trackage under roof measures four miles. The roof has three rows of trusses, the middle span being 228 feet, the side spans, 177 feet each. In the construction of this mammoth building there were used as follows: 43,000 piles, nearly 16½

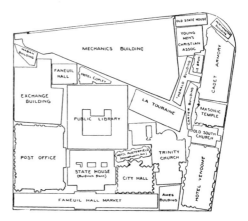

Plan showing how twenty-four large buildings in Boston might be placed within the area covered by the South Terminal Station.
(From [J. H. Tewksbury], Historic Boston: Sight-Seeing Tours around the Hub, *[Boston]: Young Men's Christian Associations, 1901, p. 153.)*

million bricks, 106,000 cubic yards of stone and concrete masonry, 15,000 tons of steel, 200,000 cubic feet of cut stone, 90,000 barrels of cement, 14,500 barrels of pitch and asphalt, 425 tons of tarred paper, 212 tons of sheet copper, 5,000,000 feet of pine, 8 tons of solder, about 3½ acres of wire glass, and about 20 tons of putty to set the same. The paint used, reduced to a single coat, would cover 200 acres (Tewksbury 156).

Although the train shed is long gone and the extensive wings of the original granite head house[2] were shorn by urban renewal in the 1970s, the remaining head house has been refurbished inside, preserving at least the outlines of its Victorian grandeur and providing the weary traveler with a bite to eat and a place to sit and watch the world go by.

When Commonwealth Pier was developed after the turn of the century, Summer St. was extended as a viaduct over the vast freight yards in South Boston, and connected by Viaduct St. to the upper (or passenger) level of Commonwealth Pier. This grade-level separation allowed passengers to be whisked swiftly and stylishly from train to ship far above the congestion of the sea-to-rail freight transfer below, which completed the advanced transportation network of the new Boston waterfront. It was the grand culmination of Victorian Boston's drive to design an ever-larger, ever more efficient, ever more grandiose waterfront, and it marked the end of the era when such a waterfront was needed.

The Red Line's South Station T stop has several entrances within and around the head house of South Station.

TOUR 2

BOSTON'S SOUTH END: MID-NINETEENTH-CENTURY URBAN PLANNING AND ARCHITECTURE

by Margaret Supplee Smith and Richard O. Card

Tour Location: See Downtown Key Map for the location of the Tour and its T stop, page xli.

About Walking the Tour: At the start of the twenty-first century, the South End has once again become, as it had a century and a half earlier, a popular residential neighborhood for middle-class and professional Bostonians. In an era when the condominium has become far more common for city living than the single private home, new construction on this level area has tended to be on a much larger scale, but a substantial portion of the gracious nineteenth-century neighborhood remains to be savored today.

Thumbnail Sketch of Sights: See Introduction, page xxxiii.

Approximate Walking Time: 2½ hours.

T Stop: Back Bay/South End T Station, Orange Line.

Begin at: The Cyclorama Building of Boston Center for the Arts, 539 Tremont St. (Leave the Back Bay/South End station by the rear exit to Clarendon St. Turn right onto Clarendon St. and follow it for a few blocks until it ends at Tremont St. Turn left on Tremont St. and stop in front of the second building on the left.)

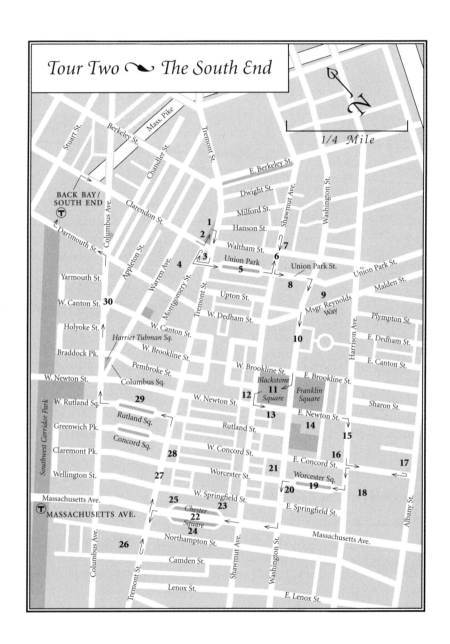

Tour Two ∾ The South End

1/4 Mile

BACK BAY / SOUTH END Ⓣ

Stuart St.

Berkeley St.

Mass. Pike

Chandler St.

Tremont St.

E. Berkeley St.

Dwight St.

Milford St.

Shawmut Ave.

Washington St.

Dartmouth St.

Columbus Ave.

Clarendon St.

Appleton St.

Hanson St.

1
2

Waltham St.
3

Union Park
5

Union Park St.

7
6

Union Park St.

Malden St.

Warren Ave.

Montgomery St.

4

Upton St.

Tremont St.

W. Dedham St.

8

9

Msgr. Reynolds Way

Plympton St.

E. Dedham St.

Harrison Ave.

Yarmouth St.

W. Canton St. **30**

Holyoke St.

Braddock Pk.

W. Newton St.

Harriet Tubman Sq.

W. Canton St.

W. Brookline St.

Pembroke St.

Columbus Sq.

10

E. Canton St.

W. Brookline St.

Blackstone
Square
11

E. Brookline St.

Franklin
Square

Southwest Corridor Park

W. Rutland Sq.

29

Rutland Sq.

Concord Sq.

W. Newton St.

12

13

Sharon St.

E. Newton St.
14

15

Greenwich Pk.

Claremont Pk.

Wellington St.

Rutland St.

W. Concord St.

28

27

Worcester St.

E. Concord St.

16

Albany St.

17

Massachusetts Ave.

Ⓣ MASSACHUSETTS AVE.

25

Chester
22
Square
24

23

W. Springfield St.

21

Worcester Sq.
19

20

18

E. Springfield St.

Columbus Ave.

26

Tremont St.

Northampton St.

Camden St.

Shawmut Ave.

Washington St.

Massachusetts Ave.

Lenox St.

E. Lenox St.

INTRODUCTION

Two unique residential districts were developed in Boston in the mid-nineteenth century—the Back Bay and the South End. Singular in the magnitude of their scale, planning, and execution, both projects were, however, typical of the Victorian period, involving considerable foresight, enterprise, and audacity. Common to both developments were extensive landfill operations to create "new" land from the marshy Back Bay and South Cove waters, and comprehensive plans by which each district was realized as an area of broad streets lined by rows of substantial town houses and varied by planted open spaces. The Back Bay is well known as the model of the prosperous Victorian urban neighborhood, its distinctive brownstone houses epitomizing the bourgeois respectability of the proper Bostonians dwelling within them. Although the South End developed slightly earlier and is the largest Victorian urban residential district remaining in the United States, it is less widely known.

The South End was conceived and planned as a residential area as early as 1801, but for half a century received only nominal attention from both the City of Boston and private investors. Then, in the 1850s, it became the center of real estate activity in Boston. The city, faced with a dearth of land for expansion on its limited peninsula, was forced into more systematic development of the area in hopes of offsetting the exodus of native Bostonians to the surrounding suburbs.

The nucleus of the present South End was the narrow "Neck" of barren land that provided the original land access into Boston from the mainland (see "Boston Neck," Preface, and p. xlvi). The geographical limits of the South End were determined by the traditional territorial boundaries of Boston and by the newer nineteenth-century speculative ventures into railroads and landfill operations. East Berkeley St. (formerly Dover St.), sometimes considered the northern boundary, is the site of the narrowest section of the Neck, where it spanned only some forty yards and was frequently under water during high tides. The southern terminus, Lenox St., is near the old boundary line separating Boston and Roxbury. The western boundary is described by the old Boston & Providence and Boston & Worcester railroad tracks, which at one time crisscrossed the waters of the Back Bay and whose disruption of the tidal flow was instrumental in the Back Bay's ultimately being filled. Albany St., the eastern boundary, is built entirely on land reclaimed from the South Bay.

Although there are public buildings, hotels, hospitals, schools, and factories in the district, the characteristic architecture of the South End is the brick, bow-fronted, high-stooped town house, which continues the conservative, English-influenced tradition of residential building found on Beacon Hill and the streets bordering the Public Garden (see T5, T6, T8). Although much of the area has been altered or demolished, enough remains to convey the physical structure and architectural forms of a mid-nineteenth-century urban community.

As you begin your tour, you may walk through an area of smaller, more modest homes built in the 1860s. These replicate the form, although not the elaborate ornament, of the more monumental town houses that set the style in the South End of the 1850s.

1. **Cyclorama Building** (1884), 539 Tremont St., by Cummings and Sears

This two-story circular building originally displayed turrets (still visible from across the street) and battlements, with two larger towers facing Tremont St. (the present facade is a later modification). It was designed to house *Cyclorama of the Battle of Gettysburg*,[1] a four-hundred-foot-long panorama executed by the French artist Paul Philippoteaux. Faux terrain with actual objects suggesting a battlefield heightened the realism of the painting, which completely surrounded the viewing platform. Cycloramas were extremely popular with the Boston public, and a number of other works, ranging from *Custer's Last Fight* to the Hawaiian volcano *Kilauea*, were later exhibited at this site. The Cyclorama Building admirably demonstrates the flexibility necessary to survive in an urban setting, variously serving as an arena for roller polo, boxing tournaments (with an 1894 appearance by John L. Sullivan), roughriding drills, and a bicycling academy. After use as a factory for three-wheeled electric automobiles and then as the location of

The Cyclorama Building, 539 Tremont St., detail of original program (ca. 1884). Designed to house the four-hundred-foot-long *Cyclorama of the Battle of Gettysburg*. (Courtesy of the Richard O. Card collection.)

Bostock's Animal Arena, it became a garage, in which Albert Champion invented the spark plug. Housing the Boston Flower Exchange from 1923 to 1970, the old Cyclorama Building has been the nucleus of the Boston Center for the Arts since 1970 (see Cummings and Sears T4, T5).

2. **Smith American Organ Company** (1865), 551 Tremont St.

Now part of the Boston Center for the Arts complex, this building was built as the factory of the Smith American Organ Company, whose reed organs were found in many New England homes. The building's mansard-roofed top story was never restored after an 1885 fire. Here later came the George Frost Company, manufacturers of the Gentleman's Boston Garter and Velvet Grip Hose Supporter for ladies. After the 1940s the site was used by florists associated with the nearby flower market. It now contains artists' studios, a gallery, and a restaurant.

3. **St. Cloud Hotel** (1869–70), 565–569 Tremont St., by Nathaniel J. Bradlee

Providing an effective terminus to Union Park, this marble-faced French Academic building is an early example of an apartment hotel. In contrast to the generally vertical pattern of living in the South End, here one lived horizontally in "French flats," as this type of living arrangement was called at the time. Built shortly before the land values started to decline in the South End, the building had become derelict prior to its 1985 renovation into condominiums, artists' studios, and commercial space (see N. J. Bradlee Site 8, and T4, T5, T10, T11).

Now walk a little way up Montgomery St., behind the St. Cloud building. On your right is the **Clarendon Street Baptist Church**, *built*

The Boston English High and Latin School, Dartmouth and Montgomery Sts., engraving. The corner tower was never actually built. (*From* King's Hand-Book of Boston, *9th ed., Boston: Moses King, 1889, p. 153.*)

in 1869 from a design by Samuel J. F. Thayer. Gordon College originated from this church in 1889. The original congregation remained here until the building was largely destroyed by fire in 1982. It was renovated into condominiums in 1987.

4. The English High and Latin School

(1877–81; nonextant), **Warren Ave., Montgomery St., and Dartmouth St.,** by George A. Clough

The elaborate brick, sandstone, and terracotta building that originally stood next to the church on the site of the McKinley (formerly Mackey) School was considered the largest free public school in the world at the time of its construction. It was 420 feet long with a drill hall that would seat three thousand persons. The Boston Latin School facade was on Warren Ave., while the English High faced Montgomery St. Before the construction of the Boston Public Library in Copley Sq., this building was considered as a possible location for the expanded library facilities. Used by English High until 1949, it was then demolished and the present building erected.

Now turn left on Union Park and follow the crosswalk across Tremont St.

5. Union Park

This small residential square was designed under the direction of Ezra Lincoln by city engineers, who were responsible for creating the mid-nineteenth-century South End, which included three new residential squares. The small size of Union Park was dictated by the radiating street pattern of the South End, which narrows at the Neck and widens toward Roxbury. Lots were auctioned in November 1851 and the square developed through the 1850s, with the houses showing a variety of architectural sources, such as Greek Revival (45 Union Park), and a picturesque Boston bowfront version of Italianate (42–52 Union Park). The elaborate lintels of the latter are of cast iron.

Many substantial Boston citizens resided on the square, including the grocer S. S. Pierce[2] (5 Union Park) and Alexander H. Rice, mayor of Boston (1856–57), congressman, and thrice-elected governor of Massachusetts (34 Union Park).

Residential parks, not widely adopted in early-nineteenth-century Boston because of space limitations, became the focus of a

Union Park with a waiting carriage, seen from near Shawmut Ave. (ca. 1870). (*Courtesy of the Richard O. Card collection.*)

gracious neighborhood wherever they were used. The small parks scattered throughout the South End were obviously intended to evoke associations with the prestigious Tontine Crescent (designed by Charles Bulfinch in 1793, demolished in 1858) and Louisburg Sq., completed in 1844 (see Louisburg Sq. T6, T8). Designed not so much for public use as to beautify the city and to increase property values, the residential squares reflect the enclosed and intimate sense of neighborhood space favored in English planning. Although the original Union Park fence had been replaced about 1903, the original fountains were restored and new trees planted to replace the lost elms as part of the 1990–92 Restoration Master Plan.

Continue past the park and turn left on Shawmut Ave.

6. Shawmut Ave.

Originally called "Suffolk Street," this is one of the oldest streets in the South End. Laid out parallel to the major thoroughfare of Washington St., the street was built initially with smaller frame houses, which were mostly replaced with brick structures in the 1840s and 1850s. 281–293 Shawmut Ave. (ca. 1852) form an unusual group of row houses, featuring stepped and curved Flemish Revival gables. The facades of these houses were originally covered with a stucco finish made to look like stone.

Shawmut Ave. from Pelham St. (ca. 1870), Josiah Johnson Hawes, photographer. *(The Josiah Johnson Hawes Collection, courtesy of the John Fitzgerald Kennedy Library, Boston.)*

7. Zion German Lutheran Church (1847), Shawmut Ave. and Waltham St.

This simple brick Greek Revival church was built by the German Evangelical Lutheran Society of Boston and dedicated on Christmas Day 1847. The South End in this period was absorbing a substantial German immigrant population, many employed in the woodworking crafts and, subsequently, in the Boston pianoforte industry (see piano factories T1). This congregation later built the larger church (1899) on West Newton St., and then moved, in 1955, to its present home on the corner of Marlborough and Berkeley Sts. Subsequently the original church became a restaurant for a time, and it is now used only for storage.

Now retrace your steps on Shawmut Ave. and turn left on Union Park St.

8. South Congregational Church (1861), Union Park St., by Nathaniel J. Bradlee

This brick amalgamation of Renaissance and Romanesque Revival features was designed and built for the South Congregational Church (actually Unitarian and unrelated to Old South Church). The tower was originally topped by a belfry with twelve slender columns, now missing, and there was a rose window on the facade. The pastor to the church for the entire quarter century here was Edward Everett Hale, the great orator and author, probably best known today as the writer of *The Man without a Country* (1869) (see E. E. Hale T6). In 1887, after the congregation had moved to the Back Bay, this building was sold to Temple Ohabei Shalom, an important Reform Jewish synagogue that remained here for nearly forty years. In 1925 the present Greek Orthodox Church of St. John the Baptist was established and took over the building, the interior of which was later decorated in the Byzantine tradition. A collapsed ceiling in 1995 required extensive restoration of the church.

Continue to Washington St. and turn right.

9. The Cathedral of the Holy Cross

(1866–75), **Washington St.**, by Patrick C. Keely

The genesis of the cathedral took place in 1860 when Bishop Fitzpatrick, yielding to the combined pressures of business and traffic, sold the original Holy Cross Church on Franklin St. (designed by Charles Bulfinch, built 1800–1803). By purchasing land for the new church on Washington St. in the newly developed South End, Fitzpatrick was following the western settlement pattern of Boston, although theretofore mostly Protestant churches had been built in the South End and few Catholics lived in the area. By the time the church was finally completed, many Catholics had moved into the South End, so its location proved convenient after all. Reminders of the discrimination some-

South Congregational Church, Union Park St. (ca. 1870), Josiah Johnson Hawes, photographer. *(The Josiah Johnson Hawes Collection, courtesy of the John Fitzgerald Kennedy Library, Boston.)*

times endured by Catholics in Boston are in the vestibule arch of Holy Cross Cathedral: the bricks saved from the Ursuline convent in Charlestown (burned by a mob in 1834) and reused.

An impressive building, constructed of Roxbury pudding stone (see also Site 28) with granite and sandstone trim, Holy Cross was completed in the same year that Boston was elevated to an archdiocese (1875). It has an area of some forty-six thousand square feet. Spires were initially planned but never built. The cathedral's great 1875 Hook and Hastings organ, now once again in playing order, is the largest surviving nineteenth-century organ in the country. The magnificent nineteenth-century stained glass has also required extensive recent restoration work.

10. Washington St.

The location of the original road connecting Roxbury to Boston, this street was celebrated for its superb sleigh racing before the Victorian development of the South End. In 1856 its first horsecar line was constructed, running from Scollay Sq. to Roxbury. The elevated trains followed at the turn of the century and ran here until 1987.

Proceeding along Washington St., past the Blackstone School, you will see Blackstone Sq. on your right and Franklin Sq. on your left. With the demolition of the elevated tracks, dedicated rapid transit Silver Line bus lanes

Cathedral of the Holy Cross as originally planned, engraving. *(From Edward Stanwood, Boston Illustrated, Boston: James P. Osgood and Company, 1872, p. 84.)*

have been set up along Washington St. At each bus stop there are new kiosks whose panels commemorate, with period pictures, scenes in the South End over the past two centuries.

11. Blackstone Sq.

The location of Blackstone and Franklin Sqs. dates back to the original plan for the Neck lands by the Boston selectmen in 1801. As chairman of the selectmen, Charles Bulfinch is thought to have been the major contributor to the plan, which included straight, right-angled streets and large blocks, with an elliptical grass plot called Columbia Sq. as the focal point of the new district. This plan represented an early attempt to break from the organic and curvilinear street pattern characteristic of old Boston.

Initially the squares were viewed less as residential squares and more as public

ornaments. After nearly half a century of neglect this area became a center of residential activity in the late 1840s and early 1850s. Columbia Sq., divided by Washington St., became Franklin and Blackstone Sqs. The original mid-nineteenth-century fountains in the parks, ornamented with dolphins, have survived and were restored in the early 1980s. Improvements at that time included installation of new fencing, benches, and tree plantings.

Cross Blackstone Sq., on your right, to Shawmut Ave., which is parallel to Washington St.

12. 425–435 Shawmut Ave. (1847)

These fine row houses, facing Blackstone Sq. on the west, are characteristic of Greek Revival urbanity, with their strong impression of surface continuity, brick and granite facades, subtle bowfronts, and moderately pitched roofs.

Turn left onto West Newton St., beside the park.

Blackstone Sq., looking toward corner of Shawmut Ave. and West Brookline St. (ca. 1860s). *(Courtesy of the David R. Hocker collection.)*

Italianate houses facing Blackstone Sq. along West Newton St. (ca.1860s), stereograph. *(Courtesy of the Society for the Preservation of New England Antiquities.)*

13. 35–45 West Newton St. (early 1850s)

The correct and academic application of architectural motifs, unusual in the South End, makes this group of brownstone town houses unique and reflects the interest during the 1850s in the Italianate palazzo style. In England Sir Charles Barry revived the style, which is exemplified in the United States by such buildings as the Philadelphia Athenæum (1845), designed by John Notman. In the early 1870s, before his invention of the telephone, Alexander Graham Bell lived and taught deaf-mutes on the parlor floor of 35 West Newton St. (see Bell T12).

West Newton St. becomes East Newton St. as one crosses Washington St.

14. St. James Hotel (1867–68), 11 East Newton St., facing Franklin Sq., by John R. Hall

Along with the residential construction of the 1850s and 1860s came the establishment of churches, schools, and public buildings, many in this Washington St. area. Built for the editor of *Ballou's Pictorial*, Maturin M. Ballou, the St. James Hotel was considered the most fashionable in the South End and was host to such guests as President Ulysses S. Grant (1869) and waltz king Johann

Strauss, Jr. (1872). The seven-story building, with its projecting central and side pavilions, central domes, superimposed orders, and mansard roof, reflects the influence of the then-new Boston City Hall (1861–65), designed by Gridley J. F. Bryant and Arthur Gilman, one of the early monuments of the French Second Empire style in the United States (see Old City Hall p. xxxi, Introduction, and T4). The history of this building emphasizes the adaptation necessary to survive in the city. It remained a hotel only fourteen years, afterwards becoming the New England Conservatory of Music (1882–1901), then a large nonprofit hotel for young working women, the Franklin Square House, which it remained from 1902 until 1970. In the latter period it was extended to Washington St. Today the still-handsome building has been transformed into apartments for senior citizens.

Continue along East Newton St. and turn right on Harrison Ave.

St. James Hotel/New England Conservatory of Music/Franklin Square House, Franklin Sq., engraving. *(From* King's Hand-Book of Boston, *9th ed., Boston: Moses King, 1889, p. 159.)*

15. Harrison Ave.

Originally named "Front Street," this was the site of the first land-filling activities in the South End. When first projected in

1804, a seventy-foot-wide street laid in a completely straight line was a novelty in Boston.

16. Immaculate Conception Church

(1858–61), **761 Harrison Ave.,** by Patrick C. Keely

Despite opposition to their intention to build a new church and college in Boston, Catholics were finally able to realize their plans on this South End site. It was not quite as convenient as the original North End location on which they had intended to build, but it was ultimately more desirable for its accessibility from surrounding towns (see early Catholic churches T3). Designed by the same architect as Holy

Church of the Immaculate Conception and Boston College (ca. 1865), stereograph. *(Courtesy of the Richard O. Card collection.)*

Cross Cathedral, Patrick C. Keely,[3] the white New Hampshire granite church has classical motifs and an elaborate interior planned by Arthur Gilman, some of which was destroyed in a controversial remodeling done in the 1980s to create a Jesuit Urban Center (see Keely T9).

The original building of Boston College, to the right of Immaculate Conception, was designed by Louis Weissbein and built concurrently with the church next door. It was not

intended to serve as a college until the church could provide sufficient revenue and was used between 1860 and 1863 as a retreat for Jesuit scholars. The first college students entered in September 1864. The redbrick complex, formerly crowned with a cupola, served Boston College until the school moved to its suburban campus in Chestnut Hill in 1913, and later was the home of Boston College High School. A recent building now connects it to the church.

Turn left and proceed along East Concord St. The old Homeopathic Hospital is on your left, on the corner of Albany St.

17. Massachusetts Homeopathic Hospital

(1875–76), 82 East Concord St., by William R. Emerson

This redbrick Victorian Gothic building, with its picturesque roofline and ornate wooden entrance porch, once faced a formal French garden. Its architect, William Ralph Emerson, also designed numerous Shingle-style country houses and the Boston Art Club at Newbury and Dartmouth Sts. (see William Ralph Emerson T4, T5, T9, T12; Boston Art Club T5).

Now part of Boston Medical Center, this was originally a homeopathic hospital

Boston University School of Medicine (left) and Massachusetts Homeopathic Hospital, East Concord St., engraving. *(From King's Hand-Book of Boston, 9th ed., Boston: Moses King, 1889, p. 149.)*

renowned for its cure rate, especially with seemingly hopeless cases. Homeopathic medicine, popular in the nineteenth century, relied on limited dosages of simple medications carefully tailored to the symptoms of the individual patient rather than on surgery or the harsh overuse of drugs characteristic of the orthodox medical practices of earlier times. When surgery was deemed necessary, the patients were wheeled across the courtyard to the Boston University School of Medicine, which in 1874 had united with the New England Female Medical College, the first medical school to admit women, and occupied an adjacent building, now demolished. Known in its day for its sunny, modern hospital rooms, the remaining portions of the original Massachusetts Homeopathic building have recently been renovated to house the Boston University School of Public Health.

Now return to Harrison Ave. and turn left.

Boston City Hospital, Harrison Ave., engraving. *(From* King's Hand-Book of Boston, *9th ed., Boston: Moses King, 1889, p. 227.)*

18. **Boston City Hospital** (1861–64), **Harrison Ave. facing Worcester Sq.,** by Gridley J. F. Bryant

After twenty years of discussion concerning the need for a municipal hospital, the city finally allocated seven acres of land in the newly developed South End for that purpose in late 1860. Designed by the same architect as the Old City Hall on School St. (see Introduction, p. xxxi, and T4), the hospital featured a central iron-domed administration building (nonextant) connected by colonnaded walkways to flanking mansard-roofed medical and surgical pavilions. It was set in the midst of elegant French ornamental gardens. Subsequent additions in response to the hospital's ongoing need for more space have obscured the original building complex beyond recognition, although two of the mansard-roofed flanking buildings survive and have been restored. In 1996 Boston City Hospital merged with Boston University Medical Center Hospital to form Boston Medical Center.

Worcester Sq. is on your right, opposite the hospital complex.

19. **Worcester Sq.**

This elongated elliptical park created a gracious and symmetrical approach to the Boston City Hospital, whose central domed administration building once provided a focus for the square. The city embellished the park in the early 1850s, but the house lots were not auctioned until 1859. Building proceeded rapidly at that point, and the square was completed within two years. With its uniform cornice line, brick bowfront facades, and high-stooped entrances, Worcester Sq. presents the most cohesive appearance of all the South End squares.

Walk to the other end of the square, where it meets Washington St. The Allen House is on the left corner.

Aaron Allen house, Washington St. and Worcester Sq., engraving. *(From Edward Stanwood,* Boston Illustrated, *Boston: James P. Osgood and Company, 1872, p. 89.)*

20. **Aaron H. Allen House** (1859–60), **1682 Washington St.,** by John J. McNutt

Providing an impressive entrance to Worcester Sq., this brownstone house was unusual for the South End in its scale, material, and pretension. With its similar front and side elevations, the mansion acknowledged its importance to both Washington St. and Worcester Sq. John McNutt, presumed from contemporary accounts to have been both designer and builder, later was proprietor of the Novelty Wood Works (corner of Malden and Wareham Sts.) and did considerable theatrical work as well as homes, stores, and offices. Allen was a furniture dealer and many of the architectural details show an affinity to furniture design of the period. Like William Dean Howells's upwardly mobile protagonist in *The Rise of Silas Lapham* (1885), who moved from the South End to the Back Bay, Allen sold his South End house after twelve years and moved to Beacon St (see *Rise of Silas Lapham*, Introduction, T6).

The building served successively as headquarters for the Central Club (a South End men's club founded in 1869) until 1881, the Catholic Union of Boston (which was responsible for the brick auditorium attached to the rear of the house) from 1894 to 1937, Boston College High School (which used the building as an annex until 1941), and the Lebanese-American Club of Boston after 1941. It then entered a period of deterioration, which ended ultimately with the City of Boston taking over the property in 1958. Sold for $5,500 to a private individual at public auction in 1960, the house lost its cupola in a fire a decade later and also suffered further indignities. Stabilized by the city in 1994, this endangered landmark has since been redeveloped into condominiums, with extensive exterior restoration, including replacement of the missing cupola.
Now look diagonally across Washington St.

21. **Deacon House** (1848), **Washington, West Concord, and Worcester Sts.,** by Jean Lemoulnier

Here an elegant brick mansion, designed by a French architect working briefly in Boston, was once a Boston showplace. Only a remnant of the original house survives. The Deacon House featured the first mansard roof in Boston, a gatehouse, and elegant interiors that included a set of decorative panels by Claude-Nicholas Ledoux and a pair of large paintings by François Boucher (both now in the Boston Museum of Fine Arts). Exhibiting much grander scale than the typical South End brick row house, the Deacon House was little used after the death of Mr. Deacon and was auctioned off in 1871. The Massachusetts Normal Art School (now the Massachusetts College of Art) moved here in 1881. After a fire, part of the building was removed and the remainder remodeled as a dance hall

Edward Preble Deacon house, Washington, West Concord, and Worcester Sts. Woodcut print. *(From* Gleason's Pictorial Drawing-Room Companion, *January 28, 1854; courtesy of the Richard O. Card collection.)*

and club rooms. The sign "1897 Deacon Halls," still visible behind modern construction, dates from this period. Fragments of the once-magnificent house later served as a storeroom for a hardware store. The remnant of the original house has now been converted into apartments.

Turn left on Washington St. and follow it to Massachusetts Ave. On your left, at 1724 Washington St. (1806), you should notice what is probably the only pre-Victorian structure remaining in the South End. Actually, this is a mirror-image double-house, with entrances on the sides, built in 1806 for William Porter and his son. The exterior appearance of this Federal-style building, which for years housed a barroom, was returned to its original aspect in a recent renovation into condominiums.

On your right is the Smith Block, built about 1859. Upper floors originally were used as a ballroom and social club, and there were four storefronts at street level. Much of the interior was destroyed by several fires in the 1980s. The building was remodeled into an antiques center in the late 1990s, and recently renovated again (with two large additions) as Minot Hall Residences.

At Massachusetts Ave., turn right and proceed across Shawmut Ave. to Chester Sq.

22. Chester Sq.

Larger than Union Park or Worcester Sq., Chester Sq. originally had elaborate gardens and a three-tiered fountain in its central park, with planted malls extending out to either side. Providing an effective terminus to the South End, the square reflects the widening street pattern toward Roxbury. Designed by engineer Ezra Lincoln, Chester Sq. was considered one of the most prestigious addresses in Boston for a period after its development. House lots on the square were auctioned in October 1850, although actual construction did not begin until the mid-1850s and continued through the 1860s. The 1½-acre park was devastated in 1952 when traffic-clogged Massachusetts Ave. was thrust through it, leaving only two small strips of green space.

Chester Sq. (ca. 1870), stereograph. *(Courtesy of the Society for the Preservation of New England Antiquities.)*

The town houses, rather more pretentious and grandiose than found elsewhere in the South End, epitomize the height of architectural taste in midcentury Boston with their brick swelled fronts, mansard roofs, and ornamental ironwork. Architectural detail is lavish and includes such varied styles as Italianate, Moorish, Gothic, and Academic Renaissance. Several houses deserve close attention, for instance:

23. 558 Massachusetts Ave. (1858)

Built in 1858 for William R. Carnes, a dealer in rosewood and mahogany, this lavishly ornamented house (originally 39 Chester Sq.) has been occupied since 1920 by the League of Women for Community Service. The architectural treatment of stringcourses and quoins on 558 and 560 Massachusetts Ave. is unusual for the South End, as is the quality and extent of the cast-iron ornament (see mahogany T1).

24. 545–547 Massachusetts Ave. (ca. 1853)

This pair of Renaissance Revival houses (originally 54–56 Chester Sq.), built around 1853, provides a focus within the square and is distinguished by greater scale, flat facades, restrained ornament, and brownstone material. Both still have their original cupolas.

25. 532 Massachusetts Ave. (1859), by Luther Briggs, Jr.

One of relatively few houses in the South End that can be definitely attributed to an architect, this brick bowfront house (originally 65 Chester Sq.) features the accentuated cornice and bold profile characteristics of the fully developed Italianate row house. It was built for Paul D. Wallis, a Roxbury builder and merchant who was active in both the South End and surrounding suburbs, and was first occupied by Francis Dane, a prominent businessman and shoe manufacturer. The house is now the headquarters of the South End Historical Society, a group of individuals interested in the history, preservation, and restoration of this urban neighborhood.

Proceed though the square and turn left on Tremont St. Tremont and many other South End streets were laid with horsecar track during the nineteenth century, and a large horsecar barn was nearby on Tremont St. Cars of rival lines were painted in different colors as an aid to those who could not read. Lines were later consolidated and electrified, and continued to run along this part of Tremont St. until 1961.

26. Chickering Building (1853–54), 791 Tremont St., by Edwin Payson

Constructed for the Jonas Chickering and Sons Piano-Forte Manufactory, one of many piano and organ builders in the South End during the nineteenth and early twentieth centuries, this brick building with the central cupola was said to be the largest manufacturing building in the United States. It was built around a large, open courtyard and, though bearing Italianate features, has been described as "plain American" in style. Used by a variety of small businesses after 1930, it was developed in 1973–74 by the Piano Craft Guild to provide housing and studios for artists (see piano factories T1).

Now turn back and continue along Tremont St. as far as West Concord St.

27. Tremont St.

Although most South End streets developed as small residential enclaves, Tremont St. exhibits a more monumental and boulevard aspect, which is reinforced by the conscious grouping of houses into cohesive and formal arrangements.

28. Tremont Street Methodist Church

(1860–62), **corner of Tremont and West Concord Sts.**, by Hammatt Billings

Widely praised in its day for its stylish Gothic Revival exterior, this church was the first in Boston to be constructed of Roxbury pudding stone, a variegated and irregular stone, quarried locally, which became extremely popular for church building in the 1860s and 1870s. The original E. E. Howard clock is still in the tower. New Hope Baptist Church, now located here, has done much to restore the church building.

Turn left at the next street, by the South End Branch Library and its little park.

29. 3–23 Rutland Sq.

Rutland Sq. is one of the smaller Victorian squares, built in the late 1860s and early 1870s to evoke associations with Chester Sq. and Union Park. These modest houses, with their wood and stone fronts and their Venetian Gothic detailing, deserve attention. Other houses on this square exhibit head keystones, unusual features that do, however, occur elsewhere in the South End.

*Walking through Rutland Sq., you will see the Union United Methodist Church directly in front of you on Columbus Ave. Originally the **Union Congregational Church** (1870), it was built of Roxbury pudding stone from a design by Alexander Estey (who also did Emmanuel Church in the Back Bay). The stone spire was not completed until five years later.*

Turn right on Columbus Ave., and con-

tinue past the park, Harriet Tubman Sq. (see Tubman; Tubman statue T8), to the intersection with West Canton St.

30. Columbus Ave., West Canton St., and Appleton St.

This corner is depicted in the well-known painting *Rainy Day, Boston* by Childe Hassam (1859–1935), an American Impressionist who lived on Columbus Ave. in the mid-1880s. Built in the early 1870s, this boulevard visually and literally connects the South End with downtown Boston. Initially paved with wooden blocks to mute the sound of passing vehicles, and intended to become a second Beacon St., Columbus Ave. instead followed the pattern of slow decline that characterized the rest of the South End. Private homes were converted into lodging houses, sometimes with storefronts added. Many factors contributed to this deterioration: the competition of the Back Bay district, the new emphasis on French formal planning and facades, the Depression of 1873 with its resultant collapse of speculative building and decrease in property values, and the popularity of the new streetcar suburbs. Ultimately much of the South End became, by the end of the nineteenth century, a convenient port of entry into Boston for its growing immigrant population.

From this point continue walking one block along Columbus Ave.; turn left at the red light on Dartmouth St. to return to Back Bay/South End T Station.

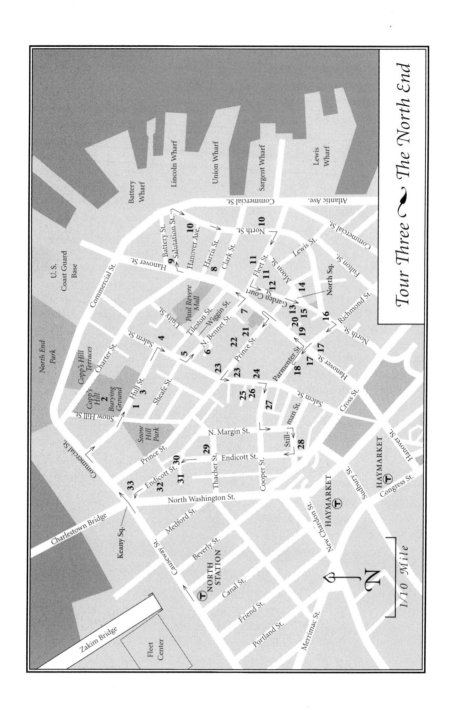

Tour Three ～ The North End

ETHNIC DIVERSITY IN THE VICTORIAN NORTH END

by Will Holton

Tour Location: See Downtown Key Map for the location of the Tour and its T stop, page xli.

About Walking the Tour: Our walking tour begins at the corner of Commercial and Hull Sts. (a few blocks from North Station) and ends at the same corner. (There are also optional directions from the last site directly to the North Station T stop.) The ascent of Hull St. is short, but  steep. However, after a moderate descent the tour continues on level ground. Keep in mind that the sites included in this tour are only a selection of the important Victorian legacy in the North End. There will be temptations to look more closely at side streets and nearby sites along the way to make one's own discoveries. Many will want to stop for Italian food, espresso and pastries, specialty groceries (for eating at home), and delicious full meals in the scores of excellent cafés and restaurants.

Thumbnail Sketch of Sights: See Introduction, page xxxiii.

Approximate Walking Time: 2 hours

T Stop: North Station, Green and Orange Lines

By Car: Parking is handy for a reasonable fee in the North End Garage on Commercial St. between Prince and Hull Sts.

Begin at: Commercial St. at the foot of the Hull St. hill. (Upon leaving the North Station T by the main exit, turn right onto Causeway St. for two blocks. The large intersection at Causeway St., North Washington St., and the foot of the Charlestown Bridge is called Keany Sq. Continue straight across; shortly after this, Causeway St. becomes Commercial St. Hull St. will soon appear on the right-hand side.)

INTRODUCTION

This walking tour is organized with several themes mingled throughout. Attention is paid to the social importance of lingering Protestant "yankees" and their institutions in the North End, sailors and maritime enterprises, Irish Catholic, Italian, and Jewish immigrant communities, benevolent activities, and industry in the North End. Some buildings dating from before the Victorian period are included to give a flavor of how the area looked at that time, and to cover how older buildings were used in new ways. Victorian structures included in the tour range from plain and cheap wooden houses and brick tenement buildings occupied by the poor to solid brick apartment houses, ornate brick and stone commercial buildings, and churches and public institutions.

Poverty, substandard housing, and ethnic diversity characterized the North End throughout the Victorian period. Through the eighteenth century the North End was a desirable residential neighborhood, with the homes of royal governors and other wealthy residents. By the early nineteenth century, however, the tremendous expansion of shipping on the nearby waterfront (T1) brought many sailors and undesirable activities in their wake. By 1837 the Irish Catholic immigration to Boston had begun in earnest, with the North End becoming the primary destination. In 1850 poor Irish immigrants made up between one-third and one-half of the approximately twenty thousand people who lived there. German immigrants were also a significant group here during this period. After that, the crowded neighborhood grew more slowly and peaked at about twenty-nine thousand in 1900. The North End remained mostly Irish American until after 1880.

By 1880 small and compact Jewish, Italian, and Portuguese communities had begun to form. Jewish immigrants from Russia, Hungary, Poland, Lithuania, Latvia, and other Eastern European countries settled in the North End. The Jewish community, centered on Salem St. south of Prince St., expanded between 1890 and 1910. Jewish residents then sought better housing in Roxbury and other areas so rapidly that the North End enclave had nearly disappeared by 1925. The Portuguese community remained small and never expanded much beyond two blocks east of Hanover St. and north of North Bennet St.

The Italian population of the North End grew and spread steadily after a small beginning in the 1870s. Throughout the fifty-year growth of the Italian community, referred to by 1900 as "Little Italy," immigrants clustered within the North End along regional lines owing to their various dialects and strong allegiance to their native towns. Starting in 1880 the Avellinesi (from Avellino, just east of Naples) expanded rapidly from a beginning just north of St. Leonard's Church, whereas Genovesi (from Genoa) remained concentrated south and west of North and Richmond Sts. Beginning around 1895, the Siciliani (from Sicily), many of whom were fishermen, settled on or near North St. close to the fishing docks and in a smaller area between Charter and Commercial Sts.

Intergroup conflict was a fact of life in the North End throughout the Victorian period. The Irish immigrants were greeted with scorn by the "native" English-Protestant residents. Soon after the beginning of the Victorian era, the Know-Nothing Party gained strength in Boston and fueled prejudice against the rapidly growing Irish Catholic group. Throughout Victorian times "no Irish need apply" was a common phrase in announcements of job openings, and the group was limited to the most menial and low-paying occupations. Over several decades violence frequently erupted on the Charlestown bridge, which separated Protestant Charlestown from the Irish North End. In turn, when the Italian and Jewish groups began to enter the North End, conflict erupted between them and the established Irish-American community. Ethnic slurs and harassment were targeted against all newcomers. Before and after the turn of the century, Irish and Italian "corner gangs" of young men clashed over control of prime turf in the North End. The Jewish residents seem to have largely avoided open conflict, but not verbal harassment.

During the Victorian period, proper Bostonian society seems to have largely overlooked the North End because it was a poor immigrant district that did not fit the desired image of their city. Many guidebooks of the time mentioned the Old North Church but little else, and Paul Revere's house had been greatly altered and was used for stores and apartments. When describing the Copp's Hill Burying Ground, Edwin Bacon (1889) wrote: "It is an attractive spot, in a part of the city, which, once quite aristocratic, now possesses little attraction" (241). An exception was *Rambles in Old Boston* by the Reverend Edward G. Porter, which discusses the "antiquarian relics" in the North End. Porter's efforts eventually led to the restoration of the Paul Revere House in 1908. Even recently the North End has not been considered to be of Victorian interest. In fact, this walk is one of the first published treatments to consider the Victorian significance of the North End.

We begin by ascending Hull St. As we climb the hill from Commercial St., the left side presents a streetscape of small apartment buildings that date mostly from the Victorian period. No. 55, in the middle of the block, is a wood building that somewhat predates the era; however, the site of the garage on the right saw the first manufacturing of gas for lighting purposes in New England in 1828. This was the Boston Illuminating Gas Company works (nonextant), which continued to operate here until at least 1930, and some residents still call nearby Snow Hill Park "the gassy."

1. 44 Hull St. (ca. 1804), Joseph Eustis, builder

At the top of the hill on the right is 44 Hull St., a small wooden structure built in about 1804. Joseph Eustis, a housewright, bought the land in 1804 and built the house for his family's home. In 1837, at the outset of the Victorian era, this house was owned by Thomas Neely, who was a "watchmaker" of Boston. No. 44 is supposed to be Boston's narrowest house, ten feet and six inches wide. The only survival of the second-growth wooden buildings in the area, with a back garden, the house is surrounded by late-Victorian and early twentieth-century brick apartment houses.

We enter the Colonial cemetery crowning Copp's Hill by way of steps and a gate that are directly opposite 44 Hull St.

2. Copp's Hill Burying Ground (1660); renovated twice during the Victorian era

{View of Boston Harbor, USS Constitution ("Old Ironsides"), Charlestown Navy Yard, Charlestown, and the Bunker Hill Monument}
The finely carved slate tombstones in

Copp's Hill Burying Ground reflect the Puritan beginnings of the North End, and there are a few Victorian monuments. Records indicate that the northwest section of the cemetery holds about one thousand graves of African American residents who lived on the slope of Copp's Hill from the seventeenth century until about 1800. Unfortunately, few gravestones are in this section, either because few were placed or because many have been removed. However, the highlight of this section, under a tree, is the Victorian black granite column for Prince Hall, Revolutionary War soldier and founder of the African American Masonic Order in America. Victor Young, historian of Boston's Prince Hall Masonic Lodge, tells us that the monument was unveiled on June 24, 1895, by John J. Smith, then Grand Master of the Prince Hall Masons, Jurisdiction of the Commonwealth of Massachusetts. African American Masons hold an impressive ceremony at the Prince Hall monument every Memorial Day (see Hall; Smith T7).

In 1891 Edward MacDonald, the superintendent of Copp's Hill, published the small book *Old Copp's Hill and Burial Ground with Historical Sketches,* which gives us insight into the nineteenth-century treatment of this Colonial legacy. He wrote

Copp's Hill Cemetery (1890). John W. Robbins, photographer. *(Courtesy of The Bostonian Society/Old State House.)*

in May 1833 that "fifty dollars was appropriated by the city authorities toward purchasing trees for ornamenting the grounds, and from that date the whole appearance of the Hill began to change and resume its ancient popularity" (30–31). MacDonald explains that other changes came soon after: "In 1838, new avenues and walks were laid out; grave stones were removed for that purpose, thus affording opportunities for pleasant promenades, which are by no means neglected. Considerable care was used when laying out the paths to place the tomb-stones as near as possible to their original positions" (31).

But this good Victorian start for the Copp's Hill Burying Ground was followed by hard times. MacDonald tells us that the cemetery was in poor condition until he became its superintendent: "Until within a few years the Hill has been very much neglected, and boys have been allowed to run wild through the grounds six months in the year. No one having charge during the winter months, the West and North End Boys would meet and imitate the North- and South-Enders on Pope Day, and it frequently required a squad of police to drive them away; but this has changed" (31).

He wrote that by 1891 the trees of 1833 had been removed and 180 trees "of a more agreeable character" replaced them. MacDonald, showing evidence of a city official's concern for an important Boston site, says that the Board of Health then took charge of the Copp's Hill Burying Ground, making improvements and restoring gravestones that had been buried or moved to cover the doors of tombs.

From the Charter St. side of the cemetery, we can see across the Copp's Hill Terraces.

Copp's Hill Terraces, designed by the firm of Olmsted, Olmsted and Eliot

The terraces were part of the original plan for North End Park, which extended across Commercial St. to the Waterfront. Money for construction of this three-acre park was raised largely through the efforts of City Councilor John Fitzgerald, the grandfather (Sites 8, 12; T6 note 12) of John Fitzgerald Kennedy. The plan called for a pedestrian bridge over the street, connecting to a two-level "promenade pier" that jutted into the harbor in an L-shape, protecting a small bathing beach. The bridge was not built because it would have interfered with the elevated transit line, which was built along Commercial St. in 1901. Twentieth-century changes have obliterated the beach and substantially

Christ Church ("Old North") (ca. 1890), Salem St. *(Courtesy of The Bostonian Society/Old State House).*

altered the park on the north side of Commercial St. The terraces with their massive stonework remain much as the Olmsted firm planned them.

Return to the Hull St. gate to exit Copp's Hill Burying Ground.

3. Hull Street Settlement and Medical Mission (1901), 36 Hull St., by Walter R. Forbush

Just to the left of the cemetery's Hull St. gate, the ornate Flemish gothic or Moorish structure with fine brickwork, stained glass, and a peaked top facade was opened as a medical clinic for immigrant women in 1901. The architect was Walter R. Forbush.

The Methodist Episcopal Church sponsored the Women's Home Missionary Society, which provided much-needed prenatal, obstetrical, and other services, as well as around-the-clock nursing care, at ten cents per case, seven days a week. When the clinic opened both Italian and Jewish immigrant women lived in crowded conditions in the blocks nearby. The building is now an apartment house.

As we descend Hull St., we see at its base

4. Christ Church ("Old North") (1723), Salem St.; commemorative tablet above the door set in 1878

This fine Wren-style Colonial church is Boston's oldest church building. It has remained Anglican (Episcopal) and active through several waves of ethnic immigration, largely because of its Revolutionary significance. During the Victorian period, guidebooks to Boston gave considerable attention to this church for its historic significance, although they said little else about the immigrant neighborhood of the North End. Henry Wadsworth Longfellow visited Christ Church on April 5, 1860, and wrote in his diary that a "Mr. H. who acts as a guide" told him about Revere's lanterns. The next day, Longfellow began writing "Listen, my children, and you shall hear / Of the midnight ride of Paul Revere" ("Paul Revere's Ride," in the "The Landlord's Tale," *Tales of the Wayside Inn.*).

Written just before the Civil War, the poem was intended, in part, as an alarm call to rouse the opponents of slavery (see Revere; Longfellow T6). Edwin Bacon[1] (1903) mentions the tablet above the door that reads, "The signal lanterns of Paul Revere displayed in the steeple of this church April 18, 1775."

Some of the tombs beneath Christ Church had an interesting use during the Victorian period. George W. McConnell, in *The Memorial History of Christ Church, Boston, Massachusetts* (1886), explains that a "stranger's tomb" was added in 1812 when the church was short on funds. Similar tombs for public interments were added over the years. One tomb would be filled up and sealed. Later, when room was needed for more burials, "the first tomb used was opened and the bones in it were collected and thrown into a large vault or well that was built for the purpose in the cellar." The two "bone wells" were closed in about 1851; in 1860 "the vestry voted to seal up all the tombs belonging to the church."

Christ Church Sexton's House (1850), 193 Salem St., George W. Pope, builder

The Victorian residential structure to the left of the church at 193 Salem St. was built by mason George W. Pope under an agreement with Christ Church. He had use of the building for twelve years, and then it became the sexton's house. This handsome building in brick has a recessed doorway and a paneled wood door with side and top lights. It remains in use as the sexton's residence and for choir practices.

Turn right on Salem St., and walk to the corner of Tileston St.

5. North Bennet Street Industrial School, 171–173 Salem St.; the Salem Street Church (1828); the Boston Seaman's Friend Society Building (1874)

The 1828 Salem Street Church, a beautiful Classic Revival church, stood on this corner. It had a wide bow-fronted vestibule and a seventy-one- by seventy-four-foot sanctuary with high, narrow, granite-topped windows on the sides. Two of the original window openings of the 1828 church are barely visible from the Tileston St. side because the present Victorian Gothic structure was built around the core of the original church. The remaining section of the 1874 Boston Seaman's Friend Society building on Salem St. has unusual corbeled brickwork under the eaves and a mansard roof. In 1879 fifty women volunteers from the Associated Charities rented rooms here and started giving classes in sewing and laundry for "worthy poor" women. Soon the North End Industrial Home was leasing the entire building. Pauline Agassiz Shaw (1841–1917) established a day nursery there, one of the first in the nation. In 1884 a Mrs. Adams and others bought the building.

Since 1885 this structure has been the home of a crafts school, incorporated as the North Bennet Street Industrial School. For several decades the building also housed a public library delivery station, and it was an early meeting place of the Saturday Evening Girls (ca. 1899), an organization that began as a reading club for Jewish and Italian teenage girls. The North Bennet Street School, which received its current name in the late 1980s, continues to train skilled artisans in traditional carpentry, cabinetmaking, and other crafts; short-term courses are also offered.

Turn left on North Bennet St. A bricked tunnel on the right, opposite Wiggin St., gives entrance to North Bennet Ct., a hidden space with a block of four brick row houses.

6. North Bennet Ct., pedestrian passageway through the building, between 34 and 36 North Bennet St.

Each row house in North Bennet Ct. has a low arch over all of its doors and windows. Built before 1867, these solid structures are much more substantial than most of the housing that was erected in Boston's alleyways for Irish Catholic immigrants. Nevertheless, these row houses were doubtless tenements during the height of immigration. Note the original gaslights, which are among Boston's few surviving nineteenth-century illumination fixtures. (Most of the gaslights in the city today are recent installations to give neighborhoods a "historic" flavor.)

Continue down North Bennet St. to its end. Turn right on Hanover St. and stop near the corner.

7. First Universalist Church (1838),
   332 Hanover St.

This simple, square, Greek Revival building is the First Universalist Church, built on the site of a 1742 two-story wooden church. John Murray, who brought Universalism to the United States from England, organized a church in Gloucester, Mass., in 1772, and came to this location in 1795. The present building was constructed by the Universalists in 1838, and Reverend Sebastian Streeter preached here for many years. Universalists opposed the doctrine of eternal damnation because it was inconsistent with belief in a just and loving God.

Owing to financial difficulties, the congregation was dissolved and the building was sold to the Boston Baptist Society in 1864. The society maintained it as the Baptist Bethel to serve and save visiting sailors through the later Victorian period. (A bethel is a place of worship for seamen; several of these were located in the North

End.) The Hanover St. facade has been entirely modernized, although a hint of the triangular window in the front gable is still apparent. Note that the words "SAMARITAN HALL" are still visible, cut in brownstone over a doorway on the North Bennet St. side. The present cupola is also smaller and less attractive than the original. Today the building is used as a community health center.

Walk one block north on Hanover St. and cross to the other side.

8. St. Stephen's Church (in name since the 1860s), formerly the New North Congregational Church (1804), by Charles Bulfinch

The only remaining Bulfinch church in Boston, this structure cost $26,570 to build for the New North Congregational Society in 1804. The story of St. Stephen's Church reflects the ethnic changes in the North End during the Victorian period. Protestant descendants of the early Puritans held on to

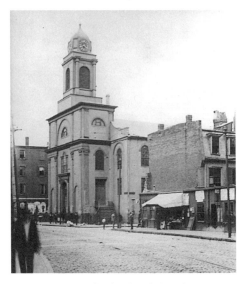

St. Stephen's Church (1890),
Hanover and Clark St. *(Courtesy of The Bostonian Society/Old State House.)*

this church for about four decades after Irish Catholics began to come into the neighborhood. Finally, the New North Church was sold to the Roman Catholic Diocese of Boston in 1862 for $35,000 (see early Catholic churches T2). The church was moved back twelve feet to accommodate a street-widening project and was renamed. Soon afterwards, the church was raised six and a half feet to make room for a parish hall. Curved outside stairs at the sides of the vestibule were added, and the new cupola sported a clock on each of its four sides. This was considered to be the parish of well-to-do Irish families in the late nineteenth and early twentieth centuries: Rose Fitzgerald (Kennedy) was christened here in 1890. The etching of the sanctuary in 1881, on display in the vestibule, shows the heavy decoration of the walls and ceiling during the Irish period. After fires badly damaged the sanctuary in 1897 and also in 1929, it was redone, and the 1920s decorations are shown in the 1950 photograph in the vestibule. St. Stephen's present appearance is the result of Cardinal Cushing's attempt in 1965 to restore it to the Federal style, lowering the sanctuary back to sidewalk level and creating a stark Congregational atmosphere, which is probably not true to the original.

Continue up Hanover St. to the corner of Salutation St.

9. 443–445 Hanover St. (ca. 1870)

This is an unusually large wood-frame structure dating from about 1870. In spite of major alterations, the mansard roof and rounded corner are still evident.

Walk east on narrow Salutation St., which gives the feeling of earlier times. At the end of the block turn right on Commercial St.; then bear right immediately on North St. The junction of Commercial and North Sts. marks

the northeast corner of the original North End shoreline (see map, p. 32).

10. 372 and 293–297 North St.

Around 1700 North St. had three names. "Ann St." extended northward from the Blackstone Block (T1) near Faneuil Hall, changed its name to "Fish St." at Cross St., and was called "Ship St." north of Fleet St. Several larger buildings here were added for the Irish and later Portuguese residents. Notice the large number of buildings along these streets that have inscriptions indicating the construction date and/or the original owner's name. For example, 372 North St., at the corner of Hanover St., has "T. D. WALSH 1895" carved on it. No. 293–297 North St. consists of two four-story wooden buildings that were built around 1860. The modern siding probably covers clapboards, and there used to be simple wooden cornices with brackets. The Y.M.C.A. guidebook *Historic Boston: Sight-Seeing Tours around the Hub* (1901) noted, "Wholesale business occupies much of the region though 'Little Italy,' a crowded Italian quarter, claims a section of it" (46). Remnants of the Sicilian community are found along North St. today; families trace their roots to dory fishermen who sailed from docks on Atlantic Ave.

Turn right on Fleet St. and walk to 38 Fleet St., a handsome three-story brick Federal-style home with a side entrance. It is a rare survivor from the early nineteenth century with a hip roof.

11. The Piscopo Hotel, 28 Fleet St. (1899), and 23½–25 and 16 Fleet St.

Another Fleet St. building worthy of comment is the Piscopo Hotel, a redbrick building with limestone trim, which includes entrance, window surrounds, and quoins. "18 PISCOPO 99" is carved over the entrance. The storefronts and cornice have been altered. The Piscopo Hotel, built at a cost of $51,000, was actually an apartment building with forty units and two stores on the ground floor.

Across the street, at 23½–25 Fleet St., a simple, four-story Federal brick building carries an old, faded painted Portuguese name: "FAYAL HOTEL MANUEL R. JACINTHO, PROPRIETOR." Fayal (or Faial) is an island in the Azores from which many fishermen came to Boston, Gloucester, and New Bedford. This "hotel" was probably a tenement or boardinghouse for newer immigrants.

No. 16 Fleet St., a commercial building with apartments upstairs, was built in about 1888. (Like its neighbor at 14 Fleet St., it has an interesting pressed-metal cornice.) With its five stories it exemplifies the larger brick structures that transformed the North End in the late nineteenth century.

Before reaching Hanover St., turn left on Garden Court St. This small street was solidly Irish from about 1840 until almost 1900. The 1834 house previously at 10 Garden Court St. (nonextant), whose top two floors had been added in 1911, was built when the street was widened. It was once the home of Franklin Webster Smith, who later founded the Y.M.C.A. and was a charter member of the Republican Party.

12. **6** and **4 Garden Court St.**

No. 6 Garden Court St., a bowfront brick structure in Greek Revival style, was constructed in about 1850, with granite trim and a recessed doorway topped by a stone lintel. Most bowfront buildings were later extended out to the street line, having their front walls flattened in the process.

The previous building at 4 Garden Court St. was identical to No. 6. John F. and Josie Fitzgerald moved to No. 4 (subse-quently demolished) and Rose Fitzgerald (Kennedy) was born there on July 22, 1890. Fitzgerald kept his family in the neighborhood after most Irish Catholics had left his "dear old North End." The present building at No. 4 was built in 1913.

Continue into North Sq.

13. **The Mariners' House** (1847), 11 North Sq.

This solid Federal-style building was built by the Boston Port Society as a temporary residence for sailors. The Mariners' House has a recessed double doorway with a fanlight framed in granite and unusually large windows on the first floor. At the top are four dormers and an impressive cupola, which was called "the lookout" because guests could go there to watch for ships. The Mariners' House is L-shaped, with a generous garden for summer activities. It was built by "Father" Edward Thompson Taylor of the Seamen's Bethel (Site 14) on the other side of North Sq.; Taylor's pulpit is preserved in a meeting room on the second floor. The Boston Port and Seamen's Aid Society operates the Mariners' House today. Because of a large endowment, merchant marine sailors still room and board here for low prices.

14. **The Seamen's Bethel** (1833), Sacred Heart Church (since the 1880s), **14 North Sq.**

Look across the triangular park space to Sacred Heart Church. This structure was the Seamen's Bethel, built in 1833 by the Port Society for the City of Boston and Vicinity at a cost of $28,000. "Father" Taylor, a former seaman, was its colorful first pastor. During the Victorian period, famous people who came to hear Taylor speak included Jenny Lind, Walt Whitman, and Charles Dickens. Dickens visited the bethel in 1842 with Longfellow and Charles Sumner and described his visit in *American*

Notes (1842). "Father" Taylor served as a model for Father Mapple in chapters 8 and 9 of Herman Melville's *Moby-Dick* (1851). John Harris tells us that Ralph Waldo Emerson, a close friend of Taylor, called him "the Shakespeare of the sailor and the poor," and that Whitman called Taylor the only "essentially perfect orator" (243) he had ever heard (see Whitman; Dickens; Emerson T6; Lind T8).

Most of the businesses in this area were related to the sea. In 1867 a "boat builder" was still located on Sun Ct. opposite the side of the bethel. The Seamen's Bethel was sold in the 1880s to the Society of Saint Mark; the money to purchase the bethel was raised by Italian Americans who wanted their own church. In 1888 the Reverend Francesco Zaboglio came to Boston and had the building deeded to Archbishop John J. Williams. The present facade, ornamented with religious sculptures, was dedicated in 1911. Since about 1900 the Sacred Heart congregation has been mostly of Sicilian heritage. By 1900 the North Sq. area was well known as "Little Italy" and a large apartment building called the "Hotel Rome" stood on the site of the small playground at the corner of North Sq. and North St.

15. Paul Revere House (ca. 1680), 19 North Sq.

Paul Revere's house had been expanded and rebuilt extensively by the late Victorian

Seamen's Bethel, North Sq. (ca. 1865), Father Taylor's Church. Josiah Johnson Hawes, photographer. *(Courtesy of The Bostonian Society/Old State House.)*

period. Photographs of the building at this time show a third floor, added for apartments, and businesses on the first floor. A "BANCO ITALIANO" sign is particularly striking in some photographs. Paul Revere House was purchased by the Paul Revere Memorial Association in 1907 and then restored to its assumed seventeenth-century appearance.

Walk south to the corner of North and Richmond Sts.

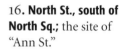

16. North St., south of North Sq.; the site of "Ann St."

Soon after 1840 this area attracted many Irish immigrants. During the 1840s Ann St. had a reputation as a rough and immoral area dominated by sailors and laborers. Cheap rooming houses were home to a racially diverse group of single men, including most of the North End's "persons of color" after the primary African American community had moved to the north slope of Beacon Hill. Taverns, brothels (one dubbed the "Beehive"), and other decidedly un-Puritan establishments enlivened Ann, Fish, and Ship Sts. In the "Ann Street Descent" of 1851, police arrested 153 persons, including 92 women charged with prostitution. The name of the whole street was changed to North St. by 1854 to improve its image, and the street was widened in 1859.

Turn right on Richmond St. and go one block to Hanover St.

Paul Revere House, North Sq. (1890), and neighborhood boys. John W. Robbins, photographer. *(Courtesy of The Bostonian Society/Old State House.)*

17. **267–275** and **256–262 Hanover St.**

In the 1840s and 1850s this street, and the alleyways off it, housed many early Irish immigrants in the most crowded and unsanitary conditions. However, by the late nineteenth century the North End showed signs of prosperity as the Irish population gained a foothold in Boston's economy.

On the near corner to the left is **267–275 Hanover St.** (ca.1880), a three-and-a-half-story brick building built for commercial space and apartments; cast-iron columns between the first floor windows and a wide stone course above them distinguish this structure. It also has attractive stonework above the windows and an impressive mansard roof and angled corner.

No. **256–262 Hanover St.** (1878) is a massive stone building, which seems out of place in the North End. This building was constructed by Joel Snow in 1878, but a new stone facade[2] was added about 1910.

Walk into Parmenter St., opposite Richmond St.

18. **30 Parmenter St.,** former address of the North End Union (est. 1892; nonextant)

The third building on the left, 30 Parmenter St., was the North End Union, a social service agency that opened on January 1, 1892. This Protestant organization was founded and operated by the Benevolent Fraternity of Churches in Boston. A pamphlet published by the North End Union in 1893 stated: "Its object, as stated at the outset, was 'to make a social home for young men, stimulate mental activity, promote good citizenship, and lend a hand wherever needed.' Situated in the midst of a population, many of whom are foreign born, composed almost entirely of Hebrews and Catholics, it was clear that the work should be absolutely unsectarian. Recognizing that self-respect and independence are endangered by the giving of something for nothing, a small fee for the privileges of the Union was required" (1).

From the beginning, the North End Union provided a playroom for small children in the Children's House at 32 Parmenter St. The North End Union recently dissolved after the building was sold.

Return to Hanover St. and turn left (north).

19. **Seaman's House** (ca. 1870s), 287 Hanover St.; became the Congregational Bethel after 1892 (site of the New Brick, or "Cockerel," Church, demolished 1844)

Across Hanover St., and just north of Parmenter St., is the second Boston Seaman's Friend Society building (the first, Site 5, was on Salem St.). It is a large Victorian Gothic structure with panel brickwork that probably was built in the 1870s. The corner tower, with a wrought-iron fence around its square top and part of an ornate weather vane, is the dominant feature of the building. This building became, after 1892, the Congregational Bethel (operated by the Seaman's Friend Society) that had been originally founded in 1827 by Reverend Lyman Beecher, the father of Harriet Beecher Stowe.

At an earlier time the New Brick, or "Cockerel," Church was located here. Between 1829 and 1832 this church was Ralph Waldo Emerson's pastorate. The Methodist Episcopal Church then constructed a stone building here that was later damaged by a storm and the consequences of street widening. The Methodists built the present structure and later sold it to the Boston Seaman's Friend Society. In 1901 it was estimated that 160,000 sailors annually visited Boston. The 1901 Y.M.C.A. guidebook described the Seaman's House as follows: "Its chaplains and missionaries supply relief to the destitute seamen, comfort the sick in hospitals, and bury the dead. They give social entertainments to men in port, and good reading matter to those going to sea. They hold frequent religious meetings of a kind attractive to seamen, encourage men to sign the pledge (of sobriety) and save their earnings, and impart to thousands a powerful influence toward a better life" (171).

The Seaman's House facility had lodgings for fifty-two men, a library, a chapel, and recreation rooms.

Enter Lathrop Place, off Hanover St., through a passageway between 309 and 315 Hanover St. (A new metal gate may be locked, preventing all but a narrow peek into Lathrop Place.)

20. Lathrop Place

Lathrop Place has three small wooden houses jammed together, which were built in about 1836 by housewrights John Perkins and Jonathan Robinson. Although newer siding and composition shingles cover the original clapboards, the simple design and economical construction indicates their long use as immigrant housing. Nos. 7 and 8 have smaller window openings and windows between floors that probably light a stairwell.

Handlin, in *Boston's Immigrants,* describes Victorian North End alleys such as Lathrop Place as having dilapidated sheds and shacks occupied by many desperately poor Irish immigrant families. He includes a diagram and an etching of the dilapidated wooden buildings "in the rear of 136 Hanover St." (103). The 1901 Y.M.C.A. guidebook says of Hanover St.: "We notice as we pass, the narrow passageways which, if followed, would reveal to us other rows of dwellings behind those facing the street, and all densely inhabited" (45).

Continuing on Hanover St., just to the north, note the sign on a gate to the right for the back entrance to the Mariners' House. Keep walking until you pass Prince St. The garden of St. Leonard's Church will be on the left.

21. St. Leonard's Church (1891–99),

by William Holmes {The main entrance on the side facing Hanover St. is located behind the Peace Garden.}

St. Leonard's parish was founded in 1873 as the first Italian Roman Catholic Church in New England. The first church, called St. Leonard of Porto Maurizio (Port Morris), was built in 1876 on Prince St. This second 1891–99 Romanesque building, by the architect William Holmes, cost $160,000. There is a dome over the crossing and a cross on the transept. The highly decorated interior, with its interesting color scheme, in the Italian style, was reportedly created by immigrant craftsmen who were parishioners. The church's entrance on Prince St. is rarely used today; most people enter the church through the entrance leading from the beautiful Peace Garden on Hanover St. St. Leonard's is usually open to visitors, and regular services are held, including devotions to St. Anthony (see schedule of services). A passageway leads from the Peace

Garden to North Bennet Place, which was settled by early Genovese immigrants.

Leaving St. Leonard's Peace Garden, turn right on Hanover St. and right again on Prince St. The south side of Prince St., west of Hanover St., boasts a variety of Victorian buildings. 26–28 and 30–32 Prince St. have unusual carved limestone window surrounds and pressed metal ornamentation over the storefronts. 42 Prince St. is probably a pre-Victorian wooden house that has been altered with siding.

22. **Paul Revere School** (1898), 61 Prince St., by Peabody and Stearns

This public elementary school, designed by Peabody and Stearns in 1898, was the first school building in New England built entirely of incombustible materials and the first with bathing facilities for the students. After being used as a Catholic school it was converted to condominiums in the 1980s. Some features of this large building suggest the classic revival style, and the decoration includes carved wreaths around the letter "R" and horns of plenty with ribbons (see Peabody and Stearns T1, T4, T5).

23. **Prince and Salem Sts.** (two corners)

At the end of the block, on the left corner is **58–68 Prince St. and 137–139 Salem St.**, a five-story tenement complex, which wraps around the corner onto Salem St. Built in 1895, when this section was part of the Jewish community, the building features spectacular copper oriels and brick with multiple stone courses. This building was owned by Nelson W. Howard in 1898 and then by Max Lebowich into the 1920s.

The four-story wooden Federal-style building with a hipped roof on the opposite corner of Prince and Salem Sts., **71 Prince and 149 Salem Sts.**, was built around 1800. A historic plaque on its Salem St. side tells of a song about Solomon Levy's clothing store:

> My name is Solomon Levy
> At my store on Salem Street
> That's where you'll find your coats
>   and hats
> And everything that's neat.

The streetscape on Prince St. beyond Salem St. is more complete in its late-Victorian aspect. Outstanding copper- and tin-fronted oriels are found on 88 and 89 Prince St.

But we'll turn left now onto Salem St.

24. **133, 115–121,** and **113 Salem St.**

This section of Salem St., from near Prince St. south to Cross St. and beyond, was the center of Boston's Eastern European Jewish community from the 1880s into the 1920s. Most new arrivals were poor and took on work such as peddling goods door-to-door until they could establish regular businesses. The home of Russian-born Sophie Tucker (1884–1966), from the age of three months to eight years, was on Salem St., closer to Haymarket. In her long career as a singer and actress, she became famous as the "Last of the Red-Hot Mamas." Buildings of many different eras and styles flank Salem St. as it curves gently southward.

No. 133 Salem St. is a former fire station, Engine Company Number 8, built in 1868 and renovated to Beaux Arts Classic style with cast-stone ornamentation in 1916. An interesting feature is that the round ceiling hole used by firemen to slide down the fire pole is still visible inside Sheldon's Bargain Outlet store.

No. 115–121 Salem St. is a large brick building with "1884" and "LEWIS & BERMAN" carved on the fifth-floor level. **No. 113 Salem St.**, built around 1845 by Enoch Robinson, is an early Victorian brick bowfront, which has had a newer storefront added in front.

25. Baldwin Place

The Second Baptist Society built its church, in 1811, at the far end of Baldwin Place facing Salem St. By 1865 the building was used by the Baldwin Place Home for Little Wanderers (later known as the New England Home for Little Wanderers), which remained there until at least 1898. At the turn of the century, the old church was occupied by the Baldwin Place Shul. After the synagogue moved, the old building was replaced by a health center, which is now owned by the Knights of Columbus.

Congregation Beth Israel, 5 Baldwin Place

This building, on the right side, was occupied during the late Victorian period by Congregation Beth Israel, the largest Jewish synagogue in the North End. Its facade has subsequently been modernized. Across the street, 4 Baldwin Place still has a faint Star of David design in an archway above the third-floor level, but this seems to have been an apartment building owned by J. M. Rabinowitz.

Notice the next alley on the right, known as Jerusalem Place, which has no street sign at present. Access to Jerusalem Place is blocked by a gate, which may be locked.

26. Jerusalem Place (1903); formerly "Carroll Place"

This alley, between Baldwin Place and Cooper St., was "Carroll Place" until 1903, when the name was changed because the alley led to the synagogue of Congregation Beth Hamidrash Sharai Jerusalem (1902). Although the synagogue's building at the end of Jerusalem Place is now gone, this synagogue (that is, the congregation itself) remained until 1944, making it the last one in the North End, whereas most moved

around 1930. Near the end, on the left, a three-story brick building, with arched windows on the top floor, was the synagogue's religious school. Painted black letters are still visible on the brick arch above the door that read, "HEBREW SCHOOL."
Turn right onto Cooper St.

27. 18 Cooper St. (1896) and 20 Cooper St. (1893)

Two ornate buildings with carved stone ornaments and attractive oriels reflect the lifestyles of somewhat higher-status Jewish families around the turn of the century. No. 18 Cooper St. has copper work from the second to the fifth floors, with "SEGEL" molded at the bottom, and "1896" at the top. No. 20 Cooper St. is a four-story building with tin oriels and the date "1893." Decorations include a beautifully carved stone doorway and terra-cotta panels below the windows.
Turn left on North Margin St. and right on Stillman St. Then cross Endicott St. and look back to the southeast corner.

28. Waitt and Bond Cigar Factory (1891), 63–69 Endicott St.

The large industrial structure at the corner of Endicott and Cooper Sts. was built in panel brick style as the Waitt and Bond cigar factory. The company name remains carved in brownstone. This building is characteristic of those built by the owners of industries near North Station in the late nineteenth century. Endicott St. was described in 1901 as "Named for Governor Endicott and now crowded with foreigners" (Tewksbury 44).
Walk up Endicott St., away from the Central Artery corridor.
St. Mary's Church (nonextant), an 1877 design by Patrick C. Keely (see Keely T2, T9), occupied most of the block on the west side of Endicott between Cooper and Thacher Sts.

where the Casa Maria Apartments for the elderly are now. The Victorian Catholic church with high twin towers was razed in the 1970s, after its Irish American congregation had dwindled and few of the Italian Americans living nearby attended the "Irish" church. On the corner of Thacher St., in the elderly housing complex, is Saint Mary's Chapel, which can be seen through the first-floor windows.

At the northeast corner of Endicott and Thacher Sts. is the next site.

29. 157 Endicott and 13–19 Thacher Sts. (1871)

The carved stone lintels over the former storefront at this first-floor corner "misspell" both street names and have the date of 1871. Small plaques at the second-floor level on both sides of the building note its origin as housing built by the Boston Cooperative Building Company. This organization was founded by Boston philanthropists to alleviate slum-housing conditions. In all, the Boston Cooperative Building Company invested in seventy-eight buildings for 311 families. In 1908 the organization was cited as a success for producing improved housing at rents of $.72 to $1.05 per room per week. No. 157 Endicott St. apparently passed into private ownership in the mid-1920s, and then was a facility of the Waitt and Bond cigar company.

30. McLaughlin Building (1875), 175–179 Endicott St.

This commercial structure, at a prominent corner location, has granite post-and-lintel construction on the first-floor level. Decorative touches include arched windows with keystones and a carved floral design. "MCLAUGHLIN BUILDING 1875" is carved on the facade.

Take note of Endicott Ct., the alley on the left.

31. Endicott Ct.

This land was fill in the former Mill Pond (see "Old and New Boston," p. xlvi, Preface). On opposite sides of the alley are two wooden double houses dating from about 1845, which are additional examples of the cheap housing built for Irish immigrants in the mid-nineteenth century. The doors show faint Greek Revival influence, and there are single windows on each floor above the doors. No. 8 Endicott Ct. still has a Greek Revival dormer (see inexpensive housing T7).

32. 210 Endicott St. (ca. 1842)

This wooden single-family home has two stories plus a gable roof with a dormer. Built in about 1842, it also demonstrates Greek Revival style features. Most of this section near North Station was transformed into an industrial district in the late nineteenth century, leaving just a few remnants of early architecture like this.

33. Minard's Liniment Manufacturing Building (1898–99), 221–223 Endicott St., by F. A. Norcross

As we approach the end of our fascinating exploration of the diversity offered by Victorian Boston's North End, note this five-story panel brick structure in Queen Anne style. It was designed by F. A. Norcross and built as the Minard's Liniment Manufacturing Building. An advertisement in the Boston City Directory (1900) proclaimed: "A GOOD THING, MINARD'S 'KING OF PAIN' LINIMENT: RUB IT IN."

Continue a short distance on Endicott St. and turn right to return to the start of the tour. Or, to return to the North Station T stop, continue a short distance on Endicott St. to Keany Sq. Turn left on Causeway St.

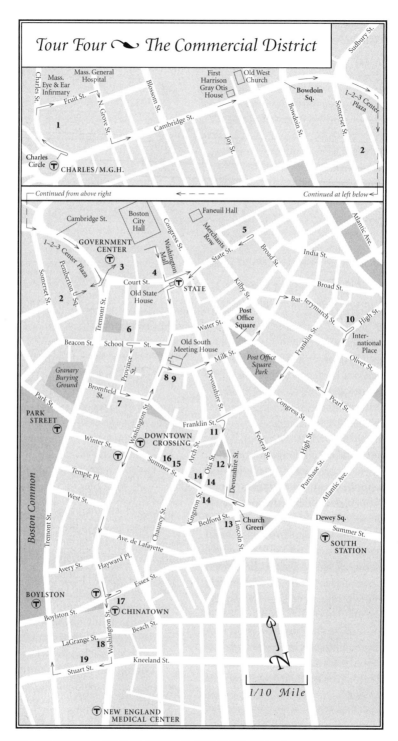

Tour Four ～ The Commercial District

Charles St.
Mass. Eye & Ear Infirmary
Mass. General Hospital
Fruit St.
N. Grove St.
Blossom St.
Cambridge St.
First Harrison Gray Otis House
Old West Church
Bowdoin Sq.
Bowdoin St.
Somerset St.
Sudbury St.
1–2–3 Center Plaza
Joy St.

1

2

Charles Circle
Ⓣ CHARLES / M.G.H.

— Continued from above right →   ← – – – →   Continued at left below ←

Cambridge St.
Boston City Hall
Faneuil Hall
Merchants Row
5
Atlantic Ave.
India St.
Congress St.
GOVERNMENT CENTER
Ⓣ
1–2–3 Center Plaza
Washington Mall
State St.
Broad St.
Broad St.
Somerset St.
Pemberton Sq.
3
4
Court St.
Old State House
Ⓣ STATE
Kilby St.
Bat-terymarch St.
High St.
2
Tremont St.
6
Water St.
Post Office Square
Franklin St.
10
Inter-national Place
Oliver St.
Beacon St.
School St.
Old South Meeting House
Milk St.
Post Office Square Park
Granary Burying Ground
Province St.
8 9
Devonshire St.
Congress St.
Pearl St.
Park St.
Bromfield St.
7
PARK STREET
Ⓣ
Washington St.
Franklin St.
11
Federal St.
High St.
Purchase St.
Winter St.
DOWNTOWN CROSSING
Ⓣ
Ⓣ
Summer St.
Arch St.
Otis St.
16 15
Devonshire St.
12
Atlantic Ave.
Temple Pl.
14
14
Boston Common
West St.
Kingston St.
14
Bedford St.
13
Church Green
Dewey Sq.
Summer St.
Ⓣ SOUTH STATION
Tremont St.
Chauncy St.
Lincoln St.
Ave. de Lafayette
Avery St.
Hayward Pl.
Essex St.
BOYLSTON
Ⓣ
17
Ⓣ CHINATOWN
Boylston St.
Beach St.
N
LaGrange St.
18
Washington St.
19
Kneeland St.
Stuart St.

1/10 Mile

Ⓣ NEW ENGLAND MEDICAL CENTER

·TOUR 4·

THE COMMERCIAL DISTRICT: WITH A PRIOR LOOK AT BOSTON'S MID-NINETEENTH-CENTURY CHARLES STREET JAIL

by Robert B. MacKay

Boston meant business.
—Henry Adams, *The Education of Henry Adams* (1907)

Tour Location: See Downtown Key Map for the location of the Tour and its T stop, page xli.

About Walking the Tour: Our tour offers a choice of beginning sites, depending on the time and energy available to the walker. We rove widely throughout the level Commercial District, and conclude at Jacob Wirth's, a Victorian German restaurant that opened in 1868.

Before we plunge into the Commercial district: if you have chosen to start with Site 1, we will begin with the long-neglected Charles Street Jail, a building whose inmates were safe from the disastrous Boston Fire of 1872, which drastically altered the appearance of the Commercial District. From the jail, near the foot of Beacon Hill, we shall wend our way up Cambridge St., a ▲ mild and then short, moderate ▲▲ incline, to the Government Center, passing some of the municipal accomplishments of the present period to reach Site 2, the Suffolk County Court House, at Pemberton Sq., located behind Center Plaza.

Whether you choose to start with the Charles Street Jail, Site 1, or the Suffolk County Court House, Site 2, when we enter the Commercial District we will pass into the "burnt-over" zone of the 1872 fire, where, because of the great conflagration, architectural styles of the later Victorian decades are still seen in most streets. (I cannot think of another city where you can see as many types and styles of Victorian buildings in such proximity.) Alas, there is not sufficient space here to deal with all the structures of architectural interest in our tour area, but we hope this tour will lead you to streets that you may not have passed before and to stop in front of edifices from the reign of Victoria Alexandrina.

Thumbnail Sketch of Sights: See Introduction, page xxxiii.

Approximate Walking Time: 2½–3 hours (depending on your choice of beginning site)

T Stop Alternative for Hearty Walkers: Charles/MGH T Station, Red Line; descend to begin at the Charles Street Jail (Site 1); or

T Stop Alternative: Government Center/Scollay Sq. T Station, Green Line, to begin at the Suffolk County Court House (Site 2) in the Commercial District

Begin at: See alternatives above

INTRODUCTION

A disaster to one century can be a blessing to the next, and so it was with the Great Fire of November 9–12, 1872, which leveled downtown Boston from Milk St. to the harbor, and between Washington St. and Batterymarch St. The fire has provided Victorian architectural buffs of the twenty-first century with the opportunity to see a rich diversity of architectural styles and building materials. Sweeping away 766 buildings, many of them with the solid granite facades for which Boston was famous, the fire provided immense opportunities for a new generation of architects with commissions that they never could have hoped for in normal times. Even the prolific Gridley J. F. Bryant, a stalwart of the "Boston Granite School," who had been responsible for 152 buildings in the burnt-over district before the fire and who was recommissioned to design 111 afterward, could not keep up with the demand. Owners were forced to turn to young practitioners who enlivened the downtown area in the wake of the fire with

new styles, such as the Ruskinian Gothic and the French influenced Neo-Grec.

Many of these new styles required polychrome and decoration that could not be easily achieved in granite. Moreover, improvements in transportation were bringing a polychromatic selection of new stones from afar, and there was growing interest in easily constructed and economical cast-iron facades that were changing the face of the downtown commercial district. Where granite had been king, white marble from Vermont, brownstone from the Connecticut River Valley, red granite from New Brunswick, bluestone from Ohio, and other materials were now in evidence.

Charles Street Jail (Site 1) is close to the Charles/MGH T station; in fact, you can view the jail from the windows on the outbound train platform. To comprehend the jail's size, keep the Charles Street Jail visible on your right, walk to Fruit St., and turn right for a closer view of the jail's north wing.

1. **Charles Street Jail** (1848–51),
215 Charles St. at Charles Circle, by
Gridley J. F. Bryant; Suffolk County Jail

Looming behind Charles Circle are the soot-covered granite walls of one the city's most maligned buildings, the Charles Street Jail, officially the Suffolk County Jail. Now shorn of many original features, including its lantern and distinctive window sash, the jail was long unoccupied after the last inmates were removed under federal order in 1991, making it hard to believe that the ancient "poke" was one of Boston's most significant civic achievements of the nineteenth century. Moreover, it was considered a seminal design in correctional architecture and was to become the first realized U.S. architectural plan to be published (1849) in the important London periodical *The Builder.*

Designed by Gridley J. F. Bryant in collaboration with the prison reformer the Reverend Louis Dwight, the Boston jail adapted the inside cellblock introduced at the Auburn (N.Y.) penitentiary and popularized at the Ossining (N.Y.) penitentiary (a.k.a. "Sing Sing") to a radical plan: the cruciform. Widely visited by prison officials and embraced as the last model plan of the "Auburn System" of prison discipline, it earned its designers dozens of commissions across New England and the Midwest and was copied in later decades by the architects of such institutions as the Concord (Mass.) Reformatory and the District of Columbia Jail, and even by H. H. Richardson at his Allegheny Courthouse and Jail (1884) in Pittsburgh. The Charles Street Jail is also one of the finest surviving examples of the late Boston Granite School. As this book goes to press the Charles Street Jail is in the process of being reused as a luxury hotel (see G. J. F. Bryant Sites 6, 8; and T1).

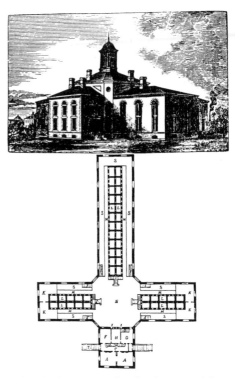

The Charles Street Jail with a diagram of the interior. *(From* 24th Annual Report of the Board of Managers of the Prison Discipline Society, Boston, Boston: T. R. Marvin, 1849, p. 8.)

Continue past the jail to North Grove St. (entrance to the Massachusetts General Hospital). Turn right here, and return to Cambridge St.

Turn left and stay on the left side of Cambridge St.; walk five blocks. The hill's moderate incline will begin shortly, and you will pass, on your left, the historic Harrison Gray Otis House (1796), designed by Charles Bulfinch and now headquarters of Historic New England (formerly SPNEA), 141 Cambridge St. {www. spnea.org; (617)-227-3956, tours, archives}, and the Old West Church (1806), by Asher Benjamin.

Cross New Chardon St. Turn right to cross

Cambridge St. Follow along its south side. Beyond Somerset St., you'll walk under the arcade of the 1-2-3 Center Plaza. To your left, you'll see Boston's massive "new" City Hall (1968). Continue to the entrance of 3 Center Plaza. Ascend the large double staircase/escalator on your right. At the top of the stairs the facade of the Suffolk County Court House will be directly in front of you.

To begin at Site 2 use the Government Center/Scollay Sq. T Station (Green Line).

If you have chosen to begin in the Commercial District (Site 2), you emerge from the T onto the redbrick City Hall Plaza. We shall return to this location, near the Government Center T exit/entrance, shortly.

But first, in order to begin at the Suffolk County Court House (Site 2), face Boston City Hall. Turn sharply right, and walk with your back to Boston City Hall. Using the triangular traffic island in the middle of Cambridge St., cross Cambridge St. Ascend the large double staircase escalator marked "3 Center Plaza." The facade of the Suffolk County Court House (Site 2) will greet you with its handsome gold-lettered clock face. Pemberton Sq. in the Victorian era was an elegant residential development of early-nineteenth-century brick town houses.

2. Suffolk County Court House (1895), Pemberton Sq., by George A. Clough; upper floors added in 1909; now the John Adams Court House

This exuberant essay in municipal architecture stands in contrast to the faceless buildings of the 1960s, which constitute so much of nearby Government Center. The massive Court House was built in 1895 to the designs of George A. Clough, who was also responsible for the upper floors added in 1909. Allegorical figures by Domingo Mora and a grand staircase greet those who enter its vast lobby.

We'll return now to City Hall Plaza. Retrace your steps down the double stairs at 3 Center Plaza. Recross Cambridge St. When you reach the redbrick surface of City Hall Plaza, notice the large suspended Steaming Kettle (1873), by coppersmiths Hicks and Badger, which was commissioned by Oriental Tea Company. The kettle's capacity is written on one side, a favorite sign from the Scollay Sq. era, now on the corner of Court St.

3. Sears Block; and the Sears Crescent, City Hall Plaza

Sears Block (ca. 1845), at the Court St. corner end of the Crescent; renovated by Stahl-Bennett, 1969 (the immense Steaming Teakettle is suspended over its entrance)

The four-story trabeated (post and lintel) facade of the Sears Block is typical of the granite-faced buildings that were omnipresent in the commercial district in the middle of the nineteenth century and that contributed greatly to the district's sense of place. Pictures of Boston after the Great Fire of 1872[1] often depict these facades as freestanding after the wooden floors and brick sidewalls behind them had collapsed.

Aftermath of the Great Fire of 1872.
James W. Black, photographer.
(Courtesy of the Boston Athenæum.)

The building adjoining it on the left is the Sears Crescent—whose name is written on its central facade.

The Sears Crescent (1816), 100 City Hall Plaza; remodeled 1850s; renovated by Don Stull Associates (1969)

The curvilinear brick building, with brownstone corners, facing City Hall Plaza is actually a Victorian alteration (1850s) of a Federal-era commercial structure. On its rear wall, in the back passageway, one may see its splayed Federal window cornices and some of the earliest extant post-and-lintel granite former storefronts in the city. It owes its present appearance to Don Stull Associates, who rehabbed it again in 1969. The Sears Crescent's graceful, curving facade conformed to what was once Cornhill, and a similar curve is reflected in the modern office building at 1-2-3 Center Plaza (1966–69), by Welton Becket and Associates (seen facing us across Cambridge St. from City Hall Plaza).

Face the grasshopper weathervane of Faneuil Hall (to the right of and behind City Hall), and continue bearing right around the Sears Crescent. Washington Mall opens on the right. Turn right at One Washington Mall, and walk along the bench-lined mall one block. No. 1 Court St. will be on your right. Boston's Colonial Old State House,

The Ames Building (1889), engraving. *(From* Boston: Its Commerce, Finance and Literature, *New York: A. F. Parsons, 1892, p. 263.)*

with its impressive golden eagle, will be across the street.

4. Ames Building (1889), 1 Court St., by Shepley, Rutan and Coolidge

Designed by Shepley, Rutan and Coolidge, successors to Henry Hobson Richardson, the splendid Ames Building's massive, thirteen-story masonry structure is both a lexicon of Richardsonian Romanesque design and an engineering marvel. It is the second tallest bearing-wall building in the world built before the advent of the steel frame. It dominated the Boston skyline in its early decades [2] and was commissioned by the Ames family of railroad and shovel fame,[3] for whom Richardson was to do so much of his work (see Shepley, Rutan and Coolidge T1, T5, T12).

Turn left on State St.; the Custom House tower's clock face will confirm your direction. We will digress momentarily to walk down State St. two blocks to the Richards Building.

5. Richards Building (ca. 1859–67), 112–116 State St., by Edward Cabot; upper floors added in 1889

Time has not always been kind to the Richards Building. Its upper floors were added in 1889 and its bottom stories were obliterated by an unsympathetic reworking in the 1950s. However, the building was

The Richards Building (ca. 1869). *(Courtesy of The Bostonian Society/Old State House.)*

beautifully restored about fifteen years ago; the 1950s rehab had simply covered over the circa 1859 cast-iron facade, which was still intact under the accretions. Iron-fronted buildings that employed the same "curtain wall" construction methods used in the glass towers of the present age are associated more with New York's SoHo district and the rapidly expanding cities of the West, but they were not unknown in Boston before the fire: dozens were erected thereafter. The Richards Building facade, a particularly handsome example in this Italian Renaissance Revival style, is one of the few left in Boston. The architect, according to the Landmark Commission records, was Edward Cabot.

Retrace your steps up State St. to the Old State House and Washington St. while enjoying the view of the magnificent upper stories of the Ames building. The Old State House (1713), 206 Washington St., is headquarters of The Bostonian Society {open daily; www.bostonhistory.org; museum, library; (617)-720-

1713}. On its south side the National Park Service Visitor Center may be seen across a pedestrian plaza. Walk through that plaza, turn left on Washington St. for one block, and turn right at School St. Walk up a slight incline to find on the right

6. Old City Hall (1861–65), 41–45 School St., by Gridley J. F. Bryant and Arthur Gilman

The beautifully scaled three-tiered Chelmsford granite Old City Hall was one of the first major examples of the French Second Empire style in the United States and helped popularize the style. It was also one of the first buildings of its period to be designated a National Historic Landmark. Following the completion of Boston's new Government Center, the fate of this Parisian wedding cake was in doubt and Roger S. Webb's not-for-profit corporation, Architectural Heritage, Inc., came to its rescue, convincing skeptical officials that the city-owned building should be preserved and renovated for offices and restaurant use.

Today, the 1969–70 adaptive reuse project, for which Anderson, Notter Associates were the architects, is considered to have been a precursor to the entire adaptive reuse movement in the United States. In fact, the preservation of Old City Hall was honored by its appearance on the cover of the 1975 edition of *Victorian Boston Today* (see p. xxxi Introduction). Flanking the entrance are statues of the Boston-born Benjamin Franklin (sculpted by Richard S. Greenough in 1855—note the vignettes from Franklin's life on the base) and Josiah Quincy (sculpted by Thomas Ball in 1878), the Boston mayor and Harvard president for whom the nearby Quincy Market is nicknamed (see Quincy Market T1).

In front of the Old City Hall, cross School St. at Province St.. Walk down Province St.

one block to Bromfield St. *The Great Fire of 1872 spared Bromfield St., near the western edge of the burnt-over district, and two interesting granite buildings situated here have survived. Facing you across Bromfield St. will be*

7. 32–36 Bromfield St. and 20–30 Bromfield St.

Wesleyan Association Building (1870), 32–36 Bromfield St., by Hammatt and Joseph Billings

The Wesleyan Association Building, a generation newer than its neighbor to the left, and designed by the gifted brothers Hammet and Joseph Billings, is typical of the French Second Empire buildings of its period. Window cornices at the second-floor level and a projecting central pavilion relieve the otherwise austere facade.

20–30 Bromfield St.
(ca. 1848)

The senior of the granite pair made up of the business block between Wesleyan Place and Washington St., but for its stylized Greek Revival capitals, is almost devoid of decoration. The architectural historian Henry-Russell Hitchcock (1903–87) called this starkness imposed by the nature of granite "an original sort of basic classicism," and these buildings have long been seen by architectural scholars as

The Boston Transcript Building (1873), engraving. *(From* King's Hand-Book of Boston, *9th ed., Boston: Moses King, 1889, p. 306.)*

an influence on later developments in architecture, particularly on the development of the great nineteenth-century architect Henry Hobson Richardson (1838–86) (see H. H. Richardson T5, T12; Bromfield St. T6).

Walk one block down Bromfield St. to Washington St. Turn left on Washington St. to see the steeple of the Old South Meeting House (1729), saved with tremendous effort during the Great Fire.

8. Transcript Building (1874), corner of Milk St. at 322–328 Washington St., by Gridley J. F. Bryant

The Boston Transcript Building, home of a well-known Republican paper, the *Boston Evening Transcript* (1830), was erected[4] two years after the fire, in 1874. It is a rather sober and traditional granite building. The architect was the conservative Gridley J. F. Bryant, the commercial architect trusted by the business community[5] to be not too flamboyant.

Turn right at Milk St. Continue along Milk St.

9. Boston Post Building (1874), 17 Milk St., by Peabody and Stearns

Benjamin Franklin again greets us (between Washington and Arch Sts.) at the Boston Post Building at 17 Milk St., where his bust, marking the site of his birthplace, is incorporated into the facade of a most unusual building. Once the home of the *Boston Post,* a Democratic daily newspaper, this eclectic cast-iron masterpiece exhibiting Gothic, Neo-Grec, and other detailing, was designed by the talented young firm of Peabody and Stearns in 1874, and it was one of the most interesting buildings to rise after the Great Fire. As mentioned earlier, iron-fronted buildings were both expedient and economical to construct and could provide a lot of elaboration for the dollar (see Peabody and Stearns T1, T3, T5).

The Boston Post Building (1874), engraving. *(From* King's Hand-Book of Boston, *9th ed., Boston: Moses King, 1889, p. 307.)*

Keeping the Old South Meeting House behind you on your left, continue walking down Milk St. five blocks. You will pass through Post Office Sq. Turn right when you reach Batterymarch St., and walk up Batterymarch until you pass Franklin St. At the next alley on your left, look up to see the ornate shot tower at the rear of the the 1887 Chadwick Lead Works building. Then continue to the corner of Batterymarch and High Sts. to view the next two buildings.

10. Chadwick Lead Works (1875), 172 High St.

At 172 High St., on the corner of Batterymarch, is one of the finest extant examples in the city of what Back Bay historian Bainbridge Bunting dubbed the "Panel Brick Style." Popular between the late 1860s and 1870s, this use of imbricated (i.e., overlap-

ping like fish scales) brickwork actually predated the Queen Anne style, with which it is usually associated. Characteristic of this economical nonacademic local style are the recessed panels, stepped corbel tables, and staccato effects.

Chadwick Lead Works (1887), 184 High St., by William G. Preston

The handsome Romanesque Revival Chadwick Lead Works (with the shot tower) was built to the designs of William G. Preston (see Preston T5, T6). Commercial buildings in the Romanesque style, popularized by H. H. Richardson, were to become the rage in Boston in the late 1880s and are characterized by multistory arches capped by an attic story. This building once contained all aspects of Chadwick's industrial enterprise, from fabrication to management. The company later acquired the adjacent building at 172 High St. and used it as a warehouse.

Go back on High St., past Batterymarch, to Pearl St. Turn right on Pearl, and walk one block to Franklin St. Turn left on Franklin St. and walk three blocks to Devonshire St. On the far left corner will be the Wigglesworth Building.

11. Wigglesworth Building (1873), 89–93 Franklin St., at Winthrop Sq., by N. J. Bradlee and W. T. Winslow

Squeezed between Winthrop Sq. and the Franklin Street Crescent, the curving brick

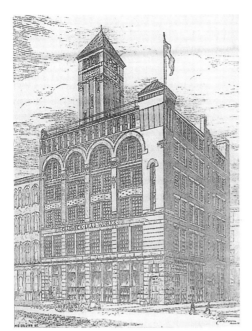

Chadwick Lead Works (1887). *(From Charles Durell,* A Half Century of Boston's Building, *Boston: Louis P. Hager, 1895, p. 204.)*

facade of the Wigglesworth Building gracefully conforms to a difficult site. Erected to the designs of N. J. Bradlee and W. T. Winslow for Abraham French and Company (importers of china and crystal), it was the first building to be completed after the Great Fire. The architects utilized cornices, stringcourses, and even the fenestration to reinforce the dynamic effect of the curving facades that *King's Handbook of Boston* likened in 1878 to "the top of a liberty cap." The handsome Italianate building[6] also marked the reemergence in the 1870s of brick facade with granite trim, a combination that had been out of fashion in the downtown area for three decades (see Bradlee and Winslow T10).

North of here on Franklin St. are a number of postfire facades, including a fine little Neo-Grec building by Cummings and Sears

(1878) at 74 Franklin St. From Franklin St. walk behind the Wigglesworth Building, going south on Devonshire St. In front of you will be Winthrop Sq. and

12. 1 Winthrop Sq. (1873), the Beebe Block, by William Ralph Emerson and Carl Fehmer

One Winthrop Sq. has had a varied history. An office building since it was adaptively reused by the Raymond Cattle Company (Childs, Bertman, Tseckares Associates were the architects) in the 1970s, it is probably best remembered by Bostonians as the publishing plant of the *Boston Record American,* when it was known as the New England Press Building. However, in its first life, after the fire, it was "The Beebe Block," which had replaced an earlier block of the same name by Gridley J. F. Bryant, which had been one of the commercial wonders of the city before the Great Fire. In fact, it

The Wigglesworth Building (1873). Photograph (ca. 1970s) by Robert B. MacKay.

was at this location that the fire's holocaust got out of hand and spread in all directions across the commercial district. The present eclectic and unconventionally massed structure seems at peace with itself and its site, despite the seemingly top-heavy flanking pavilions, but it could be greatly enhanced by the removal of the reflective glass, which replaced the original sash in 1974. Designed by a young pair of innovators, William Ralph Emerson (cousin of Ralph Waldo Emerson) and Carl Fehmer, in 1873, the building housed the Boston branch of A. T. Stewart's, the famous New York department store (see William Ralph Emerson T2, T5, T11, T12; and Ralph Waldo Emerson T6).

Go up Devonshire St., along the left side of 1 Winthrop Sq., for one block, and turn left on Summer St. for half a block. Stop and look across the street to your right. The building with the stained glass clock (a modern update), is the Bedford Building.

13. **Bedford Building** (1875–76), **99 Bedford St.**, by Cummings and Sears

The Bedford Building, at the triangular intersection of Summer, Bedford, and Lincoln Sts. (Church Green), is a polychromatic Ruskinian Gothic building, with Viollet-le-Duc–inspired iron balconets, and was erected as a retail shoe center in an area that had been leveled by the Great Fire. Designed by Cummings and Sears, it was the first building in the city to utilize red granite from New Brunswick in conjunction with the already popular white marble (which in this case came from Tuckahoe, N.Y.) and terra-cotta panels. The variety of colors in building materials was one of the most striking phenomena of the postfire downtown, and the Ruskinian Gothic style was particularly dependent on polychrome bands and patterns using natural building materials.

The Bedford Building (1875–76).
(Collection of Robert B. MacKay.)

Go back down Summer St., past Devonshire St. for one block, to the corner of Otis St.

14. **Three Summer Street Corners,** by Emerson and Fehmer, and **71 Summer St.**

Nos. 72, 74–78, and 87 Summer St. are attributed to the firm of Emerson and Fehmer (the attribution was made on the basis of a plate of details in an 1877 issue of *American Architect and Building News*). These three corners of the intersection of Otis, Kingston, and Summer Sts. are graced by commercial buildings in the Neo-Grec (not to be confused with the Greek Revival) style of the 1870s. The distinguishing features of this French style, which grew out of the Second Empire and was popularized by the publications of the French tastemaker César Daly (1811–93), are classical decorative devices such as triglyphs, metopes (in both academic and the derived form of channeling and medallions), frets, rosettes, acroteria (the "ears" along the roof line), and guilloches.[7] Neo-Grec detailing seems easier to read when it has been articulated in white marble, as can be seen at 87 Summer St., vis-à-vis the decoration on the buildings across the street, which was executed in granite.

Continue along Summer St. for another block.

71 Summer St.

71 Summer St., on your left, is all that remains of an iron block that once belonged to Jacob Sleeper, one of Boston University's founders, and which was part of his bequest to the university. It was erected after the fire by George Pope, a South End developer.

Cross to the south side of the street to view the next site. After the intersection of Chauncy and Arch Sts., the next site (formerly Long's Jewelers) will be the second building on the right.

15. **40-46 Summer Street** (1873–74), by Charles K. Kirby

One of the first buildings in the city to open its doors after the Great Fire, 40–46 Summer St. is typical of the cast-iron

40–46 **Summer St.** (1873–74). Photograph (ca. 1970s) by Robert B. MacKay.

fronted buildings erected in great numbers for the dry goods and clothing business after the fire along Washington and Summer Sts. Tile-ground floors, wrought-iron spanning beams, and brick insulation made them a good deal more fire resistant than their wooden-floored predecessors. Yet the overly elaborate High Victorian Italianate style, in which iron fronts almost always appeared, gave them a bad name. Particularly galling to the city's new crop of Beaux Arts–educated architects was the use of classical "orders" above the street level and their use in conjunction with nonacademic design (notice the roofline ornamentation).

87 **Summer Street**, "Neo-Grec" detail. Photograph (ca.1970s) by Robert B. MacKay.

16. 26–38 Summer St. (ca. 1873)

This piece of Yankee masonry is the largest panel brick facade in the city. Like many buildings along Summer St., it was built for the dry goods industry, and it still housed a department store in the early 1980s. After a major preservation battle, the entire building, except for the facade, was demolished to make way for the 101 Arch Street Tower (1989). The lower two floors of the Summer St. frontage were completely recreated. Be sure to look up Hawley St., the side street beyond the building, to see the grand arch framing a service entrance.

Continue up Summer St. to Washington St. At Washington St. turn left, keeping Macy's department store (formerly Jordan Marsh) on your left. Walk four blocks to Essex St. At Essex turn left. The third building on the right side of Essex is 15 Essex St.

17. 15 Essex St. (1875), by Cummings and Sears

This former sewing machine manufactory is a high point of Boston's remaining Victorian Gothic. Note the finely articulated collinesque capitals and the confrontation of massive and delicate shapes and forms (see Cummings and Sears near Site 11, Site 13, and T1, T5).

Return to Washington St. Turn left on Washington and walk one block; look across the street to see the large stone building on the corner of LaGrange St.

18. Hayden Building (1875), 681 Washington St., by Henry Hobson Richardson

This Longmeadow sandstone building was designed by H. H. Richardson for the estate of his deceased father-in-law, Dr. John C. Hayden. It is of particular interest to architectural historians because the post-and-lintel construction of the fifth floor seems to link Richardson with the Boston Granite School (represented by a number of mid-nineteenth-century buildings at the beginning of the tour).

Continue down Washington St. one block to Stuart St. Turn right on Stuart. 31 Stuart is Jacob Wirth's.

19. Jacob Wirth Company, 31–33 Stuart St. (1844–45), by Greenleaf C. Sanborn; opened as restaurant (1868)

By now you may be feeling your feet have turned to granite, having covered half the city on foot, and you are probably in need of respite. With one of the best-preserved Victorian storefronts and interiors in the city, "Jake Wirth's"—a German restaurant established in 1868—has long been a favored Boston watering spot. The translation of the Latin motto over the bar, "Suum Cuique," is "To Each His Own." Try the knockwurst or sauerbraten and call for a stein with which to toast Victoria Alexandrina, queen of the United Kingdom of Great Britain and Ireland (1837–1901) and empress of India (1876–1901)!

This tour concludes at Jacob Wirth's. To reach the closest T stop, continue up Stuart St. to the corner of Tremont St. Turn right on Tremont, and walk two blocks to Boylston St. On the Common are two entrance kiosks (inbound and outbound) to Boylston station. Nearby Park Street Station and Boylston were the first two subway stations in the United States to open, on September 1, 1897. Unlike its busier neighbor, Boylston has been spared numerous remodelings and still retains hints of its Victorian interior.

TOUR **5**

TOURING THROUGH TIME TO THE HEART OF BACK BAY: BOYLSTON AND DARTMOUTH STREETS WITH COPLEY SQUARE

by Margaret Henderson Floyd

Tour Location: See Downtown Key Map for the location of the Tour and its T stop, page xli.

About Walking the Tour: This tour over level landfill begins on Arlington St., the mid-nineteenth-century border of the marshy Back Bay. We will look first at no. 12 and then enjoy Arlington Street Church. With our eyes tuned both to the skyline and closer prospects, we follow commercial Boylston St. with its prominent later buildings to landmark Copley Sq. Then, turning north, we move into the residential heart of the district along Dartmouth St. (taking in corner views of Newbury and Marlborough Sts.). We return via Commonwealth Ave. Exeter and Boylston Sts. provide a final memorable view across Copley Sq.

Thumbnail Sketch of Sights: See Introduction, page xxxiv.

Walking Time: Approximately 1¼ hours (excluding building interiors).

T Stop: Arlington St., Green Line.

Begin at: John Bates House, 12 Arlington St. (From the Arlington St. T, locate the steeple of the Arlington Street Church on the corner of Arlington and Boylston Sts. Walk along Arlington St., past the church, the Ritz-Carlton Hotel, and Commonwealth Ave., to reach 12 Arlington St.)

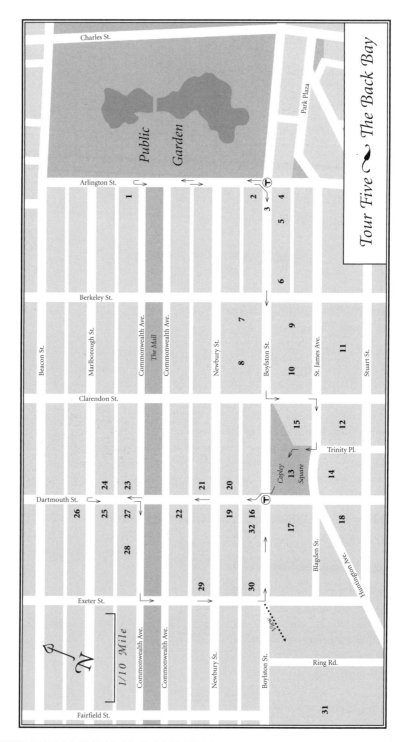

Charles St.

Public Garden

Park Plaza

Tour Five ～ *The Back Bay*

Arlington St.

1

2 4

3

5

6

Berkeley St.

Beacon St.

Marlborough St.

Commonwealth Ave.

The Mall

Commonwealth Ave.

Newbury St.

7

8

Boylston St.

9

10

St. James Ave.

11

Stuart St.

Clarendon St.

15

12

Trinity Pl.

Copley Square

13

14

24

23

21

20

Dartmouth St.

26

25 27

22

19

32 16

17

18

Blagden St.

Huntington Ave.

28

29

30

Exeter St.

1/10 Mile

N

Commonwealth Ave.

Commonwealth Ave.

Newbury St.

Boylston St.

Mall

Ring Rd.

Fairfield St.

31

INTRODUCTION

Boston's Back Bay is unrivaled in the United States as an ambitious and progressive program in urban design. Its lavish buildings are the tangible record of the late nineteenth century, when Boston was the cultural and architectural leader of the nation. During the twentieth century, the residential character of this district has been maintained, and Copley Sq. is recognized as one of the nation's most intriguing public spaces.

In 1857 the Back Bay, one of the largest landfill operations in history, began between the Boston peninsula and the mouth of the Muddy River on the Brookline shore. Moving gradually westward from Arlington St. and the recently completed Public Garden, the fill reached Dartmouth St. by 1870, and new houses and public buildings rose on pile-driven foundations. The grid plan of the streets in the newly filled area contrasts with the irregularity of the early streets of Boston itself and the occasional curving crescents of the new South End that, in the early 1850s, had been the first outward expansion from Boston proper (see landfill, Preface, and p. xlvi).

The Back Bay street plan (1856) was made by Arthur Gilman (1821–82), who was also the architect of its earliest public building, the Arlington Street Church (Site 2). Gilman modeled the area on the great boulevard system that Baron Haussmann had devised for contemporary Second Empire Paris, from which Gilman had recently returned. Thus it is not surprising to find French standards of architectural design—the mansard roof, the common cornice line, the restricted height—appearing in the Back Bay as well. Maps reveal a clearly discernible rectangle, axially aligned on Commonwealth Ave., with its mall as the central east-west boulevard, and Dartmouth St., one hundred feet wide, forming the north-south axis leading down into the then fashionable South End.

These initial premises were enhanced in 1867 when a French Ecole des Beaux Arts curriculum was established at the first architectural school in the United States—the Massachusetts Institute of Technology (MIT) on Boylston St. (Site 8). But the redbrick and brownstone Queen Anne Revival elevations of most Back Bay buildings erected between 1870 and 1886 reflect Boston's longstanding affinity to England, resembling London's South Kensington more than Paris. Development during that period became an English architectural game on a French playing field, which yielded a streetscape unique in the United States.

Arlington St. (ca. 1867), view from the Beacon St. corner of the Public Garden. (*From* King's Handbook of Boston, *9th ed., Boston: Moses King, 1889, p. 30.*)

Arlington St.

Walk along Arlington St. past the Arlington Street Church, Newbury St., and Commonwealth Ave. to reach "12 Arlington St." (today 1 Commonweath Ave.)

1. **The John Bates House** (1860), formerly 12 Arlington St., now 1 Commonwealth Ave., by Arthur Gilman

Arlington St. was the first in the Back Bay to be completed, with rows of substantial houses from the 1860s. Each block combined several of these houses into symmetrical pavilioned facades that evoked Parisian concepts of urban design. The John Bates[1] House, on the north corner of Commonwealth Ave., was one of the first of these; it was enlarged in 1893 and joined to 1 Commonwealth Ave. by Mrs. J. Montgomery Sears. On the south corner, the Ritz-Carlton Hotel (1931) by Strickland and Blodgett, with its 1981 addition by Skidmore Owings and Merrill of Chicago, has replaced earlier houses on Arlington St. and Commonwealth Ave. (see also Gilman Site 2; T2, T4).

Retrace your steps past the hotel to the nearby corner of Boylston and Arlington Sts.

2. **Arlington Street Church** (1858–61), by Arthur Gilman; restoration by Robert Neiley (1985) and Goody and Clancy (1996) {Unitarian Universalist; side entrance 351 Boylston St.; www.asc-boston.org; (617)-536-7050}

Arlington Street Church (1858-61), by Arthur Gilman. Photograph by Josiah Johnson Hawes. *(Courtesy of the Society for the Preservation of New England Antiquities.)*

The first public building in the Back Bay, Arlington Street Church, brought Boston architecture up to international standards for the first time. Gilman, the primary architectural theorist of his day, had traveled in England and on the Continent, and the monumental, correct scale of this baroque design was unique in Boston. The exterior, with its 190-foot spire, was executed in stone brought from Belleville, N.J.; it was adapted from the English design of James Gibbs's St. Martin's-in-the-Fields (1727), Trafalgar Sq., London. Gibbs's pattern books provided the models for dozens of small churches built throughout Federal New England.

The Arlington Street Church interior drew inspiration from the basilica of Santa Annunziata in Genoa (1587), the city of Christopher Columbus's birth, and is one of the most spectacular spaces in Boston. Enhanced with rich baroque ornament, a monumental arcade of Corinthian columns supports the gallery, rising to a barrel-vaulted ceiling that recalls Peter Harrison's much smaller King's Chapel (1749), Boston's only stone church from colonial times. A spectacular series of Tiffany windows designed by Frederick Wilson were planned in 1898 and installed in the following decade, and a pulpit carved in the style of Grinling Gibbons now fills the entire sanctuary at the front of the nave. This was designed in 1911 by Alexander Wadsworth Longfellow, Jr., a prominent Boston architect and the nephew of the poet Henry Wadsworth Longfellow. In 1903, this architect also arranged for a statue of the congregation's famed minister William Ellery Channing (1779–1842) by sculptor Herbert Adams to be set at the edge of the Public Garden·opposite the Church (see A. W. Longfellow T12; H. W. Longfellow T3, T6, T12; Channing T6, T8).

The distinguished history of the Arlington Street Church congregation extends from Colonial times, but its historical apogee was reached at its now-demolished Federal Street Church (1803) by Charles Bulfinch with the founding of the American Unitarian Association under Channing's leadership in 1825. Subsequent activities of the congregation have likewise been notable in maintaining their church as a national sanctuary for the oppressed, both individuals and groups, including those persecuted during the Civil War, participants in civil disobedience actions, and objectors to the Vietnam War.

At the corner of Arlington and Boylston Sts., remain on the church side (north side) of Boylston St. Turn right (the side and back of the church will be on your right). You should now be facing west for a view of Boylston's streetscape. Before proceeding west toward Copley Sq., view Sites 3, 4, and 5.

3. Boylston St. (View west)

Although Boylston St. is semicommercial in use, numerous private homes were built initially here with projecting bays and French mansard roofs, such as those still visible farther down Boylston on the south (left) side, above the entrance of 406–410 Boylston St. (1861). Most of these houses were replaced in the early twentieth century by stores and shops of modest size. Many of the huge new buildings erected on Boylston St. since 1950 have stimulated severe con-

troversies not only because of their proximity to the residential Back Bay but also because of their juxtaposition with the historic and landmark buildings of Copley Sq.

An exception on the north (right) side is 399 Boylston St. (1982–84), by Childs, Bertman and Tseckares, where the bulk and scale are deliberately deconstructed through variation of surface materials, with only seven to eleven of its thirteen stories affecting the view from the street. This new structure was combined with restoration of a fine classical building on the same side at 415–421 Boylston St., the Warren Chambers (1896), by Ball and Dabney.

We will pass the sites above shortly. However, while still near the corner of Arlington and Boylston Sts., look across Boylston St. at 330 Boylston St., Shreve, Crump and Low, and 356 Boylston St., the former site of the Women's Educational and Industrial Union, several storefronts farther west.

4 and 5. Shreve, Crump and Low, 330 Boylston St. (1930), by William Aldrich; and 356 Boylston St. (1906), by Parker Thomas and Rice; restored (1973) by Shepley Bulfinch Richardson and Abbott

With their elegant detailing of bronze and glass, Boston's most famous jewelry store and 356 Boylston St. are notable examples of the refined classical designs that distinguished Boston architecture following the turn of the century, here and in the financial district. Under zoning restrictions in the early twentieth century, new construction comported well with earlier buildings, such as No. 356, in both limited height and ornate materials.

Proceed now along the right side of Boylston St. toward Copley Sq. (west). 420 Boylston is on the left side.

Berkeley Building, 420 Boylston St. (© Steve Rosenthal, photographer; courtesy of Steve Rosenthal.)

At the corner of Boylston and Berkeley Sts., cross Berkeley for a closer look at our next facade, 234 Berkley St.

7. The Museum of Natural History (1863), 234 Berkeley St., by William Gibbons Preston

This Italian renaissance palazzo was designed in Paris, where Preston, the architect also of the elegant iron footbridge (T6) in the Public Garden, was studying. The combination of brick and stone and the elimination of most of the architectural sculpture that Preston had projected in his original drawings were economy measures, but the elaborate Corinthian pilasters and fine proportions of the monumental freestanding building were unique (see W. G. Preston T4). It also is important as the site of one of Boston's earliest cultural institutions.

Return to Boylston St.

6. The Berkeley Building (1905), 420 Boylston St., by Codman and Despradelle; restored (1988) by Anderson Notter Finegold Alexander

This is the most spectacular historic Edwardian (1901–10) structure on Boylston St. east of Copley Sq. Desiré Despradelle, professor of design (1893–1912) at the nearby MIT Architectural School, had trained at the Ecole des Beaux Arts in Paris, and this is his most important remaining building in Boston. The steel frame is clad in ornate glazed terra-cotta, copper, and glass. The design is brought together by the large central entrance arch, the sophisticated treatment of the narrow lateral bays along Boylston St., and the bay windows that project on the Berkeley St. elevation. Evoking great commercial store designs, such as Franz Jourdain's "Samaritaine" (1907) in Paris, the Berkeley Building has one of the most festive facades in Boston, and its small-scale ornament complements the streetscape of the Back Bay, although its style is unique.

8. Site of the Massachusetts Institute of Technology (1864; nonextant), by William Gibbons Preston; now New England Mutual Life Insurance Building (1938–42), 501 Boylston St., by Cram and Ferguson.

Founded in 1863, MIT's original building was similar to the Museum of Natural History and stood on the northwestern segment of this block until the late 1930s, when MIT moved to Cambridge. Although the present New England Life building is a fine example of the "Federal Classicism" exploited in Massachusetts in the 1930s, the massive addition to its original E-shaped plan, raising the wings and eliminating an open courtyard facing south, initiated the breakdown of Boylston St.'s coherence as urban design.

9 and 10. The New England/222 Berkeley St. (1990), by Robert A. M. Stern; and **The New England/500 Boylston St.** (1989), by Johnson and Burgee

Determined to create an architectural statement that would upstage both the Hancock and Prudential towers, in 1989 the New England Life Insurance Company commissioned Philip Johnson of New York to design a pair of twenty-five-story frontal towers along the south side of this block on Boylston St. Rigorously symmetrical and gigantic in scale, they were wholly out of context with the Back Bay.

Boston Y.M.C.A., by Sturgis and Brigham. *(From King's Hand-Book of Boston, 9th ed., Boston: Moses King, 1889, p. 204.)*

222 Berkeley St. (left), by Robert A. M. Stern; **500 Boylston St.,** by Johnson and Burgee; **Museum of Natural History,** by W. G. Preston. Perspective rendering by Frank Costantino for Robert A. M. Stern Architects. *(Courtesy of Robert A. M. Stern Architects.)*

Under the pressure of intense public protest but after the first tower at 500 Boylston was well under construction, New England Life submitted the eastern corner tower to redesign by Robert A. M. Stern, also of New York, who introduced brick and limestone as cladding to create an articulated surface, changed its scale and shape by reducing its height to twenty stories, and turned it 90 degrees to become 222 Berkeley St. The imperious axial symmetry embodied in the initial proposal was thereby alleviated, leaving the first tower at 500 Boylston St. as a bulky and lonely Gulliver marooned amid smaller and more picturesque neighbors.

This important site at the corner of Boylston and Berkeley Sts. was earlier occupied by Sturgis and Brigham's picturesque Boston Y.M.C.A. (1882, nonextant),[2] rebuilt after a fire as the five-story Coulton Building (1910) by Putman and Cox (nonextant). Incorporating some of the walls and gables of the earlier building with a brilliant syncopated series of rectangular glass oriel windows that echoed the materials of the adjacent Berkeley Building (Site 6), the Coulton Building (at 500 Boylston St.) became one of the most admired and contextual structures in the commercial Back Bay until its demolition in 1989. This corner was rehumanized in 1990 by sculptor Robert Shure's bronze *Teddy Bear,* commissioned by FAO Schwarz.

Continue west along Boylston St. toward Copley Sq.

Apartments and hotels designed by some of Boston's most distinguished nineteenth-century architects formerly occupied Boylston St. from Clarendon to Dartmouth Sts., including Levi Newcomb's Bristol Hotel (1879), Peabody and Stearns's Brunswick Hotel (1877), and J. P. Putnam's Hotel Cluny (1876). All of these were demolished by the redevelopment of Boylston St. as the insurance center of the city.

Turn left on Clarendon St., and walk behind Trinity Church one block to St. James Ave., where the first John Hancock Building will be on your left, on the east side of Clarendon St. between St. James Ave. and Stuart St. Not visible here but behind the first Hancock Building is

11. John Hancock Life Insurance Company Building (1946–49), by Hoyle Doran and Berry, successor firm to Cram and Ferguson

No. 200 Berkeley St. is the address of Boston's second skyscraper—the Custom House Tower (T1) was the first, in 1917. At the end of this tour the top of the Hancock may be viewed from the west side of Copley Sq. You will see that its profile echoes that of Trinity Church. The twenty-six-story Hancock Building was the second structure to be built by the insurance company. The granite First Hancock Building (1922) by Parker Thomas and Rice (here at 197

Clarendon St.) was initially four stories high; four additional stories were added later to achieve a total of eight. The second building, situated on Berkeley St., much influenced by developments in New York and Hugh Ferriss's drawings of skyscrapers, introduced the genre to Boston, where severe height restrictions had long been honored.

Diagonally across the intersection of Clarendon St. and St. James Ave. is the main entrance to the new John Hancock Building, often referred to as the Hancock Tower.

12. John Hancock Tower, the new John Hancock Building (1967–75), 200 Clarendon St., by Henry Cobb of I. M. Pei

The John Hancock Insurance Company, whose earlier building (Site 11) had been exceeded in height by the Prudential Center tower, finally responded with this 790-foot, sixty-story, sleek rhomboid skyscraper just south of Trinity Church. This shining structure provides a striking backdrop as we move along Boylston St. But in full view from the west across Copley Sq., its towering presence is rendered benign through a reflective cladding that, especially on sunny days, causes the building effectively to disappear, to evaporate against the sky while reflecting the adjacent Trinity Church at the ground. Although initially this third Hancock Building was plagued by structural problems and occasional unexpected shedding of its windows, its minimalist yet picturesque shape provides an elegant accent for Boston's skyline. It is recognized widely as one of the world's great skyscrapers.

Turn to the west and cross Clarendon St. As you walk along St. James Ave., Trinity Church will be on your right and the Hancock Tower will be on your left. The striking total effect of its presence will be viewed from the northwest corner of Copley Sq. later in the tour; here, with its stunningly large mirror reflection, it provides a double of Trinity Church (see the cover).

Continue into Copley Sq.

13. Copley Sq.

The awkward intersection of Huntington Ave., Dartmouth St., and St. James Ave., marking the southwestern corner of Copley Sq. where Dartmouth St. leaves the southern edge of the Back Bay, was a dusty construction site in 1870. In this same year the final decision was made to build a Museum of Fine Arts, first of the great nineteenth-century public museum buildings in the United States, on the southeastern corner of the intersection. It was from this point, said Walter Muir Whitehill, that Copley Sq., "never properly or reasonably laid out . . . [began] . . . to stumble into shape" (171). From uncertain beginnings, called "Art Sq." at the time, Copley Sq. has evolved into not only a great cultural center of Boston but also one of the most famous urban spaces in the United States.

Monumental institutional buildings have defined Copley Sq. over time, but its function as either an intersection or a plaza has been problematic. Charles McKim's 1890 vision of a central fountain in front of his Boston Public Library was followed by a series of proposals brought forward by prominent architects, from Ralph Adams Cram to C. Howard Walker. No action was taken until 1966, when Sasaki Dawson and DeMay won a national competition to redesign Copley Sq. Their sunken concrete plaza and fountain mandated by the competition program rerouted traffic, but its wall separated the plaza from Boylston St. both visually and physically, so that the scheme never worked as a pedestrian space. In 1983, for the centennial celebration of the naming of Copley Sq., another round of planning was initiated with another competition. Finally, in 1989 a new design by Dean Abbott with Clarke and Rapuano was implemented with articulated brick walkways, sycamore trees, landscaping, seating, and a redesigned fountain to create an urban park. Graham Gund's elegant ticket kiosk (1993) now ornaments and brings coherence to the northeast corner of the square.

We look next at the south side of Copley Sq.

14. Site of Boston's Museum of Fine Arts (1870–76; nonextant), by Sturgis and Brigham; now the **Fairmont Copley Plaza Hotel** (1912), by Henry J. Hardenbergh

The Museum of Fine Arts that stood on the south side of the square faced wide Dartmouth St. and was the first public building on Art Sq. However, when the South End fell on hard times and Trinity Church (1872–77) construction began to the northeast, it became clear that a great boulevard along Dartmouth St. would never be needed. The completion of the original design for the museum was abandoned and its north side (on Copley Sq.) became its

Museum of Fine Arts, Art (now Copley) Sq., by Sturgis and Brigham, engraving. (*From* King's Hand-Book of Boston, *9th ed., Boston: Moses King, 1889, facing p. 128.*)

primary facade. The redbrick Ruskinian Gothic structure, encrusted with imported English terra-cotta ornament, had a profound effect on subsequent building design. Although it is virtually unknown today as a structure, the museum's focus on an English program of decorative arts, drawn from that of London's South Kensington Museums, introduced the ornamental new style of London to the Back Bay and to the United States; this quickly led to the melding of Arthur Gilman's French grid of the Back Bay with an essentially English streetscape (see Sturgis and Brigham Sites 24, 27, 28; T6, T12).

The U.S. terra-cotta industry, which was to supply the decorative cladding for most of the commercial buildings erected throughout the nation between 1890 and 1930, was begun soon after 1870 by English experts who immigrated at the time of the museum project. The Museum of Fine Arts was razed shortly after 1909, when the institution moved to Huntington Ave. and the Fens; its present neoclassical quarters were designed by Guy Lowell.

Standing on the site of the Museum of Fine Arts, the Copley Plaza Hotel (1912), unlike its predecessor, faces the square. Richly ornamented and monochromatic, its contained classical silhouette reflects the Ecole des Beaux Arts training of Hardenbergh, who had studied with Detlef Lienau, one of the best-known and earliest of

Trinity Church, by H. H. Richardson; **Hancock Tower,** by I. M. Pei and Henry Cobb; Copley Sq. (*© Steve Rosenthal, photographer; courtesy of Steve Rosenthal.*)

French-trained architects working in pre–Civil War New York. As the preeminent hotel architect of his day, Hardenbergh also designed the Plaza Hotel (1907) and the old Waldorf Astoria (1893) in New York City, and the famous terra-cotta-clad Willard Hotel in Washington, D.C. The horizontal design of his Copley Plaza well complements the Boston Public Library, giving unity and monumental presence to the square.

Turn for a view of the front of Trinity Church.

15. Trinity Church

(1872–77), by Henry Hobson Richardson {Episcopal; open, visitors enter (except Sunday) through the Parish House Bookshop near the corner of Boylston and Clarendon Sts.; fee; www.trinityboston.org; (617)-536-0944}

Unlike most late-nineteenth-century buildings, Trinity Church has been admired continuously, and is perhaps the best-known building by H. H. Richardson. Praised internationally from its opening on February 9, 1877, Trinity's plan and round-arched design drawn from historic precedents marked Richardson's decisive move from Gothic to Romanesque forms. Like the adjacent original Museum of Fine Arts, Trinity was the result of a major competition, and the winning design was altered several times before completion, including a switch on the exterior from Roxbury pudding stone, used by Richardson earlier on the Brattle Square Church (1869–73) two blocks north of Trinity (now the First Baptist Church), to granite and Longmeadow sandstone. The central tower was lowered from its projected height (because of problems of weight on the pile-driven foundations), and the western Galilee Porch (in front) was added in 1898 by Shepley, Rutan and Coolidge, the inheritors of Richardson's practice (see Shepley, Rutan, and Coolidge T1, T4, T12). Also at this time the western towers, already built, were both lowered and altered.

Too frequently overlooked in discussions of the building are the sculpture, the plan, and the mural decoration of the interior. As we walk from the square into Trinity, the stylized Romanesque ornament of the western porch appears obviously different from the sculpture on the actual facade. At the doorway is foliate ornament typical of the 1870s. Carved by the Scottish sculptor John Evans, who later did much work for Richardson and most other major Boston architects, the details of the carving on the Trinity facade are botanically correct as to species of plant and leaf, and deeply undercut. This architectural foliage reflects the widespread interest in natural science and botany that resulted, for example, in the foundation of Louis Agassiz's Museum of Natural History at Harvard in 1858. Despite the Romanesque aspects of the building, this ornament, derived in large measure from the books of the English architect J. K. Colling, was fashionable detailing—the same sort of design appeared in terra-cotta on the museum next door and on the New Old South Church on the corner opposite.

The Greek Cross or centralized plan of Trinity Church gave maximum exposure to its popular rector, Phillips Brooks (1835–93), who was closely in touch with the building committee during the competition. Unlike the long, narrow Latin Cross

plan advocated by the High Church faction of the Episcopal Church (in which a raised chancel and screen separated the clergy from the congregation), the Trinity plan followed the new broad church policy voted by the Anglican ecumenical council in 1866. The lantern above the crossing brought clergy and laity together into one great central space. Richardson's plan was unique in the competition, and it may well have been the decisive factor in his selection as architect (see H. H. Richardson T4, T12).

The mural decorations of John LaFarge on the interior of Trinity were another innovation for art in the United States and had been planned with Richardson from the beginning. In light of many failures in fresco painting, whereby the artist paints directly onto the plaster of the wall, the technological success of John LaFarge is astounding, for this was the first major fresco installation to be executed by artists in the United States. LaFarge, who had trained in France, developed both the wax-based formula for the paint and the designs. His name and those of his assistants appear above the chancel: F. D. Millet, Augustus Saint-Gaudens, G. W. Maynard, Francis Lathrop; others were easel painters who later went on to become leaders of the American Society of Mural Painters following the Chicago Columbian Exposition of 1893. Here at Trinity they learned with LaFarge, helping to execute the designs of the narrative panels *Christ and the Women of Samaria* and *Christ and Nicodemus,* the paintings in the central tower, and the Byzantine decorative stenciling of the interior.

Although LaFarge had trained in France, and this background is reflected in the large masses and spatial disposition of the figurative panels, the red, green, and gold color scheme for the banding and patterning of

the wall surfaces is based more closely on contemporary English systems of wall decoration. The subdivision of the large surfaces into a series of small areas, decorated with stenciling, reflects this source rather than contemporary French mural painting.

Funding limitations prevented LaFarge from executing his decorations in the chancel. This was redesigned by Maginnis and Walsh in a Byzantine style with marble and gold leaf in 1938. It was here at Trinity that John LaFarge first became aware of the overpowering effects of daylight through clear glass on the colors of the decoration. This concern led to his experiments, beginning in the mid-1870s, with stained glass. His objective of controlling light through the effects of color is well illustrated in his huge blue *Christ in Majesty* above the west portal.

When emerging from Trinity, pause to read about the next site, New Old South Church, best viewed from Copley Sq.

16. **New Old South Church** (1874), 645 Boylston St., by Cummings and Sears {United Church of Christ (Congregational); **Old South Church,** architecturally labeled "new" when this building replaced the original building; www.oldsouth.org; (617)-536-1970}

As we look across Copley Sq. from the portal of Trinity to the northwest corner of Boylston and Dartmouth Sts., the picturesque silhouette, tall tower (now lowered twenty-five feet below its original height), and copper lantern of the New Old South present a marked contrast to the low-lying symmetry of the Boston Public Library (1887–95) by McKim, Mead and White. The classical library looks to the architectural future, whereas the church is one of the most prominent surviving examples of Ruskinian Gothic design in Boston and the United States. Its architect, Charles Cummings, has clearly provided us with a centrifugal design, a textbook sample of the theorems of the nineteenth-century English art critic John Ruskin, whose famous books *The Seven Lamps of Architecture* (1849) and *The Stones of Venice* (1851–53) popularized the polychromatic, or Venetian Gothic, style in the United States.

Cummings, like Ruskin (and unlike the French-trained Richardson and McKim), designed his church as a series of superb details that are remarkably close to Ruskin's own illustrations for his books. For example, as we stand in the square the total independence of the east elevation from that of the south becomes apparent. This is an additive, rather than a unified, composition, and for full enjoyment of the building we should look at it this way too. The walls are brilliantly banded and randomly punctured with pointed Gothic arches and arcades of varying derivation, complete with polychromatic voussoirs and Norman nail-head and zigzag moldings. The luxuriance and quality of the foliate carving on the exterior make New Old South the finest remaining example in stone of the sort of undercut Gothic ornament that appeared in less expensive terra-cotta on the Sturgis and Brigham Museum of Fine Arts to the south. Particularly distinguished are the foliate stringcourses that are utilized by Cummings as the sole unifying device common to both elevations. These and the sculpture were carved by John Evans, the young sculptor from Scotland, who also carved the facade and exterior sculpture of Trinity Church for Richardson.

Although the central lantern was influenced by Trinity Church, the New Old South interior mirrors Cummings's philosophy that church architecture should reflect liturgy or use. The timbered roof trusses and nave piers are exposed and remain along with the original furnishings in the recently repainted and restored interior. These "Reform Gothic" details clearly reveal their construction, with diagonal boarding and chamfering. With its wide crossing and shallow transepts and apse, and without aisles, New Old South illustrates a new solution for late-nineteenth-century American church architecture, a centralized meetinghouse with an open plan, but in a Gothic envelope (see Cummings and Sears Site 28; T2, T4).

17. **Boston Public Library** (1887–95), Dartmouth St., by McKim, Mead, and White {Use Dartmouth St. entrance; restaurants; tours; www.bpl.org; (617)-536-5400}

In 1880 land had been given by the city for a library on Dartmouth St., abutting the west edge of what was then still called Art Sq. It was not until 1887, however, that the final design of Charles F. McKim was accepted and work on the present building actually began. Clearly influenced by the architect's training in Paris at the Ecole des Beaux Arts and by Henri Labrouste's Bibliothèque Ste. Genevieve (1844) in that city, the low, symmetrical, monochromatic structure of the library led the way to the classicism that came to control the direction of American public building for the next several decades. When designed in 1887, it was to be the greatest combined work of architect, painter, and sculptor produced in the United States up to that time.

The building opened in March 1895 without all its embellishments completed, but with the monumental lions of Augustus Saint-Gaudens mounted on the grand staircase of yellow Siena marble. Three major mural painting cycles had been commissioned and were partly installed. *The*

Allegory of Wisdom by French Symbolist Puvis de Chavannes, in pale colors, enhances the yellow marble of the staircase. *The Quest for the Grail* by Edwin Austin Abbey brought Arthurian medievalism to the book delivery room on the second floor and was to bring the Philadelphia illustrator Abbey, who was then living in England, into the realm of mural painting for the first time. The fantastic *World Religions* by John Singer Sargent in the third-floor gallery was also the first attempt of this artist at mural painting, but it brought full recognition to the art form with which John LaFarge had begun experimenting ten years earlier on the opposite side of Copley Sq. at Trinity Church. All these later murals were executed on canvas in Europe,[3] not in fresco (directly on the plaster), as LaFarge had done. Both the Abbey and Sargent cycles incorporate areas of gold-leaf relief sculpture executed by Saint-Gaudens after the installation of the canvas. More sculpture and painting were added to the library in the following decades, including the bronze doors by Daniel Chester French, culminating with the great figures of Art and Science (1912) by Bela Pratt, which face the square from the entrance. When completed, the building incorporated the work of some of the most distinguished American artists then working in this country and abroad (see Boston Public Library T8).

A Library Addition (1966–72), designed by Philip Johnson (Site 9), was attached to the rear of the McKim building, with an entrance on the Boylston St. side, which we pass at the end of the tour. Replacing the red brick of Van Brunt and Howe's demolished Harvard Medical School (1883), the library addition is of monumental scale. Its unornamented slabs of stone reflect the New Brutalism of the 1960s, which inspired Boston's Government Center and new City

Harvard Medical School, by Van Brunt and Howe, engraving. *(From* King's Hand-Book of Boston, *9th ed., Boston: Moses King, 1889, facing p. 142.)*

Hall (see Government Center, New City Hall T4; Van Brunt and Howe T12). Despite Johnson's duplication of the size and rectangular shape of the original library building as requested by his client, the two back-to-back segments of the institution fail to communicate in either exterior visual or interior functional terms. Incorporating expanded but isolated functional arrangements while duplicating the proportions of the original building, Philip Johnson's lowering granite-faced walls, devoid of ornament, mock the delicate carving and detailing of the earlier building and are best seen from Exeter St. at the end of the tour.

18. Site of S. S. Pierce Store (1887; nonextant), by S. Edwin Tobey; now **Copley Place** (1980–84), by The Architects Collaborative and Hugh Stubbins

After 1883, when Copley Sq. was officially renamed and the original museum entrance on Dartmouth St. abandoned, Boston's S. S. Pierce Company commissioned Edwin Tobey to erect a picturesque yet tough little building opposite the museum on the triangular space at the southwest corner of the square. With heavy walls of quarry-faced ashlar and a complex gabled roof, which evoked Trinity Church, and an oriel with a rounded tower at the southwest corner of Dartmouth St. and Huntington Ave., this comparatively small building became the visual keystone for enclosing the space of Copley Sq. Following the demolition of S. S. Pierce in 1956 to create ramps for the Massachusetts Turnpike, the triangular lot reverted to a dusty construction site—its condition in 1870 before the museum was built. After almost thirty years of debate and resolution of daunting legal and engineering challenges associated with use of air rights over the Massachusetts Turnpike, Copley Place, a vast urban mall and residential and office complex

Pierce Building (1887), Copley Sq., by S. Edwin Tobey, steel engraving by C. A. Walker (1887). *(From Richard Herndon, compiler,* Boston of To-day: A Glance at Its History and Characteristics, with Biographical Sketches and Portraits of Many of Its Professional and Business Men, *ed. Edwin M. Bacon, Boston: Post Publishing Company, 1892, facing p. 72.)*

with two hotels, finally was erected on the S. S. Pierce Store site and adjacent land behind. This key corner of Copley Sq. has thereby been reestablished with the foyer of the Westin Hotel, which connects the common cornice lines of the adjacent Boston Public Library and Copley Plaza Hotel, serving the same visual function as the earlier S. S. Pierce Store. Picturesque articulation of the different components of Copley Place, with the huge Marriott Hotel tower set back from the south side of Huntington Ave., allows its rough horizontal banding, stonelike texture, and surface color to enhance its linkage with the historic buildings on the square.

Proceed to the northwest corner of Copley Sq. near the ticket kiosk and cross Boylston St. The New Old South Church will be on the left as we walk north on Dartmouth St. to the Boston Art Club (at the end of the block on the left).

Boston Art Club, corner of Dartmouth and Newbury Sts. (1883), by William Ralph Emerson. Photograph by Baldwin Coolidge. *(Courtesy of the Society for the Preservation of New England Antiquities.)*

19. **Boston Art Club** (1881), 270 Dartmouth St., by William Ralph Emerson

The Boston Art Club is one of the few, and surely the most distinguished, urban building by Boston's famous country house architect, William Ralph Emerson. Although picturesque, it has an overall cohesion and horizontality, which is lacking in the polychromatic and vertically oriented New Old South Church. The low,

bulbous tower and centered gables barely break the line of the roof, while the irregularity of the lateral fenestration is resolved by the introduction of a dominant central bay. Seen from the north on Dartmouth St., the Art Club forms a single picturesque composition with the lantern and tower of the New Old South Church behind (see William Ralph Emerson T2, T4, T11, T12).

The ornament is an excellent example of the finest type of terra-cotta decoration, executed with hand-sculpted clay blocks, as large in size and high in relief as was possible to manufacture without warping and twisting in firing. The redbrick walls are trimmed with quarry-faced brownstone and decorated with irregularly spaced panels of this dense, comparatively small-scale baked clay ornament, which evokes in nineteenth-century terms the fine cut-brick designs found in early eighteenth-century England during the reign of Queen Anne.

20. **Hotel Victoria** (1886), 275 Dartmouth St., by J. L. Faxon

Designed by another local architect, the building opposite the Boston Art Club is clad entirely with brilliant red molded commercial terra-cotta. The exotic eclecticism of the ornament is less significant than the way in which the material reveals its mode of manufacture. In contrast to the high relief and hand-crafted quality of Emerson's decoration, the sheathing of the Hotel Victoria is composed of very small terra-cotta blocks, imprinted with a sharp design in low relief. Made with only a few different molds used over and over again, the resulting ornament is both lavish and repetitive and was produced at comparatively low cost. The lack of marked horizontal projection and the restriction in the size of the individual block allowed for accuracy and quality control in production. Thus, stringcourse and sills, ordered and manufactured wholesale for the architect, were sure to lay up true to scale. Such use of terra-cotta anticipates applications by Louis Sullivan in Chicago and its use as sheathing for skyscrapers. Natural slip-glazed terra-cotta preceded the less durable colored enamel–glazed terra-cotta of the Berkeley Building (Site 6), which became available after the 1890s.

Hotel Vendome (ca. 1908), by W. G. Preston. Postcard published by Reichner Brothers, Boston. *(Courtesy of the Society for the Preservation of New England Antiquities.)*

Look across Dartmouth St.[4] before crossing Newbury St. On the northeast side of Dartmouth you will find

21. **J. P. Putnam House** (1878), 277 Dartmouth St., by J. Pickering Putnam

At the northeast corner of Dartmouth and Newbury Sts. Putnam designed his own private residence. Educated at Schinkel's Bauacademie in Berlin, where he went after a few months at the Ecole des Beaux Arts in Paris, upon his return to Boston Putnam quickly adopted the new Queen Anne Revival style that began to sweep through the Back Bay beginning in 1870. The piled-up, picturesque, and polychromatic surfaces of such a design differ markedly in style and ornament from the academic classicism of Arthur Gilman's buildings

along Arlington (Site 1 and 2) and Berkeley Sts. Despite its complexity, this design is tightly controlled, with limestone courses pulling together its bays and projections. The multiple gables and towers create a syncopated counterpoint of shapes against the sky, anchoring the structure and turning the corner with finesse to achieve the picturesque silhouette so highly prized in the late nineteenth century.

Continue north along Dartmouth St. to the corner of Commonwealth Ave.

22. **Hotel Vendome** (1871), southwest corner of Commonwealth Ave. and Dartmouth St., by William G. Preston; additions by J. F. Ober (1881) and Stahl-Bennett (1972)

Although the Hotel Victoria conjures up British association in the 1880s, the pale gray Hotel Vendome, designed a decade earlier, evokes Second Empire Paris. Indeed, its architect, William G. Preston, who had studied there, designed the Museum of Natural History (Site 7) on Berkeley St. in 1863 while in that city. Returning to Boston, he developed this more French, axially aligned mansardic structure that faced Dartmouth St. with a central projecting pavilion. The Vendome is further distinguished in the Back Bay because of the incised Neo-Grec ornament that adorns its monochromatic marble walls. This machine-crafted classical detailing had been widely publicized through the work of César Daly, the French publisher of *Revue de l'Art*.

Like many other Second Empire buildings, for example Boston's Old City Hall (1861–65) on School St. by Bryant and Gilman (see p. xxxi; T4, T6), the outmoded Vendome precipitated a heated preservation controversy in the 1960s and early 1970s, when attempts were made to demolish it. This controversy and associated problems were exacerbated by a disastrous fire that occurred in the southeast section of the original building on Dartmouth St. in 1972, when renovation of the structure was nearly completed. A monument to the nine firefighters who died when the burned section collapsed has been installed on the Commonwealth Avenue Mall at Dartmouth St. A 1972 addition to the Vendome by Stahl-Bennett replaced the destroyed portion of the hotel; it reflects the New Brutalism of the 1960s. A remodeling of the remaining portion of the old building by Irving Salsberg mildly reflects the Vendome's tradition of catering to famous Victorians by converting it to luxury apartments, with offices and stores on the ground floor and in the basement.

From the east side of Dartmouth St. (the side closer to the Public Garden), cross the eastbound side of Commonwealth Ave. to its central Mall. The nearby memorial to the firefighters killed in the Vendome fire is visible here. Continue on Dartmouth St. across the westbound side of Commonwealth Ave. No. 303 Dartmouth is on the northeast corner of Dartmouth and Commonwealth Ave.

23. Arthur Hunnewell House (1876), 303 Dartmouth St., by Shaw and Shaw

Construction of permanent buildings on Dartmouth St. began from both ends; the central section was completed only in the 1880s. At the heart of the Back Bay, the block from Commonwealth Ave. to Marlborough St. is particularly distinguished for its domestic architecture. A more free use of classical formulae appears on this house, designed by Robert Gould Shaw, architect brother-in-law of Hollis Hunnewell. The axial three-bay composition of the facade is similar to that of both the Hotel Vendome (Site 22) and the Thomas F. Cushing House (Site 26). Although he was attracted to classicism from early in his career, Shaw's work is of the "Free Classic" rather than a rigorously disciplined mode. For example, the oriel windows and the changes in the surfacing material of the building from the stone basement to the brick superstructure reveal concurrent influences from France and the English Queen Anne Revival.

Continue north on Dartmouth St. No. 315 will appear on the right.

24. Hollis H. Hunnewell House (1869), 315 Dartmouth St., by Sturgis and Brigham

Hollis H. Hunnewell House (ca.1901), 315 Dartmouth St., by Sturgis and Brigham; residence of T. Jefferson Coolidge. Photograph by Baldwin Coolidge. (*Courtesy of the Society for the Preservation of New England Antiquities.*)

The one-story wing of the Hollis Hunnewell House and even the mansardic towers that give the building its superb pyramidal massing were added following a fire in 1881. The robust stone trim, elegant detailing and paneling of the brick walls, and the tiled cornice are all original. The house is thus one of the earliest instances of exterior ceramic ornamentation on a building in Boston. In the following year its architects introduced terra-cotta on their Museum of Fine Arts (Site 14) at the other end of Dartmouth St. The picturesque silhouette, multimedia surfaces, and articulation of the facades were deftly aligned.

At the intersection of Dartmouth and Marlborough Sts., turn left (west) to cross Dartmouth, where the Crowninshield House is located on the southwest corner.

25. Benjamin Crowninshield House
(1869), 164 Marlborough St., by H. H. Richardson

The assurance with which the English-trained John Hubbard Sturgis worked with tile and brick opposite, at the Hollis Hunnewell House, is in marked contrast to the awkward design developed by H. H. Richardson for his first house in Back Bay. Here he attempts, rather unsuccessfully, to combine bald brick walling, incised ornament, and tile with an ornate iron-door hood that evokes the pavilions of Paris's Bois du Boulogne. The frontality and symmetry of this house, its curious tar-dipped Salomónic columns on the corners of the entrance bay, and the tiles inset at the belt course and cornice after Richardson saw the Hunnewell House provide a fascinating glimpse of the young Richardson experimenting ten-

tatively in the Queen Anne Revival before he developed his own Romanesque aesthetic.

The Cushing House, next, is opposite the Crowninshield House.

26. Thomas F. Cushing House (1871), 165 Marlborough St. (the Cushing-Endicott House), by Snell and Gregerson

Tall simple bays, elegant proportions, and classical ornament mark this house as one of the most distinguished French Academic designs in the Back Bay. Its architects, Snell and Gregerson, led one of Boston's outstanding firms of the period, and their work was characterized by much use of brick with Nova Scotia sandstone trim and by subtle manipulation of detail to achieve an effect of symmetry. Here, blind windows and careful design of the elevations achieve that end. Snell and Gregerson (see also Site 28) habitually favored a low ceiling on the ground level to allow a *piano nobile* for the public rooms above. The interiors were originally as notable as the elevation, which incorporates three houses into a single massive composition. Inside, the ebony furniture, the mantel, and cornice were imported from the Orient by the first owner, Thomas F. Cushing.

Thomas Cushing House, by Snell and Gregerson. *(Courtesy of the Boston Athenæum.)*

Return to the corner of Dartmouth St. and Commonwealth Ave.

27. Frederick L. Ames House (1882), 306 Dartmouth St., by John Hubbard Sturgis; formerly the S. V. R. Thayer House (1872), by Peabody and Stearns

The Dartmouth St.–Commonwealth Ave. intersection was complete by 1882, a fitting architectural anchor to the north, which balances the great public buildings to the south on Copley Sq. In this year John Hubbard Sturgis, architect of the museum, executed a complete remodeling and two additions to the simple mansardic S. V. R. Thayer House (1872), by Peabody and Stearns, here on the northwest corner of the intersection. From this earlier structure only the exterior walls and part of the roof at the corner remain. Sturgis added a two-story glazed conservatory on Commonwealth Ave., a tower with a great battered chimney emblazoned with the initials of Frederick L. Ames, and a porte cochere to extend the Dartmouth St. elevation.

Six years later, at the time of the death of the architect (1888), a Boston newspaper noted that "the most beautiful example of his work was Mr. Ames' house . . . which possesses a wrought iron gate and some carved exterior panels which are not surpassed by anything in this country and by very few pieces of modern work anywhere." Indeed, the sophistication of the ornamentation, drawn from Owen Jones's *Grammar of Ornament* (1856), is far more erudite than that which appears on most buildings in the United States—for example, across the street in the work of Shaw and Shaw (Site 23). Sturgis, who had studied and trained in England, designed here his major American statement of London's Queen Anne Revival that he so ably stimulated with his museum on Copley Sq. Typically

English is the use of multiple materials in a single composition. Beneath the arch of the porte cochere, terra-cotta plaques appear, as had been used at the museum. These are incorporated adroitly with brick, stone, wood, and glass to produce a design of consummate finesse.

Setting the standard for the decorative arts in Boston, Sturgis created a palatial interior for the Ames House, reached by a mosaic-lined staircase rising from the street to a great hall eighteen by sixty-three feet and forty feet high, where mirrors and balconies open up the space. Lined in carved oak of magnificent quality, the stairwell rises four stories, adorned with a mural cycle of Justinian by the French academician Benjamin Constant and stained-glass windows by John LaFarge. The house has been converted to offices under the auspices of the Raymond Cattle Company and the architects Childs, Bertman and Tseckares.

Turn west (right) on Commonwealth Ave. to walk the block to Exeter St.

28. Commonwealth Ave. (Dartmouth to Exeter Sts.)

The lavish sculptural detail, Queen Anne Revival invention, articulation, towers, turrets, and ornament of Commonwealth Ave. in the late 1870s are a distinct departure from the severe earlier style of Arthur Gilman on Arlington St. in the 1860s. John Sturgis's Museum of Fine Arts introduced the Queen Anne Revival of Richard Norman Shaw and other English architects designing contemporaneously in South Kensington. Not only did the English-inspired designs of the Back Bay set a standard for American architecture in the fifteen years following the opening of the museum, but the streetscapes of this largest upscale residential district in the late nineteenth-century United States remain largely intact today. Boston's most prominent late-nineteenth-century architects designed houses on the north side of Commonwealth Ave. between Dartmouth and Exeter for some of Boston's leading citizens to produce a vigorous ornamental streetscape:

165 Commonwealth Ave. (1879), by Cummings and Sears, was designed for John Erskine, 167 Commonwealth Ave. (1880), by Sturgis and Brigham, for E. Rollins Morse.

169 Commonwealth Ave. (1879), for J. S. Fay, 173 Commonwealth Ave. (1879), for Roger Wolcott, and 175 Commonwealth Ave. (1881), for Charles Merriman, were all designed by the firm of Peabody and Stearns, whose principals would sustain their national practice for another thirty-six years (see Peabody and Stearns T1, T3, T4). (The first two of these Peabody and Stearns designs, Nos. 169 and 173, were completely remodeled in Federal Revival style by Parker Thomas and Rice after World War I.)

171 Commonwealth Ave. (1877), for Abbott Lawrence Lowell, 177 Commonwealth Ave. (1882), for John Quincy Adams, and 183 Commonwealth Ave. (1878), for Frank Merriman, were all by Snell and Gregerson.

179 Commonwealth Ave. (1879), by Carl Fehmer, was for William Bradley, and 181 Commonwealth Ave. (1878), by fashionable Clarence Luce, was for Charles Whitney.

Meanwhile, on the corner the **Hotel Agassiz** (1872), 191 Commonwealth Ave., by Weston and Rand, was designed for Henry Lee Higginson, founder of the Boston Symphony Orchestra and son-in-law of Harvard's naturalist Louis Agassiz (who, after the death of his first wife, married Elizabeth Cary Cabot [Agassiz], first

president of Radcliffe College) (see E. C. Agassiz T6; P. Agassiz T3).

Turn left (south), and walk on the left (east) side of Exeter St. Walk one block from Commonwealth Ave. to Newbury St., where the Spiritualist Temple is on the northeast corner.

29. **Spiritualist Temple** (1884), **corner of Exeter and Newbury Sts., by Hartwell and Richardson (Exeter Street Theater)**

The battered, quarry-faced granite walls and sandstone trim of this blocky building show the strong influence of H. H. Richardson, with whom the younger partner in this firm should not be confused. Texturally, polychromatically, and stylistically, the "Richardson Romanesque" style of the temple derives from such buildings as Trinity Church and Austin Hall at Harvard. The detailing of the composition here lacks the subtlety of the mature designs of H. H. Richardson. For example, central bays are used to articulate the subdivision of the symmetrical elevations, breaking through the cornice, beltcourse, and roof. Yet the monumentality and texture of the design give it importance as a landmark of the Back Bay streetscape where its former peers on Exeter St., such as the Boston Athletic Association (1886) by John Hubbard Sturgis, have been demolished.

After rehabilitation by Childs, Bertman and Tseckares, the same architects who renovated the Frederick L. Ames House at 306 Dartmouth St. (Site 27), the Exeter Street Theater housed a restaurant, cabaret, and offices on the third floor, in addition to the theater. This theater was later removed, and the slate roof and copper spire of the building were damaged severely by fire in 1995. Even more exciting than the architectural impact of the building is the importance of its associations with the religious history of

Boston, which in the late nineteenth century was a center not only of Transcendentalism, but also of Spiritualism, Swedenborgianism, Christian Science, and the Gothic Quest of Ralph Adams Cram (see Transcendentalism T6; Christian Science T8; Cram T12).

Continue south on Exeter St., across Newbury, to the intersection with Boylston St. One Exeter Place is on the northeast corner.

30. **One Exeter Place** (1984), at the northeast corner of Boylston and Exeter Sts., by Jung Brannen

When we return to Copley Sq. at the end of the tour, we'll look west on Boylston St. to this intersection. This view will reveal more effectively the slick green glass of what is known as the notorious fourteen-story "Darth Vader"5 building, rising on the north side of Boylston at Exeter St. Rebuilding without contextual awareness of or concern for scale and materials has been the tragedy of Boylston St. on the north side of Copley Sq., where flimsy modern structures have replaced the substantial Second Church (1873) by N. J. Bradlee and the many ornate hotels that created the nineteenth-century streetscape (see N. J. Bradlee T2, T4, T10, T11). These new, taller buildings are short on the quality of Despradelle's Berkeley Building (Site 6) and I. M. Pei's Hancock Tower (Site 12), lacking a sense of scale in their application of modern industrial materials that dissociates them from the Back Bay as if they had been sent from Mars. Yet, despite these twentieth-century changes, the magic of Boston's monumental Copley Sq. still remains.

A glance to the west from the intersection of Boylston and Exeter Sts. reveals to the left (Site 17) the Boston Public Library Addition (1966–72), best seen here. To the right the
flat-topped Prudential Tower may be seen in the distance.

31. **The Prudential Center** (1959–65), 800 Boylston St., west of Copley Sq., by Charles Luckman and Associates

In the late 1950s, as urban renewal gained momentum, Hartford's Prudential Insurance Company projected a huge new complex here; the final design, executed in the 1960s, included the 750-foot tower, which was taller than the 1946 Hancock Building (Site 11). At this time Harvard's Walter Gropius proposed tall buildings for every other corner of Commonwealth Ave. This threat to the integrity of the Back Bay aroused a broad civic concern for preservation of that historic residential district. Competition for skyline prominence between the Hancock and Prudential companies led the Boston Society of Architects to urge that a narrow band south of historic Back Bay be designated as space for aligning a "High Spine" track for tall buildings between the financial center on the waterfront and the huge unarticulated Prudential Center. Boylston St. today forms the northern edge of this high spine, which has been executed with varying degrees of design success. In the 1880s, houses were built to the west of the New Old South Church on Boylston St., but only a few remain.

Turn left from the intersection of Boylston and Exeter to walk east on the north (left) side of Boylston St. back toward Copley Sq. No. 647 will be on the left.

32. **Haberstroh Building** (1886; copper bay and entrance added), 647 Boylston St., by George Wilton Lewis

The ornate copper design on the facade of this remodeled house adjacent to the New Old South Church makes this structure a

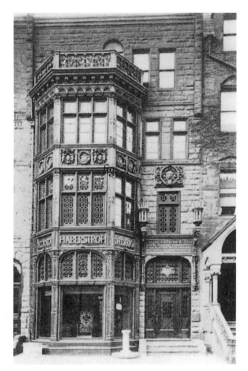

Haberstroh Building, Boylston St., detail from E. Van Noorden Company's advertisement showing their execution of the copper front of Haberstroh and Sons. *(From the* Yearbook of the Boston Architectural Club Exhibition, *1907, p. 141; courtesy of the Boston Architectural Center Memorial Library Collection.)*

The quarry-faced ashlar surface of the house worked well with the adjacent New Old South Church from the start. Then in 1905, after Dr. Whittier's death, an elaborate four-story copper bay and entrance were added by Albert Haberstroh, owner of a prominent design firm formerly located with the Society of Arts and Crafts on Beacon Hill (at 9 Park St., Charles Bulfinch's Amory-Ticknor House opposite the State House, T6). With its elaborate Gothic and Elizabethan ornament executed in copper for Haberstroh by the Van Noorden sheet metal company, the facade of this small Boylston St. building to the west of Copley Sq. is as festive and elegant as that of the contemporaneous Berkeley Building (Site 6) to the east.

Walking back to Copley Sq., we see the original skylit backdrop for Trinity Church interdicted by the blocky silhouette of 500 Boylston St. (Site 10), but the church is reflected magnificently in the mirror glass sheathing of I. M. Pei's Hancock Tower (Site 12). The skyline to the east is punctuated even more poignantly by Hoyle Doran and Berry's second Hancock Building (Site 11), rising behind Trinity Church as a more modest contextual reflection of H. H. Richardson's masterpiece for Boston's Back Bay.

Near the corner of Boylston and Dartmouth Sts., beside the Boston Public Library on Boylston St., you will see the vintage Copley Sq. T stop entrance kiosk (ca. 1914).

singular landmark. Originally built on speculation, it became between 1888 and 1902 the home of Dr. Edward Newton Whittier, a Civil War hero who was on the staff of the nearby Harvard Medical School.

BOSTON'S VICTORIAN AUTHORS:
THINKERS IN THE CENTER
OF THE PLANET

by Eugenia Kaledin and
Mary Melvin Petronella

> Books remained ... a source of life; as they came out
> they were devoured.
>
> —Henry Adams, *The Education*
> *of Henry Adams* (1907)

Tour Location: See Downtown Key Map for the location of the Tour and
its T stop, page xli.

About Walking the Tour: Our literary tour, divided for convenience into
parts I, II, and III, meanders; walkers should feel free to begin at any
point, stop for refreshment, skip parts, or return later if fatigue sets
in. There are promising settings for spontaneous revival: the first on
the Common, between parts I and II; the second on Charles St.,
sandwiched between parts II and III, where numerous cafés provide
delectable delights and coffee is an essential to rekindle the pleasure
of discovery. Our tour ends at the Public Garden, a refreshing Victorian landscape in which to recuperate.

Please note that part II, which includes the lovely, lofty, literary sites
on Beacon Hill, also includes steep ▲▲▲ and moderately ▲▲
hilly terrain. Although most residences in the Beacon Hill area are
private, there are two wonderful exceptions: Prescott House on Beacon St. and the Nichols House Museum on Mt. Vernon St. Our itinerary offers two optional digressions: West St. and Smith Ct.

Thumbnail Sketch of Sights: See Introduction, page xxxiv.

Approximate Walking Time: Estimate 2½ hours for entire tour (excluding
building interiors).

T Stop: Park St., Red and Green lines; a central downtown T intersection. The Park St. kiosks, by Edmund Wheelwright (Wheelwright and Haven), are two of the four that marked the country's groundbreaking Tremont St. subway (1897) when Henry James returned to Boston in 1904. The Tremont St. subway is a National Historic Landmark.

By Car: Parking: The Boston Common Garage, under the Common, on Charles St. between Boylston and Beacon Sts.

Begin at: The Park and Tremont Sts. corner of the Common, near the Park St. T.

INTRODUCTION

Boston's literary history is vital in defining the United States. The strong individualism and civic morality that characterized the early New England writing of Jonathan Edwards and Benjamin Franklin continued with Ralph Waldo Emerson and Harriet Beecher Stowe, and the same qualities remained apparent in the writing of Robert Lowell and may still be found in that of Ellen Goodman. Boston's nineteenth-century literary history provides the fertile territory of today's tour. However, because every vital tradition reaches beyond time and place, we shall occasionally cross over into other centuries and accept fictional situations as "reality." And the special truth that can make literature "more real" than life persuades us to include at times the streets and addresses of Boston's residents in fiction and imagined literary events along with those historical incidents that define Boston's literary heritage.

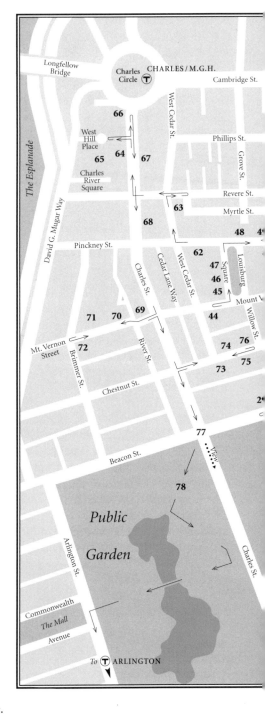

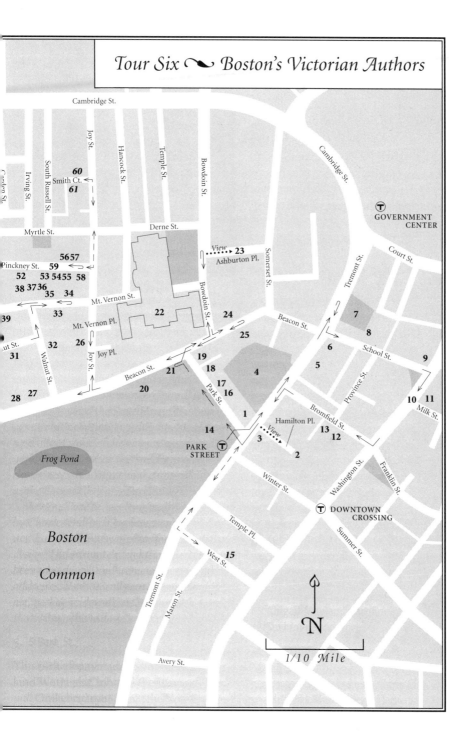

Cambridge St.

Joy St.

Hancock St.

Temple St.

Bowdoin St.

South Russell St.

Irving St.

Garden St.

Smith Ct. **60**
61

Cambridge St.

ⓉGOVERNMENT
CENTER

Myrtle St.

Derne St.

Court St.

Tremont St.

View ▸ **23**
Ashburton Pl.

Somerset St.

56 57
Pinckney St. **59**
52 53 54 55 58
38 37 36
35   34

Mt. Vernon St.

Beacon St.

7

8

39

33

Mt. Vernon Pl.

22

24

25

6

School St.

9

Province St.

32 **26**

Joy St.

Joy Pl.

19

18

5

nut St.

31

Walnut St.

Beacon St.

21

17

16

4

Bromfield St.

10 11
Milk St.

28 27

20

Park St.

1

Hamilton Pl.

13

12

Washington St.

Franklin St.

14

PARK
STREET Ⓣ

3

2

View ▸

Frog Pond

Winter St.

ⓉDOWNTOWN
CROSSING

Summer St.

Boston

Common

Temple Pl.

Tremont St.

West St. **15**

Mason St.

N

Avery St.

1/10 Mile

PART I. From the Common to the Old Corner Book Store (with a return via Bromfield St.)

Standing on the Common, near the corner of Park and Tremont Sts., we crane our necks up to see the steeple of Park Street Church.

1. **Park Street Church** (1809–10), One Park St., by Peter Banner. {See entrance for scheduled open hours; www.parkstreet. org; (617)-523-3383}

Park Street Church "persistently 'holds the note'" (238), said an appreciative Henry James in *The American Scene* (1907). He voiced concern when he learned, in 1904, that "the fat shoulder of financial envy" had recently pushed to replace Park Street Church with a "business block." Pleading for the preservation of "a memorial object" made sense to James, who described Park Street Church as a "landmark," exemplary of the "charm [of Boston past, which] only

Henry James (1843–1916), by his nephew William James, Jr. (1882–1961); oil on canvas. *(Courtesy of the Isabella Stewart Gardner Museum, Boston.)*
"Boston . . . a city of culture."
—Henry James, *The Bostonians* (1896).

Tremont Street Mall (ca. 1890) with Park Street Church. *(Courtesy of the Bostonian Society/Old State House.)*
"The perfectly felicitous 'Park Street Church.'"
—Henry James, *The American Scene* (1907).

asks that . . . we know it and love it. When we fail of this . . . we can never get it back" (238–40).

With James's concern for the preservation of Boston's historic buildings in mind, we pause to imagine the diminutive Henry Adams attending elementary school in the basement and recall that Harriet Beecher Stowe's father, Lyman Beecher, and her husband, Calvin Stowe, preached here, as did William Lloyd Garrison, who delivered Boston's first antislavery speech (1829) with John Greenleaf Whittier in attendance. And in 1888, the "thunderous voice" of Frederick Douglass (1818–95) "poured forth his eloquence," echoing in the ears of the young, Boston-born, African American poet William Stanley Braithwaite (1878–1962): Braithwaite recalled that he "left the church, in my spirit eternally woven the image of Frederick Douglass" (quoted by Butcher 187–88, 191).

Frederick Douglass (1817[20?]–1895), unidentified artist; former attribution: Elisha Livermore Hammond (1779–1882); painting (ca. 1844), oil on canvas, 69.9 cm x 57.1 cm (27½ x 22½ in.), NPG.74.45. *(Courtesy of the National Gallery, Smithsonian Institution.)*
"In the right *one* is a majority."
—Frederick Douglass quoted by T. W. Higginson, *Contemporaries* (1899).

Cross Park St. We'll stay on the Park Street Church side of Tremont St. while we look across Tremont to locate the short cul de sac, Hamilton Place. Look right down to the facade of the building at the far end.

2. **Hamilton Place, the Music Hall** (1852; interior, nonextant, by Snell and Gregerson); repeatedly remodeled

Behind the wall facing us at the end of Hamilton Place (its facade now labeled "The Orpheum Theater") is the location of the framework of Boston's famous Music Hall (1852). Within the extant old structural walls of the Music Hall, Emerson delivered his lecture "Immortality," Theodore Parker preached to huge audiences, and in 1878 Louisa May Alcott performed "Mrs. Jarley's Waxworks" from Dickens's *Old Curiosity*

Shop. The hall's original Victorian interior provided the setting in *The Bostonians* (1886) for the final humiliation of Henry James's Women's Rights advocate, Olive Chancellor, and for the beginning of Verena Tarrant's tears as she fled from the public world of Boston reformers into the private arms of the southern gentleman Basil Ransom. In 1882 Oscar Wilde's live wit and uncharacteristic conservative attire kept the attention and goodwill of his Boston audience despite a standing-room-only crowd and the presence of sixty Harvard undergraduates wildly dressed as Wilde "look-alikes" (Lewis and Smith 335). Here also, writers Booker T. Washington and William James helped in 1897 to dedicate Saint-

Interior of the Boston Music Hall (1852). Wood engraving by C. W. Wright published in *Gleason's Pictorial*, December 18, 1852, facing p. 384. *(Courtesy of the Boston Athenæum.)* Basil Ransom "had never been in the Music Hall before, and its lofty vaults and rows of over-hanging balconies made it to his imagination immense and impressive. . . . He had a throb of uneasiness at his private purpose of balking it of its entertainment, its victim—a glimpse of the ferocity that lurks in a disappointed mob."
—Henry James, *The Bostonians* (1886).

Gaudens's great monument, the *Robert Gould Shaw and the 54th Regiment Memorial* (Site 21).

We'll look next at the right-hand corner of Hamilton Place and Tremont St.

3. 124 Tremont St.

This corner, opposite Park Street Church, is the site of the second or "new corner" location of Ticknor and Fields's well-known bookstore and publishing firm. Here Longfellow, Lowell, Holmes, Whittier, and Emerson[1] were frequent visitors to the "Author's Parlor," and here William Dean Howells, editor (1871–81) of the *Atlantic Monthly*, had his first meeting, as described in *My Mark Twain* (1910), with Samuel Clemens (1835–1910): "Clemens . . . was wearing a sealskin coat, with the fur out, in the satisfaction of a caprice, or the love of strong effect which he was to indulge through life. I do not know what droll comment was on Fields's mind with respect to this garment, but probably he felt that here was an original who was not to be brought to any Bostonian book in the judgment of his vivid qualities" (4).

Twain had reason to observe that in Boston every man saw himself a critic (Brooks, *New England* 8). His "humorous" celebratory speech at John Greenleaf Whittier's seventieth birthday supper (1877), amid illustrious contributors to the *Atlantic Monthly,* was received as irreverent and confirmed the idea that even as gifted a writer as Mark Twain could be made uncomfortable by judgmental Boston. Howells recalled Twain's jesting with "joyous self-reliance" as he described a Western miner who had been swindled by three "tramps" named Emerson, Holmes, and Longfellow: the first was "a seedy little bit of a chap," the second "fat as a balloon," and the last "built like a prize fighter" (Twain,

quoted by Kaplan 210). Regrettably, Twain's Western humor misfired in the midst of his *Atlantic* audience. He had underestimated the cohesive loyalty and adulation that existed among Boston's fraternity of literary friends. With the exception of one uncontrollable giggler (Howells), the silence was deafening (Howells, *My Mark Twain* 59).

Walk up Tremont St. and descend the steps to the old Granary Burying Ground, on which Louisa May Alcott once stood to watch the horrendous Boston Fire of 1872 (Delamar 107) (see Great Fire T4).

4. Granary Burying Ground {See flat map of gravesites, to the left, along path}

Upon reaching this oasis, we may feel, as Nan Prince did in Sarah Orne Jewett's *A Country Doctor* (1884), that "the quiet Granary Burying Ground" resembles "a bit of country which the noisy city ha[s] caught and imprisoned" (151). Actually, in 1877, when graveyard locations had looked promising as the possible sites for a new courthouse or a city hall extension (Holleran 127), the Boston Board of Health suggested that they were possible health hazards. The legend that here lay Mother Goose (Elizabeth Foster Vergoose), and the fact that the old Granary Burying Ground was the resting place of Samuel Sewall (1652–1730), whose diary writing nourished a Boston tradition, mattered little to those tempted by the open space. And although Longfellow's literary "resurrection" of Paul Revere (buried here) rang in the Victorian ear as "Paul Revere's Ride" (1860), it was inconsequential that he and Hawthorne, inspired by the city's old burial grounds, had peopled their works with colonial heroes (see Copp's Hill T3). Fortunately, the respected physician and poet Dr. Oliver Wendell Holmes (1809–94) refuted the health hazard theory and described the land along Tremont St. as "'a positively beneficial influence . . . an open breathing-space in a crowded part of the city'" (Holmes, quoted by Holleran 127).

We welcome the "bit of country" Holmes helped to preserve. If it were not for authors such as Holmes and later Amy Lowell (1874–1925), the old Granary Burying Ground might have been "entombed" by skyscrapers. Today the windows of the Boston Athenæum (Site 25) are its quiet background setting.

We look next across Tremont St. down Bosworth St.

According to Holmes, part of the "charm" of Boston's past was lost forever on the far left-hand corner of Bosworth St., the site of his former home (1841–59, non-extant). In *The Autocrat of the Breakfast-Table* (1872) Holmes, in the persona of the Professor, describes to the schoolmistress the consequence of the loss of his former home to invading commercialism. "My friend, the Professor, lived in that house at the left-hand next the farther corner, for years and years. He died out of it, the other day.—Died?—Said the Schoolmistress.—Certainly,—said I.—We die out of houses just as we die out of our bodies. A commercial smash kills a hundred men's homes for them, as a railroad smash kills their mortal frames and drives out the immortal tenants" (241).

The pressure of Boston's expanding and powerful commercial interests would persist in haunting Holmes, as we shall see.

Walking along Tremont St., we stay on the same side as the Granary Burying Ground for the best view of Tremont Temple across the street.

5. Tremont Temple (1896), 88 Tremont St., by Clarence H. Blackall; the fourth Tremont Temple on this site; its auditorium, seating three thousand, was described in 1901 as the handsomest in the city {Baptist; www.kingdomrise-kingdomfall.org/tremonttemple; (617)-523-7320}

The first integrated church in the United States, Tremont Temple reminds us that the speeches of many Victorian orators became a part of our literary heritage. Within Tremont Temple, Abraham Lincoln addressed a Free Soil Rally in 1848, the fiery abolitionist Wendell Phillips (1811–84) orated (see Phillips T7), and the self-emancipated writer Frederick Douglass, author of *My Bondage and My Freedom* (1855), spoke. Thomas O'Connor points out, "The printed page alone could not confine the vigorous energies of the Boston writers. . . . They missed few opportunities to take to the lecture platform" (*Hub* 102). In fact, the usually restrained Ralph Waldo Emerson tried to use the Tremont Temple's pulpit in an attempt to praise John Brown (Site 12) as a saint. Here also Charles Dickens (1812–70) presented selected readings from *Pickwick Papers* (1836–37), *A Christmas Carol* (1843), and *David Copperfield* (1849–50), on each occasion drawing great crowds.

Upon reaching the School St. corner, look across Tremont to today's Parker House, once the "palace-inn" of Oliver Wendell Holmes's poem "The Saturday Club."

6. The Parker House (est. 1855); rebuilt (1927) by Desmond and Lord {Saturday Club memorabilia in the lobby}

In *Literary Friends and Acquaintance* (1900), William Dean Howells (1837–1920) recalled what to him became a "visionary" dinner in the Parker House when James Russell Lowell, Oliver Wendell Holmes, and James T. Fields welcomed the young midwesterner to Boston. "I would gladly have glimmered before those great lights in the talk that followed, if I could have thought

of anything brilliant to say" (39), recalled Howells, who eventually was to assume Fields's job as editor of the *Atlantic Monthly* (1857), a powerful influence on American literary taste. The liberal, non-Harvard Howells managed before leaving for New York to describe his sense of awe regarding Boston and also his doubts in a series of novels about its pretensions.

The Parker House was the first meeting place of the Saturday Club. This prestigious group of literary intellectuals, among them Emerson, Holmes, Lowell, Longfellow, Whittier, Henry James, Sr., Prescott, Dana, Hawthorne, and Fields, met on the last Saturday of the month for conversation, fellowship, and a generous multicourse dinner. In an area that prided itself on freedom of thought there were individuals, of course, who questioned the assumptions of even such august groups. Henry David Thoreau (1817–62) was one. In corresponding to a friend, he wrote:

> As for the Parker House, I went there once, when the club was away, but I found it hard to see through the cigar smoke, and men were deposited about in chairs over the marble floor, as thick as legs of bacon in a smoke house. It was all smoke.... The only room in Boston I visit with alacrity is the Gentlemen's [waiting] room at the Fitchburg Depot, where I wait for the cars [trains], sometimes for two hours, in order to get out of town. It is a paradise to the Parker House, for no smoking is allowed ... and I am pretty sure to find someone there whose face is set the same way as my own (401–2).

As we leave the Parker House, we remember that before its series of expansive renovations, Dickens stayed on the third floor [2] on his second visit to Boston. In fact, "the

great mirror [mezzanine-level hall] before which Dickens used to rehearse his talks— may still be seen" (Harris 118). We might also remember that Victorian-born Willa Cather (1876–1947) lived here for almost a year gathering material on Christian Science for *McClure's Magazine.*

We head next across Tremont and School Sts. and past the front of King's Chapel, a National Historic Landmark. {See entrance for scheduled open hours.} Here Louisa May Alcott's "Marmee," Abigail May, was married to Bronson Alcott in 1830.

7. King's Chapel Burying Ground
{See flat map of gravesites inside the gate to the left}

The austere facade of King's Chapel (1749– 54) reminds us that Nathaniel Hawthorne's colonial minister, Arthur Dimmesdale, lived on this very spot with the evil Chillingworth in *The Scarlet Letter* (1850), and that in the adjacent 1630 burial ground lie the remains of Hester Prynne. Let's enter the burial ground where little Pearl in "perverse merriment ... skipped irreverently from one grave to another" and danced on "a broad, flat, armorial tombstone" (Hawthorne, *Scarlet Letter* 92).

We take the path toward King's Chapel to the right, turning left along the chapel's wall until we come to the sixth gravestone from the corner.

This is the grave of Elizabeth Pain (d. 1704). By long tradition it is the very grave that inspired Hawthorne's conclusion to *The Scarlet Letter:* "On this simple slab of slate—as the curious investigator may still discern ... there appeared the semblance of an engraved escutcheon" (178). The heraldic shield, or escutcheon, is certainly carved in the slate, but are you one of the viewers who immediately perceive the letter "A"? Upon viewing the tombstone, some Hawthorne enthusiasts will see a large A at first glance, but others may not see any letter at all!

To find the A, look on the upper left-hand side of the gravestone. The large raised capital A shape can be made out within the pattern of the heraldic shield. (The center of the shield forms the capital A's straight left side, and the A's diagonal right side moves from the center of the shield, the tip of the A, down through the center of the shield's pattern to the right-hand side.) Once the A is seen, it is difficult to look at the shield without seeing it. A Hawthornesque symbol, to be sure, it combines his love of ambiguity with optical illusion.

We return to the corner[3] *of Tremont and School Sts. On School St., just below the lower end of King's Chapel, we pass the site of the third building that was part of the Victorian evolution of Boston Latin, the first public school in the United States (see Boston Latin T2). Among the distinguished Victorian literati who were pupils were Emerson and the young Edward Everett Hale (1822–1909), who entered Harvard at age thirteen and became one of Longfellow's students (Mead, "Foreword," viii) and in time a leading Unitarian minister and author of* Man without a Country *(1869) (see Hale's South Congregational Church T2).*

Within the courtyard in front of Boston's Old City Hall,[4] *a National Historic Landmark (see p. xxxi), is a statue of Benjamin Franklin.*

8. Benjamin Franklin (1856), by Richard S. Greenough, front left of Old City Hall (1861–65), by Bryant and Gilman

Benjamin Franklin, whose writing career began nearby while working for his brother James's *New-England Courant*, was the subject of Boston's first portrait statue (1856) (see Franklin; Old City Hall T4). In Edward Everett Hale's best-known short story, "My Double and How He Undid Me" (1869), the narrator recalls: "Richard Greenough once told me, that, in studying for the statue of Franklin, he found that the left side of the great man's face was philosophic and reflective, and the right side funny and smiling. If you go and look at the bronze statue, you will find he has repeated this observation there for posterity" (174–75).

After an inquisitive look at Greenough's depiction of Franklin's face and Thomas Ball's statue of Josiah Quincy (1878), the mayor of Boston (1823–24) when Victoria was still princess, we continue down School St., anticipating Bela Pratt's impressive interpretation of the "Grand Old Man," Edward Everett Hale himself, a favorite presence in the Public Garden.

9. Old Corner Book Store (building ca. 1718), 135 Washington St., a National Historic Landmark

On the corner of School and Washington Sts. is the Old Corner Book Store, Ticknor and Fields's first publishing house (1845–65), whose list of writers included American and British literary stars, among them Hawthorne, Emerson, Whittier, Julia Ward Howe, Harriet Beecher Stowe, Longfellow, Margaret Fuller, Thoreau, Holmes, Thackeray, Tennyson, Robert (but not Elizabeth Barrett) Browning, Dickens, and Matthew Arnold. Poet and essayist Nathaniel Parker Willis (1806–67), who celebrated James T. Fields's domain as "Parnassus Corner," described the convivial publisher as "the hub in which every spoke of the radiating wheel of Boston intellect ha[d] a socket—the central news giver, listener, sympathizer, gossip and adviser" (quoted by Tryon 221). Victorian tourists whose footsteps we follow here include Horatio Alger, Edmund Gosse, Charles Dickens, and the British

physician who created Sherlock Holmes, Sir Arthur Conan Doyle.

10. Washington St.

Numerous nineteenth-century newspapers and publishers did business on Washington St. In fact, Edgar Allan Poe found a publisher here for his first book, the anonymous *Tamerlane and other Poems by a Bostonian* (1827). However, it is Washington St.'s seemingly countless stores that astounded Julian West after his long dream about living in the year 2000 in Edward Bellamy's *Looking Backward: 2000–1887* (1888): "Stores! Stores! Stores! Miles of stores! Ten thousand stores to distribute the goods needed by this one city, which in my dream had been supplied with all things from a single warehouse, as they were ordered through one great store in every quarter, where the buyer, without waste of time or labor, found under one roof the world's assortment in whatever line he desired" (257).

Bellamy (1850–98) wrote that he intended his book "in all seriousness, as a forecast . . . of the next stage in the industrial and social development of humanity" (273). Certainly his vision of shopping in the year 2000 sounds remarkably like the "one great store" available for universal shopping on the Internet's world-wide web.

James T. Fields *(From Mary Caroline Crawford,* Romantic Days in Old Boston, *Little, Brown, 1910, facing p. 375.)* "He had the publishing instinct developed almost to genius. He had an intuitive grasp of what the public wanted or should want, the latter knowledge, perhaps being the more important. He was an educator of public taste." —Lilian Whiting, *Boston Days* (1902).

The area's bookstores are tempting, but we cross Washington St., and turn right. We are heading toward the steeple of the Old South Meeting House, in whose chamber was situated the Reverend Thomas Prince's "New England Library" (looted by the British; Governor Bradford's History of New Plimouth, *discovered in England, was recovered). The remainder of Prince's collection was moved, in 1866, to the Boston Public Library (Swift 22).*

11. Old South Meeting House[5] (1729), 308 Washington St. {Check entrance for visiting hours; www.oldsouthmeetinghouse.org; (617)-482-6439}

Rescued by extraordinary means from the Great Fire of 1872, this National Historic Landmark was a church involved in political issues from its beginning. Two centuries of Bostonians used this place to articulate new ideas. At Old South Meeting House visitors might hear echoes of Julia Ward Howe, Wendell Phillips, James Russell Lowell, Ralph Waldo Emerson, and Louisa May Alcott, who worked in the 1870s to preserve once more the historic building where radicalism and religion often came together.

Passing Old South, we continue along Washington St. and turn right up Bromfield St.

12. 20 Bromfield St.

Dr. Samuel Gridley Howe's Bromfield St. office "was a center for antislavery fund raising" (Harris 166). An organizer of the Vigilance Committee to protect fugitive slaves, Dr. Howe had told his wife that she would meet the man who "wished to be the savior for the negro race" (J. W. Howe 254). Julia Ward Howe (1819–1910) met John Brown twice—the second time here. She described Brown as "a Puritan of Puritans, forceful, concentrated, and self-contained"

Bromfield House (ca. 1860).
(Courtesy of the Boston Athenæum.)
This "picturesque hostelry," with an interior courtyard for horse-drawn vehicles and a popular dining room, served good New England food, claiming to shun French or "ambiguous" entrées. Besides baked beans and brown bread, menu items included "boiled salt fish with pork scraps, hashed calf's head and dropped eggs, corned beef and cabbage, cottage pudding and cranberry pie!" —Mrs. Kate Gannett Wells, quoted in Mary Caroline Crawford, *Romantic Days in Old Boston* (1910).

(254). Later her "Battle Hymn of the Republic" (1861) was set to the tune of the popular Civil War army song "John Brown's Body." Less well know is her poem "The First Martyr," a ballad recalling the reaction of her five-year-old daughter, Maud, to learning about Brown's plight in prison (see Bromfield St. T4; Vigilance Committee T7).

13. Bromfield House (nonextant), the site of the stagecoach entry, remains to the right of 36 Bromfield St.

This is the site of Bromfield House, the inn to which Dr. Oliver Wendell Holmes came at the request of Sophia Hawthorne in order to evaluate her ailing husband, who had "absolutely refused to see a physician officially" (S. Hawthorne, quoted in J. Fields 121). Holmes, playing his part, accompanied Hawthorne on a casual walk, adeptly assessed his friend's condition, and offered practical suggestions. Annie Fields's diary entry on May 11, 1864, reads, "[Holmes] thinks the shark's tooth is upon him [Hawthorne], but would not have this known" (A. Fields, quoted by M. A. Howe 27). It is from this site that Hawthorne (1804–79) and former President Franklin Pierce, his friend since college days, set out toward New Hampshire (Miller 517) for Hawthorne's last train journey.

Turn left at Tremont St. and return to the Common. We may wish to rest on the Common, where Ralph Waldo Emerson once tended his mother's cow. Perhaps a bench nearby was the very one where once sat Julian West, the dazed hero of Edward Bellamy's utopian novel, who found "an interest merely in watching the throngs that passed" (263).

14. The Common, a National Historic Landmark

It was on the Common, at the edge of Frog Pond (see map, pp. 84–85), that little Louisa May Alcott slipped and fell. She long remembered the strong arms and face of a young African American who pulled her up from the suffocating water. Alcott forever regretted not being able to thank him properly and felt the experience influenced her strong views on abolition (Delamar 7–8).

Optional Digression to West St.: *It is possible, either before or after a refreshing break on the Common, to make an optional roundabout jaunt to West St. Proceed along the Common's Tremont St. Mall, parallel to Tremont St., to the Visitor Information Booth (contains rest rooms). At this point West St. is across Tremont St.*

15. 15 West St.; formerly 13 {Plaque}

This location deserves tribute as a literary shrine. Here, from 1840 to 1854, Elizabeth Palmer Peabody (1804–94) lived with her parents, Dr. and Mrs. Nathaniel Peabody, and her two sisters, Mary and Sophia. In a modest back parlor of her home, Elizabeth's sister Sophia was married to Nathaniel Hawthorne in 1842. It had been Elizabeth Peabody who had interested Sophia in Hawthorne by telling her he was "as handsome as Lord Byron" (Elizabeth Peabody, quoted in Hoyt 177) (see West St., Elizabeth, Mary, Sophia T8). Elizabeth not only managed her "Foreign Bookstore" here but also published *The Dial* (1840–44) and *Aesthetic Papers,* in which the first version of Thoreau's revolutionary essay "Civil Disobedience" appeared in 1849.

Here also Margaret Fuller and Emerson, as editors of *The Dial,* helped the world learn about American Transcendentalism, succinctly defined as "a philosophy that held that the innate qualities of individuals transcended their actual experiences, and that the soul had the inherent power to

grasp the truth" (O'Connor, *Hub* 100).

Margaret Fuller (1810–50), the model, it is thought, for Zenobia in Hawthorne's *The Blithedale Romance* (1852), conducted her famous "Conversations" (1839–44) with bright women of Boston, among them "the wives of Emerson, Theodore Parker, and George Bancroft, Channing's [eldest] daughter [Mary], Lydia Maria Child, and Maria White who became [James Russell] Lowell's wife" (Bacon, *Literary Pilgrimages* 301). It was Emerson who recalled that "in discourse, [Fuller] was quick, conscious of power, in perfect tune with her company" (337). Her seminars were to enrich *Woman in the Nineteenth Century* (1845), her published work on the rights of women (see p. 147; Fuller T8).

9–11 West St. The Brattle Book Shop has been in business since 1825. Recalling the role that bookstores, both new and antiquarian, played in what Edwin Bacon called Boston's "literary workshop" (*Book of Boston* 125), walkers interested in antiquarian books and bargains in second-hand books will find here irresistible attractions and distractions.

Return to the Common,[6] *whose dignified appearance was of particular interest to Robert Grant's "simon-pure" Bostonian, Mr. Harrison Chippendale, who "kept an eye on the Common—to preserve its integrity"— but "took a feverishly passive part in politics" (Grant 77).*

PART II. From the Common over Beacon Hill to the Charles Street Meeting House

During our break on the Common, we recall that six-year-old Louisa May Alcott had energy to spare when she ran with her stick and hoop, without once stopping, around its circumference (Meigs 51). Now for the most delightful lap of our tour, we head toward the State House and Beacon Hill's "literary precinct," as William Dean Howells described it.

"The Long Path" (the diagonal path to our far left as we face the State House, which crosses the Common from Boylston St. and ascends to the Joy St. corner of Beacon St.) suggested to Oliver Wendell Holmes, in *The Autocrat of the Breakfast-Table* (1858), the long path two individuals choose to walk together in marriage. Holmes, who defined himself as Brahmin, and is known for the phrase "Boston State House is the hub of the solar system" (125), wrote to instruct about Boston as well as to celebrate his own heritage. Although some of his ideas are now deemed parochial (for example, his view that descendants of the signers of the Declaration of Independence were genetically superior), he deserves high praise for his inspiration to others as a physician, his psychological perception, and his work on *The Contagiousness of Puerperal Fever* (1843) as he strove to improve conditions for women in childbirth.

For traffic-free viewing of the sites along Park St., ascend the Park St. Mall on the Common.

16. 4 Park St.; now the location of the Paulist Fathers Center and the Holy Ghost Chapel (1956).

After 1880, display windows filled with the latest publications of the "Book Room," at 4 Park St., marked the habitat of Houghton, Mifflin and Company, by then the sole authorized publisher of Harriet Beecher Stowe, Emerson, Hawthorne, Holmes, Longfellow, Lowell, Whittier, and Thoreau. Houghton Mifflin, "having the appearance more of a finely equipped library than a place of business" (Bacon, *King's Dictionary*

64), occupied three floors and housed the editor of the *Atlantic Monthly,* William Dean Howells, in a "tiny sanctum" on the second floor. A subsequent editor (1881–90) and wit, Thomas Bailey Aldrich, in the company of his pipe and his Irish setter, "Trip," occupied a back room on the third floor, which overlooked the Granary Burying Ground, "where as he liked to say were those who would never submit any manuscript" (Greenslet 142).

The site of the formative plans of the founding of the Boston Browning Society (est. 1885) was at 4 Park St. in the drawing room of Mr. and Mrs. Samuel E. Sewall. Among the society's early members were Louisa May Alcott, James Freeman Clarke, Edward Everett Hale, William Wetmore Story, Thomas Wentworth Higginson, and Lilian Whiting. Today, as the oldest continuing Browning Society[7] in existence, it is a genial group that welcomes those interested in learning about the Victorian world of Robert and Elizabeth Barrett Browning and features lectures about their poetry, friends, travels, letters, and memorabilia.

17. 5 Park St.; now the Paulist Fathers Center and the Holy Ghost Chapel (1956)

At No. 5 Julia Ward Howe, and later Lucy Stone, edited *The Woman's Journal.* Both women fit F. Marion Crawford's apt description, in *The American Politician* (1884), of the "school of Boston women, who 'see to things' themselves in the intervals of literature, gossip, and transcendental philosophy" (131). Editor William Dean Howells recalled that Howe made one of the finest speeches he had ever heard. "It gave me for the first time a notion of what women might do in that sort if they entered public life" (*Literary Friends* 132) (see Howe; Stone T8).

Farther up the hill is

18. The Union Club, 7–8 Park St. (1801)

The Union Club was formed in 1863 by a group of former Somerset Club (Site 27) members who were Union sympathizers during the Civil War. A founding member, Levi Thaxter, husband of poet Celia Thaxter (1835–94), was an elocution teacher. His public readings of Robert Browning's poetry helped spread the poet's popularity in the United States (Brooks, *New England* 53). It was to the Union Club's compatible setting that the Saturday Club moved. Oliver Wendell Holmes, a member of both the Union and Saturday Clubs, was fond of describing his early years with Boston's literati: "If you have seen a cat picking her footsteps in wet weather, you have seen the picture of Emerson's exquisite intelligence, feeling for its phrase or epithet" (Holmes, quoted in Morse 188–189). In his poem "The Saturday Club," Holmes described the presence of Nathaniel Hawthorne.

> The Essex wizard's shadowed self is
>   there,—
> The great ROMANCER hid beneath his veil
> Like the stern preacher of his somber tale;
> Virile in strength, yet bashful as a girl,
> Prouder than Hester, sensitive as Pearl.
>   (Holmes, *Poetical Works* 359)

The white-pillared doorway at 9 Park St. marks the entrance to George Ticknor's home. Let's find a bench, get our bearings, and preview the attractions of Sites 19, 20, 21, and 22 before we reach the Beacon St. sidewalk (above), which abuts heavy traffic that is not "sightseer-sensitive."

19. Amory-Ticknor House (1804), 9 Park St., by Charles Bulfinch

We pay tribute to George Ticknor (1791–1871), whose large personal library became the core of Boston's great Public Library (known affectionately to Bostonians as the BPL). Nathaniel Hawthorne, when describing Ticknor's "stately" library, mentioned that a portrait of Sir Walter Scott hung over the fireplace (*Passages* 472). Ticknor, professor of modern languages at Harvard, whose pupils included Thoreau and James Russell Lowell (S. Wilson 25), wrote the three-volume *History of Spanish Literature* (1849; final revision 1872). He was typical of the well-traveled and -educated Boston Brahmin willing to share on his own terms his advantages with average citizens.

At his elegant corner home Ticknor entertained the young Lydia Maria Child (1802–80), author of *Hobomok, A Tale of*

Nathaniel Hawthorne, engraving. *(From W. D. Howells,* Literary Friends and Acquaintance, *New York: Harper and Brothers, 1900, facing p. 56.)* Hawthorne "liked on Sundays to mouse about among . . . [my] books and there are few volumes . . . which he had not handled or read. . . . One summer morning I found him as early as four o'clock reading a favorite poem, on Solitude."
—J. T. Fields, *Yesterdays with Authors* (1871).

George Ticknor's Second-Floor Library at
9 Park St., engraving. *(From Justin Winsor, ed.,*
The Memorial History of Boston, *vol. III,*
Boston: James R. Osgood and Company, 1881, p.
662.) Visible over the fireplace is Leslie's portrait
of Sir Walter Scott, painted expressly for
Ticknor. The bookcases along the left wall
contained "German, French, and English
literature." History books were closest to the
fireplace, and on its right were his biography
and theology volumes. The cupboards below
were full of books, and his Spanish books filled
"the whole end of the room opposite the
fireplace"; his Greek, Latin, Italian, and other
books were in other parts of the house.
—Anna Eliot Ticknor, quoted in Justin Winsor,
ed., *Memorial History of Boston* (1883).

Early Times (1824), our first historical novel
that daringly recorded a brief, happy marriage between a white woman and a Native
American. Deeply committed to abolition
as well as to women's rights, Child found
herself taken off Ticknor's guest list when
she published *An Appeal in Favor of That
Class of Americans Called Africans* (1833).
Undaunted, she went on to publish a series
of books, among them *History of the Condition of Women* (1835) and *Appeal for Indians*
(1868). It was Lydia Maria Child who edited
Harriet Ann Jacobs's *Incidents in the Life of
a Slave Girl: Written by Herself* (1861) and
also negotiated a publishing contract for

her. Jacobs (1813–97), after her escape in
1842, had come to reside in Boston (O'Connell 151) (see Child T7, T8).

Anna Eliot Ticknor played a little-known
but inspiring role in the Amory-Ticknor
house. Two years after her father's death,
she devoted herself to directing women's
education by founding, at the Ticknor mansion, the Society to Encourage Studies at
Home (1873–97), an endeavor committed to
encouraging women over sixteen, throughout the United States and beyond, "to
develop intellectual habits while pursuing
their ordinary occupations" (Smith 83).
Members not fortunate to live near libraries,
museums, or colleges were sent (Lawrence
92) not only personal correspondence but
also books, engravings, photographs, and

Lydia Maria Child. *(From Elizabeth Stuart
Phelps,* Chapters from a Life, *Boston: Houghton,
Mifflin, 1896, facing p. 184.)*
"In our earliest recollections she came before us
less as author or philanthropist than as some
kindly and omnipresent aunt . . . some one
gifted with all lore, and furnished with
unfathomable resources."
—T. W. Higginson, *Contemporaries* (1899).

maps and were encouraged "to devote some part of every day to thorough and systematic reading" (Sweetser 161).

With a lending library of only 1,308 volumes gathered from her own bookshelves and those of her teacher-managers—Fanny Appleton (Site 27); Elizabeth Cary Agassiz (see E. C. Agassiz T5); Anna Eliot Ticknor, her mother, hostess of the Ticknors' well-known literary salon; Katherine Peabody Loring (Site 25); and Alice James (Site 70) (Strouse 175)—Ticknor and her instructors, numbering 183, held annual meetings in her father's library, where their students had an opportunity to meet the teachers with whom they had been corresponding about English, German, and French literature (also science, art, and history). Alice James, a professor of history in the society, wrote a revealing comment about the value of the endeavor: "We who have had all our lives more books than we know what to do with can't conceive of the feelings that people have for them who have been shut out from them always. They look upon them as something sacred. . . . I have to write between thirty and forty letters every month. . . . It is what I care most about right now" (A. James, quoted in Strouse 176).

The arduous work of one-to-one teaching by handwritten correspondence had rewards; two-thirds of the society's at-home students had completed its English Literature course by 1883 (see also Women's education, Girls High School T8, Radcliffe T12). Editor William Dean Howells featured Anna Eliot Ticknor's correspondence school in an *Atlantic* article. Her book collection, invaluable to her at-home students, was given to the Boston Public Library upon her death (Whiting 350).

As Park St. Mall ends, we see to our left Beacon St. Mall (parallel to Beacon St. above).

20. Beacon St. Mall

Perhaps it is no accident that the loftiest part of the Common reflects the democratic tensions of those members of Boston society who wanted to stand for quality. Here it was that the boy Henry Adams and the "Beacon St. Cowards" faced the intrepid Conky Daniels and his gang in snowball fights, fleeing up over the hill as they learned that blackguardism "had the charm of force and freedom and superiority to culture and decency." Adams went on to wonder whether during the Civil War, "when these same boys were fighting and falling on all the battlefields of Virginia . . . whether their education on Boston Common had taught Savage and Marvin how to die" (*Education* 41–42).

On the tree-lined Beacon St. Mall, one of the liveliest literary debates that ever took place in Boston occurred (1860). Here Walt Whitman (1819–92) argued with Ralph Waldo Emerson (1803–82) about the importance of keeping the overtly sexual references in "The Children of Adam" section of *Leaves of Grass*:

> Up and down this breadth by Beacon Street, between these same old elms, I walked . . . with Emerson, then in his prime, keen, physically and morally magnetic, arm'd at every point. . . . During those two hours he was the talker and I the listener. It was an argument-statement, reconnoitering, review, attack, and pressing home . . . of all that could be said against that part (and the main part) in the construction of my poems, *Children of Adam*. More precious than gold to me, that dissertation. . . . Then I felt down in my soul the clear and unmistakable conviction to disobey all, and pursue my own way (Whitman, *Specimen Days* 302–3).

Like our other great nineteenth-century poetic individualist, Emily Dickinson, Walt Whitman took inspiration from Boston but followed his own instincts (see Whitman; Emerson T3).

The Mall was also the remarkable setting for a "poet's promise" that led to three well-deserved Pulitzer Prizes. Here the African American poet, critic, and literary editor of the *Boston Transcript* (1908–29), the anthologist William Stanley Braithwaite[8] (Site 1), urged and successfully convinced the modest Victorian-born Edwin Arlington Robinson[9] (1869–1935) that it was "time for a collected edition" of his works: "'Will you make me a promise . . . ask your publisher to bring out a collected edition of your poems?' 'Who'd want a collected edition of my poems?' [Robinson] responded. 'Will you do it?' I insisted" (Braithwaite, quoted in Butcher 214).

Within six months Robinson had written to Braithwaite: "Since you were crazy enough to suggest that I should have a collected edition of my verse, I think you ought to be the first to know . . . Macmillan agreed." Therewith, Robinson's "fame skyrocketed," much to the satisfaction of Braithwaite, who astutely championed Robinson as the "greatest poet" in the United States (Braithwaite, quoted in Butcher 215).

Before we climb the steps to look at the stirring Beacon St. side of Saint-Gaudens's great Civil War monument, let's read the names of the African Americans of the 54th Regiment who fought with Robert Gould Shaw at Fort Wagner inscribed on this side of the monument (1982). Their sacrifice lives as well in the movie Glory *(1991).*

21. ***Robert Gould Shaw and the 54th Regiment Memorial*** (1884–97) by Augustus Saint-Gaudens; setting for the monument by Charles F. McKim of the architectural firm McKim, Mead and White (see p. 133).

"Look at that monument and read the story,"[10] directed William James in his Music Hall dedication speech (quoted in Boston City Council, *Exercises* 40). For James "the story" of the 54th was doubly poignant, because Adjutant Garth Wilkinson "Wilky" James, William and Henry James's younger brother, had joined Colonel Shaw's 54th Regiment and had suffered grievous wounds during the 54th's charge at Fort Wagner in 1863 (Edel 185). Underneath the sculpture the words of James Russell Lowell (1819–91), great-granduncle of Robert Lowell (1917–77), tell of the admiration that contemporaries Emerson and Parkman felt for Robert Gould Shaw as the heroic ideal of Yankee Boston.

Later writers have also responded to the monument's symbolic power. The African American poet Paul Laurence Dunbar (1872–1906), John Berryman (1914–72), and Robert Lowell, whose "For the Union Dead" (1960) makes us think about the contrast between American political reality and the ideal of equality that the men in the sculpture represent, all derived inspiration from Shaw and the 54th Regiment.

Still securely situated on the Beacon St. Mall, we are able to enjoy the magnificent gilded dome and facade of the State House looming above us.

22. **The State House** (1795–98), by Charles Bulfinch (dome first gilded 1874). Brigham Extension in rear (1889–94), by Charles E. Brigham; East and West Wings (1914–17), by William Chapman, Robert Andrew, and R. Clipston Sturgis {The State House entrance is now behind the equestrian statue (1903) of Major-General Joseph Hooker (1814–79) by Daniel Chester French, and his horse

by Edward C. Potter. Regularly scheduled weekday tours; www.state.ma.us/sec /trs/trsidx.htm; (617)-727-3676}

The impressive facade of the State House, a National Historic Landmark, reminds us that democratic idealism was revived among writers when Edna St. Vincent Millay (1892–1950), Dorothy Parker (1893–1967), John Dos Passos (1896–1970), and Upton Sinclair (1878–1968), each a child of the Victorian age, were in the midst of the many picketing here to protest Sacco and Vanzetti's execution (1927), seen as a hysterical reaction and betrayal of the dream of equality. The untutored letters[11] of these two Italian-born alleged anarchists remain part of our literary heritage as well. "'Never in our full life can we hope to do such work for tolerance, for justice, for man's understanding of man as now we do by accident'" (Vanzetti/Dos Passos "Newsreel LXVI" in *The Big Money*). Millay also took up the distressing Sacco and Vanzetti story in "Justice Denied in Massachusetts" (1928), as did Upton Sinclair in his two-volume novel *Boston* (1928). Ironically, Sinclair's work was banned in the very city whose name it bears.

As we take a closer look at the Bulfinch State House, we like to imagine Henry James above on the platform looking for "old more definite Boston," while admiring the "uplifted front of the State House . . . a thing of beauty, more delightful and harmonious even than I had remembered it" (*American Scene* 230). Here James (1843–1916) realized that his once "small homogeneous Boston" had drastically changed when all whom he observed coming up from the Common were "laboring wage earners" and "aliens" speaking Italian rather than English. To James these immigrants were a "measure of the distance by which the general movement was *away*, always and everywhere, from the old presump-

tions" (*American Scene* 231). Yet in the twentieth and twenty-first centuries, reaching back to the preachers of the seventeenth, many writers, both Yankee and the descendants of more recent immigrants, have persisted in finding roles as social critics and public consciences for the broader society.

To add another star to the galaxy of writers associated with the State House, we should mention that sixteen-year-old Emily Dickinson (1830–86), during her September 1846 visit to Boston, named the historic sites she had visited. Yes, she had "been upon the top of the State House" (Dickinson 8)! We find it exhilarating to imagine the young poet walking upon the State House dome and seeing the panoramic views of Victorian Boston from its lantern (see lantern and p. xlv; State House T8).

Let's rally now, mount the steps, and enjoy the sites we have just reviewed. We'll aim for the crosswalks of this busy intersection. At the traffic light, we first cross Park St. to arrive beside the Amory-Ticknor House. This was a pivotal corner in nineteenth-century Boston. Bostonians could actually see the harbor from this intersection. Today it is our best view, across Beacon St., to the statue of Mary Dyer (see Dyer T8) on the lawn in front of the State House wing.

Major Molineux's House

The corner site of the State House wing evokes a recurring question in Hawthorne's "My Kinsman, Major Molineux" (1832): "I pray you to tell me whereabouts is the dwelling of my kinsman, Major Molineux?" ("My Kinsman" 4). The Molineux house (nonextant), formerly on the site of the State House wing, was actually the residence of the patriot (not the royalist as in the story) William Molineux (Lawrence 134). However, in spite of his poetic license,

Hawthorne's story about the hostility of a Revolutionary crowd's tarring and feathering a loyalist in the streets of Boston continues to haunt us in the twenty-first century.

We'll use the crosswalk to reach the corner of Bowdoin and Beacon Sts. and continue a short block along Bowdoin St. to the first corner on the right for a peek down the canyon of Ashburton Place.

23. Ashburton Place

In 1904 Henry James returned to Ashburton Place, an "eminently respectable byway" (*American Scene* 228), to revisit the exterior of No. 13, his former home (1865–66). But he was jolted when he returned four weeks later to savor a second look—the house had been leveled. "If I had often seen how fast history could be made I had doubtless never so felt that it could be unmade still faster" (229). To James his home had "old secrets to keep and old stories to witness

Ashburton Place (ca. 1890s), looking toward Bowdoin St. When James returned, the homes still exemplified redbrick Boston. *(From M. F. Sweetser,* King's How to See Boston: A Trustworthy Guidebook, *Knights Templars ed., Boston: Moses King, 1895, p. 190.)*
"Both houses had been leveled and the space to the corner cleared. . . . The act of obliteration had been breathlessly swift. . . . It was as if the bottom had fallen out of one's own biography, and one plunged backward into space without meeting anything."
—Henry James, *The American Scene* (1907).

for" (229). Those of us who have experienced the discontinuity caused by the loss of a building intimately associated with our own youth will sympathize with James's response: "It was as if the bottom had fallen out of one's own biography, and one plunged backward into space without meeting anything" (229), an experience certain to intensify James's impression that "the moral material social solidities" (234) of nineteenth-century Boston had evaporated. To James commercial interests alone seemed to shape the city.

Having witnessed with James the effect of the commercial destruction of sites on Ashburton Place, we return now to Beacon St. to see the condition of the historic "solidity" at the crest of Beacon Hill. Turn left and walk a quarter of a block. On our left is the elegantly ornamented

24. Hotel Bellevue (1899), 21 Beacon St.; replaced the former Bellevue Hotel at 17 Beacon St.

This site of the former Bellevue Hotel[12] was a frequent home over a period of sixteen years (1868–84) for Louisa May Alcott, whose life as an author often illustrated a woman's need to get away from domesticity even as she wrote about it. Alcott (1832–88), who had worked as a housemaid, seamstress, and teacher, sympathized with Hannah, in *Little Women,* when she declared, "Housekeeping ain't no joke" (114). Having recently completed the first part of *Little Women* (1868), Alcott stayed at the Bellevue while she finished *Little Women, or Meg, Jo, Beth, and Amy, Part Second* (1869). Believing that marriage wasn't "the only end and aim of a woman's life," her response to those readers who wondered whether Jo and Laurie would ever marry was, "I won't marry Jo to Laurie to please anyone" (quoted by Delamar 89).

The Boston Athenæum, across the street, in which young Louisa May Alcott "liked best of all" the statue of Beethoven (Myerson, Selected Letters 15), is admired most effectively from the "Bellevue" side. It is a view of the library that Alcott and her sister May saw often.

25. Boston Athenæum, 10½ Beacon St.

(1849), by Edward Clarke Cabot and George Minot Dexter; complete renovation, 1913–15, fourth and fifth floors added; major renovation, 1999–2002 {Tours by reservation—see tour days and hours beside the entrance; www.bostonathenaeum.org; (617)-227-0270, ext. 27}

The Boston Athenæum. Photograph (1889) of Beacon St. looking from Bowdoin St. to Somerset St. *(Courtesy of The Bostonian Society/Old State House: Henry P. Curtis Collection.)* The Boston Athenæum and neighboring buildings as James remembered their pleasing scale. It is unlikely that the arches of the facade, complemented by the entrances to the adjoining buildings, would have been lost on James's sophisticated eye. High in the old Bellevue Hotel, within the bowfront town houses opposite, had been Alcott's retreat. However, it was today's Hotel Bellevue (1899), that James found facing the Athenæum in 1904.

The Boston Athenæum, a National Historic Landmark, is an oasis of Boston culture. Ralph Waldo Emerson, the son of a founder, loved to visit the library, as did Oliver Wendell Holmes. Hawthorne, who chose the Boston Athenæum as the deadly quiet setting for his tale "The Ghost of Dr. Harris," delighted in spending "delicious hours" exploring old advertisements in the library's newspaper files (J. Fields 62). In 1901 the proposed relocation of the Athenæum to a new site, which had been already purchased on the corner of Newbury and Arlington Sts., met the strong opposition of young Amy Lowell (1874–1925), her friend Katherine Peabody Loring (Site 19), and Richard Henry Dana, Jr. (Sites 71 and 76), all resolute Athenæum proprietors. The controversy was finally resolved by the library's renovation in situ (Slautterback 71ff).

Henry James, whose Olive Chancellor entwines a dense "web" of authority and dependence around Verena Tarrant as they plunge together into their studies within "innumerable big books from the Athenæum" (*Bostonians* 175), described the library as the "honored haunt of all the most civilized" (*American Scene* 232). However, upon his return to Boston in 1904, he hated the tall buildings, which he thought made the library seem less significant. Moreover, he found little compensation in the massive new Boston Public Library (1895).

We head back toward the State House side now, crossing

Beacon St. at the crosswalk once more in order to enjoy the ambiance of the front gate, steps, and ample lawns of the State House, and begin our descent of the Beacon St. slope. From now on we must be vigilant about our footing. Beacon Hill's notoriously uneven brick sidewalks will be a challenge.

If we happen to walk along this stretch— late on a Tuesday or Friday morning—our odds of a face-to-face encounter with a literary "manifestation" increases, for a Brahmin of the strictest habits, a "rigid gentleman in black," might possibly be seen leaving his home just below us. "His hat firm on his head, his scarf pinned, his gloves buttoned, and his umbrella tightly rolled," Mr. Nathaniel Alden, who "always turned left, for never, except to funerals, did Mr. Nathaniel Alden walk down Beacon Hill" (16).

George Santayana's careful description of Alden and the location of his residence, in The Last Puritan *(1935; set in 1870), gives us an opportunity to evoke a Victorian diversion, a "literary séance," as we approach the prestigious address that corresponds to Alden's residence, Boston's Parkman House[13] at 33 Beacon St. (1825).*

Beside it on the corner of Joy St. and also by Cornelius Coolidge, 34 Beacon St. (1825) was the longtime headquarters (after 1909) of Boston's Little, Brown, and Company (est. 1837), known for its role in the literary careers of James Russell Lowell, Francis Parkman, and Louisa May Alcott (after 1898). We'll take a small sideways jog now. Turn right and walk about two-thirds of a block up steep Joy St. to No. 3 (on the left).

26. 3 Joy St.

In this home (1863–66), and at "Greenpeace," their home near the Perkins Institution for the Blind in Dorchester, the abolitionist and suffragist Julia Ward Howe and her husband, Samuel Gridley Howe (1801–

76), entertained the fashionable nineteenth-century Hungarian patriot Louis Kossuth (Brooks, *New England* 125). Dr. Howe, who had been a freedom fighter for Greek independence, had few problems with those who were willing to fight for a country's liberty. John Greenleaf Whittier's poem "The Hero" was written expressly about Dr. Howe.

> Wherever rise the peoples,
> Wherever sinks a throne,
> The throbbing heart of Freedom finds
> An answer in his own. (192–93)

Just beyond No. 3, on the right-hand side, is Mt. Vernon Place. Here, close to the Common, lived Miss Lucretia Daintry, the quintessential Bostonian woman whom James described in "A New England Winter" as wearing "her bonnet as scientifically poised as the dome of the State house" (340).

We retrace our steps now and continue our Beacon St. descent.

27. The Appleton House (1818), 39 Beacon St., by Alexander Parris

No. 39 Beacon St., a National Historic Landmark, was the home of Waltham/Lowell textile magnate Nathan Appleton. Longfellow's marriage to the manufacturer's lovely daughter, Fanny Appleton (1817–61), took place here on July 13, 1843 (see F. Appleton; Longfellow T12). Within a week of Fanny's acceptance of the poet's proposal, on May 16, 1843, she wrote to her mother's sister, her aunt Martha Gold, the following:

> Dearest Aunt Matty,
>   Rejoice with me in my great, inexpressibly great joy! I am engaged to Henry Longfellow! This news will astonish you doubtless, as it is just beginning to many others, but it is true nevertheless

true—to me a true dream—brighter than all my fictitious ones . . . words are not needed; the fact that a nature so noble and gifted and gentle and true had been bestowed upon unworthy me is eloquent enough.

Good bye.

Your happy and grateful Fanny

We should note also that Edgar Allan Poe was once purportedly ushered out of this house for his inappropriate behavior in the Bostonian world he called "Frogpondium." This Boston legend was no doubt based on the fact that Poe's review of Longfellow's *Hyperion* (1839) described the novel as a "triumph of Tom O'Bedlam"—an affront not only to Longfellow but also to Fanny Appleton. It is no wonder that Poe, as a critic, was known as "the tomahawk man." Born in Boston (1809) but raised in Richmond, Va., Poe returned to his birthplace to serve in the U.S. Army at Fort Independence, in Boston Harbor, before attending West Point (1830–31). He became a bitter critic of Boston writers, whom he called "the Humanity *clique*."

28. **The Somerset Club** (1852; at this site since 1872); **David Sears House** (1819), 42 Beacon St., by Alexander Parris, a National Historic Landmark

The list of Victorian literary lions who have

Francis Elizabeth Appleton, painting by George Peter Alexander Heal. *(Courtesy of the National Park Service, Longfellow National Historic Site.)* "Her face had a wonderful fascination in it. It was such a calm, quiet face with the light of the soul shining peacefully through it."—Henry Wadsworth Longfellow, *Hyperion, A Romance* (1839), describing Mary Ashburton, a character inspired by Fanny Appleton.

been guests at the Somerset Club is impressive. Club members entertained not only American literati Nathaniel Hawthorne, Henry James, James Russell Lowell, F. Marion Crawford, but also many of Victorian England's literary stars: Thackeray, Trollope, Wilkie Collins, Oscar Wilde, Matthew Arnold, and Rudyard Kipling (Committee 25–26).

As we pass 44 Beacon St., the family home of Robert Gould Shaw, whose likeness we saw in Saint-Gaudens's sculpture in front of the State House, we recall Whittier's words describing Shaw as the poet witnessed the departure of the 54th Regiment from Boston: "The very flower of grace and chivalry, he seemed to me beautiful and awful, an Angel of God come down to lead the host of Freedom to victory" (Whittier, quoted by S. Wilson 30) (see 54th Regiment T1, T7).

29. **William Hickling Prescott House** (1808), 55 Beacon St., by Asher Benjamin, a National Historic Landmark {See schedule of tour days and hours; headquarters of the Society of Colonial Dames of Massachusetts; www.nscda.org/ma/ william_hickling_prescott_house.htm; (617)-742-3190}

This was the home, from 1845 to 1859, of the partly blind romantic historian William H. Prescott (1796–1859), author of two testimonies to nineteenth-century commitment to the course of empire: *The Conquest of Mexico* (1843) and *History of the Conquest of Peru* (1847, written here). Able to mentally revise his memorization of "as many as three chapters . . . seventy-two pages of printed text" (Brooks, *New England* 138), Prescott wrote with a noctograph, recording his letters on carbon paper with an ivory stylus. The story of two crossed swords (now at the Massachusetts Historical Society,[14] but originally in the Prescott home), one worn by Prescott's grandfather (Colonel Prescott) and one by his wife's grandfather (Captain Linzee), each man on opposing sides at the Battle of Bunker Hill, inspired Prescott's friend the British author William Thackeray (1811–63) to write *The Virginians* (1859) (see Colonel Prescott statue T9).

Those who may have difficulty with steep ascents should continue to descend Beacon St. here in order to rejoin the tour at the Charles St. sites below.

Next we'll retrace our steps up Beacon St. a half block to Spruce St., the first street on the left. Ascend Spruce St.; then turn right onto Chestnut St., the street dubbed by Mrs. Harrison Gray Otis [15] "the capital of Massachusetts" in her opening chapter of The Barclays of Boston *(1854).*

Trudging up the steep incline, we pass on our left 29A Chestnut St., the home for a time of the Shakespearean actor Edwin Booth, brother of John Wilkes Booth. Here Thomas B. Aldrich, after tapping repeatedly on a window to get the attention of his good friend late at night, brought Booth to the door holding a cocked revolver (Greenslet 159).

Beyond on the right is 18 Chestnut St., where the poet Robert Lowell (1917–77) was born in the home of his maternal grandfather Winslow. Given Lowell's familiarity with the hill, how could he not sense the power of Julia Ward Howe and the spirit of "the Conscience

Whigs" when he meditated about slavery and the Civil War in "For the Union Dead." Near the top on the left, we find*

30. 13 Chestnut St. (1806), by Charles Bulfinch, a National Historic Landmark

At No. 13 lived the free-spirited New Yorker Julia Ward Howe (see p. 151), in what she called "the frozen ocean of Boston life." Poet of *Passion Flowers* (1853) and "The Battle Hymn of the Republic" (1861), Howe, yet to write *Is Polite Society Polite?* (1895), often felt isolated from Boston's social elite, in part because of her fondness for men and women who were considered eccentrics. When Howe lived here (1863–66), she composed a satiric cantata, "The Socio-Maniac," about members of "The Brain Club."

Then, as now, it was easy to organize small groups with social and intellectual commitments such as the Radical Club (1867–80), which subsequently held its Monday meetings in the parlor of this Bulfinch-designed house when No. 13 was the home of Mrs. John T. Sargent and the abolitionist minister John Turner Sargent (1807–77). Among the members, literati, distinguished clergy, and writers of conscience were Lydia Maria Child, Emerson, Whittier, Elizabeth Peabody, Longfellow, Holmes, William Lloyd Garrison, Thomas Wentworth Higginson, Henry James, Sr., Edwin Whipple, Julia Ward Howe herself, and Louisa May Alcott, who often attended Radical Club meetings during her many extended stays in Boston (see 13 Chestnut St. T8).

On the opposite side of street we find

31. 8 Chestnut St.

Nathaniel and Sophia Peabody Hawthorne's youngest daughter, Rose Hawthorne Lathrop (1851–1926), lived here with her husband (Swift 7). George Parsons Lathrop (1851–

98), associate editor (1875) of the *Atlantic Monthly* (when Howells was editor) and subsequently editor of the *Boston Courier* (Valenti 61), wrote *A Study of Hawthorne* (1876), a book that troubled Rose's brother, Julian Hawthorne. The Lathrops surprised Victorian Boston when they converted to Catholicism. Yet to come was Rose's postpartum breakdown, separation from Lathrop, subsequent role as Mother Mary Alphonsa of the Third Order of St. Dominic, her publication of *Some Memories of Hawthorne* (1897), her devotion to the care of destitute cancer victims (treated as lepers at the time), and her publication of the periodical *Christ's Poor* (Valenti 194).

As we approach the top of Chestnut St., notice No. 5, where Judge Robert Grant (Site 42) grew up. Slightly below the intersection with Walnut St. we see

32. 8 Walnut St.

This is the Parkman family home, where Dr. George Parkman, a pioneer in mental health, lived at the time of his infamous murder in 1849. At the trial of the alleged murderer, Harvard professor Dr. John Webster, Dr. Oliver Wendell Holmes, then dean of Harvard Medical School and Harvard's Parkman Professor of Anatomy (previously named in honor of the missing Parkman) testified. The trial and surrounding controversy captured the curiosity not only of Boston but also of the Victorian world. Charles Dickens, who had observed after his first visit to Boston (1842), "If I were a Bostonian, I think I would be a Transcendentalist" (50), asked Dr. Holmes during his second visit to Boston (1867–68) to show him the site of the body's gory disposal in the old Harvard Medical School building (nonextant). The mystery of the Parkman murder has been the subject of several twentieth-century speculative books, Helen

Thompson's *Murder at Harvard* (1971), Robert Sullivan's *The Disappearance of Dr. Parkman* (1971), and Simon Schama's *Dead Certainties: Unwarranted Speculations* (1991). In 2003 the PBS television production *Murder at Harvard,* inspired by Schama's interpretation, caused Bostonians to dispute once more the guilt or innocence of Webster.

We now journey up Walnut St., a short, steep incline, and turn right onto Mt. Vernon, a street that still represents social "stability." Henry James described the street's crest as pausing here as if to rest "like some good flushed lady of more than middle age" (*American Scene 243*). Here we recall Henry Adams's wry observation: "Viewed from Mt. Vernon St., the problem of life was as simple as it was classic. . . . Social perfection . . . was sure" (Education 33).

Turn right to see

33. 32 Mt. Vernon St.

Another in the series of the Boston residences (1870–72) of the Howe family, here we can imagine Julia Ward Howe in the company of her adventuresome husband, Samuel Gridley Howe, receiving Ulysses S. Grant or serving "buckwheat pancakes and maple syrup" to Bret Harte (Elliott, *Three Generations* 127), perhaps telling each about a literary relic that belonged to Dr. Howe. "Visitors were always interested in Byron's helmet" (Elliott, *Lord Byron's Helmet* 29). Young Dr. Howe had assisted the Greeks as a doctor and as a freedom fighter. Inspired by Byron, he had reached Greece just after the poet's death in 1824. However, he was able to purchase the poet's helmet, an intimate fixture of the Howe household. Years later their daughter, Maud Howe Elliott, personally returned the helmet to Greece.

A little farther up, on the level summit, on the left-hand side of the street we see

34. 49 Mt. Vernon St.

Massachusetts Chief Justice (1830–60) Lemuel Shaw, a defender of the Fugitive Slave Law (Site 36), a judge in the Parkman murder trial (Site 32), and the father-in-law of Herman Melville, moved to No. 49 in 1831. Chief Justice Shaw recorded that for his daughter Elizabeth's coming-out party, to which two hundred were invited, the 10:30 P.M. supper consisted of "scalloped and stewed and fried oysters, sliced ham, tongue, and sandwiches, rolls, blancmange, patés, truffles, etc., etc., ices, lemon, vanilla, etc., salad, lemonade, sherry wine, champagne, claret" (Chase 292). We may assume that a similar carte du jour was served at Miss Shaw and Herman Melville's [16] wedding (1847). The ceremony was held at home, rather than at New South Church (nonextant; see Church Green Site 13, T8), in order to avoid the crowds that were likely to gather to gawk at the writer, whose fact-based literary adventures in *Typee* (1846), involving an American mariner's romantic relationship with a native girl in the South Seas, had made him a celebrity. The novel that had caused the sensation was dedicated to "Lemuel Shaw, Chief Justice of the Commonwealth of Massachusetts."

Before we turn back to descend Mt. Vernon St., we'd like to take a close look at the exterior of 45 Mt. Vernon St., particularly at the architectural details around the entrance. We need to recall them soon in order to disentangle a "Mt. Vernon St. Literary Legend." As literary sleuths, we'll work to resolve this William Dean Howells "mystery" during our descent. But first, we'll retrace our steps to find 55 Mt. Vernon.

35. Nichols House Museum (1804),

55 Mt. Vernon St., attributed to Charles Bulfinch {See schedule of tour days and hours, www.nicholshousemuseum.org; (617)-227-6993}

The Nichols House Museum is the former home of Victorian-born Rose Standish Nichols (1872–1960), who founded and long presided over the Beacon Hill Reading Club. One of her prized possessions was a bronze relief of Saint-Gaudens's *Robert Louis Stevenson.* Nichols, founder of the Women's International League and author of *English Pleasure Gardens* (1902) and *Italian Pleasure Gardens* (1928), lived in this inviting home acquired by her parents in 1885. Here the fortunate visitor gains insight about what living at the crest of Mt. Vernon St. was really like (see Nichols T8).

Beside and below we see

36. 57 Mt. Vernon St.

It is said that Daniel Webster lived here for a short time. Webster's talents as an orator made him particularly formidable when he came out in support of the Fugitive Slave Law in 1850 (see Fugitive Slave Law T7 and the handbill on p. 137). Later, he was indirectly attacked for that support by the Quaker poet John Greenleaf Whittier,[17] who often stayed as a guest at No. 63, down the hill (Swift 10). Whittier's poem "Ichabod" left little doubt as to his opinion of Webster's action.

> So fallen! So lost! the light withdrawn
> Which once he wore!
> The glory from his gray hairs gone
> Forevermore! (186–87)

In 1842 No. 57 was the home of Charles Francis Adams (1807–86), scion of presidents, appointed by Lincoln to be Civil War minister to England (1861), founder of the Republican Party, and father of Brooks and Henry Adams (1838–1918), important commentators on American society. Henry Adams, who satirized the Brahmin attitude that "Boston had solved the universe" (*Education* 34), maintained, in *The Education of*

Henry Adams (1907), that in the course of his education he had "learned the most" during the contented hours he spent "reading 'Quentin Durward,' 'Ivanhoe,' and 'The Talisman'" (37–38). Post–Civil War disillusionment with democracy began to invade the writings of both brothers. Henry (see Introduction) published the novel *Democracy* (1880) (anonymously) and *The Degradation of the Democratic Dogma* (1918), Brooks *The Law of Civilization and Decay* (1895).

*As we begin our descent, the historic patina of Mt. Vernon St. reminds us once again of Henry James, who described the street's "deviations" from the common norm as a welcome relief from the too-new "blankness of the American street-page" (*American Scene 244*).

37. 59 Mt. Vernon St. (1837), by Edward Shaw

This was the Beacon Hill home of Thomas Bailey Aldrich's prosperity (see also Site 62). Illustrations of the entrance to no. 59 were used as frontispieces—emblematic "openings"—to two contemporary life stories[18] about the Aldriches. Their home's striking street front symbolized not only "home" to the Aldriches but also "tasteful Brahmin architecture" to the doorway's admirers. "To reach [Thomas Bailey Aldrich's study], which was the heart of the house, one climbed a fascinating flight of winding stairs,—giving glimpses here and there of all kinds of beautiful things, Oriental rugs, pictures and bits of statuary,—or else entrusting oneself to a tiny iron cage [elevator], was literally lifted, by a man above and a woman below,—right into the presence of the poet" (M. C. Crawford 386).

Born in Portsmouth,[19] N.H., Aldrich (1836–1907), who claimed to be "Boston-plated," succeeded Howells as editor of the *Atlantic Monthly* in 1881. Although he ex-

59 Mt. Vernon St., the Aldriches' home. *(From Ferris Greenslet,* The Life of Thomas Bailey Aldrich, *Boston: Houghton Mifflin, 1908, p. 152.)* "The large drawing-rooms, up one flight, after the manner of the old-time mansions of Boston, are interesting in their relics of travel and quaint carvings and old pictures." —Lilian Whiting, *Boston Days* (1902).

pressed his concern about Boston's vast immigrant population in his poem "Unguarded Gates" (1895), Aldrich befriended Irish-born John Boyle O'Reilly (1844–89), described by contemporary writers as "'the most romantic figure in literary Boston'" (M. C. Crawford 403) and as "a royal soul" (Whiting 447).

The life of O'Reilly, a Fenian, which reads like romance, is highlighted by his adventurous escape from horrific Dartmoor Prison, his recapture, subsequent escape by sea from a West Australian penal colony, and his Melvillesque rescue by the New Bedford whaler *Gazelle*, after he missed his crucial rendezvous at sea with the whaler *Vigilant*. (Forbes 57–58). His book *The Moondyne* (1879) is a reflection of his Australian experiences. However, it was his poetry, such as his "Crispus Attucks," a memorial[20] poem (which begins, "Where shall we seek for a hero, and where shall we find a story?") read at Faneuil Hall in praise of the patriotism of the African American Attucks in the Boston Massacre, that attracted literary Boston.

> [We give] honor to Crispus Attucks, who
>   was leader and voice that day,—
> The first to defy, and the first to die, with
>   Maverick, Carr and Gray.
> Call it riot or revolution, his hand first
>   clenched at the crown;
> His feet were the first in perilous place to
>   pull the king's flag down;
> His breast was the first one rent apart
>   that liberty's stream might flow;
> For our freedom now and forever, his
>   head was the first laid low.
>   . . . .
> And we who have toiled for freedom's
>   law, have we sought for freedom's
>   soul?
> Have we learned at last that human right
>   is not a part, but a whole?
> That nothing is told while the clinging sin
>   remains part unconfessed?
> That the health of the nation is perilled if
>   one man be oppressed?
>   . . . .
> And so we must come to the learning of
>   Boston's lesson today;
> The moral that Crispus Attucks taught in
>   the old heroic way,—
> God made mankind to be one in blood,
>   as one in spirit and thought;
> And so great a boon, by a brave man's
>   death, is never dearly bought!
>   (O'Reilly 51, 53–56)

The "first Irish-American writer . . . to break into the inner sanctum of Boston culture" (O'Connell 118), O'Reilly became editor (1870–89) of *The Pilot* and president of the Boston Press Club. He was an outstanding help in reconciling the Yankees and the Irish (Brooks, *New England* 311; O'Connor, *Boston Irish* 134) (see p. 182; O'Reilly T9).

Ever-vigilant of Mt. Vernon St.'s uneven brick footing, we look down as well as up while searching for street numbers. When we see on the right the name "CABOT" *written large above the door, we have found*

38. 65 Mt. Vernon St.

This was the site of the residence of George Cabot Lodge (1873–1909), a son of the respected Bostonian political family. Dramatist and author of *The Soul's Inheritance and Other Poems* (1909), Lodge died young —doomed, his biographer Henry Adams believed, by the indifference of his environment: "a society which commonly bred refined tastes, and often did refined work but seldom betrayed strong emotions" (Adams, *Life* 6).

We continue our descent recalling that it was in the refined ambiance of the Corey family residence on Beacon Hill that William Dean Howells placed the former Vermont farmer Colonel Silas Lapham,[21] *who was unused to the custom of drinking alcohol at meals. In* The Rise of Silas Lapham *(1885), he became tipsy, lost his reserve, and began to boast about his wealth: "At last he had the talk altogether to himself; no one else talked, and he talked unceasingly" (183). Still read in college courses, Howells's classic novel gives us an apt picture of Victorian Boston's social customs while it asks important questions about the nature of ethics and success in a "society" bound by tradition (see Boston society, Introduction).*

39. **48 Mt. Vernon St.:** A Literary Legend Revised

The current belief that the lovely present-day No. 48 Mt. Vernon St. was the address that inspired Howells's depiction of the Coreys' home in *The Rise of Silas Lapham* is due to confusion that began with author and literary enthusiast Frances Weston Carruth's *Fictional Rambles in and about Boston* (1902). A rather engaging literary muddle has ensued. When we look at the doorway of no. 48, Carruth's specified site for the Coreys' faded aristocratic residence on Beacon Hill, we find that the entrance is not at all compatible with Howells's description, and its street number places it on the wrong side of Mt. Vernon St. Although the streetscape matches Howells's evocative description—where the "dwellings are stately and tall, and the whole place wears an air of aristocratic seclusion" (165), Carruth's citing Howells's inspiration for the Coreys' residence as even-numbered, while saying it is located on the well-known "Otis-residence-No. 41's-odd-numbered-side," is befuddling.

This is just the sort of tangle that literary sleuths cannot resist. In spite of the writer's craft, which hinders definitive "unraveling," and the plausibility that Howells, using poetic license, created a composite of several homes, in the same way that he identified the Coreys' "handsome, quiet old street" on Beacon Hill as "Bellingham Place" (the name of a small private way just off Revere St.), we are keen to find the actual site that Carruth had in mind as the inspiration for the Coreys' house. Howells describes its entrance as one with "a wooden portico, with slender fluted columns, which have always been painted white, and which, with the delicate moldings of the cornice, form the sole and sufficient decoration of the street front" 165)—a classic Beacon Hill entry.

Equipped with Howells's text as "evidence," additional "clues" from the Victorian Carruth, knowledge that street numbers sometimes change, and that typos exist, our investigation,[22] in the end, reveals that the proper address is situated within the scope of our tour. It is 45 Mt. Vernon St., pointed out in passing, located just "above" Melville's father-in-law's home (Site 34). Our deduction that No. 45 is the Coreys' address is confirmed by Carruth's 1902 photograph—"nothing could be simpler and nothing could be better" (165).

On our right-hand side as we travel downward we soon catch sight of

40. **The Club of Odd Volumes,** 77 Mt. Vernon St. {Sarah Wyman Whitman's former home; not open to the public}

The Club of Odd Volumes (1887), a convivial and intellectual group devoted to the adventure of discussing all aspects of books and literary scholarship, was founded for literary and artistic purposes. In addition to collecting fine books, members create periodic exhibitions of notable texts, develop a program of topical lectures, pursue literary outings, and meet for dinner (Williams 43–44). Once happily described as "a gregarious coterie of poets, scholars, and bibliomaniacs" (Hogarth 60), the club formerly owned property across Mt. Vernon St. (Nos. 50, 52, and 54) and moved, in 1936, to this attractive Beacon Hill town house, which had been the home of Sarah Wyman Whitman (1842–1904), a leading graphic designer of attractive book bindings for Houghton Mifflin (Smith 282).

Whitman, also a writer and fabricator of stained glass, was a friend of Sarah Orne Jewett and a participant in the Charles St. salon of Annie Fields. She designed book covers for works by James Russell Lowell, Harriet Beecher Stowe, William Dean Howells, Oliver Wendell Holmes, Nathaniel Hawthorne, Celia Thaxter, and Sarah Orne Jewett, who in turn dedicated *Strangers and Wayfarers* (1890) to Whitman.

41. 83 Mt. Vernon St. {Plaque}

William Ellery Channing (1780–1842), whose house has long been distinguished with a bronze marker, was a leading theologian, liberal Unitarian minister, and man of letters who shared the intellectual independence of so many of his contemporaries. Van Wyck Brooks points out that "Channing was the father of half the reforms that characterized the Boston of his age" and explains that the essence of Channing's *The Importance and Means of a National Literature* (1830) is the belief that a nation's leaders are those "who determine its mind, its modes of thinking, and that writers are the originators of all those currents of thought by which nations and people are carried forward" (Brooks, *Flowering* 110). In 1842, during his first visit to Boston, Charles Dickens breakfasted here with Channing (Harris 44). Surely Dickens proved the essence of Channing's beliefs when he exposed the plight and exploitation of England's poor, and "determined" recognition of the need to assist the unfortunate on both sides of the Atlantic (see Channing T5, T8).

On the opposite side of the street is

42. 62 Mt. Vernon St.

Judge Robert Grant (1852–1942), author of *The Chippendales* (1909), a thoroughly Bostonian novel set in the 1880s and 1890s, was born here at No. 62. Grant,[23] who grew up at 5 Chestnut St. (noted in passing), "spent his entire lifetime within walking distance of his Beacon Hill birthplace" (Warner 8). At Harvard Law School, he edited *The Lampoon* and anonymously published a popular pamphlet titled *The Little-Tin-Gods-on-Wheels, or, Society in Our Modern Athens* (1879). A writer of social comedy, Grant, known for his wit, his "delicate sympathy with life" (Swift 29), and his "intuitive line of interpretation of social life" (Whiting 436), is now known for having "served with presidents A. Lawrence Lowell of Harvard and Samuel W. Stratton of MIT on Governor Fuller's pardon review panel, and h[is] join[ing] with them [after almost seven years of litigation] to recommend no reprieves [for Nicola Sacco and Bartolomeo Vanzetti]" (Warner 13).

On the odd-numbered side of the street at the head of an upward curving cobblestone driveway, we see

43. 87 Mt. Vernon St. (1805), by Charles Bulfinch {Plaque}

Designed to be Bulfinch's own home, this lovely, high-set mansion was instead first owned by Stephen Higginson, Jr., the father of Thomas Wentworth Higginson. Colonel Higginson's Civil War memoir, *Army Life in a Black Regiment* (1870), tells of his own war experience and at once suggests parallels with that of Robert Gould Shaw and the 54th Regiment:

> I used to think that I should not care to read "Uncle Tom's Cabin" in our camp; it would have seemed tame. Any group of men in a tent would have had more exciting tales to tell. I needed no fiction when I had Fanny Wright, for instance, daily passing to and fro before my tent with her shy little girl clinging to her skirts. . . . She had escaped from the main-land in a boat with that child and another. Her baby was shot dead in her arms, and she reached our lines with one child safe on earth and the other in heaven. I never found it needful to give any

elementary instructions in courage to Fanny's husband, you may be sure (192–93).

Although a successful minister, author, lecturer, and proponent of women's rights, Higginson referred to his correspondent Emily Dickinson as his "half-cracked" poetess in Amherst.[24] Yet it is very likely that his concern and encouragement played an important role in helping the great poet define herself as a writer. Her April 26, 1862, letter to Higginson is quintessential Dickinson: "Mr. Higginson,—You inquire my books. For poets I have Keats, and Mr. and Mrs. Browning. For prose, Mr. Ruskin, Sir Thomas Browne, and the Revelations. . . . You ask of my companions. Hills, sir, and the sundown, and a dog large as myself, that my father bought me. They are better than beings because they know, but do not tell" (quoted in Higginson, *Carlyle's Laugh* 253–54). The Higginson-Dickinson correspondence illumines the poetic imagination in much the same manner as Walt Whitman's debate with Emerson did.

More than two decades after the Civil War, Higginson, who had met Robert Browning and studied his poetry, became president (1887–89) of the Boston Browning Society (Site 16) during the last two

Thomas Wentworth Higginson,
Colonel of the First South Carolina Volunteers.
(From Mary Caroline Crawford, Romantic
Days in Old Boston, *Boston: Little, Brown,
1910, facing p. 203.)*
"All the soldiers in the black regiment of which
Thomas Wentworth Higginson of Cambridge
was chosen colonel had been slaves."
—Mary Caroline Crawford, *Romantic
Days in Old Boston* (1910).

years of Browning's life.

Mrs. Mason Hayne's Brick House on Mt. Vernon St., "The Lamp of Psyche"

As we continue to descend Mt. Vernon St., Higginson's heroic Civil War service brings to mind Mrs. Hayne in Edith Wharton's "The Lamp of Psyche" (1895). It is from Mrs. Mason Hayne's "swell-fronted" brick house on Mt. Vernon St. that she carried on her reforms with an "inflammatory zeal for righteousness in everything from baking powder to municipal government" (48).

Her telling question to her niece, Delia, about her cultured husband, Corbett, a dilettante with whom her niece is totally and happily in love, strikes an insightful blow: "Why shouldn't he [Corbett] have been in the [Civil] war?" asks Mt. Vernon St.'s Mrs. Hayne. The question reverberates though Delia's psyche. The possibility that cowardice could have been the motive for her American husband's pleasant "career" of doing nothing in Europe reduces her "passionate worship" of Corbett to a subdued and "tolerant affection."

Before we walk along the lower side of Louisburg Sq. (pronounced "Lewis"-burg), we continue to descend Mt. Vernon St. a little farther, remembering that Henry James, a historic preservationist at heart, observed that descending Mt. Vernon St. afforded "a brush with th[e] truth [that] . . . we like the sense of age to come, locally, when it comes with the right accompaniments, with the preservation of character and the continuity of tradition" (American Scene 244).

44. 102 Mt. Vernon St.

At No. 102 Henry James wrote the "happy-ending," dramatic version of *Daisy Miller* (story 1879; drama 1883), which he read to his friend Isabella Stewart Gardner at her 152 Beacon St. home (nonextant, the site at present is "150" Beacon St.) (see p. xxx and location of her museum, Introduction; and Gardner T8). At 102 Mt. Vernon James planned his plot for *The Bostonians* in part to show that "'I *can* write an American

story'" (James, quoted in Lewis 359). He lived here (see also Site 70) from time to time in 1882 and 1883, when his friend William Dean Howells lived just above in Louisburg Sq.

We return upward now to the lower side of Louisburg Sq. Robert Lowell defined Louisburg Sq. as the "Hub of the Hub," the focal point of old Boston's "cold roast elite" (Life Studies 15). It remains one of the most harmonious and exclusive areas of the city. Here the feeling for aristocracy characteristic of Boston since the Puritans looked for signs of grace emerges in a setting characteristic of the "best" in urban life.

45. 4 Louisburg Sq.

No. 4 Louisburg Sq. was the residence of William Dean Howells when he was editor of the *Atlantic Monthly.* At No. 4 he began his story about Silas Lapham, whose moral qualities would triumph over his unschooled taste, asserting the natural superiority of democratic man. Howells's novels also celebrated the strength and wit of women, often his most memorable characters, and helped his readers appreciate the need for women's rights. Howells was a master of realism, and his sensitivity to the living conditions of Boston's immigrants in *The Rise of Silas Lapham* and his observation of the plight of the city's destitute in *A Minister's Charge* (1886) did not increase his popularity among those Bostonians who preferred to overlook any negative

William Dean Howells with Daughter, Mildred, by Augustus Saint-Gaudens (1848–1907). Bronze relief, 21 x 33.5 cm. (8¼ x 13¼ in.), 1898, NPG.65.65. *(Courtesy of the National Portrait Gallery, Smithsonian Institution. Transfer from the National Gallery of Art; gift of Miss Mildred Howells, 1949.)*
"I arrived [1866] in Boston . . . when the greatest talents were literary." —W. D. Howells, *Literary Friends and Acquaintance* (1900).

aspects of their native city (see poverty and proper Bostonian society T3).

46. 10 Louisburg Sq.

Caring for both older and younger generations at once, Louisa May Alcott moved here (1885), with May's daughter, little Lulu (see Site 48), and her ailing father, Bronson Alcott, an educator of children as well as a social idealist, whom she called "Plato." It is easy to explain Louisa's compulsion to make money in view of Bronson's failure to do so, but she remained a devoted daughter and respected his transcendental spirit. Louisa died in 1888 on the day of her father's funeral (see 10 Louisburg Sq. p. 160, T8; Alcott T8).

47. 16 Louisburg Sq.

By the time William Dean Howells (1837–1920) lived here in 1882, after retiring from his highly influential editorship of the *Atlantic*, few remembered that its subscription list lapsed after his approval, as a young assistant editor, of the publication of Harriet Beecher Stowe's sensational assessment of "The True Story of Lady Byron's Life" (1869). Stowe's attempt to justify the standpoint of Byron's wife, "by exposing the whole story of Byron's incest, broke like a bombshell on the readers of the *Atlantic*" (Kirk 62).

The Victorian-born author of *The Atlantic Monthly and Its Makers* (1919), Mark A. DeWolfe Howe (1864–1960), a Boston aficionado and director of the Boston Athenæum (1922), also lived at No. 16 (H. Howe 354; S. Wilson 48). Howe, a faithful protégé of Annie Fields, removed from the Fields-Jewett letters the childlike nicknames Annie Fields and Sarah Orne Jewett used for each other, "Fuff" for Annie and "Pinny" for Sarah, fearing the possibility of "all sorts of people reading them

wrong" (H. Howe 84) (see Fields; Jewett T8).

At the far end of Louisburg Sq., we'll turn right onto Pinckney St.,[25] but let's pause a moment first to consider the homes opposite us across Pinckney St., for one of the homes addressing us

"With its front windows fac[ing] Louisburg Square" (164) was the Pinckney St.[26] home of Jean Stafford's Miss Lucy Pride in *Boston Adventure* (1944), set around 1912, The Victorian-born Miss Pride, with a telling last name, takes on a shoemaker's daughter, Sonie Marburg, as her pet "cause." While having tea with Sonie in the library, Miss Pride informs her that "literary people were often 'brainy' and that she did not enjoy brains when she was relaxing at her tea-table" (167). Following the tradition of Howells's realism, but in a more pointedly critical vein, Stafford (1915–79) suggests that aristocratic Boston had become decadent and that moral quality had passed to the children of the new immigrant. This did not increase Stafford's popularity on the Hill.

Also facing us across Pinckney St. is No. 81, the house where Louisa May Alcott lived before she moved to 10 Louisburg Sq.

48. 81 Pinckney St.

Alcott's *Work: A Story of Experience* (1873) "explored the possibilities of self-realization for unmarried women" (O'Connell 67) and by the time she lived in No. 81 (1880) Alcott was her own best example. After the tragedy of the early death (in Europe) of her sister May Alcott Neiriker ("Amy" in *Little Women* and *Good Wives*), Louisa May Alcott, during the last decade of her life, took on the role of mother for her namesake and charge, May's baby, LuLu (Louisa May Neiriker). In September 1880 Alcott wrote in her journal: "My heart is full of pride & joy, & the touch of the dear little hands seems to take away the bitterness of grief. I often go at night to see if she is *really* here, & the sight of the little yellow head is like sunshine to me" (quoted in Meyerson and Shealy 227).

Leaving Louisburg Sq., we'll turn now to head up Pinckney St., at this point a short, steep rise. A few doors up on the left we see

49. 71 Pinckney St.

Publisher James Osgood was "the Boston Bantam" who won Charles Dickens's six-mile "Great International Walking Match" with Annie Fields's assistance. Her administration of brandy, during his final lap in the snow (A. Fields 162), may have given him the edge over Dickens's manager, Mr. Dolby. Osgood, who had become James Fields's "right-hand man," triumphed once again when he bought this house with proceeds from the sponsorship of Dickens's American lecture tour during the winter of 1867–68. To his credit, Osgood also supported Walt Whitman at a time when many Bostonians disapproved of the poet's barbaric yawp. After Osgood joined Ticknor and Fields, the company underwent various incarnations, among them Fields, Osgood and Company; a second James R. Osgood and Company; Houghton, Osgood, and Company (James Osgood retired in 1880); and finally Houghton Mifflin (Mead, "Boston Memories" 13).

Practically opposite No. 71 is

50. 74 Pinckney St.

This was the home of the Boston historian Marjorie Drake Ross (McVoy 89). Her *Book of Boston: The Victorian Period 1837–1901* (1964) provides a rare, focused overview of the era. Ross was director, for a time, of Gibson House (now a National Historic Landmark), a distinctive Victorian house museum, which formerly belonged to three generations of the family of the author and poet Charles Hammond Gibson (1874–1954). Gibson, who sometimes used the pseudonym "Richard Sudbury," and whose family connections to Brahmin Boston were numerous, joined (1903) the Boston Authors Club, founded by Julia Ward Howe and Thomas Wentworth Higginson (Flagg 116–17). Braithwaite included Gibson in his *Anthology of Massachusetts Authors* (1922). Gibson House, definitely worth a visit for those interested in Victorian Boston, is also home to the New England Chapter of the Victorian Society in America. {Gibson House Museum, 137 Beacon St., Back Bay between Arlington and Berkeley Sts.; www.thegibsonhouse.org; for tour days and hours: call (617)-267-6338}

Farther up on the right-hand side, just past the opening of Anderson St., we find

51. 54 Pinckney St.

Man of letters, orator, lawyer, U.S. District Attorney, and scholar George Stillman Hillard (1808–79) wrote the nineteenth-century school textbook series *Hillard's Readers*. He is credited with having "instilled a love of good literature, and a knowledge of the best English writers to generations of American[s]" (Bacon 265). Hillard, who also lived at 62 Pinckney (1848), opened No. 54, his first home on Pinckney St., to Nathaniel Hawthorne, who wrote in the introduction to *The Scarlet Letter* that he "gr[ew] fastidious by sympathy with the classic refinement of Hillard's culture" (20). Nevertheless, Hawthorne did not share his host's political philosophy. "Why," wrote Edward Everett to Hillard, in an effort to come to terms with the writer's Jacksonian persuasion, "is Hawthorne on the side of barbarism and vandalism against order, law and constitutional lib-

erty?" (Everett, quoted by Schlesinger 370) (see Everett T9).

Legend claims that it was from this house that Hawthorne[27] wrote his marriage proposal to Sophia Peabody.[28]

He did, in fact, write the following to James Freeman Clarke from this address.

No. 54 Pinckney Street
Boston, July 1842

My Dear Sir.—Though personally a stranger to you, I am about to request of you the greatest favor which I can receive from any man. I am to be married to Miss Sophia Peabody; and it is our mutual desire that you would perform the ceremony. Unless it should be decidedly a rainy day, a carriage will call for you at half-past eleven o'clock in the forenoon. Very respectfully yours,

Nathaniel
Hawthorne

He omitted, however, both the place and the date of the wedding.

As we approach more level ground, on the right-hand side is

52. **30 Pinckney St.**

This was the home of Edwin D. Mead (1849–1937), a cousin by marriage of William Dean Howells, who had married Elinor Mead of Brattleboro,

Vt. Author of *Martin Luther: A Study of the Reformation,* Edwin D. Mead, a lecturer on American literature, scholarly essayist, and expert on Kant (Whiting 476), became editor (1889–1901) of the *New England Magazine.* He had worked, when a youngster, as a clerk in the counting room at Ticknor and Fields Publishing House at 124 Tremont St. (Site 3), happily meeting the leading literary figures of Victorian Boston.

As the street levels off, we find on the right

53. **20 Pinckney St.**

Louisa May Alcott's room here was on the third floor during a period (1852–55) when the Alcott family had little means. Here Louisa published her first story, "The Rival Painters: A Tale of Rome" (1852), and enjoyed the publication of her first book, *Flower Fables* (1854; dedicated to Ralph Waldo Emerson's daughter, Ellen), telling her mother in a note that in "your Christmas Stocking I have put 'my first born' knowing that you will accept it with all its faults (for grandmothers are always kind), and look upon it merely as an earnest of what I may yet do; for, with so much to

Louisa May Alcott (1862). Portrait.
(Courtesy of the Boston Athenæum.)
"She knew she was no nightingale,/Yet spite of much abuse,/She longed to help and cheer the world,/Although a plain gray goose."
From "The Lay of a Golden Goose" (1870), by the "golden goose" herself, Louisa May Alcott. A delightful happenstance is Marmee's recipe called "Bird Nest Pudding," in Abigail May Alcott's *Receipts and Simple Remedies: Best Way of Doing Difficult Things All Tried and Proved* (1856), ed. Nancy L. Kohl, N. L. Kohl, and Louisa May Alcott Memorial Association (1980).

cheer me on, I hope in time to pass from faeries and fables to men and realities" (quoted by Meyerson and Shealy xxx) (see 20 Pinckney; Alcott T8).

54. 16 Pinckney St.

Near the back of the State House, at No. 16, lived the poet and essayist Louise Imogen Guiney (1861–1920) when she was working on her fourth book of poems (Bacon 268). Credited as being a "driving force behind" the Aesthetic movement of the 1890s in Boston (*History Project* 87), Guiney, the Irish-American daughter of a respected Civil War general, attempted to reconcile the Irish and Yankees through a common poetic tradition. A member of Isabella Stewart Gardner's circle of literary friends (Shand-Tucci 131), she was affectionately referred to as "The Linnet" by Annie Fields and Sarah Orne Jewett (M. A. Howe 288). She was known for her scholarship on the English Romantic poets, and her *Songs at the Start* (1884) had won early approval from Boston literati. It is to Guiney that William Stanley Braithwaite (Sites 1 and 20) dedicated his poem "Mater Triumphalis." Van Wyck Brooks describes Guiney as "liv[ing] in a dream of the seventeenth century" (Brooks, *New England* 451).

Edwin Munroe Bacon (1844–1916), whose Victorian *Literary Pilgrimages in New England* (1902) has led us to several delectable literary morsels, described Guiney's poetry as "delicately refined" (268). Bacon, a trustworthy "connoisseur of New England, historical and literary" (Swift 14), lived, for a time, in the very same "modest little house" (Bacon, *Literary Pilgramages* 268). Antiquarian, journalist, and managing editor (1873–78) of the *Boston Globe*,[29] Bacon was the author of numerous books about Boston and New England. Bacon also lived at 36 Pinckney; his neigh-bor Edwin D. Mead (Site 52) tells us that Edwin Bacon "loved Boston as Charles Lamb loved London, and relished his morning walk around Boston Common as Doctor Johnson relished a walk down Fleet Street" (Mead, "Boston Memories" 22).

55. 14 Pinckney St.

No. 14 was the home of William D. Ticknor (1810–64), responsible for founding Ticknor and Company. With its headquarters at the Old Corner Book Store (Site 9), the pub-lishing house became a prime instrument in fostering Boston's nineteenth-century literary heritage when Ticknor teamed up with his junior partner, James T. Fields, establishing Ticknor and Fields (1843). Ticknor's death dealt a devastating blow to Nathaniel Hawthorne, who had written to James Fields, "As regards nursing, he shall have the best that can be obtained; and my own room is next to his, so that I can step in at any moment; but that will be of almost as much service as if a hippopota-mus were to do him the same kindness. Nevertheless, I have blistered, and pow-dered, and pilled him and made my obser-vation on medical science" (quoted by M. A. Howe 66). Hawthorne himself was to live but a month longer (Site 13).

On the left-hand side, practically opposite, is

56. 15 Pinckney St.

This is the site of the location where Eliza-beth Peabody, from 1862 to 1863, continued her early kindergarten work. She was be-lieved to be the model for the gentle reformer Miss Birdseye in *The Bostonians*, though Henry James denied this. He described Miss Birdseye as having "a sad, soft, pale face, which . . . looked as if it had been soaked, blurred and made vague by exposure to some slow dissolvent. . . . She

wore a loose black jacket, with deep pockets, which were stuffed with papers, memoranda of a voluminous correspondence.... She looked as if she had spent her life on platforms, in audiences, in conventions in phalansteries, in *séances*; in her faded face there was a kind of reflection of ugly lecture-lamps" (26–27).

Whether or not this is a portrait of Boston's first woman publisher, Thomas Wentworth Higginson's recollection of his own last meeting with Peabody, whom he refers to as "the Grandmother of Boston" is a good rival portrayal:

> I chanced to pick her out of a snowdrift into which she had sunk overwhelmed during a furious snow squall, while crossing a street in Boston. I did not know her until she had scrambled up with much assistance, and recognizing me at once, fastened on my offered arm, saying breathlessly, "I'm so glad to see you, I have been wishing to talk to you about Sarah Winnemucca. Now Sarah Winnemucca"—and she went on discoursing as peacefully about a maligned Indian protégée as if she were strolling in some sequestered moonlit lane, on a summer evening (*Cheerful Yesterdays* 87) (see p. 146; Peabody; Winnemucca T8).

Longfellow recalled first meeting Elizabeth Peabody when she was inside a carriage. "Hearing his name mentioned, she leaned forward and said, "Mr. Longfellow, can you tell me which is the best Chinese Grammar?" (A. Fields, quoted by M. Howe, *Memories* 119).

On the left-hand side a few steps farther we see

57. 11 Pinckney St.

The genial Mr. and Mrs. Edwin Percy Whipple, whose books "looked as if they had been the every-day property of a book-loving household" (Whiting 211), held their "Sunday Evenings" in their two parlors at 11 Pinckney St. for thirty years. Lowell, Longfellow, Emerson, John Boyle O'Reilly, Thomas Wentworth Higginson, Louisa May Alcott,[30] Whittier, the Hawthornes, the Fieldses, the Holmeses, and the Howes were among their attending friends (Parsons 69). Lilian Whiting explains that it was "not easy to estimate the influence on a young school of literature of such a mind as" Whipple's (212). In the role of influential intellectual and literary critic, he encouraged Nathaniel Hawthorne and the early literary talents of Louisa May Alcott (205). Applauded by Thomas Macaulay, Edwin Whipple's "essay on George Eliot drew from her the exclamation, 'This man understands me'" (quoted by Bacon, *Literary Pilgrimages* 272–73).

On the right-hand side just a little farther we find

58. 4 Pinckney St.

No. 4 was home for a time to Henry David Thoreau (Freely 215), and also for a while (1831–32) to Jacob Abbott (1803–79). Edwin M. Bacon (Site 54) explains that Abbott's establishment of Boston's Mt. Vernon School was "one of the first in the country to give young women the same standard of education as young men" (*Literary Pilgrimages* 168). Elizabeth Stuart Phelps (1844–1911), author of *The Gates Ajar* (1868), was Abbott's student at the Mt. Vernon School, and Abbott, from Maine, had once had Portland-born Henry Wadsworth Longfellow as his pupil (D. Johnson). Abbott, best known for his twenty-four-volume series for children, the Rollo books, wrote nineteenth-century America's "first fictional series for children" (D. Johnson)—the Harry Potter books of the day.

59. Upper End of Pinckney St.

William Dean Howells particularly liked this street in back of the State House. According to Carruth (21–22), whose *Fictional Rambles in and about Boston* and whose unusual enumeration of the location of diverse sites in Boston fiction has been an inspiration for visiting several sites on this tour, Pinckney St. was Howells's model in *A Modern Instance* (1882) for Rumford St. (59). In one of our earliest novels about divorce, Howells's character, Ben Halleck, a resident of Rumford (i.e., Pinckney) St., expresses his chauvinistic pride about being born in Boston, while Howells satirizes Victorian Boston's endemic provinciality: "'I don't think there is any place so well worth being born in as Boston. . . . Even Boston provinciality is a precious testimony to the authoritative personality of the old city. . . . we're antique, we're classic'" (211–12).

Optional Digression to Smith Ct.: *Boston's African American community was well established on Beacon Hill's north slope in the nineteenth century. At the crest of Pinckney St. at the corner of Joy St., Smith Ct. is easily accessible below us (see p. 138; Pinckney St. T7). Energetic walkers may wish to include this downward and steep upward return. If so, turn left onto Joy St., proceed down the hill, and take the second left into Smith Ct.*

60. 3 Smith Ct.

No. 3 Smith Ct., a National Historic Landmark, was home for over a decade to the African American historian William C. Nell (1816–74). Born on Beacon Hill, Nell had gained work and writing experience at William Lloyd Garrison's *Liberator*. A historian, Nell wrote *The Colored Patriots of the American Revolution,* for which Harriet Beecher Stowe wrote (1855) the introduc-

tion (S. Wilson 44). Stowe had visited the home of Lewis Hayden (see p. 136; Hayden T7, T8) at nearby 66 Phillips St. {Plaque} while doing research for *The Key to Uncle Tom's Cabin: Presenting the Original Facts and Documents upon Which the Story Is Founded. Together with Corroborative Statements Verifying the Truth of the Work* (1853). The Haydens' home was a refuge for many fugitive slaves as well as lecturing abolitionists (see Nell T7).

61. The African Meeting House (1806),

8 Smith Ct.; facade an adaptation of an Asher Benjamin town house design; interior restored to its known 1854 design. {Check current hours and tours; www.afroammuseum.org; (617)-725-0022}

The African Meeting House, a National Historic Landmark (see African Meeting House p. 140; and T7, T8), was a primary site for abolitionist speakers. Here Frederick Douglass, author of *The Narrative of the Life of Frederick Douglass: An American Slave* (1845), "enlist[ed] soldiers for the 54th Massachusetts volunteers, who fought under Colonel Robert Gould Shaw. Two of Douglass's sons were among the first recruits" (S. Wilson 45) (see Douglass, Sites 1, 5, 69).

Hike back now up to Joy and Pinckney Sts.; from now on it's almost all downhill.

As we reverse direction in order to see No. 84, one-half block below Louisburg Sq., let's enjoy the nature of Pinckney St.'s intimate streetscape, which appears to change with the very direction of our steps. Often portrayed as Victorian "Boston's Bohemia," Pinckney St., the acknowledged dividing line between the Beacon St. and the Cambridge St. sides of Beacon Hill, was described in 1903 as the city's "most interesting thoroughfare" (Swift 13). Retracing our steps gives us a rare chance

to appreciate the neighborly atmosphere of the street's upper end without the distraction of looking for street numbers.

Just below Louisburg Sq. we find

62. 84 Pinckney St.

Here Thomas Bailey Aldrich began *The Story of a Bad Boy* (1870) (see setting of story in note 19). James Fields's account of bringing Charles Dickens to tour the Aldriches' cheerful honeymoon house with its "open fires, flowers," and "table set for dinner with . . . silver and glass" (Aldrich 104) is an appealing one. The housekeeper's daughter, Lizzie, age six, served Dickens wearing a "mouse-colored dress reaching almost to the ground . . . [her] hair braided on each side of her brow, and tied with the same mouse-colored ribbon in a prim bow" (104–5).

Longfellow's tour found the house decorated in "white muslin" with pink and blue ribbons. He was shown the crimson-walled study, with its flowers, and "crowded shelves of books," the Aldrich bedroom, with its "blue chintz hangings . . . painted with blue birds," and also the Aldriches' "round table for two," which inspired Longfellow's poem "The Hanging of the Crane" (102, 108–9):

For two alone, there in the hall,
Is spread the table round and small;
Upon the polished silver shine

Thomas Bailey Aldrich, engraving.
(From W. D. Howells, Literary Friends and Acquaintance, *New York: Harper and Brothers, 1900, facing p. 134.)*
Aldrich "always knew when to stop, an unusual virtue . . . exceedingly pleasant in a world that was used to poets who went on and on."
—Van Wyck Brooks, *New England: Indian Summer* (1940).

The evening lamps, but, more divine,
The light of love shines over all;
Of love, that says not mine and thine,
But ours, for ours, is thine and mine.
(Longfellow 308)

At the corner of West Cedar we'll turn right and proceed. On the right-hand side of West Cedar, just before we reach Revere St., is

63. 43 West Cedar St.

A child of the Victorian age, John P. Marquand (1893–1960) moved here in 1927. He opened his novel *The Late George Apley* (1937) in 1866, a quarter century before his own birth. The book, once described as "'a detailed Valentine to a city— Boston—such as no other American city can expect'" (Birmingham 88), won Marquand a Pulitzer Prize. Walking along West Cedar St., we understand why Boston itself is considered to be "a character" in Marquand's work (H. H. Adams i), for here the atmosphere is certainly conducive to an encounter with a literary "manifestation" of George Apley, saying of himself, "'I am the sort of man I am, because environment prevented my being anything else'" (1).

A few houses above the corner of West Cedar and Revere Sts., on the left-hand side, is 91 Revere St. This house is immortalized in

Robert Lowell's forthright chapter "91 Revere Street" in his Life Studies (1959). Lowell (1917–77) described his childhood address as "looking out on an unbuttoned part of Beacon Hill" (14), where "houses, changing hands, changed their language and nationality" (15). His Victorian-born mother described the address as "perched on the outer rim of the hub of decency" (15). Her Winslow family home (18 Chestnut St., noted as we passed) had been safely ensconced on the "right" side of the hill.

Turn to descend Revere St. Upon reaching Charles St., turn right. Here the literary pilgrim returns to the role of literary sleuth. The street's numbers have undergone changes and much has been demolished (street widening), particularly on the even-numbered Charles River side. However, lovers of literature, not short on imagination, will want to investigate the landscape knowing that the Fieldses, Aldriches, and Holmeses were close neighbors on this, the "Cambridge-Street-end," of Charles St. As we walk toward Cambridge St., we find that the site of 148 (once 37), the Fieldses' Charles St. residence, is best evoked in an unusual location.

64. Site of James T. and Annie Fields's Home

(nonextant), 160 Charles St.; formerly No. 148 (and before that No. 37); now the Charles St. Garage

Henry James, upon returning to Charles St. in 1904, was disappointed by its "soiled and sordid" look and was relieved to find Annie Fields's home a "votive temple to memory" (*American Scene* 244–45). It was Annie Fields's wish that her home be demolished after her death to avoid its further degradation from the encroachment of Charles St. commercialism (Roman 165). Hence, we find today, just as Willa Cather did upon her own return, a parking garage where the house once stood.

AND SHE IN WHOM SWEET CHARITIES UNITE
THE OLD GREEK BEAUTIES SET IN HOLIER LIGHT

Annie Adams Fields (1834–1915), miniature, watercolor on ivory (ca. 1890) by Lucia Fairchild Fuller (1872–1924), based on a daguerreotype taken by Southworth and Hawes (ca. 1855); it reads: "And she in whom sweet charities unite the old Greek beauties set in holier light." (*Courtesy of the Boston Athenæum.*)

"July 26, 1863—What a strange history this literary life in America at the present day would make." —Annie Fields, *Memories of a Hostess* (1922).

We need to make our way into the large brick Charles St. parking garage, which may be entered through its second "driveway" entrance—the one most distant from Beacon St., a right of way.

Walk into and through the parking garage, but not under the archway, into West Hill Place (Harris 273–74). On our immedi-

ate left, adjacent to the garage's back wall, we may clearly see (through the widely spaced vertical bars of a tall black iron gate) a pedestrian passage, which culminates in a private garden.

To "open the door" to the Fieldses' house from our vantage point here, in the face of the solid immensity of the back wall of the parking garage, requires that we be ready for discovered treasure, unearthed by the chief means available: a literary "dig." Perhaps we can inspire twenty-first-century Victorian enthusiasts to commemorate the site of the Fieldses' house-museum with a plaque.

Encouraged by the discoveries from our "dig," we enter, in our mind's eye, the brick house described as "high-set and bare in a row of houses all high-set and bare ... with brownstone trimmings" (Shackleton 39). The front door opens directly on Charles St., under the facade's bay window.

Publisher James T. Fields (1816–81), author of *Yesterdays with Authors* (1872), and his wife, Annie Adams Fields (1834–1915), of *Authors and Friends* (1896), entertained luminaries in their home, among them Longfellow,[31] Emerson, Lowell, Hawthorne, Whittier, Mark Twain, and their British houseguests, literary lions such as Dickens, Thackeray, Trollope, Matthew Arnold, and Charles Kingsley (M. C. Crawford 401). After her husband's death, Annie Fields conducted her literary salon in her house-museum, inviting her friends, such as Thomas Bailey Aldrich, Celia Thaxter, and her intimate friend Sarah Orne Jewett

The Fieldses' library, Mrs. James T. Fields at the window, Sarah Orne Jewett at the right. *(Courtesy of the Boston Athenæum.)* "Mrs. Fields showed me from shelf to shelf in the library, and dazzled me with the sight of authors' copies, and volumes invaluable with autographs and ... penciled notes." —W. D. Howells, *Literary Friends and Acquaintance* (1900).

(1847–96), author of *The Country of the Pointed Firs* (1896). Jewett made her home at No. 148 during the winters.[32] In fact, it was at Annie Fields's home that Jewett met (1908) Willa Cather, who wrote of their subsequent friendship: "Sometimes opening a new door can make a great change in one's life" (52).

Upon our "entering" the Fieldses' home we pass the "small reception room" (Cather 53), glimpse "spacious rooms, wide halls, easy stairways, and generous fireplaces" (Wolfe 89), even the Fieldses' green library furniture (Roman 12). On the far side of the house, the windows of all five stories, including the large rooftop lookout, afford tempting views over the garden to the Charles River. In the refined comfort of the rooms below, the Fieldses' literary treasures[33] offer us countless tempting choices. We may view the portrait of Hawthorne in the dining room (Howells, *Literary Friends*

45), pause to examine a "youthful [oil] portrait of Dickens in the drawing room" (Cather 54), or admire Sir Joshua Reynolds's skillful portrait of Alexander Pope (Tryon 214). A lock of Keats's hair under glass along with Severn's drawing of Keats, gifts of the artist to Annie (Cather 60), are prized literary keepsakes not to be missed. Finally, it is impossible to omit at least a cursory dreamlike glance at the collection of first editions, letters, and handwritten manuscripts within the Fieldses' influential literary mecca, in Henry James's words, a "waterside museum."

We're grateful today that the Fieldses' private garden remains to enhance the story of our "reconstruction." Yes, thanks to Annie Fields's will, her large garden—the property was originally bought to preserve the river view behind their home—remains a garden.

65. Literary Boston's "Secret Garden"

To the Fieldses' garden, "with its benches," trees, and flowers (Carruth 58), luminaries brought "roses and flowering shrubs," explains Willa Cather (57). A tall tree and the respite of green vegetation is visible as we peek down the passage to see the back private corner of the Fieldses' former garden. From our vantage point, looking through the gate, we suspect that the ivy mitigating the tall expanse of the back of the garage may be a descendant of that which was once described as "latticing" the Fieldses' dining room windows.

At the Charles River end, formerly the river's edge, of the Fieldses' long garden, a high brick wall effectively blocks traffic noise from the David G. Mugar Way and successfully restricts the passerby's view into the garden, allowing it to remain, as Annie Fields wished, a quiet and private oasis. For the closest approximation of the Fieldses' garden-level view of the Charles River, however,

glance through and past the open archway into West Hill Place. In clement weather bright sailboats still ply the Charles.

Olive Chancellor's Home on Charles St., *The Bostonians* (1886)

Olive Chancellor (Sites 2 and 25), Henry James's domineering, elegant reformer, maintained her sophisticated home on Charles St. Basil Ransom, observing his kinswoman's home, "wandered to the windows at the back, where there was a view of the water" (James 15). From Mississippi, Ransom "had always heard that Boston was a city of culture, and now there was culture in Miss Chancellor's tables and sofas, in the books that were everywhere, on little shelves like brackets (as if a book was a statuette),

The Charles River side of the Fieldses' home (ca. 1900), from the end of their garden. *(From Lindsay Swift,* Literary Landmarks of Boston, *Boston: Houghton Mifflin, 1903, p. 18.)*
"We breakfasted in the pretty room whose windows look out through leaves and flowers upon the river's coming and going tides, and whose walls were covered with the faces and autographs of all the contemporary poets and novelists."
—W. D. Howells, *Literary Friends and Acquaintance* (1900).

View from the Fieldses' "Waterside Museum," from the drawing room window over their garden toward the Charles River.
(From W. D. Howells, Literary Friends and Acquaintance, *New York: Harper and Brothers, 1900, facing p. 46.)*
"Directly above the garden wall lay the Charles River and, beyond, the Cambridge shore."
—Willa Cather, "148 Charles Street," in *Not Under Forty* (1936).

in the photographs and watercolors that covered the walls" (James 16). There is little doubt that the interior of the Fieldses' home evoked Olive Chancellor's home: "He had never seen an interior that was so much of an interior" (James, *Bostonians* 16).

As we retrace our steps back through the garage's "right of way" passage to Charles St., Oliver Wendell Holmes's nearby residence comes to mind.

66. Oliver Wendell Holmes's Charles St. Residence (nonextant)[34]
—"A commercial smash kills a hundred men's homes for them" (Site 4).

Oliver Wendell Holmes, living at 164 Charles St. (formerly no. 21), was a waterside neighbor (1859–70) of the Fieldses. His house was so similar to theirs that he actually explored their house when making the decision to buy his (A. Fields 114). On William Dean Howells's first visit to Holmes's house on Charles St., he was

offered an English breakfast tea. Holmes described it as "the flower of the Souchong; it is the blossom, the poetry of tea" (Holmes quoted by Howells, *Literary Friends* 44). The two conversed, recalled Howells, about "intimations of immortality . . . forebodings and presentiments. . . . In the gathering dusk, so weird did my fortune of being there and listening to him seem, that I might well have been a blessed ghost, for all the reality I felt in myself" (44–45).

Victorian Boston's Poet Laureate, Holmes, with his "Old Ironsides" (1830) had helped save the USS *Constitution* from demolition. It is now a National Historic Landmark (see view of USS *Constitution* T3, and its location on map T9).

Oliver Wendell Holmes.
(From Hezekiah Butterworth, Young Folks' History of Boston, *Boston: D. Lothrop, 1881, facing p. 410.)*
"Holmes, you are intellectually the most alive man I have ever known," said by Henry James, Sr., quoted in W. D. Howells, *Literary Friends and Acquaintance* (1900).

Many of Holmes's memorable and chauvinistic Boston witticisms were written when he lived on Charles St. In *The Professor at the Breakfast Table* (1860), "Little Boston" crows that "Boston has opened and kept open, more turnpikes that lead straight to free thought and free speech and free deeds than any other city of live men or dead men" (3–4). The same little gentleman boldly claims that Boston is "the thinking centre of the continent, and therefore of the planet" (83). Holmes's *Elsie Venner* (1861) was a forerunner of the modern psychological novel, and his "My Hunt after the Captain" describes his search for his wounded son (the future Justice Oliver Wendell Holmes) during the Civil War. Annie Fields recalled that, in 1864, "during the terrible days of the war" (126), Dr. Holmes dropped by one Sunday afternoon, precisely to make some needed changes in a poem: "'I am ashamed,' he said, 'to be troubled by so slight a thing when battles are raging about us; but I have written: "Where Genoa's deckless caravels were blown." Now [Christopher] Columbus sailed from Palos, and I must change the verse before it is too late'" (Holmes, quoted by A. Fields 126). When Dr. Holmes finally moved to 296 Beacon St. (Back Bay) in order to avoid Charles St.'s growing commercialism, he quipped that he was "committing justifiable domicide." Ironically, none of Dr. Holmes's Boston residences remains completely intact in spite of his fame in the city, the United States, and Britain.

As we turn to walk back along Charles St. (toward Beacon St. and the Common) we see on the left-hand side

67. 127 Charles St.

This was the home for a time of Lucretia Peabody Hale (1820–1900), originator of the children's book *The Peterkin Papers* (1880),

rare in that it demonstrated Bostonian humor. Van Wyck Brooks embellishes Hale's own humor when he explains that she satirized Boston's leading literary families:

> the Alcotts, the Howes, or the Hales. With their innocent pedantry, their breezy gullibility, their high-minded faith in life and utter lack of common sense, the [Peterkins] carried the traits of these families to a pitch of the absurd. Their "educational breakfasts" were one of the notes of a nonsense-Boston that might have been conceived by Edward Lear. Their bent for self-improvement, their conundrums at picnics, their zest for the acquisition of Sanskrit and Turkish, their joy in making life an object-lesson,— studying the butter at table and including the cow,—could only have been possible in a world that had known Elizabeth Peabody and the candours of transcendental Concord. (Brooks, *New England* 332)

Hale, a "favorite" student of Elizabeth Peabody, was once considered, through her writing and her literary and correspondence "classes," to have had an influence and "discipleship" comparable with that of Margaret Fuller (Wolfe 99; Parsons 65; Whiting 435). In 1888 Lucretia's brother, Edward Everett Hale (Site 8) organized Boston's Tolstoy Club (Kirk 112).

Just a little farther is

68. 103 Charles St. {Plaque}

Born in Boston, the civil rights activist and charter member of the Boston Chapter of the National Association for the Advancement of Colored People (NAACP) Josephine St. Pierre Ruffin (1842–1924) lived on Charles St. for over two decades. She had been sent as a child to Salem in order to attend a desegregated school (see school

desegregation; Nell; Abiel Smith School T7). She was married to George Lewis Ruffin, who had become the first black judge in the North after attending Harvard Law School, and the two helped to recruit soldiers for the Massachusetts 54th and 55th Regiments. Four years after being widowed, Ruffin financed and edited (1890–97) *Women's Era,* a monthly paper that emphasized the necessity of women's active participation in striving for racial justice (Rothman, "Hear Us"). *Women's Era* was "the first newspaper in America created by and for Black women" (S. Wilson 33) (see Ruffin T8).

Now, before we attempt Part III, our last lap, let's consider selecting a spot to get a snack and rest—perhaps even within the National Historic Landmark, the Charles Street Meeting House at the corner of Charles and Mt. Vernon Sts. A cup of coffee, a sandwich, or an ice cream may help us assess whether we have the stamina to tackle our final, shortest circuit, which rambles a bit from the straight before we reach our respite in the Public Garden.

PART III. From the Charles Street Meeting House to the Public Garden, but not as the bird flies

For those who have revived sufficiently to rekindle a yen for discovery, we'll take a closer look at

69. **The Charles Street Meeting House** (1807), 70 Charles St., by Asher Benjamin; formerly the Third Baptist Church; subsequently the African Methodist Episcopal Church (1876) (see p. 135)

This splendid historic Asher Benjamin building (1807), now a shell of its former self with shops and offices within, plays a role in William Dean Howells's *An Impera-*

tive Duty (1892) when Rhoda Aldgate discovers that she has African American blood and comes to worship with the free African Americans who used this building as a church. Frederick Douglass once spoke here,[35] as did Harriet Tubman (see Charles Street Meeting House T7; Tubman T8).

Turn right onto Mt. Vernon St. and walk along the flat end of the street. About half a block down on the right-hand side we find

70. **131 Mt. Vernon St.**

"It is a very pleasant little house in a most convenient situation for housekeeping and for father," wrote Alice James (1848–92) about 131 Mt. Vernon in the spring of 1882 (quoted by Strouse 203). Henry James, Sr., had moved here with his daughter "to the heart of the bookstore district" (Lewis 340). On New Year's Eve, during the winter of 1882–83, Henry James, Jr., arrived here in the late evening, having traveled posthaste from England. He had missed his father's funeral by just half a day. That same evening James left No. 131 and sought his father's wintry grave in Cambridge Cemetery[36] in order to read aloud a letter from his brother, William, which had also arrived too late. After addressing the elder James as "Darling old Father," William's letter read,

> And it comes strangely over me in bidding you good-bye how a life is but a day and expresses mainly but a single note. It is so much like the act of bidding an ordinary good-night. Good-night, my sacred old Father! If I don't see you again—Farewell! a blessed farewell!!
> Your
> William

At the corner of Mt. Vernon and Brimmer Sts. we find an architectural gem:

71. **Church of the Advent** (1879–83), by Sturgis and Brigham {Plaque inside honors

the memory of two founders of the parish: Richard Henry Dana, Sr., and his son, Richard Henry Dana, Jr., Sites 25 and 76}

The Episcopal Anglican Church of the Advent is a Victorian High Gothic treasure with a lovely stained-glass Nativity window inside the Brimmer St. entrance. In *The Puritans* (1898), Arlo Bates (1850–1918), who lived nearby (Site 73), refers to the Advent as "the Church of the Nativity" and describes its renowned musical programs and acoustics as "most elaborate, the very French millinery of sacred music" (318). The Advent still resounds with exquisite music (see Church of the Advent T8; Sturgis and Brigham T5, T12).

On the opposite corner we see

72. 44 Brimmer St.

This is the location of the home of the Brahmin literary historian and autobiographer Samuel Eliot Morison. The author of *One Boy's Boston, 1887–1901* (1962) reminisced about poring over the illustrated books in his grandfather's library, recalling that his cousin had given him for Christmas in 1894 Seawell's *Decatur and Somers,* which kindled his interest in naval history. "For that I bless Cousin Lily, albeit she was a Victorian of Victorians. She always dressed her hair like the picture of Princess Victoria . . . and she worked through all the English poets in her father's library, blacking out the lines in Byron and Shelley which she considered erotic" (15).

As we retrace our steps back to Charles St., we appreciate the intriguing personalities who were contemporaries of Boston's Victorian authors and who rival their fictional characters. We've met the "Grand Old Man of Boston" (Edward Everett Hale), "the most romantic figure in literary Boston" (John Boyle O'Reilly), "the Grandmother of

Boston" (Elizabeth Peabody), "Little Boston" *(in the persona of Oliver Wendell Holmes),* "the tomahawk man" *(Edgar Allan Poe in his role of critic), and finally the "Victorian of Victorians" (Morison's Cousin Lily). Nineteenth-century Boston was literally as well as literarily peopled with originals.*

At Charles St. turn right (toward Beacon St.). And at Chestnut St. turn left for our last brief, moderately steep trek upward to see three literary houses on the lower slope. On the right-hand side, just opposite the opening of West Cedar St., we find

73. 62 Chestnut St.

At the turn of the twentieth century this was the home of Arlo Bates (1850–1918), author, poet, professor of English literature at MIT, and editor of the *Boston Sunday Courier.* Lindsay Swift, whose scarce but reliable *Literary Landmarks of Boston: A Visitor's Guide to Points of Interest in and about Boston* (1903), points out that Bates, after the departure of Howells, was "the resident novelist of Boston life, especially of its artistic and Bohemian side" (9). In his late-nineteenth-century Boston novels, now out of print, *The Pagans* (1884), *The Philistines* (1889), and *The Puritans* (1898), Bates emphasized the provinciality of Boston's residents. And he observed in *Love in a Cloud* (1900) that it was "the moral duty of every self-respecting Bostonian to be . . . related to everybody who was socially anybody" (260).

Above West Cedar St. on the left-hand side of the street we find

74. 51 Chestnut St.

This was the home of the minister of Old West Church (T4), the Reverend Charles Lowell, before he acquired (Harris 52–53) "Elmwood," the family's country estate in Cambridge (see Elmwood T12 and note 6).

His son, James Russell Lowell, abolitionist, poet, author, and first editor (1857–61) of the *Atlantic Monthly,* began his poem "The Street" with words that anticipate T. S. Eliot's[37] "The Hollow Men":

> They pass me by like shadows, crowds on
>   crowds,
> Dim ghosts of men, that hover to and fro,
> Hugging their bodies round them like
>   thin shrouds
> Wherein their souls were buried long ago.
> (24)

Right above on the right-hand side of "crowd-less" Chestnut St. we see

75. **50 Chestnut St.,** a National Historic Landmark {Plaque}

Perhaps the most distinguished of Beacon Hill's nineteenth-century historians, the romantic writer Francis Parkman, settled here between 1865 and 1893. For over twenty-five years Parkman recorded his "vision" of the French in America with a series of books, beginning with *France and England in America* (1865). In his urban third-floor study, surrounded by books and Native American artifacts, he struggled against fierce physical disabilities to write the "history of the American forest" (Parkman, quoted by Brooks, *New England* 173). His first book, *Oregon Trail* (1849), which chronicles his 1846 summer with Native Americans, became a classic. "What he called 'the improved savage' was Parkman's favorite type," wrote the cultural historian Van Wyck Brooks, "delicate in his feelings and decent in behavior and also virile, natural, resourceful and strong" (*New England* 176–77). The Victorian author and journalist Lilian Whiting portrayed Parkman as "a magician who had devised the secret spell by which to conjure up the entire living panorama out of the buried past" (320).

Not far above on the left-hand side of the street is

76. **43 Chestnut St.**

This was the family home of the poet Richard Henry Dana, Sr. (1787–1879), an early critic of American national literature and a founder of the *North American Review* (1812). His son, Richard Henry Dana, Jr. (1815–82), known as "the sailor's lawyer" (Brooks, *Flowering* 308), wrote *Two Years before the Mast* (1840), an account that was a positive influence against the brutal flogging of sailors (see Dana Sites 25 and 71; T12). Henry Adams described Dana as "a man of rather excessive refinement trying with success to work like a day-laborer . . . he suffocated his longings with grim self-discipline, by mere force of will" (30), a description that Adams knew would apply to many Bostonians. Dana's failure to get a much-sought-after ambassadorship to England—in the tradition of Hawthorne and James Russell Lowell—suggests a declining cultural influence of American writers on political leaders.

We'll retrace our steps down to Charles St. and turn left. On Charles St. we follow the path of Robert McCloskey's (1914–2003) parade of ducklings to their home in the Public Garden in Make Way for Ducklings *(1941), a joy to children of every age. The entire mallard family, cast in bronze (1987) by Nancy Schön (b. 1928), may be found inside the gate.*

77. **View from the corner of Charles and Beacon Sts.**—"Hester Prynne's Thatched Cottage"

As we wait for our traffic-free chance to cross to the Public Garden, we recall that Charles St., the straight thoroughfare that stretches out before us now between the Common and the Public Garden, was once the irregular salt-mud shoreline of Boston's Back Bay.[38] Hawthorne set *The Scarlet Letter* not in Victorian but in Colonial Boston and described the setting of Hester's previously abandoned thatched cottage "on the shore looking across a basin of the sea [the Back Bay] at the forest-covered hills, toward the west" (57). Hence, the edge of the Common, Boston's Colonial shoreline, is the elusive location that Hawthorne had in mind for Hester Prynne's "lonesome dwelling."

Fatigue necessarily limits forays beyond the hill,[39] but Boston offers much in every direction for those in pursuit of Victorian writers. Let's cross now to the corner entrance of the Public Garden, a National Historic Landmark, to enjoy its inviting and restful surroundings.

78. The Public Garden (est. 1837—the year Princess Victoria was crowned queen)

After viewing the ducks in the Public Garden, both live and bronze, don't miss the statue (1913) of Edward Everett Hale (Site 8), the Grand Old Man of Boston, by Bela Pratt (1867–1917), to the left, just inside Charles St.'s main (central) cast-iron gate.

Sitting in the flower-bedecked Public Garden, we can enjoy the Swan Boats as we remember Miss Allston, in Margaret Allston's *Her Boston Experiences* (1899), greeting lonely Mr. Warren Hartwell as he sat facing "the lake where already the swan-boats had begun to ply" (162). "I had no idea," said Miss Allston, "that a Bostonian would do anything so plebeian as to sit in the Public Garden on a bench" (165). Class and social distinctions remain alive in Boston, the most British of U.S. cities (see "Victorian" Boston, Introduction). In *The American Politician* (1884) F. Marion Crawford recognized the social tensions of the Victorian Public Garden: "There is a smell of violets and flowers in the warm air, and down on the little pond the swan-shaped boats are paddling about with their cargoes of merry children and calico nursery maids, while the Irish boys look on from the banks and throw pebbles when the policemen are not looking, wishing they had the spare coin necessary for a ten minute voyage on the mimic sea" (281).

A Victorian voyage in a Swan Boat (1877) around the tranquil lagoon (1861) may be our choice for "the end" of our literary tour. Or we may wish merely to linger, collapsing on the shady grass. Yes, William Dean Howells's words ring true: "The great Boston authors . . . have left their inspiration in Boston. In one sense the place that has known them shall know them no more forever; but in another sense it has never ceased to know them" (*Imaginary Interviews* 25).

The closest T Stop is Arlington St. Its entrance may be reached by walking over the Victorian pedestrian bridge (1869), by William Gibbons Preston, in the direction of the equestrian statue (1869) of George Washington by Thomas Ball. Once through the impressive central gate to Arlington St., turn left and walk beside the Public Garden's decorative cast-iron fence until you reach Boylston St. You will see the Arlington St. T entrance ahead.

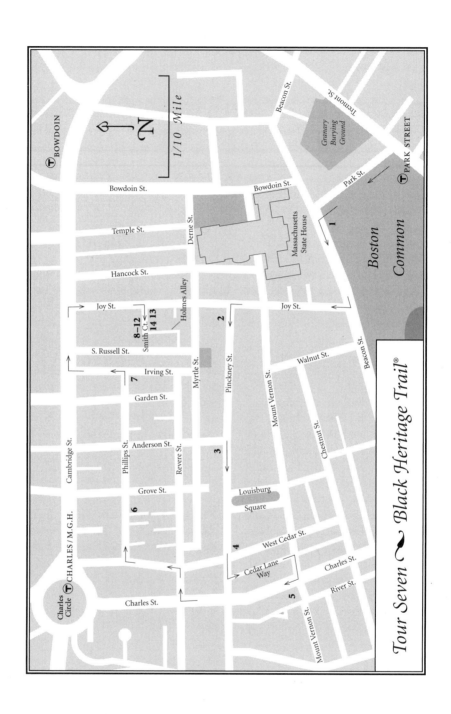

Tour Seven ∽ Black Heritage Trail®

BLACK HERITAGE TRAIL®

The Black Heritage Trail® concept was devised by Sue Bailey Thurman. The Trail was refined by J. Marcus and Gaunzetta L. Mitchell. This tour was originally researched by the Honorable Byron Rushing, Massachusetts State Representative, and edited by the Staff of the Museum of Afro-American History. The Black Heritage Trail® is a registered trademark of the Museum of Afro-American History, Inc., Boston, Mass., USA.

We express our sincere gratitude to the Museum of Afro-American History for granting us permission to reprint "Black Heritage Trail.®" The Museum of Afro-American History in partnership with the Boston African American National Historic Site offers guided tours of the Trail. Information: Museum of Afro-American History Administrative Offices, 14 Beacon St., Ste. 719, Boston, MA 02108; www.afroammuseum. org.; (617)-725-0022.

Tour Location: See Downtown Key Map for the location of the Tour and its T stop, page xli.

About Walking the Tour: Please Note: The historic homes on the Black Heritage Trail® are not open to the public, being private residences. Only the African Meeting House [see p. 140] and the Abiel Smith School [see p. 138] may be entered, because they are part of the Museum of Afro-American History. [At times this tour includes steep ▲▲▲ and moderately ▲▲ hilly terrain.]

Thumbnail Sketch of Sights: See Introduction, page xxxv.

Approximate Walking Time: 1½ hours; 1.6 miles.

T Stop: Park St., Red and Green lines; a central downtown T intersection.

By Car: Parking: The Boston Common Garage, under the Common, on Charles St. between Boylston and Beacon Sts.

Begin at: *The Robert Gould Shaw and 54th Regiment Memorial.* (Turn left after leaving Park St. T Station. Follow the path up the Common that parallels Park St. Before climbing the steps at the top of the path toward the gold dome of the Massachusetts State House, look at the back of the monument to your left. At the top of the steps, turn left before you cross Beacon St. The sculpture will be on your left.)

INTRODUCTION

The Black Heritage Trail® is a walking tour that explores the history of Boston's nine-teenth-century African American community. Between 1800 and 1900, most of the African Americans who lived in the city lived in the West End, between Pinckney and Cambridge Sts., and between Joy and Charles Sts., a neighborhood now called the North Slope of Beacon Hill.

The first Africans arrived in Boston in February of 1638, eight years after the city was founded. They were brought as slaves, purchased in Providence Isle, a Puritan colony off the coast of Central America. By 1705 there were over four hundred slaves in Boston and the beginnings of a free black community in the North End.

The American Revolution was a turning point in the status of Africans in Massachu-setts. At the end of the conflict, there were more free black people than slaves. When the first federal census was enumerated in 1790, Massachusetts was the only state in the Union to record no slaves [see statistics, by decade, showing population of African Americans in nineteenth-century Boston, p. 134]. The all-free black community in Boston was concerned with finding decent housing, establishing independent support-ive institutions, educating [its] children, and ending slavery in the rest of the nation. All of these concerns were played out in this Beacon Hill neighborhood.

1. **Robert Gould Shaw and 54th Regiment Memorial,** Beacon and Park Sts., Boston Common

Responding to pressure from black and white abolitionists, President Lincoln admitted black soldiers into the Union forces in 1863. The 54th Regiment of Massa-chusetts Volunteer Infantry was the first black regiment to be recruited in the North. Robert Gould Shaw, a young white officer from a prominent Boston family, volunteered for its command [see Shaw family home T6]. The 54th Regiment trained in Readville (in the present-day Hyde Park neighborhood of Boston). On July 18, 1863, the 54th Regiment became famous for leading an assault on Fort Wag-ner as part of operations to capture the Confederate city of Charleston, S.C. In the hard-fought battle Shaw and many mem-bers of the regiment were killed. Sergeant William Carney of New Bedford was wounded three times in saving the Ameri-can flag from Confederate capture. Car-ney's bravery earned him the distinction of the first African American to be awarded the Congressional Medal of Honor. A pho-tographic reproduction of the 54th's saved national flag is on display across the street in the State House's Hall of Flags.

For eighteen months of service, the 54th Regiment refused to accept a salary lower than their white counterparts. Ultimately, Congress relented and increased their pay retroactively.

This high-relief bronze memorial to Colonel Shaw and the 54th Regiment was erected through a fund established by Joshua B. Smith in 1865. Smith, a fugitive slave from North Carolina, was a caterer,

Robert Gould Shaw and the 54th Regiment Memorial (ca. 1905–15). Photograph by Thomson and Thomson. *(Courtesy of the Society for the Preservation of New England Antiquities.)*

a former employee of the Shaw household, and a state representative from Cambridge. The sculpture is by Augustus Saint-Gaudens, and the architectural setting by Charles F. McKim of the architectural firm McKim, Mead and White.

The monument was dedicated on May 31, 1897, in ceremonies that included Carney, veterans of the 54th and 55th Regiments, the 5th Cavalry, and several speakers, including Booker T. Washington [see Music Hall dedication T6]. The inscription on the reverse side of the monument was written by Charles W. Eliot, then president of Harvard University.

The sixty-two names listed on the lower portion of the monument are those soldiers who died during the assault on Fort Wagner. They were added in 1982 [see *Robert Gould Shaw Memorial* T6; 54th Regiment T1; see also J. A. Andrew T11].

[After viewing the 54th Regiment Memorial, cross Beacon St. toward the State House using the crosswalk. Turn left and follow Beacon St. downhill. Turn right at Joy St. and

climb the hill. At the second street, Pinckney St., turn left. The Middleton house is the third building on the right.]

2. George Middleton House,
5–7 Pinckney St.

Built in 1797, this is the oldest extant home built by African Americans on Beacon Hill. Its original owners were bachelor friends George Middleton (1735–1815), a liveryman, and Louis Glapion, a French mulatto hairdresser. Both Middleton and Glapion were members of the African Lodge of Masons founded by black educator Prince Hall [see Hall T3].

George Middleton was a veteran of the American Revolution. Honorifically called "colonel," Middleton supposedly led the all-black company, the "Bucks of America." John Hancock, in front of his house[1] on Beacon St., was documented by William C. Nell as having presented the company with a painted silk flag bearing the initials "JGWH," a pine tree, a deer, and a scroll bearing the name of the company. During the Civil War, Nell donated the flag to the Massachusetts Historical Society[2] where it is preserved today.

Bucks of America Flag (ca. 1776). *(Courtesy of the Massachusetts Historical Society.)*

Middleton in his old age on Pinckney St. was remembered by Lydia Maria Child:[3]

It became a frolic with the white boys to deride them on this day [the anniversary of the abolition of the slave trade, celebrated in June] and finally . . . to drive them . . . from the Common. The colored people became greatly incensed by this mockery of their festival, and rumor reached us . . . that they were determined to resist the whites, and were going armed with this intention. . . . Soon, terrified children and women ran down Belknap Street [now Joy St.] pursued by white boys, who enjoyed their fright. The sounds of battle approached; clubs and brickbats were flying in [all] directions. At this crisis, Col. Middleton opened his door, armed with a loaded musket, and, in a loud voice, shrieked death to the first white who should approach. Hundreds of human beings, white and black, were pouring down the street. . . . Col. Middleton's voice could be heard above every other, urging his party to turn and resist to the last. His appearance was terrific, his musket was levelled, ready to sacrifice the first white man that came within its range. The colored party, shamed by his reproaches, and fired by his example, rallied. . . .

[Child, quoted by Nell 26]

[Continue down Pinckney St. to Anderson St., the next intersection.]

The Phillips School. (Courtesy of the Boston Athenæum.)

3. The Phillips School, Anderson and Pinckney Sts.

This architecture is typical of nineteenth-century Boston schoolhouses. Erected in 1824, this school building was open only to white children until 1855; it was the English High School until 1844 and the Phillips Grammar School until 1861. The school was then moved to a larger building at the corner of Anderson and Phillips Sts. and renamed the Wendell Phillips School [see W. Phillips T6].

Before 1855, black children who lived in the neighborhood had to attend the school on the first floor of the African Meeting House or, after 1834, the Smith School. When segregated schools were abolished by legislative act [see Site 13], the Phillips School became one of Boston's first schools with an interracial student body.

[African American] Population in Nineteenth-Century [Boston]

Year	Number	% of Total City
1820	1,690	3.90%
1830	1,875	3.05%
1840	2,427	2.60%
1850	1,999	1.46%
1860	2,261	1.27%
1870	3,496	1.40%
1880	5,873	1.62%
1890	8,125	1.81%

[Keep following Pinckney St. downhill. The next site is on the left, after Louisburg Sq., at the corner of West Cedar St.]

4. John J. Smith House, 86 Pinckney St.

Born free in Richmond, Va., on November 2, 1820, John J. Smith moved to Boston at the age of twenty-eight. Smith went west for the 1849 California Gold Rush but returned to Boston no richer than when he left. He became a barber and set up a shop on the corner of Howard and Bulfinch Sts.[4] His shop was a center for abolitionist activity and a rendezvous point for fugitive slaves. When abolitionist Senator Charles Sumner was not at his home or office, he was usually found at Smith's shop. During the Civil War, Smith stationed himself in Washington, D.C., as a recruiting officer for the all-black Fifth Cavalry [see Site 1]. After the war, Smith was elected to the Massachusetts House of Representatives in 1868, 1869, and 1872. In 1878, the year he moved to this house, he was appointed to the Boston Common Council.

John J. Smith lived at 86 Pinckney St. until 1893. He died on November 4, 1906 [see also 62 Pinckney St. T6, T8].

Charles Street Meeting House (ca. 1860).
(Courtesy of the Boston Athenæum.)

[Follow Pinckney St. downhill to the next alley, Cedar Lane Way. Turn left and walk one block down Cedar Lane Way. Turn right on Mount Vernon St. and stop at the corner of Charles and Mount Vernon Sts.]

5. Charles Street Meeting House, Mt. Vernon and Charles Sts.

This meetinghouse was built in 1807 by the white Third Baptist Church of Boston. The question arose some time later as to whether this name was not strictly the property of the African church on Smith Ct. The name was consequently changed to Charles Street Baptist Church. The segregationist tradition of New England church seating patterns prevailed here. In the mid-1830s, they were challenged by one of the church's abolitionist members, Timothy Gilbert, who invited some black friends to his pew one Sunday to test the rule. Gilbert was expelled. Joined by other white abolitionist Baptists, Gilbert went on to found the First Baptist Free Church, which became the Tremont Temple—"the first integrated church in America" [see Tremont Temple T6].

John J. Smith. *(Courtesy of the Museum of Afro-American History.)*

After the Civil War, the black population of Boston increased considerably and the largest of its churches purchased this building in 1876. The African Methodist Episcopal Church (A.M.E.) remained here until 1939. It was the last black institution to leave Beacon Hill. Today the Charles St. A.M.E. is located on Elm Hill Ave. and Warren St. in Roxbury [see Charles St. Meeting House T6, T8].

[Turn right on Charles St. and walk two blocks to Revere St. Turn right and take the next left on West Cedar St. Walk one block and turn right on Phillips St. The Hayden House will be in the first block on the right.]

6. Lewis and Harriet Hayden House, 66 Phillips St. {Plaque}

Lewis Hayden. *(Courtesy of The Bostonian Society/Old State House.)*

Lewis Hayden was born a slave in 1816 in Lexington, Ky. After escaping slavery via the Underground Railroad to Detroit, he moved to Boston with his wife, Harriet, and soon became a leader in the abolitionist movement. In Boston, Hayden's political activities were based in the clothing store he owned on Cambridge St. and in his home here on Phillips St. (then Southac St.).

The house was built in 1833. Hayden moved in as a tenant around 1849. Francis Jackson, treasurer of the Vigilance Committee, a radical abolitionist organization, purchased the house in 1853, possibly to assure that Hayden would not be harassed in his Underground Railroad activities. (Jackson's estate sold the house to Harriet Hayden in 1865.) [See Vigilance Committee T6.]

In 1850, Southern slave owners were given legal sanction by the Fugitive Slave Act to retrieve their runaway slaves [see Fugitive Slave Act T6]. Boston ceased to be a haven for escaped slaves. Hayden and his wife, Harriet, turned their home into an Underground Railroad station. William and Ellen Craft, a fugitive couple who masqueraded as master and slave, were sheltered here, as were countless other fugitive blacks [see Jacob T6; Craft, Underground Railroad, Hillard T8; Tubman T6, T8].

The Haydens reputedly kept two kegs of gunpowder under their front stoop. They greeted bounty hunters at the door with lit candles, saying that they would rather drop the candles and blow up the house than surrender the ex-slaves in their trust.

Harriet Beecher Stowe visited the Haydens' home in 1853:

> When, in 1853, Mrs. Harriet Beecher Stowe came to the Liberator Office, 21 Cornhill,[5] to get facts for her "Key to Uncle Tom's Cabin," she was taken by Mr. R. F. Wallcutt and myself over to Lewis Hayden's house in Southac Street [now Phillips St.], where thirteen newly-escaped slaves of all colors and sizes were brought in into one room for her to see. Though Mrs. Stowe had written her wonderful "Uncle Tom" at the request of Dr. Bailey, of Washington, for the *National Era,* expressly to show up the workings of the Fugitive Slave-Law, yet she had never seen such a company of "fugitives" together before. [Bearse 8; Grimké 458]

During the Civil War, Hayden was a recruiting agent for the 54th Regiment [see also Douglass; J. St. Pierre Ruffin; G. L. Ruffin; recruiting for the 54th T6]. The Haydens' only son died serving in the Union Navy. In 1873, Hayden was elected to the state legislature. From 1859 until his death in 1889 he held the position of messenger to the secretary of state.

Harriet Hayden survived her husband. In her will she established a scholarship fund for "needy and worthy colored students in the Harvard Medical School" [see H. Hayden T8].

[Continue uphill on Phillips St. 3½ blocks to the end of the street. The next site is the last house on the right, at the corner of Irving St.]

7. John Coburn House
[1843–44],
2 Phillips St.

John P. Coburn was born about 1811 in Massachusetts and died in 1873. After working as a housewright in the 1820s, Coburn established a clothing business from his small house in the cul-de-sac off Phillips St. Coburn later commissioned Boston architect Asher Benjamin to design a house for his new property on this corner between 1843 and 1844. Coburn, his wife, Emmeline, and their adopted son Wendell lived here [see A. Benjamin T6, T9].

Coburn embraced Garrisonian principles in the 1830s and went on to become treasurer of the New England Freedom Association, a petitioner in the Boston desegregation campaign, and a member of the Boston Vigilance Committee [site 6]. In the last capacity he was arrested, tried, and acquitted for the 1851 rescue of the fugitive slave Shadrach. Later in the 1850s, Coburn was cofounder and captain of the Massasoit Guards, a black military company.

Coburn also established a gaming house here with his brother-in-law Ira Gray. It was described as a "private place" that was "the resort of the upper ten who had acquired a taste for gambling." John Coburn died in 1873. He left the bulk of his estate to his adopted son.

[Turn left on Irving St., and go to the bottom of the hill. Turn right on Cambridge St.; walk two blocks and turn right to climb the hill at Joy St. Turn right at the first alley, which is Smith Ct.]

8–12. Smith Court Residences,
3–10 Smith Ct.

The five residential structures on Smith Ct. are typical of the homes occupied by black Bostonians in the nineteenth century.

No. 3 was built in 1799 by two white bricklayers. It was a double house with a common

CAUTION!!
COLORED PEOPLE
OF BOSTON, ONE & ALL,
You are hereby respectfully CAUTIONED and advised, to avoid conversing with the
Watchmen and Police Officers of Boston,
For since the recent ORDER OF THE MAYOR & ALDERMEN, they are empowered to act as
KIDNAPPERS
AND
Slave Catchers,
And they have already been actually employed in KIDNAPPING, CATCHING, AND KEEPING SLAVES. Therefore, if you value your LIBERTY, and the *Welfare of the Fugitives* among you, *Shun* them in every possible manner, as so many *HOUNDS* on the track of the most unfortunate of your race.
Keep a Sharp Look Out for KIDNAPPERS, and have TOP EYE open.
APRIL 24, 1851.

"Caution!! Colored People of Boston, One & All." *(Courtesy of the Museum of Afro-American History.)*

Smith Ct. (1890) (left to right): **Abiel Smith School, African Meeting House, and Smith Court Residences.** Photograph attributed to John W. Robbins. *(Courtesy of the Society for the Preservation of New England Antiquities.)*

entryway. Black families began renting here between 1825 and 1830. In 1865, it was purchased by black clothier James Scott. William C. Nell boarded here from 1851 to 1865. Nell was America's first published black historian, a community activist and leader in the struggle to integrate Boston's public schools before the Civil War.

No. 5 was built as income property by a lawyer between 1815 and 1828. George Washington, a laborer and deacon of the African Meeting House, purchased the house in 1849. He lived in the upper part of the house with his wife and nine children while the first floor was rented out.

No. 7 was built sometime between 1802 and 1811. **No. 7A**, behind No. 7, is in Holmes Alley. No. 7A was built as a double house in 1799 and sold the next year to Richard Johnson, a mariner, and David Bartlett, a hairdresser. In the 1860s, black chimney sweep and entrepreneur Joseph Scarlett bought both 7 and 7A as rental property. In the nineteenth century, Holmes Alley had several houses similar to 7A. They stood where there are backyards today. Such housing development in the middle of blocks, with an elaborate system of pedes-

trian alleys, was typical when African Americans lived in the West End.

No. 10, next to the African Meeting House, was built in 1853 for Joseph Scarlett. Originally, it had two brick stories with another story of dormer windows and a pitched roof. Scarlett lived on Bunker Hill St. in Charlestown [see Bunker Hill St. location T9]. At the time of his death in 1898, he owned fifteen properties. He left bequests to the African Methodist Episcopal Zion Church, then on North Bennet St. [see North Bennet St. location T3], and to the Home for Aged Colored Women, then at 26 Myrtle St. (see map p. 130)

The brick apartment houses on the west end of the court and on the corner of Joy St. are typical of the tenements developers began to build in this neighborhood between 1885 and 1915. They were built to satisfy the need for inexpensive, dense housing units for the waves of post-1880 European immigrants to Boston. Usually wooden houses were torn down to make way for these four- and five-story brick "walk-ups" [see also inexpensive housing T3].

[The Abiel Smith School is at the corner of Smith Ct. and Joy St. The original school entrance was on Joy St., but visitors today should enter at the rear using the Smith Ct. entrance.]

13. Abiel Smith School, 46 Joy St.

In 1787, Prince Hall petitioned the Massachusetts legislature for African American access to the public school system but was denied. Eleven years later, after petitions by the black parents for separate schools were also denied, black parents organized a community school in the home of his son, Primus Hall, on the corner of West Cedar and Revere Sts. on Beacon Hill. In 1808, the grammar school in the Hall home on the northeast corner of West Cedar and Revere Sts. was moved to the first floor of the African Meeting House. Not until the 1820s did the city government establish two primary schools for black children.

The Abiel Smith School was named after a white businessman who left an endowment of $2,000 to the city of Boston for the education of black children. Constructed in 1834 and dedicated in 1835, the Smith primary and grammar school replaced the Meeting House School to educate a great number of the black children of Boston. Between 1839 and 1855 [during the early years of the Victorian era], Boston became embroiled in controversy over school desegregation. William C. Nell, once a young student of the Meeting House school, spearheaded a movement for the "day when color of skin would be no barrier to equal school rights." Nell's Equal School Association boycotted the Smith School.

In 1848, Benjamin Roberts attempted to enroll his daughter Sarah in each of the five public schools that stood between their home and the Smith School. When Sarah was denied entrance to all of them, Roberts sued the city under an 1845 statute providing recovery of damages for any child unlawfully denied public school instruction. Abolitionists joined the case in 1849. Charles Sumner represented Sarah and black attorney Robert Morris acted as co-counsel. The case was argued before [Massachusetts Supreme Court] Chief Justice Lemuel Shaw, one of the most influential state jurists in the country. On April 8, 1850, Shaw ruled that Sumner and Roberts had

not proven that Smith School instruction was inferior to that of other public schools of Boston [see L. Shaw T6].

Nell and his Association then took their cause to the State House. A bill to end segregation in public schools failed in 1851, but a similar measure was passed by the state legislature in 1855 and signed by the governor in April. This bill outlawed segregation in Massachusetts public schools although the only segregated system by that time was in Boston.

By the fall of 1855, black children were finally permitted to attend the public schools closest to their homes. The Smith School closed. The building was subsequently used to store school furniture and, in 1887, became the headquarters for black Civil War veterans. Today it is part of the Museum of Afro-American History, which presents exhibits and educational programs, and operates a Museum Store in this historic space.

[The African Meeting House is the large brick building on the left side of Smith Ct.]

14. The African Meeting House, 8 Smith Ct.

The African Meeting House is the oldest black church edifice still standing in the United States. Before 1805, although black Bostonians could attend white churches, they generally faced discrimination. They were assigned seats only in the balconies and were not given voting privileges. Thomas Paul, an African American preacher from New Hampshire, led worship meetings for blacks at Faneuil Hall. Paul, with twenty of his members, officially formed the First African Baptist Church on August 8, 1805. In the same year, land was purchased for a building in the West End. The African Meeting House, as it came to be commonly called, was completed the next year. Ironically, at the public dedication on

The African Meeting House.
(Courtesy of the Society for the Preservation of New England Antiquities.)

The facade of the African Meeting House is an adaptation of a design for a town house published by Boston architect Asher Benjamin [Site 7]. In addition to its religious and educational activities, the meetinghouse became a place for celebrations and political and antislavery meetings. On January 6, 1832, William Lloyd Garrison founded the New England Anti-Slavery Society here. In the larger community this building was referred to as the "Black Faneuil Hall." The African Meeting House was remodeled by the congregation in the 1850s.

At the end of the nineteenth century, when the black community began to migrate from the West End to the South End and Roxbury, the building was sold to a Jewish congregation. It served as a synagogue until it was acquired by the Museum of Afro-American History in 1972. Its interior has since been restored to its known 1854 design.

The African Meeting House and Abiel

December 6, 1806, the floor-level pews were reserved for all those "benevolently disposed to the Africans," while the black members sat in the balcony of their new meetinghouse.

The African Meeting House was constructed almost entirely with black labor. Funds for the project were raised in both the white and black communities. Cato Gardner, a native of Africa, was responsible for raising more than $1,500 toward the total $7,700 to complete the meetinghouse. A commemorative inscription above the front door reads: "Cato Gardner, first Promoter of this Building 1806."

African Meeting House interior when it was used as the synagogue of Congregation Anshe Lebawitz (1935). Photograph by Baldwin Coolidge. *(Courtesy of the Society for the Preservation of New England Antiquities.)*

Smith School are two of the Museum of Afro-American History's four historic sites, and are open to the public. Visit the Museum's Web site (www.afroammuseum. org) for updated hour and admission information or call (617)-725-0022.

[To reach a T stop, return to Park St. T Station by turning right (from Smith Ct. onto Joy St.) and walking up and then down Joy St. until you reach Beacon St. and Boston Common. (The State House and Site 1 will be to the left.)

[Alternatively, turn left and walk downhill to the Charles/MGH T stop. From Joy St. turn left onto Cambridge St. Walk downhill seven blocks to the elevated Charles St./MGH T Station. Note that Bowdoin T Station, although nearer, is closed evenings and weekends—and there are plans to close it entirely.]

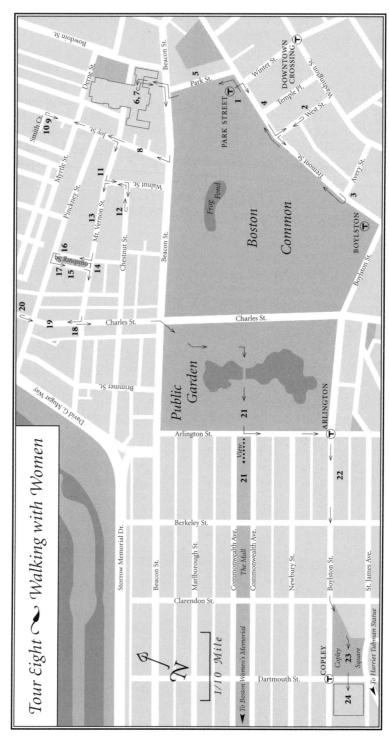

Tour Eight ∾ Walking with Women

N

1/10 Mile

To Boston Women's Memorial

To Harriet Tubman Statue

WALKING WITH WOMEN
IN VICTORIAN BOSTON

by Patricia C. Morris

Tour Location: See Downtown Key Map for the location of the Tour and its T stop, page xli.

About Walking the Tour: Our tour will consist of a walk through Boston Common to West St. We then proceed up to Boston's State House, visiting important interior sites, and tour Beacon Hill, at times negotiating steep ◢◢◢ and moderately steep ◢◢ terrain. Descending to level Charles St., we pass through the Public Garden and on to Copley Sq. During our walk with Boston's Victorian women we shall sometimes stop at the buildings where they lived, worked, or worshiped. At other times we shall pause at an address that is only a vestige of an original building that has been torn down in the cause of urban renewal without consideration of the significance it had to the story of women, Victorian Boston, or America. The lives of the Victorian women of Boston are a source of strength and survival and a reason to celebrate. Therefore, I have included their birthdays whenever possible. As you walk this route, remember that there are many other possible itineraries and countless other nineteenth-century Bostonian women whose stories deserve to be told. There are additional narratives to tell about the women of the North End, of the South End, and of each neighborhood of nineteenth-century Boston.

Thumbnail Sketch of Sights: See Introduction, page xxxv.

Approximate Walking Time: 1½ hours.

T Stop: Park St., Red and Green Lines, a central downtown T intersection.

By Car: Parking: The Boston Common Garage, under the Common, on Charles St. between Boylston and Beacon Sts.

Begin at: the Visitor Information Booth. Walk behind the Park St. subway exit and continue on the Common along the Tremont St. Mall (the walkway is parallel to Tremont St.). The popular Freedom Trail also begins at the Visitor Information Booth.

INTRODUCTION

This walk honors outstanding women and the work they did to make Victorian Boston and our own world a more decent place. As we shall see, there is, at long last, new public art that honors Victorian women, but until very recently the only two statues of women standing in all of downtown Boston were sculpted to honor women from the Colonial period of our history. We shall see these statues on our walk when we reach the State House. Anne Hutchinson was banished from Boston in 1637, exactly two centuries before the Victorian era began, and her friend Mary Dyer was hanged on Boston Common in 1660. However, in spite of Boston's scarcity of public art honoring nineteenth-century women, there are many inspiring stories to tell about Victorian women.

The route of this downtown Boston and Back Bay walk will give us the experience of walking the same streets and seeing many of the same buildings that the women mentioned in our tour lived in or worked in. Some had the help of fathers, husbands, and friends; some did not. Some married and had children; some did not. Most of the women actively created opportunities in their own lives and improved the lives of others. This tour does not pretend to furnish their complete biographies. Instead, it contains brief glimpses of their lives in their Boston context. The glimpses are presented to whet our appetite to find out more. Walking in the footsteps of the women who have shaped "our-story" reminds us that "his-tory" plus "her-story"

will give us a closer approximation of the whole story of Victorian Boston.

1. Boston Common

The Common has been a park and a playground for the city since 1634. If you stand with your back to Tremont St., with the Visitor Information Center on your right, you look into the Common where, in the Colonial era, women held spinning contests to demonstrate their willingness and ability to do without British cloth and goods. The Daughters of Liberty planned boycotts of tea and other household goods here.

Women have walked through the Common on their way to work at the schoolhouse, the poorhouse, and the State House. Some of the women who dreamed and schemed here during Victorian times include Louisa May Alcott (Site 15), who played hoops on the Common as a child. As she grew older, she worried about her mother's constant fear of eviction because her brilliant father, Bronson Alcott, could never earn enough money to give the family financial security. She also dreaded the whole grain, plain rice, and vegetable regimen that her family followed. Although this health food regimen was touted by Doctor Sylvester Graham, of Graham cracker fame, Louisa always hoped that some kind neighbor would slip her a piece of cake.

In addition, Ellen Craft (Site 10) crossed the Common to deliver her dressmaking orders and to watch for slave catchers trying to capture escaped slaves in order to return them to the South for ransom. Lydia Maria Child (see p. 97) walked through the Common to the Boston Athenæum at 10½ Beacon St. to do research for her books. She was only the second woman invited to use this prestigious library. She was "uninvited" when she exposed the racism in the North and wrote about slavery in the South. These are only a few of the women who lived and worked in Boston during the Victorian era. Thousands of women gathered on the Common for suffrage marches during the decade before and after the turn of the twentieth century. Victorian-born Florence Luscomb (February 6, 1887–1985) sold the suffrage newspaper *Woman's Journal* here. She graduated (1909) from the Massachusetts Institute of Technology (MIT) with a degree in architecture, but chose to spend her life in the suffrage, peace, and civil rights movements (see Luscomb, note 2). Nuns and nurses, political activists and prostitutes, social workers, "salesgirls," and servants walked through the Boston Common on their way to and from work or on a weekend outing.

Cross Tremont St. to West St. Walk about halfway down the street. On your left is No. 15, now a restaurant. This is the actual building where Elizabeth Peabody had her home and foreign bookshop. Step inside and read the plaque on the wall to the left.

2. **15 West St.** {Plaque}

Boston women walked down West St. on Wednesday mornings during the 1840s to listen to and participate in "Conversations" led by Margaret Fuller at Elizabeth Peabody's bookstore. These were "women only" sessions—"socials" that provided women with the intellectual stimulation and practice in debate they needed to argue effectively for women's rights and other social reforms in the coming decades. Con-

trary to the popular medical and educational opinions prevalent in the United States at this time, Elizabeth Peabody and Margaret Fuller believed that women could understand complex intellectual material and respond to powerful ideas. While the men gave sermons and speeches, Elizabeth Peabody and Margaret Fuller led "Conversations." In the 1840s it was rare for women to speak in public, attend lectures where men were present, or speak up for equal rights (see West St. T6).

Elizabeth Peabody, Mary Peabody, Sophia Peabody, and Margaret Fuller

If you attended kindergarten, then you have Elizabeth Peabody (May 16, 1804–94) to thank. Elizabeth Peabody relished her role as an eldest daughter. She often helped her mother open primary schools to earn the money necessary to support the family. She opened the first kindergarten in the United States in 1861. She and her sister Mary Peabody Mann (November 16, 1806–87) had long been proponents of cheerful, healthful education for the young, in contrast with the prevailing Calvinist belief in rigid discipline and lengthy memorization. She could be called the "Mother of Networking" because she was constantly bringing people together around a cause she believed in. Working into her eighties, she collected money to support the work of Native Americans like the Piute (also Paiute) chief Sarah Winnemucca (ca. 1844–91), who set up bilingual schools and worked to eliminate the cruel reservation system in the West (see Peabody; Winnemucca T6).

Elizabeth Peabody never married but was in "unreciprocated love" several times. All her life she assumed that she knew what was best for her family, her friends, and people in general. She would often help them, whether they wanted it or not. Her competence, energy, and generosity enabled many people to achieve the status, power, and money she never got for herself. She often forgot to sell books at the Conversation sessions because she was so involved in her ideas; her sisters and mother would encourage the ladies to purchase some reading material.

Among those she helped were her brothers-in-law. Her sisters were married at this address, in the parlor, behind the bookshop. In 1843 Mary Peabody, herself a well-respected teacher, married Horace Mann. He was to become the "Father of Public Education," and there is a statue of him on the State House (Site 6) lawn. Be assured he received considerable advice and support from his intelligent sister-in-law and his wife.

It was at 15 West St. that Sophia Peabody (September 21, 1809–71), the youngest sister and an artist, married Nathaniel Hawthorne, who was then brought into Elizabeth Peabody's circle of influential and helpful friends. Elizabeth Peabody helped Emerson, Thoreau, Channing, and others to reach a wide audience when she became the first woman publisher and bookstore owner in Boston. From 1850 to 1884 she herself wrote ten books and fifty articles and gave hundreds of lectures around the United States. Elizabeth Peabody lived to be ninety, never giving up her belief that conditions could be improved—for someone or some group—through personal action. When she was seventy-five she wrote to her sister Mary Peabody Mann: "In fact I had the success I almost always do have when I say anything to people who have faith in me for it gives me courage—I take part in discussions and when I read (my work) they say I can be heard all over the house, & I feel that I do say what I want to" (quoted in Peabody 388).

Elizabeth Peabody. *(Courtesy of the Boston Athenæum.)* Elizabeth Peabody was a teacher, an author, a publisher, a charter member of the Transcendentalist Club, a tireless social activist and the first woman publisher in Boston.

Margaret Fuller (May 23, 1810–50) was brilliant and she knew it. In fact, she said, "I now know all the people worth knowing in America and I find no intellect comparable to my own." Because she was the firstborn, her father educated her as he would have a son, encouraging her to be articulate and assertive. He regretted it during her adolescence, when he saw this would not help her fit into the accepted role of women. Subsequently, he sent her to be "finished" at a boarding school. There she learned to curb her willfulness—almost! When she was twenty-five her father died suddenly, and she became the head of the family. Always sure of her abilities, she taught school in order to support her mother and the family. In Elizabeth Peabody she met a woman who was as passionately interested in intellectual and spiritual growth as she was. They were the only two women who were members of the Transcendentalist Club, which met here on Wednesday evenings.

In 1844 Margaret Fuller became an influential journalist and foreign correspondent of the *New York Tribune*. While in New York, she visited hospitals and prisons to write about reform work. One of the correctives she suggested was "half-way houses" for discharged women convicts. At thirty-seven years of age, after an unhappy love affair, she traveled to Italy in 1847 to report on the Italian Revolution for Unification and became involved in the struggle. Later she fell in love with Giovanni Angelo, Marquis Ossoli, and had a child, Angelo Phillip Eugene. On her way home, just a few hours from landing in New York with her baby, Angelo, and the baby's father, the ship was caught in a storm and sank. Margaret Fuller died when she was only forty years old. She was a brilliant woman who questioned the unexamined assumptions of her day, a writer and activist for equality of the sexes, and a woman who constructed her life according to her own directives. "But what concerns me now is, that my life be a beautiful, powerful, in a word, a complete life in its kind. Had I but one more moment to live I must wish the same" (Fuller 177).

Cross Tremont St., return to the Common, and face West St. Look to your right; 174 Tremont (marked, at present, by the Loews Theater marquee) is the address of the school where Fannie Merritt Farmer learned to cook.

3. 174 Tremont St.
Fannie Merritt Farmer

If you have ever used a cookbook or followed a recipe, then you have Fannie Merritt Farmer (March 23, 1857–1915) to thank. Born in Boston, she was sixteen when she

Margaret Fuller. steel engraving by H. B. Hall, Jr. *(From James Parton et al., Eminent Women of the Age: Being Narratives of the Lives and Deeds of the Most Prominent Women of the Present Generation, Hartford, Conn.: S. M. Betts, 1868, facing p. 173.)* Margaret Fuller, a feminist and an author, published *Woman in the Nineteenth Century* in 1845. She led "Conversations" with her friend Elizabeth Peabody, both women intense "truth seekers."

contracted polio, which left her with a permanent limp. When her family suffered economic hardships in the 1880s, she hired out as a mother's helper. In the home of Mrs. Charles Shaw in Medford she learned to love cooking, and at the age of thirty she enrolled in the Boston Cooking School. After graduation (1889) she stayed on to become a teacher and later the principal. In 1896 she published the first cookbook to use exact measurements: *The Boston Cooking-School Cook Book.* She believed accurate measurements, such as tablespoons and cups, rather than an arbitrary "list" of ingredients, or directions such as "a pinch of," or "just enough to make the right consistency," would ensure consistent quality cooking. Considering it a risky venture, the

Fannie Farmer. *(Courtesy of the Boston Public Library, Print Department.)* Fannie Farmer was best known as a cooking teacher and the author of *The Boston Cooking-School Cook Book,* but she was most proud of her work in the field of dietetics, teaching how food can help the sick.

publisher insisted that she pay the publishing costs. The book became so popular that *The Fannie Farmer Cookbook* is still being published, and Fannie Farmer has become a household name. In 1902 she began her own school, Miss Farmer's School of Cookery (located at 40 Hereford St., Back Bay). Teaching the connection between good food and good health to doctors and nurses became the driving force of her work. Fannie Farmer was a pioneer in the science of nutrition. Dr. Elliott Joslin, famous for his study of diabetes, gave her credit for inspiring him in his work. Her passion to teach about the importance of good nutrition gave her the strength to overcome the effects of polio and, later in life, two strokes by continuing to lecture from her wheel-

chair. "I certainly feel that the time is not far distant when a knowledge of the principles of diet will be an essential part of one's education. Then mankind will be able to do better mental and physical work, and disease will be less frequent" (Farmer, quoted in Edgerly 90).

Turn to your left; walk back along Tremont St. toward Park St. and Park Street Church, where William Lloyd Garrison gave his first abolition speech. You are walking above the first subway system in the United States, opened to the public on September 1, 1897. Stop opposite the corner of Temple Place.

4. 140 Tremont St.

Known for its Beacon Hill and Back Bay clientele, the R. H. Stearns Department Store (founded in 1847) moved to this address in 1886. (Since 1977, 140 Tremont has provided housing for the elderly.) As in every era, women have worked both in and outside the home. During the Victorian era, the department store became a fixture in the United States. The women who worked in urban department stores were usually American-born, white, single, high school graduates, middle class, and needed to work to support themselves or contribute to the family income. "Salesgirls" often felt a certain prestige working in a store, even though they worked long hours, were constantly on their feet, and were paid barely enough to survive and keep up appearances. Though they earned less money, they often felt superior to immigrants and the undereducated working-class women who did physical labor in factories or domestic service.

In the Victorian era increasing industrialization and the demand for manufactured goods had moved more women out of the home and into the public workplace: stores and factories. In 1860 *Godey's Lady's*

Book, under the editorship of Sarah Josepha Hale (1788–1879), called the sewing machine, invented in 1848, the "Queen of Invention." A gentleman's shirt that took approximately fourteen hours to make by hand could be machine-stitched in an hour and a quarter. A lady's chemise that took ten hours to make by hand could be stitched in one hour. The manufacture of sewing machines led to enormous growth in the ready-made clothing industry. This invention coincided with the cheap labor available with the arrival of Irish immigrants. "In 1865[1] fully 24,101 women of native and foreign birth were employed in Boston as compared with 19,025 men. Apart from the 19,268 women workers in the clothing trade alone, there was a significant number in other occupations, including heavy industry" (Handlin 82).

Continue walking along Tremont St. Mall until you reach Park St. Walk up the Park St. Mall, inside the Common and parallel to Park St., toward the State House. You may want to sit on a park bench in the shade and read about some of the women associated with 5 Park St. when the buildings more closely resembled those to the upper left, such as the Union Club at 7 Park St.

In 1804 Park St. was originally designed by Charles Bulfinch, architect and city planner. Each building was of uniform height and design. Unfortunately, eight row houses have been torn down, and we now have only the addresses. Park St. calls out for some public art, perhaps sidewalk art, to honor the work that women have done here.

5. 5 Park St.

This is the former address of the New England Women's Club and the *Woman's Journal.* On February 16, 1868, the New England Women's Club began "to organize the social force of women of New England,

now working in small circles and solitary ways" (Hayden 87). Founded by groups of advantaged women, women's clubs were dedicated to reform. During the Civil War many women became part of the governmental system, however marginal, and women began to understand that political action was essential for change. By 1873 the New England Women's Club had four members elected to the Boston School Committee. Imagine the amount of coalition building and work that went into organizing a successful political campaign with an electorate that was totally male. When the elected women attempted to take their seats, they were denied. It took two more years to get enacted a state law confirming that women could serve on school boards across the Commonwealth. It was eleven years after their work began that women in Massachusetts could vote in municipal elections for school-related issues—the first crack in the apparently impregnable wall of male suffrage.

The women chose to rent office space here on Park St.—in sight of the State House—because they wanted not only to be seen but also to keep an eye on the legislature. They wanted to be seen and heard—to be taken seriously. They wanted a fair share in the power to effect change. This was also the address of the *Woman's Journal,* the weekly newspaper that was the national voice of woman suffrage for forty-seven years.

Abigail May and Caroline Maria Seymour Severance

Abigail Williams May, better known as Abby May (April 21, 1829–88), used the energy generated by her anger at injustice as a youth to fuel her lifelong dedication to education for girls. She was a cousin of Louisa May Alcott, and she was furious that her brothers could go to the Latin School but she could not. Girls High School had been closed in 1828, just two years after it opened; politicians felt it was an unnecessary expense and too many girls wanted to attend. It remained closed for thirty-three years. Abby May used the energy from her adolescent anger to power her determination to make sure that education for girls was a high priority on the reform agenda of the New England Women's Club (see also Lucy Stone, early woman graduate; Society to Encourage Studies at Home T6; Radcliffe T12).

During the Civil War Abby May worked with the Women's Auxiliary of the United States Sanitary Commission and was responsible for receiving and disbursing over a million dollars in money and supplies. Like many women around the country, she built on her war experience to continue public service work. She worked for the Freedmen's Aid Society and was an early supporter of Hampton and Tuskegee Institutes and other schools for freed slaves.

Abby May, perhaps more than any of the other founders, realized that it would only be through political power that women would attain any real influence. She sought a place on the School Committee to lobby for a public high school for girls, understanding that the personal is political. She became a single mother when she adopted her niece, Eleanor Goddard May, whose mother died in childbirth. Abby May was also active in the Massachusetts Society for the University Education of Women, founded in 1877, a forerunner of the American Association of University Women. She lived her belief that one person can make a difference, giving her time, her skill, and her money to the causes she believed in.

Caroline Maria Seymour Severance (January 12, 1820–1914) was one of the founders and the first president of the New England Women's Club. She spent almost seventy years of her life in reform movements. "She credited her marriage with freeing her from the bondage to authority, dogmas and conservative ideas" (Sicherman and Green III:266). At the club, women from the various reform movements would share information and strategies, support one another's causes, and present a united front to public officials.

Caroline Severance brought her interest in women's health to the New England Women's Club agenda. She had been inspired by Dr. Marie Zakrzewska (September 6, 1829–1902), a Polish immigrant who founded the New England Hospital for Women and Children in Boston in 1862. Caroline Severance influenced the New England Women's Club to sponsor lectures on health, anatomy, and physiology for teachers. The lectures were well attended and became the forerunner of what we now call sex education. The New England Women's Club supported physical education classes for girls and women's right to comfortable, healthful clothing.

Not every woman in Victorian Boston wore a corset in order to have a twenty-inch waist. As in every city, women came in all sizes, preferences, and styles; some women were slaves to fashion and some were not. Some women clung to the image of the frail, fainting female who knew her place, and some women consciously dressed for healthful, energetic, and comfortable daily living. Only a few Victorian Boston women were brave enough to wear the Bloomer outfit, a shortened skirt (about twelve inches from the ground) and pantaloons to the ankle. Although New Yorker Amelia Bloomer (1818–94) did not originate the style that was named after her, she praised and defended it in her temperance newspaper and wore it for years. In the 1850s the outfit provoked such hostility and harassment on the streets of Boston that it became unsafe for women to wear it in public.

Julia Ward Howe, Ednah Dow Littlehale Cheney, and Lucy Stone

Another of the founding members of the New England Women's Club was the woman who originated Mother's Day, Julia Ward Howe (May 27, 1819–1910). She moved to Boston in 1843 to marry Samuel Gridley Howe, a noted reformer (see J. W. and S. G. Howe T6). Her husband was nineteen years her senior, and although he admired her wit and energy before they were married, he later discouraged any active life for her beyond their home and six children. Julia Ward Howe wanted to live "intensely," and their disagreements over her "sphere" caused many a tempest. It was a stormy marriage at best. In the attempt to construct a fulfilling life for herself, she wrote, studied languages and religion, and left Samuel for a while. When her poem "The Battle Hymn of the Republic" was published and set to music in 1862, she became a well-known personality and thrived in that public role for close to fifty years.

Julia Ward Howe's appearance was often

Julia Ward Howe. (*Courtesy of the Boston Athenæum.*) Julia Ward Howe, one of the most prominent women of her time, was a popular lecturer, author, and suffragist. Today she is probably best known as the author of "The Battle Hymn of the Republic."

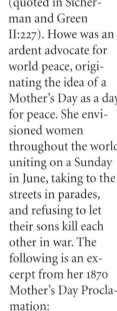

compared with Queen Victoria's and she was much loved, quoted, and interviewed. She used her name recognition to advance her goals of education and fair working conditions for women and for world peace. She lectured and traveled across the United States for the Women's Club movement well into her eighties. Of the New England Women's Club she once wrote, "One of the comforts I found in the new association was the relief which it afforded me from a sense of isolation and eccentricity" (quoted in Sicherman and Green II:227). Howe was an ardent advocate for world peace, originating the idea of a Mother's Day as a day for peace. She envisioned women throughout the world uniting on a Sunday in June, taking to the streets in parades, and refusing to let their sons kill each other in war. The following is an excerpt from her 1870 Mother's Day Proclamation:

Arise, the women of this day! . . . Say firmly, "We will not have great questions decided by irrelevant agencies, our husbands shall not come to us, reeking of carnage, for caresses and applause. Our sons shall not be taken from us to unlearn all that we have been able to teach them of charity, mercy and patience. We women of one country will be too tender of those of another country to allow our sons to be trained to injure theirs." (quoted in Richards, I:302–3).

Her design was quite different from the chocolates, flowers, greeting cards, and commercialism of Mother's Day as it is celebrated now.

Ednah Dow Littlehale Cheney (June 27, 1824–1904) was a woman who plunged into work in order to overcome grief. She traced her "awakening" to Margaret Fuller's Conversations. "To this day, I am astonished to find how large a part of 'what I am when I am most myself' I have derived from her" (quoted in Sicherman and Green I:326). Ednah Dow Cheney was widowed at the age of thirty-two and left with a baby daughter. She worked with Dr. Marie Zakrzewska for improved medical care for women and children and for the education of women as nurses and doctors. (The Dimock Health Center, the historic remnant of where they worked, can be seen in Roxbury.) She organized the Freedmen's Aid Society project to send teachers from Boston to the South after the Civil War. She was also a founder and a financial backer of the New England Women's Club and pushed for expanded career opportunities for women.

Ednah Cheney used her work to overcome the grief brought on by the early deaths of her sisters and brother and, subsequently, her husband and then her daughter, who died of typhoid in 1882. We are lucky to have the memoirs she wrote about the women she knew: Louisa May Alcott, Abby May, Susan Dimock, and Lucretia Crocker. She remained an active organizer and continued on the lecture circuit well into her eightieth year.

Lucy Stone (August 13, 1818–93) was the first Massachusetts woman to graduate from college (1847). Oberlin College in Ohio was the only college in the United States to accept women and African Americans at that time. In 1850 she was one of the leaders in calling the first National Women's Rights Convention in Worcester, Mass. She was the first to keep her birth name in a much-publicized marriage to Henry Brown Blackwell. They wrote their own marriage contract in protest of the existing legal system that denied women the right to own or inherit property, keep their own wages, or have equal say in their children's welfare. They had a marriage as partners and equals. He devoted himself to the women's rights movement, traveling, speaking, writing, and committing their financial resources to keep the weekly newspaper the *Woman's Journal* alive.

Stone's life was not just a succession of victories. In 1874, at the age of fifty-six, she wrote to a friend:

> I am so tired today, body and soul, it seems as though I should never feel fresh again. I have been trying to get advertisements for the *Woman's Journal* to eke out its expenses. Yesterday I walked miles to picture stores, crockery stores, to "special sales," going up flight after flight of stairs only to find the men out, or not ready to advertise. And for all my day's toil I did not get a cent; and when I came home at night it was to find the house cold, the fire nearly out in the furnace, and none on the hearth. . . . if only housekeeping would go on without so much looking after! (quoted in Hays 117)

However, Lucy Stone was a woman of perseverance. Early in her life she determined to find out if the Bible "really" said women should be subject to men as she was so often told in church and at home. Her father paid for her brother to go to Harvard College but thought it was ridiculous for a girl to go to college. In order to earn enough money to go to Oberlin College, she had to teach school for nine years. Women teachers earned half the salary of men teachers. At Oberlin she was the valedictorian and was invited to write the speech that a male graduate would deliver for her because it was not considered seemly for a woman to speak publicly in the presence of men. She refused! Hired by the American Anti-Slavery Society in 1847, she was soon reprimanded for relating the oppression of slaves to the denial of rights to women. Her reply: "I was a woman before I was an abolitionist. I must speak for the women" (quoted in Sicherman and Green III:388). And she went on speaking and writing for the women her whole life. Her only child, Alice Stone Blackwell (Site 23), continued her mother's work as editor of the *Woman's Journal*.

Lucy Stone died at age seventy-five, twenty-seven years before the passage of the Nineteenth Amendment to the U.S. Constitution (August 26, 1920) granted women the right to vote in all elections. A pioneer to the end, she was the first person in New England to be cremated. Her embalmed body was kept for two months until the new crematory at Forest Hills Cemetery in Boston was ready on December 30, 1893. This is only a glimpse at a few of the women who worked at 5 Park St. during the Victorian era (see Forest Hills Cemetery note 1, T11).

Continue walking up the Park St. Mall to the steps that climb to Beacon St. and the State House. On the south lawn to the right of the State House steps is the statue (1865) of Mary Peabody's husband, Horace Mann, by Emma Stebbins (1815–82). The entrance to the State House is behind the equestrian statue (1903) of Major-General Joseph Hooker (1814–79), figure by Daniel Chester French, horse by Edward C. Potter.

6. **The State House** {Regularly scheduled weekday tours; www.state.ma.us/sec /trs/trsidx.htm; (617)-727-3676}

Start in Bulfinch's Doric Hall. Just outside Doric Hall, look for the welcome new bronze medallion portraits of six Victorian women in the commemorative memorial *Hear Us* [2] (1999), by Sheila Levrant de Bretteville and Susan Sellers. Among the dedicated women represented, we have recently encountered Florence Luscomb (Site 1), become acquainted with Lucy Stone (Site 5), and will soon meet Dorothea Dix (Site 7) and Josephine St. Pierre Ruffin (Site 20).
Walk to nearby Nurses Hall.

Nurses Hall

Here Bela Pratt's *War Nurses Sculpture* (1914) honors women, often untrained and unpaid, who served during the Civil War as nurses to help ease the suffering of the soldiers. Although it reminds us of Louisa May Alcott's service as an army nurse during the Civil War and the publication of her *Hospital Sketches* (1863), it honors Civil War nurses as a group, rather than being a statue dedicated to a single Victorian woman.

Now proceed to the Senate Chamber (third floor, under the Bulfinch dome). Called by the close of the nineteenth century "Old Representatives' Hall," this hall was used as the House Chamber until 1898. Petitions and hearings were held here before the Massachusetts House of Representatives.

7. **Senate Chamber** ("Old Representatives' Hall")
Angelina Grimké, Sarah Grimké, and Dorothea Dix

It was within these chambers for over fifty years that women continued to submit petitions with the signatures of tens of thousands of citizens who wanted women to have the right to vote. It was here, on the afternoon of Wednesday, February 21, 1838, that a woman first spoke to a committee of the Legislature—the first time any woman spoke to a legislative group. Because her sister Sarah Grimké (November 26, 1792–1873) was sick, Angelina Grimké (February 20, 1805–79) delivered the oration on the abolition of slavery and connected the freedom of slaves to the demand for equal rights for women.

I stand before you as a citizen, on behalf of the twenty thousand women of Massachusetts whose names are enrolled on petitions which have been submitted to the Legislature. . . . These petitions relate to the great and solemn subject of slavery. . . . I hold, Mr. Chairman, that American women have to do with this subject, not only because it is moral and religious, but because it is political, inasmuch as we are citizens of this republic and as such our honor, happiness and well being are bound up in its politics, government and laws. (quoted in Lerner 7)

The Grimké sisters grew up on a slaveholding plantation in South Carolina. They left their family and moved to Philadelphia to escape any participation in the slave system. They became actively involved in the abolition movement and were able to speak and write from personal experience of the many evils of slavery. Hired by the American Anti-Slavery Society, they began speaking to ladies in churches and private parlors. In June 1837, at the inception of the Victorian era, over 550 women had subscribed to their New England lecture series. Their popularity grew; men started to attend the lectures. This caused a furor in New England, and the Congregational Church issued a pastoral letter warning all of the

Representatives' Hall (1856), looking south, a speaker's view. *(From Alfred Seelye Roer, The Old Representatives' Hall, 1798–1895: An Address Delivered before the Massachusetts House of Representatives, January 2, 1895, Boston: Wright and Potter, facing p. 39; Charles A. Phelps is the speaker illustrated.)* Angelina Grimké was the first woman to address a U.S. legislative body when in 1838 she delivered an oration on the abolition of slavery in Old Representatives' Hall.

dire consequences of women's moving out of their "proper sphere" of dependence. The Grimkés urged women to work for full participation in the political process and change the laws by which they were governed.

Although Sarah Grimké never married, she always had a home with her married sister and was a beloved aunt. She felt the pain and limitation of the prevailing system of limited access for women. She wrote: "Had I received the education I craved and been bred to the profession of the law, I might have been a useful member of society, and instead of myself and my property being taken care of, I might have been a protector of the helpless" (quoted in Lerner 21).

In 1838 Angelina Grimké married another abolitionist, Theodore Weld. They had five children. She was often in poor health, and Sarah became the children's co-mother. The Grimké sisters were well known for their many abolitionist and women's rights pamphlets and lectures. They continued to be involved in educational reform movements, health innovations, and the utopian communities so popular in Victorian times. In 1864 they moved to Hyde Park, Mass. The sisters were informed of the existence of two African American adult nephews, offspring of their brother and a slave woman. The aunts acknowledged, welcomed, and supported the young men, helping them attend Harvard Law School and the Theological Seminary at Princeton.

Dorothea Dix (April 4, 1802–87), the woman largely responsible for getting the mentally ill out of jails and into mental hospitals, also came to the Massachusetts Legislature. She did not find her life's work until she was thirty-nine years old. At twelve Dorothea Dix ran away from a troublesome home to her grandmother in Boston. She became a teacher, but exhaustion and burnout caused a "nervous and physical breakdown." In March 1841 this frail woman agreed to teach Sunday school at the Women's Jail in Cambridge. While she listened to the stories of the confined women, she saw "lunatics" chained and shivering with cold. She heard their pitiful cries and determined to do something. Her initial investigations found that there were few humane facilities available near Boston and that the best treatment was reserved for those who could afford to pay.

Dorothea Dix wanted to provide intelligent care for the mentally ill and initiate prison reform. Her life's work began. She visited every jail and poorhouse in Massachusetts, traveling in horse-drawn carriages in all kinds of weather. For eighteen months she scrupulously documented conditions. Influential men such as William Ellery Channing and Samuel Gridley Howe supported her work and presented her evidence and recommendations to the Massachusetts Legislature in January 1843.

"I come to place before the legislature of Massachusetts the condition of the miserable, the desolate, the outcast" (Dix, quoted in Sicherman and Green I:487). No one could argue with Dix's facts, for her research was impeccable. The legislature appropriated money to expand the mental hospital in Worcester to meet the needs of the many people who were "confined . . . in cages, closets, cellars, stalls, pens! Chained naked,

Dorothea Dix. Portrait by Seth Wells Cheney. *(Courtesy of the Boston Athenæum.)* Dorothea Dix was a teacher before she devoted her life to social reform and especially to improving conditions for the mentally ill.

beaten with rods, and lashed into obedience" (Dix, quoted in Sicherman and Green I:487). She took her crusade across the country, changing the minds and hearts and attitudes of the general public and the state legislatures. "In 1843 there were thirteen mental hospitals in the United States, by 1880 [there were] 123" (489).

It was to Boston's State House (see p. xlv) that women and men came, throughout the Victorian era, to plead for the mentally ill, the poor, children, and all those who needed state government to use the political process to create a decent life for all citizens.

While on the third floor, look also into the hall that became the "new" House of Representatives chambers in 1898.

Leave the State House and face the Common and the Augustus Saint-Gaudens Robert Gould Shaw and the 54th Regiment Memorial *(see p. 133).*

Turn right; walk along Beacon St. heading down Beacon Hill. The first building on the right is the Unitarian Universalist Association's National Headquarters. It was Unitarian women who formed the Woman's Auxiliary Conference,[3] in 1880, with Abby May (Site 5) as the first president.

Take the first right at Joy St. As you walk up the hill, observe the brick homes on the left.

8. Joy St.

A series of homes on Joy St. were built in 1832–34, before modern plumbing and lighting. Servants continued to be a necessity of life in these homes. It would not have beeen unusual for a Victorian home to have Irish maids, a French governess, a kitchen staff that prepared food on the basement level, a coach driver, and a handyman. Seasonal workers like seamstresses and chimney sweeps would be brought in several times a year. "By 1850, at a conservative

estimate, 2,227 Irish girls and women worked as domestic servants in Boston" (Handlin 61). Sometimes they were praised for their good spirits, loyalty, and cheap wages; other times they were feared and avoided because of their outspokenness and fierce tempers. Louisa May Alcott wrote warnings to friends about the dangers of Irish help. The meager but steady wages of Irish maids went to ease the poverty and starvation of families back in Ireland or to their families here in Boston and to support the increasing number of Catholic churches said by some to be built on the "nickels and dimes of serving girls" (see Joy St. T6).

Continue up hill along Joy St., passing Mount Vernon St. We will return here and walk down Mt. Vernon to Charles St. later. Stop at Pinckney St.

Pinckney St. was once the color line on Beacon Hill. More whites lived on the left (south), more African Americans lived on the right (north). Look down Pinckney St. Louisa May Alcott (see p. 116) lived in No. 20 in rented rooms with her family. It was on this street in 1861 that Elizabeth Peabody opened her first officially named kindergarten in the United States. Several houses on this street were part of the Underground Railroad. At No. 62, Mrs. Hillard may have hidden runaway slaves, unknown to her husband, George S. Hillard.[4] He was, for a time, a U.S. commissioner whose job it was to issue arrest warrants to slave catchers (Mayard 138) (see Pinckney St. T6, T7).

Continue down Joy St.

9. Abiel Smith School (1834), 46 Joy St.

This 1834 school building (see p. 138) on the corner of Joy St. and Smith Ct., now the administrative office and shop for the African Meeting House, was built in Boston for African American children. It took years of court cases and a legacy from Abiel Smith to build this public school for the African American children of Victorian Boston. The court cases continue right into our own day over equal opportunity. Some work never gets done (see Abiel Smith School T7).

Turn left after 46 Joy St. into Smith Ct.

10. **African Meeting House,** 8 Smith Ct.
{Check current hours and tours; www. afroammuseum.org; (617)-725-0022}

The African Meeting House (see p. 140) was built in 1804 by free African-American women and men, a community that could not afford to condone sex-stereotyped work. They needed to rely on all the skills of all the people.

Maria W. Stewart, Ellen Craft, and Harriet Hayden

The African Meeting House was the home of the political and religious community of Maria (pronounced Ma-rye-ah) W. Stewart, the first U.S.–born woman to speak on a public platform about political issues. She spoke to a "promiscuous audience"—men and women in the same hall. On the eve of the Victorian era, in 1832–33, she delivered four public lectures, using the Bible to preach on issues of slavery, racism, and sexism. Maria Stewart related the oppression of free African Americans and slaves to the oppression of women. Comparing these ideas was not popular and eventually she was asked to find another community.

"How long shall the fair daughters of Africa be compelled to bury their minds and talents beneath a load of iron pots and kettles? Until union, knowledge and love begin to flow among us. How long shall a mean set of men flatter us with their smiles and enrich themselves with our hard earnings, their wives' fingers sparkling with

rings, and they themselves laughing at our folly?" (Stewart, quoted by Richardson 75).

Maria W. Stewart (1803–79) was born to free African Americans but orphaned at five and "bound out" to a minister. This meant that she was a ward and servant to his family until she reached maturity at age fifteen. When she was twenty-three she was living in Boston and just married to James W. Stewart, a prosperous sailor's outfitter. Sailors often bought used clothing before they shipped out for a tour of duty and sold it for ready cash when they returned to port. The Stewarts furthered the cause of abolition by stuffing the pockets of the gear with abolition tracts and literature, which would then circulate worldwide. James Stewart died just three years after their marriage, and unscrupulous business partners defrauded Maria Stewart out of a considerable inheritance from his share of a thriving business. In order to support herself, she began her career of writing, public speaking, and teaching.

"Knowledge is power" was one of her refrains as she urged her people to take legal and political action to improve their condition. Her own community was angered that a woman presumed to tell them, quite forcefully, about equality for women as well as for African Americans. Later in life she sued the executors of her husband's estate and won. With the financial settlement she republished her speeches and writings, which are still available in the shop at the African Meeting House (see African Meeting House T6, T7).

In 1848 a young couple, newly escaped from slavery in Georgia, arrived in Boston and came to the African Meeting House to tell their story and begin their life of freedom. Ellen Craft (ca. 1826–ca. 1897) and her husband, William, after "jumping the broom" in a slave marriage ceremony, decided they would never have children in slavery and began to plot their escape. Ellen was the child of the plantation owner and a slave mother. Because she was light skinned she passed as a sickly white man in top hat and tails. Her face wrapped in a muffler, she coughed and appeared to be contagious. A sling on her arm hid the fact that she could not write, and dark glasses "hid the fear in my eyes." Her husband accompanied her in a daring escape on trains, in hotels, and on a steamer during their route to Philadelphia. They lived in Boston for only two years, until their notoriety made them targets of the slave catchers who worked for the bounty given for the return of fugitives (see the handbill on p. 137). The Crafts moved to England, had five children, and worked in a school before returning to United States after the Civil War to open a school for freed people.

Women like Harriet Hayden (ca. 1816–ca. 1893), whose homes were stops on the Underground Railroad, made room in their homes and their lives for escaped slaves. If you have made room in your home for overnight guests, you know the amount of work involved: the laundry, the food, and the change in family dynamics. Women like Harriet Hayden companioned the newly arrived through the difficult time of finding work and housing, and adjusting to the new and often strange cultural, economic, political, educational, religious, and community life of Victorian Boston. The work of these women needs to be honored and named as surely as the work of their husbands (see Hayden, Underground Railroad T7).

Retrace your steps up Joy St., and take a right onto Mt. Vernon St.

11. The Nichols House Museum,
   55 Mt. Vernon St.

This building, attributed to Bulfinch, is open for tours. It is the only private house museum on Beacon Hill. {See schedule of tour days and hours; www.nicholshouse-museum.org; (617)-227-6993}

Rose Standish Nichols

Rose Standish Nichols (1872–1964) gave her house to be preserved as a museum for the purpose of promoting international understanding. She was a member and benefactor of the Women's International League for Peace and Freedom (a pacifist organization still in existence), which protested both world wars. The league looks toward a new world order that will support continuous mediation and eliminate the causes of war. Rose Standish Nichols was a landscape architect, wrote gardening books, was a world traveler, and founded and presided over the Beacon Hill Reading Club for almost sixty years. A single woman, she was accomplished in needlework and carpentry, samples of which can be seen in her museum (see Nichols T6).

We shall continue to descend Mt. Vernon St. However, in order to take a look at 13 Chestnut St. below, you may wish to make a detour left onto Walnut St. (involves a short, steep return) and a right onto Chestnut. If you have time, take a further short digression down Chestnut St (involves a moderately steep return). It is charming.

12. 13 Chestnut St.
   Mrs. John T. Sargent and Julia Ward Howe

Julia Ward Howe lived at No. 13 during the Civil War, when she was becoming famous for her "Battle Hymn of the Republic." The Radical Club also met at this address in the home of Mrs. John T. Sargent to discuss radical ideas, such as peace and women's rights. Julia Ward Howe, Lucretia Mott, Margaret Fuller, and other radical thinkers led discussions of their essays here (see 13 Chestnut St. T6).

Return now up to Mt. Vernon St. and turn left to descend. If you wonder why Nos. 50–60 on the left look so stunted, it is because of a woman. Hepzibah Swan (1757–1825), one of the original Beacon Hill Proprietors, put into the deeds of these carriage houses that they remain thirteen feet high. They were to accompany the brick bowfront houses she had built on Chestnut St. for her three daughters.

13. 83 Mt. Vernon St. {Plaque}
Elizabeth Peabody and William Ellery Channing

This was the home, for a time, of the popular Unitarian minister William Ellery Channing and his family. He supported the work of Elizabeth Peabody and Dorothea Dix and in turn received much unpublicized help from them. Mary Channing, his eldest daughter, was a student of Elizabeth Peabody. During the 1820s and 1830s William Ellery Channing and Peabody became friends and would often go for long walks around Boston to talk about education, philosophy, and religion—the issues of the day. As we learn in her letters, she would often hear large parts of their conversations in his Sunday sermons. Happy to know that the "great man" respected her ideas enough to use them, she never asked to be credited as a contributor, nor did she mention her part in shaping the ideas when she transcribed and published his sermons in the 1840s.

Elizabeth Peabody, who later wrote *Reminiscences of William Ellery Channing* (1880), wanted this new thinking to be available to the general public. Channing's sermons are credited with the rapid spread of Unitarianism in the United States and are still read in theology schools (see Chan-

ning T5, T6). Later we will come to a large statue of William Ellery Channing on Arlington St. Channing's influential friend Elizabeth Peabody would be a good candidate for a statue, too.

14. 92 Mt. Vernon St.
Anne Whitney, Edmonia Lewis, Harriet Hosmer, and Abby Manning

Anne Whitney (September 2, 1821–1915), who annoyed many Victorians with her short hair and independent spirit, was a celebrated sculptor of the Victorian era. When she was fifty-five she bought this house and had her studio on the top floor. For almost twenty years she lived, worked, and encouraged other artists and reformers from this address. Edmonia Lewis (July 4, 1845–ca. 1909) and Harriet Hosmer (October 9, 1830–1908), two other notable sculptors of the Victorian era, were her friends and often visited her here.

Anne Whitney's works number more than one hundred and reflect her commitment to the abolitionist movement and to women's rights. She studied and worked in Europe for several years after the Civil War. There she was allowed to work from live male models, a practice denied to women artists in the United States because of Victorian rules of propriety. Her bronze statue of Samuel Adams in front of Faneuil Hall is a cast of the marble statue in Statuary Hall in the Capitol, Washington, D.C. Her memorial statue *Leif Eriksson*[5] (1887), its subject standing in the prow of a Viking ship, looks toward Kenmore Sq. on Commonwealth Avenue Mall at the intersection of Commonwealth Ave. and Charlesgate (see Eriksson and Horsford T12).

In 1875 Anne Whitney won first place in an anonymous competition with a model of a seated Charles Sumner,[6] but when the judges opened the envelopes and discovered the winner to be a woman, she was denied the commission. Anne Whitney never again entered a competition. In fact, twenty-seven years after that competition, she completed the larger-than-life statue of Senator Charles Sumner that can be seen today overlooking Harvard Sq. in Cambridge, Mass. Whitney's companion of over fifty years was Abby Manning, a painter. They lived together in what was called a Boston marriage, an accepted lifestyle in which professional women shared their homes and lives with one another in intimate friendship. Anne Whitney lived to the age of ninety-three. You can see her portrait bust of Lucy Stone (Site 5) in Bates Hall in the Boston Public Library, our last stop on this walk.

Turn right. The residents of Louisburg Sq. (houses 1834–40s) own and maintain its private park. The statues of Columbus and Aristides were donated in 1850.

15. 10 Louisburg Sq.
Louisa May Alcott

This brick bowfront fulfilled a lifelong dream of Louisa May Alcott (November 29, 1832–88). She was able to provide this secure, elegant home for her father in 1885, after becoming a best-selling novelist. As a child she often worried about finances, the rented rooms, the boarders, the evictions, and the meager diet of her family. Her childhood experiences made her determined to take care of the family, especially her mother. Louisa May Alcott was the primary breadwinner for her family from the time she was eighteen years old. She worked as a seamstress, a teacher, a nurse, and a governess as she practiced her craft of writing. Always feeling pressure to work, along with the pressure of her huge audience and the financial demands of her family, she produced over 270 published pieces

Louisburg Square, west side. *(Courtesy of the Boston Public Library, Print Department.)* It was to No. 10 that Louisa May Alcott moved in 1885 with her father, Bronson Alcott, a respected educator and philosopher.

(Sicherman and Green I:27)—and all without a word processor.

Her time as an army nurse during the Civil War was cut short when she contracted typhoid fever. She suffered the effects of mercury poisoning used in the treatment as well as other ailments for the rest of her life. Constantly consulting doctors and alternative healers such as Mary Baker Eddy (July 16, 1821–1910), she sought relief from headaches, insomnia, depression, and rheumatism. Besides supporting her extended family, she was active in many women's reform groups, often giving readings to raise money for worthy causes. Louisa May Alcott was the first woman to register to vote in Concord, Mass. (in 1879), and tried to stir up the other women to the cause of suffrage. "I can remember when

Antislavery was in just the same state the Suffrage is now, and take more pride in the very small help we Alcotts could give than in all the books I ever wrote" (Alcott, quoted in Sicherman and Green I:31). Always bound to her family, she was born on her father's birthday and died at the age of fifty-five, on March 6, 1888, the day of his funeral (see Alcott T6).

16. **19 Louisburg Sq.;** formerly the mother house of the Sisters of St. Margaret

The Sisters of St. Margaret

No. 19, the first house on the square, was built in 1834. Some three-story houses with dormered attics had the dining room in the basement near the kitchen, with the windows looking up to street level. Until recently this was the mother house of the Sisters of St. Margaret, an Episcopalian religious community of nuns who came to Boston to staff the Children's Hospital, which was founded in 1869. The Society of St. Margaret is now based on Highland Park St. in Roxbury.

17. **20 Louisburg Sq.**
    Jenny Lind

No. 20 was the town house belonging to the financial manager of Jenny Lind's American tour, the intellectual banker Samuel Gray Ward (not to be confused with Julia Ward Howe's brother Sam Ward), and the site of the 1852 marriage of the soprano Jenny Lind (October 6, 1821–87), the Swedish Nightingale. The advance publicity campaign of P. T. Barnum, combined with Jenny Lind's enormously successful and profitable concert tour of the United States, helped relieve the stigma attached to women who wished to practice their art publicly. Jenny Lind was well paid and was an accepted star; up to that time women in theater and music had been slandered and ridiculed.

Jenny Lind. *(From Mary Caroline Crawford,* Romantic Days in Old Boston, *Boston: Little, Brown, 1910, facing p. 276.)* "The Swedish Nightingale" earned $3 million a year at the height of her career in the mid-1800s. She married her accompanist at 20 Louisburg Square.

At the time Jenny Lind's popularity as a singer was growing, the public seemed unable to tolerate a woman minister preaching. Harriet Beecher Stowe (June 11, 1811–96), author of *Uncle Tom's Cabin,* said, "If Jenny Lind can sing 'I Know that My Redeemer Liveth' to thousands and get paid, I don't see why Antoinette Blackwell can't say it." Antoinette Brown Blackwell (May 20, 1825–1921) was Lucy Stone's college classmate and her sister-in-law; they married the Blackwell brothers. She became the first ordained women minister of a major denomination in the United States. Antoinette Brown Blackwell lived to exercise her right to vote in 1920 and died a year later at the age of ninety-six.

Return to Mt. Vernon St. and walk down to Charles St. Cross the street. You are now on part of Boston's landfill.

18. Charles Street Meeting House (1807)
Sojourner Truth and Harriet Tubman

The land in this area was created from mud-flats in the early 1800s. In 1807 this meeting-house (see p. 135) was a Baptist Church next to the Charles River, which was handy for baptismal ceremonies. Many abolitionists spoke here during the Victorian era, including Sojourner Truth and Harriet Tubman. In fact, Boston's first full-body statue (rather than a portrait bust) to honor an African American woman and to honor a Victorian woman is the *Harriet Tubman "Step on Board" Memorial*[7] (June 1999), by Fern Cunningham, a stirring tribute to the escaped Maryland slave and courageous Underground Railroad "conductor," unveiled in the South End just seven months before the end of the twentieth century. The sculpture shows Harriet Tubman (ca. 1820–1913) leading five runaway slaves to freedom (see location, note 7).

Walk along Charles St., passing the side of the Charles St. Meeting House.

19. Charles St.
Annie Adams Fields, Sarah Orne Jewett, Isabella Stewart Gardner, Elizabeth Cady Stanton, and Lucretia Mott

As you walk along Charles St., remember all the unnamed women, mothers and maids, aunts, artisans, as well as the prominent Bostonian women who walked and shopped, visited, worked, and lived on this street in Victorian times. Annie Adams Fields (June 6, 1834–1915) (see p. 121) was one of the most brilliant hostesses of Boston in her home on Charles St. She had a genius for gathering the well-known and the about-to-be-well-known authors and

artists of her day at her dinner parties and salons. In her position as the wife of the prominent publisher James Fields, she often promoted women writers. As a widow for thirty-four years she lived in a Boston marriage with Sarah Orne Jewett (September 3, 1849–1909), the author of *The Country of the Pointed Firs* (1896) (see p. 122). Annie Adams Fields promoted temperance and became a philanthropist to Boston charities and an author in her own right (*How to Help the Poor,* 1883; *Letters of Sarah Orne Jewett,* 1911).

Isabella Stewart Gardner (April 14, 1840–1924), whose Charles St. acquaintances were numerous, was a friend of Annie Fields and Sarah Orne Jewett. In fact, Fields and Jewett "poured tea" (Tharp 133) when John Signer Sargent's portrait (1888) of Isabella Stewart Gardner (see p. xxx) was exhibited at the St. Botolph Club. A pivotal and persevering woman in Boston's nineteenth-century art and social scene, Gardner was known and often criticized for her flamboyant joie de vivre. She was, however, a dedicated member and benefactor of the Church of the Advent on the nearby corner of Mt. Vernon and Brimmer Sts. In fact, the lovely stone altar reredos—inspired, commissioned, and given to the Advent by Gardner—depicts so many women saints that it has been described as "a glorious feminist riposte to Boston's Puritan patriarchy" (Shand-Tucci 145). Gardner is celebrated in Boston for the creation of her delightful Isabella Stewart Gardner Museum[8] (1903); however, her support of numerous women, among them Sarah Orne Jewett, the poet Louise Imogen Guiney (1861–1920), and the artist Sarah Wyman Whitman (1842–1904), is not as well-known (see A. Fields; Jewett; Guiney; Whitman; Fields; Church of the Advent T6). Gardner, a close friend of Julia Ward

Howe (Site 5), was also a "member of the New England Women's Club [Site 5], whose catalog of causes—dress reform, election of women to local school committees, admission of women to higher learning (MIT particularly), and the establishment of college preparatory schools (such as Boston's Girls Latin School, perhaps the club's most enduring achievement) reads like a roll of honor of causes led and won by women at the end of the nineteenth century" (Shand-Tucci 144–45) (see Gardner in Introduction; and T6).

We know that Elizabeth Cady Stanton (1815–1902) lived on Charles St. as a young bride in 1842. She loved Boston and the opportunities she had to meet women in reform movements and enjoyed going to Elizabeth Peabody's "Conversations" (on West St., where we began our walk).

The family moved to Seneca Falls, in rural New York, solely to advance her husband Henry's career. In 1848 she poured out her frustrations to her friend and mentor Lucretia Mott (1793–1880) at a ladies' tea. The result was the Women's Rights Convention (July 19, 1848) at Seneca Falls, N.Y. This is generally seen as the start of the first wave of feminism in the United States.

Continue on Charles St. until you reach

Elizabeth Cady Stanton. Steel engraving by H. B. Hall, Jr. *(From James Parton et al., Eminent Women of the Age: Being Narratives of the Lives and Deeds of the Most Prominent Women of the Present Generation, Hartford, Conn.: S. M. Betts, 1868, facing p. 332.)* Elizabeth Cady Stanton, author and radical feminist, co-authored, with Susan B. Anthony and Matilda Joslyn Gage, the first three volumes of *The History of Woman Suffrage.*

20. 103 Charles St. Josephine St. Pierre Ruffin

Josephine St. Pierre Ruffin (August 31, 1842 –1924), who organized African American women, was of Native American, French, African American, and English ancestry. She lived here for over twenty years. When she was a child, her parents refused to send her to the segregated Boston school system. They initiated court action in 1856 and got the law changed.

She was a friend of Julia Ward Howe and Lucy Stone and was a member of the New England Women's Club. The mother of six children, she was also active in public affairs such as education, integration of schools, and other civil rights pursuits. Her husband, George Lewis Ruffin, became a lawyer, later a judge, and was elected to city and state public office (see J. S. P. Ruffin, G. L. Ruffin T6; school integration T7).

Josephine St. Pierre Ruffin worked with Ida B. Wells (1862–1931) to bring public attention to the horrors of lynching in the South. In response to the racism she encountered at the National Convention of Women's Clubs, Ruffin organized the Women's Era Club in 1894 for African American women. A year later she called for a National Organization of African-American Women's Clubs; at their first meeting, in Boston, she said: ". . . for the sake of our own dignity, the dignity of our race and the future good of our children, it is 'meet, right and our bounden' duty to stand forth and declare ourselves and principles, to teach an ignorant and suspicious world that our aims and interests are identical with those of all good, aspiring women. . . . We are American women as intensely interested in all that pertains to us as such as all other American women" (St. Pierre Ruffin, quoted in Agger 157).

Turn back now and walk toward the Public Garden. When you arrive at the corner of Charles and Beacon Sts., use the crosswalk to enter the Public Garden at the corner entrance. We are heading for the central Arlington St. gate in front of Thomas Ball's equestrian statue (1869) George Washington. *There are several paths to reach it; one way is to use the footbridge over the lagoon.*

21. The Public Garden and View of the Commonwealth Avenue Mall

Many of the charming statues and fountains in the Public Garden were sculpted by

Lucretia Mott. Steel engraving by H. B. Hall, Jr. *(From James Parton et al.,* Eminent Women of the Age: Being Narratives of the Lives and Deeds of the Most Prominent Women of the Present Generation, *Hartford, Conn.: S. M. Betts, 1868, facing p. 371.)* Lucretia Mott, a traveling Quaker minister, abolitionist, and pioneer for women's rights, was a powerful influence on Elizabeth Cady Stanton and other suffragist leaders.

Victorian-born women, such as the *Small Child* statue and fountain by Mary E. Moore (1887–1967) and the *Boy and Bird* fountain by Bashka Paeff (1893–1979), visible near the Arlington St. gate. Although at present none of the statues in the Public Garden were sculpted to commemorate women, an inspiring response to the need to include women in public art, the landmark *Boston Women's Memorial* (2003), by Meredith Gang Bergmann, is now located between Fairfield and Gloucester Sts. on the Commonwealth Avenue Mall, the first memorial to be placed there honoring Boston women. *The Boston Women's Memorial* is an innovative grouping of three women, First Lady Abigail Adams (1744–1818), the African American poet Phillis Wheatley [9] (1754–84), and the Victorian suffragist Lucy Stone (1818–93; see Site 5), each of whom left us a legacy with her writing.

Proceed through the Arlington St. gate, and look across Arlington St. for a view down Commonwealth Avenue Mall, the central pathway on the green between the two thoroughfares that make up Commonwealth Ave. The Boston Women's Memorial can be reached at the end of our tour by a 3½-block

jaunt from Copley Sq. (see directions from the Public Library, note 12). (From our present location, the memorial is a lengthy 5½ blocks west, on the mall between Fairfield and Gloucester Sts.)

If you look to your left now, you will see Arlington St. Church (1858–61), the first building built on the Back Bay's landfill. Facing the church is the statue, mentioned earlier, of William Ellery Channing (1902), by sculptor Herbert Adams (1858–1945) (see T5). At the corner of Arlington and Boylston Sts., cross Boylston St. and look for the building recently sold by the Women's Educational and Industrial Union at No. 356.

22. Women's Educational and Industrial Union, recently sold building at 356 Boylston St. {www.weiu.org; (617)-536-5651}
Harriet Clisby, Louisa May Alcott, and Julia Ward Howe

The golden swan is the symbol of the Women's Educational and Industrial Union (WEIU) because it was founded in 1877, the same year that the swam boats were established in the Public Garden (see 356 Boylston St. T5). An English woman, Harriet Clisby, M.D., and some of her friends and associates from the New England Women's Club, such as Louisa May Alcott and Julia Ward Howe, began the Union to provide career counseling to middle-class women, training for working-class women, and school lunches for "poor children." The Women's Educational and Industrial Union continues to help women at risk, such as young single mothers, battered women, and elders.

Continue walking along Boylston St. toward Copley Sq. to the corner of Berkeley St.

Ellen Swallow Richards

The Massachusetts Institute of Technology building (1864; nonextant, see T5) was located on the north side of Boylston St. (between Berkeley and Clarendon Sts.) behind the Victorian Museum of Natural History (1863, now visible facing Berkeley St.). Ellen Swallow Richards (December 3, 1842–1911), nicknamed "Ellencyclopedia," was the first woman to graduate from MIT, in 1873, and was the first woman faculty member, in 1875. Ellen Swallow Richards was a pioneer in the scientific fields of public health engineering and home economics. She was also a fund-raiser and established a Woman's Laboratory at MIT. In her model home[10] in Jamaica Plain, always open to students and friends, she got rid of heavy drapes and other "dust collectors."

23. Copley Sq.
Alice Stone Blackwell and the "Anti's"

In 1870 the water from the Back Bay still came up to Dartmouth St. The Back Bay was filled block by orderly, alphabetical block: Arlington, Berkeley, Clarendon, Dartmouth, Exeter, Fairfield, Gloucester, and Hereford Sts. Soon churches and educational institutions moved into this more stylish section of the city. The Victorian Gothic New Old South Church, built in 1874, the Romanesque Trinity Church, built in 1877, and the classical Boston Public Library, built between 1887 and 1895, defined Copley Sq. as the new religious and educational section of the city (see Copley Sq.; New Old South Church; Trinity Church T5).

Copley Sq. was also the scene of the final years of the activity of the woman suffrage movement. Alice Stone Blackwell (September 14, 1857–1950), Lucy Stone's daughter, moved the *Woman's Journal* here. Ironically, the "Anti's," or the antisuffrage group, also kept offices on Boylston St., just beyond the New Old South Church.

24. The Boston Public Library, Dartmouth St. {Tours, restaurants; use Dartmouth St. entrance; additional entrance 700 Boylston St.; www.bpl.org; (617)-536-5400}

Mary Antin (June 13, 1881–1949), an immigrant, arrived in this country from Russia in 1894, when she was thirteen years old. In her autobiography, *The Promised Land* (1912), she captured her experience of going to the Boston Public Library. She spoke for many, including your author, when she wrote of her hours in that "palace of the people": "[I] spent rapt hours studying the Abbey pictures [and] felt the grand spaces under the soaring arches as a personal attribute of my being. The courtyard was my sky-roofed chamber of dreams" (Antin 27).

Go into the library and rest in the courtyard of this palace. Anne Whitney's (Site 14) bust of Lucy Stone (Site 5) is in Bates Hall, on the second floor.

The Boston Public Library "integrates sculpture, painting,[11] architecture and engineering" (Southworth 226). It is an experience of the best of Boston's Victorian era (see Boston Public Library T5). Truly a "palace for the people" it is available to all, rich and poor, black and white, native-born and immigrant, women and men. We find few women's names[12] carved in the facade,

but now at the end of our walk, we have gained insight. We know which women's names should certainly have been included!

This walk shows us just a small sample of the abundant energy and diversity of women's work in Boston's Victorian era. Women and men worked on issues of equality, education, health, money and labor, art, and science in Victorian Boston —just as we do today.

The site of Mary Baker Eddy's Metaphysical College (1882), and the site she chose for the Mother Church of Christian Science (1895) (the original church is incorporated into the modern complex), are within walking distance of Copley Sq. along Huntington Ave./Avenue of the Arts (turn left as you face the Boston Public Library).

If you would like to visit the Boston Women's Memorial, *walk one block past Boylston St. to Commonwealth Ave. Turn left; pass Exeter St., then Fairfield St. The memorial is on the Commonwealth Avenue Mall between Fairfield and Gloucester Sts. (Alternatively, the memorial is 1½ blocks from Site 28 in T5). To visit the Isabella Stewart Gardner Museum, see note 8. For more information about women in Boston, see note 12.*

To reach the T, face the facade of the Boston Public Library. The Copley Sq. T Station is on the right-hand side of the library on Boylston St.

· P II RT ·

FROM DOWNTOWN BOSTON TAKE THE T TO THESE TOURS

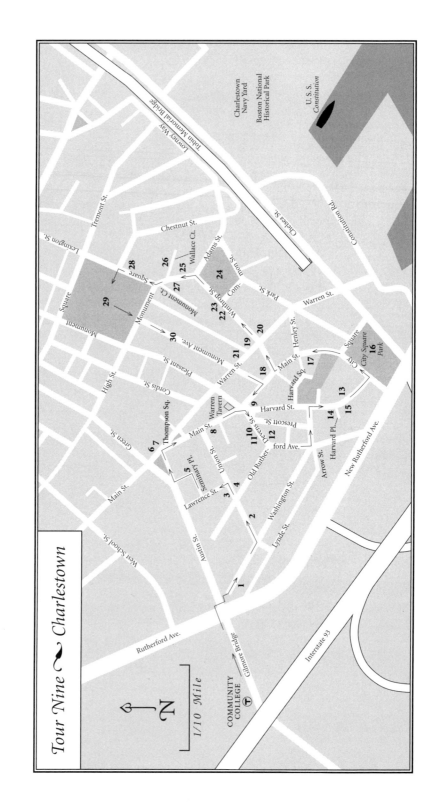

Tour Nine ～ *Charlestown*

N

1/10 Mile

COMMUNITY COLLEGE

Gilmore Bridge

Rutherford Ave.

West School St.

Austin St.

Main St.

Lawrence St.

Lynde St.

Interstate 93

Washington St.

Old Rutherford Ave.

New Rutherford Ave.

Arrow St.

Harvard Pl.

City Square Park

Square

Harvard Sq.

Henley St.

Harvard St.

Prescott St.

Main St.

Warren St.

Devens St.

Union St.

Seminary Pl.

Thompson Sq.

Green St.

High St.

Cordis St.

Pleasant St.

Monument Ave.

Monument Ct.

Monument Square

Monument Square

Lexington St.

Tremont St.

Chestnut St.

Wallace Ct.

Adams St.

Winthrop St.

Common St.

Park St.

Warren St.

Warren Tavern

Lowney Way

Tobin Memorial Bridge

Chelsea St.

Constitution Rd.

Charlestown Navy Yard

Boston National Historical Park

U. S. S. Constitution

1 2 3 4 5 6 7 8 9 10 11 12 13 14 15 16 17 18 19 20 21 22 23 24 25 26 27 28 29 30

CHARLESTOWN IN THE VICTORIAN ERA: FROM THE COMPLETION OF THE BUNKER HILL MONUMENT TO THE COMING OF THE MAIN LINE ELEVATED

by Edward W. Gordon

Tour Location: See Greater Boston Key Map for location of the Tour, page xli. See T Stop Diagram for the T stop location, page xl.

About Walking the Tour: The first part of the tour will focus on Lynde's Point and Thompson Sq. and then follow the gentle ◢ incline up Harvard Hill. We will move on to consider City Sq. in all its many incarnations—from its Colonial and early-nineteenth-century farmer's market, through its ornamental Victorian-era park, to the recent relandscaping associated with the Charlestown leg of the Big Dig mega-transportation project. The tour then meanders through the Old Training Field via Winthrop St., ascends a short, sharper ◢◢ ◢ incline to Breed's Hill, and skirts the western edge of the park containing the Bunker Hill Monument (1825–42). The tour concludes at the historic Warren Tavern, which has been serving food and drink since 1780.

Thumbnail Sketch of Sights: See Introduction, page xxxv.

Approximate walking time: 2 hours.

T-Stop: Community College Station, Orange Line; about 10 minutes from downtown Boston.

Begin at: the foot of Washington St. (From the Orange Line Community College T Station turn right, and you will be on the Gilmore Bridge, which becomes Austin St. Walk along Austin St. in the direction of the Bunker Hill Monument. Cross busy Rutherford Ave., and then turn right across Austin St. to the concrete steps leading up to the foot of Washington St.)

INTRODUCTION

Charlestown, Mass., occupies the peninsula located in Boston Harbor at the confluence of the Mystic and Charles Rivers, just to the north of Boston. Over time, Charlestown's original 424-acre land mass has nearly tripled in size because of landfill operations along its northern and (in particular) southern shorelines. Charlestown is dominated by two drumlins, Bunker and Breed's Hills. The former, at 113 feet, is the town's highest elevation. Charlestown, or *Mishawum* as it was called by Native Americans, was settled as early as 1625 by Thomas Walford. By 1629 Charlestown was more formally settled by John Winthrop and his party of English settlers. Thomas Graves, a civil engineer, was hired to set out streets at the eastern part of the town, just to the west of Market, later City, Sq. This plan is characterized by a distinctive semicircular arrangement of streets around the crest of Town or Harvard Hill. The tour route that follows meanders through this area of initial settlement.

Charlestown was originally intended to be the capital of the Massachusetts Bay Colony. Its territory once encompassed a large portion of Middlesex County, including the towns of Malden, Everett, Woburn, Stoneham, Burlington, Somerville, a large part of Medford and smaller sections of Cambridge, Reading, and Wakefield. During the Colonial period, Charlestown flourished as a seaport. Its citizens prospered in whaling, the West India trade, and shipbuilding. The town became a center for the manufacture of redware pottery, rum, loaf sugar, candles, leather, and potash. Tailors, tile makers, coopers, rope makers, glaziers, anchor smiths, and the like made Charlestown the principal industrial port in the colony during the first three-quarters of the eighteenth century. All of this commercial activity was interrupted on June 17, 1775, by the most famous event in Charlestown's history: the Battle of Bunker Hill.

Charlestown was burned to the ground by the British during this early skirmish of the Revolutionary War. Approximately 350–400 buildings were destroyed. Charlestown's population was reduced from two thousand citizens to only about one hundred townspeople. Reconstruction commenced during the 1780s and was facilitated by transportation improvements in the form of new bridge links with Boston (1786), Malden (1787), and the North Shore (Salem Turnpike, 1802), as well as the completion of the Middlesex Canal between the Merrimac River Valley and Charlestown in 1803. Additionally, the economy recovered thanks to the construction of thirteen wharves by 1785, the founding of the Charlestown Navy Yard (1800), and the establishment of a prison by 1805. By 1814 the town, with five thousand inhabitants and 670 buildings, had fully recovered from the vicissitudes of war.

Victorian Charlestown (1837–1901)

Charlestown has been essentially overlooked by historians and authors of tourist guidebooks intent on chronicling the sites associated with the Battle of Bunker Hill and the early years of the Navy Yard, the home of "Old Ironsides" (USS *Constitution*). The Victorian era, however, is colorful in its own right as a period of continued prosperity, a transportation revolution, and profound sociopolitical developments that would result in Charlestown's annexation to Boston. During the mid-nineteenth century, Charlestown's primary economic strength was as a port. Its waterfront was the focus of the ice trade made famous by Frederick Tudor, the "Ice King." Blocks of ice were cut from Boston area ponds, transported by railroad to the Charlestown waterfront, and subsequently shipped as far away as the Caribbean, South America, and Asia. By 1855 lumber and ice led the list of the products it handled, followed by the manufactures of Morocco leather, tailored goods, and baked products. At this time, two manufacturers of pickles and preserves, five furniture firms, and the Davidson Rubber Company at Sullivan Sq. contributed to the regional as well as local economy.

By the 1840s railroads had surpassed the Middlesex Canal as a fast and efficient mode of transporting goods. By the 1850s Charlestown had become the terminus for inland railroads with Boston Harbor and Charles River Bay wharves. The Charlestown branch of the Fitchburg Railroad was the first railroad line set out through the town and was followed by the Boston and Maine (1845) and the Eastern Grand Junction (1854). In 1875 the long-delayed opening of the Hoosac Tunnel in the western part of the state connected the Fitchburg Railroad with the great western trunk roads, reinforcing Charlestown's transportation-related status as "the Vestibule of Boston."

Between 1830 and 1870, Charlestown's population tripled in size, reaching 28,323 in the latter year. Population growth was encouraged by legislation that made Charlestown bridges toll-free during the early 1830s. Indeed, the construction of the *Bunker Hill Monument* between 1826 and 1842 called attention to the town, reminding inhabitants of surrounding areas that this was a desirable and convenient place to settle. On Bunker Hill during the 1840s the estates of the Adams, Kettle, and Breed families, as well as the land of the Bunker

Hill Monument Association, was subdivided to meet the demand for middle-income and upscale housing. Today, the brick- and stone-trimmed town houses of Monument Sq., Monument Ave., and High and Harvard Sts. provide physical evidence of Charlestown's early Victorian-era prosperity. By 1865, 22 percent of the population was foreign-born, of whom three-quarters were Irish. Charlestown's population growth resulted in its incorporation as a city in 1847. It was annexed to the City of Boston in 1874.

By the time of annexation, Charlestown's residential core had been almost completely built up. Interestingly, a Frederick Law Olmsted–designed park was set out over the real Bunker Hill's only remaining open expanse of rocky upland pasture during the 1890s. Commercial expansion at the town's periphery, however, continued to be a factor in Charlestown's development. Industrial concerns were developed along the shores of the Mystic River and on land created from filling in Miller's River on the southwestern side of the town. The Mystic shores were built up with rail and lumberyards, storage facilities, a gas company, and a varnish factory during the last quarter of the nineteenth century. The landfill on the south side of Sullivan Sq., formerly part of the old Mill Pond and Miller's River, was built up with a brewery and complexes concerned with the manufacture of mustard, steam gauges, and valves.

The close of the Victorian era coincides with a transportation development that would radically transform the appearance of Charlestown. Beginning in 1901, the construction of the Boston Elevated Railroad through Charlestown to Sullivan Sq., terminating in Everett, resulted in the obliteration of City and Sullivan Sqs.' charming Victorian parks and cast the entire length

of Main St. in shadows. The coming of this line attracted large numbers of working-class people, hastening the transformation of Charlestown from a neighborhood of single- and two-family homes to a quarter of apartments and boardinghouses. By 1910 Charlestown, with a peak population of 41,444, was 90 percent Irish.

After the turn of the century, Charlestown, like Boston, suffered a reduction of maritime activities, with only a brief return to economic vitality during World War II. After the war the Charlestown Navy Yard ceased to be a hive of activity and was finally shut down in 1974 by the federal government. The Navy Yard, once Charlestown's largest employer, was partly transformed into a historic park operated by the National Park Service, with the remaining portion sold for commercial and residential purposes. During the late 1960s and early 1970s, Charlestown's antique charm was discovered by young professionals and their families, who restored a number of its historic residences to their original glory. To a great degree, Charlestown is still an Irish-American enclave whose residents have a strong orientation to family and the Roman Catholic Church. The elevated train was closed in 1975 and taken down soon afterward, which helped to encourage the rediscovery of this historic neighborhood. The Central Artery (Big Dig) project, involving the demolition of elevated highways and the construction of a six-lane underground tunnel under City Sq., can only have a positive effect on Charlestown's future prospects.

Beginning at the foot of Washington St., the first part of the tour will focus on the Lynde's Point, Thompson Sq., and Harvard Hill areas, which were extensively rehabilitated and restored during the 1970s and 1980s. The first area to be explored is the old Lynde's Point neighborhood. This area is bounded by Devens St., the former shoreline of Charles River Bay (now the site of Interstate 93), Austin St., and Main St. This area was named for Joseph Lynde. He and his wife, Mary Lemmon Lynde, lived in this area for much of the eighteenth century. During the mid-1790s Captain Archibald McNeil bought twenty acres of land at Lynde's Point from Joseph Lynde's heirs. Captain McNeil's purchase was motivated, in part, by the need to build new ropewalks to replace his High St., Boston, ropewalks that were destroyed by fire in 1794. He built his mansion house (nonextant) at the center of the block bounded by Washington St., Devens St., Old Rutherford Ave., and Union St. McNeil subdivided the remaining area into house lots beginning about 1798. After the completion of the Bulfinch-designed State Prison (site of the present Bunker Hill Community College) in 1805, Lynde's Point became known as Prison Point. This area's waterfront became host to industries that included soap and turpentine manufacturing companies. In 1809 the Prison Point Bridge was built, linking Austin St. in Charlestown with East Cambridge. From about 1810 to 1835 much of Prison Point was owned by Josiah Barker, local shipyard owner, ship-model maker, and for thirty-four years the naval constructor for the Charlestown Navy Yard.

Begin at the foot of Washington St.

1. 74–90 Washington St. (1839), John W. Mulliken, builder

This redbrick, granite-trimmed Late Federal/Greek Revival row was built in 1839. Originally encompassing twelve houses, this group was built by local carpenter John W. Mulliken. The two houses adjacent to Austin St. were demolished at an undetermined date and were recreated during the late 1980s to complement the design and materials of the extant row. At the time of this row's completion, the waters of Charles River Bay (filled in during the late nineteenth century) were only one block to the southwest. The lots at Nos. 74–90 were part of an ambitious 104-lot real estate development assembled by the Charlestown Wharf Company during the mid-1830s. Timothy Thompson Sawyer in *Old Charlestown* notes: "The Charlestown Wharf Company purchased nearly all the property along the shore of the river from the wharf of the State Prison to City Sq. A granite block sea wall built for them extended along this whole line" (86). The sea wall was constructed from plans provided by Loammi Baldwin, "father of American civil engineering." Early owners of 74–90 Washington St. included builders, sail makers, tailors, grocers, and a "dye stuff broker."

Turning left from Washington St. walk north on Union St. This street was named in honor of the privateer Union, *which was built in 1815 at Captain Josiah Barker's Prison Point shipyard. By the time this ship was built, the War of 1812 was over and it was fitted for the East India trade.*

2. 35, 37, and 39 Union St. (ca. 1849–50).

This trio of well-executed, relatively rare Charlestown examples of bowfront row houses were built around 1849–50. Although vacant lots on either side of this trio suggest that they are remnants of a more extensive row, this is not the case. The first Boston bowfront town house was built about 1800 on Beacon Hill by Charles Bulfinch (see Bullfinch T1, T2, T3, T4, T5, T6, T8). Although bowfront row houses proliferated in Boston's South End neighborhood during the mid-nineteenth century (see T2), the flat-front row house was far more prevalent in Charlestown throughout the

nineteenth century. Nos. 35, 37, and 39 Union St. were built on the site of the Old Winthrop Church, which was organized in 1833. The church's congregation later built a new, larger edifice a few blocks away on Green St. in 1849. These houses were built for Elijah McIntire for $7,500 each. He owned No. 37 for many years; Nathan Tufts, a merchant, and Samuel Tufts, a clerk, owned Nos. 35 and 39, respectively.

3. 30 Union St. (ca. 1814–15)

The significance of this house is threefold. First, 30 Union St. almost certainly represents the work of the early nineteenth-century Boston architect Asher Benjamin. It is the only Federal-style house in Charlestown that can be attributed to an architect rather than a carpenter or mason (see Benjamin T4, T6, T7). Second, this house was the birthplace of Charles Devens (1820–91), attorney general under President Rutherford B. Hayes (1876–80). Third, this house is a noteworthy example of a "brick ender." It is characterized by unusually narrow brick-end walls; its main and rear facades originally were clad with clapboards.

This house was built for Apollos Field, a painter. In order to pay his debts, Field sold the house at auction on July 29, 1815. The highest bidder was Asher Benjamin of Boston, who paid $1,040. By that time Benjamin was firmly established as a master builder/architect, responsible for the design of the Charles Street Meeting House (1807) (see p. 135) and the Old West Church (1809) in Boston (see map, p. 48). Benjamin became known far beyond the limits of Boston for his series of builders' guides published between 1797 and 1830. Benjamin owned 30 Union St. for less than a year.

By 1818, this house was owned by the Reverend Walter Balfour of Charlestown's Universalist Church. His wife, Mary Devens

Balfour, was the aunt of Charles Devens, who was born in this house on April 4, 1820. Charles Devens entered Harvard at age fourteen, graduating with the class of 1838. He rose to prominence early in his life. He was a Massachusetts state senator at twenty-eight and U.S. marshal at thirty. Additionally, he was a major-general during the Civil War and was a justice of the Massachusetts Supreme Judicial Court. Although born in Charlestown, he lived in Worcester County for most of his life. No. 30 remained in the Balfour-Devens family until the early 1900s. Interestingly, Old Rutherford Ave., which runs perpendicular to Union St., was named in honor of President Rutherford B. Hayes.

4. **31 Union St**. (ca. 1807–10)

The architectural significance of this redbrick residence is twofold. First, 31 Union St. is the only double-masonry Federal-style house standing in Charlestown with both its housing units intact. Second, this house is characterized by an unusual volume that diverges from the more typical rectangular box by virtue of the odd angle of its Old Rutherford Ave. wall. The first firmly identified owner of this house was Jonathan Gilmore, "yeoman," who purchased it around 1810–15. During the mid-nineteenth century, 31 Union St. was the home of Reuben Byram, and by 1883 it was owned

Charles Devens. (*From* Souvenir of the 50th Anniversary of the Dedication of Bunker Hill Monument, *Boston: Bunker Hill Times, 1893, p. 30.*)

by Francis R. Maddox, dispatcher for the Fitchburg Railroad at Prison Point.

Turn left onto Lawrence St. and then right onto an L-shaped alley called Seminary Place, which provides passage back to Austin St.

Seminary Place was named in honor of a finishing school for girls, the Charlestown Female Seminary (nonextant), which was housed in a Greek Revival building with a monumental Ionic portico. The seminary stood at the northwest corner of Union and Lawrence Sts. Situated behind the seminary, with its sidewall bordering Seminary Place, was the First Baptist Church. The seminary and church were demolished during the early twentieth century.

5. **45 Seminary Place**

This well-preserved Greek Revival house provides evidence that Charlestown is a Boston neighborhood with architectural gems tucked away, as if for safe keeping, in alleys and cul-de-sacs in virtually every section of the town. Situated at the point where Seminary Place turns from north to west, this well-preserved Greek Revival house was built for a physician about 1845. Its main facade is noteworthy for its formal, flush-board treatment. In addition, the main facade exhibits four bays rather than the more usual three.

Continue onto Thompson Sq., turning right onto Austin St.

6. **2, 3, and 4 Dexter Row** (1836)
at Thompson Sq., Main St.,
Shadrach Varney, builder

This trio of redbrick late Federal/Greek Revival town houses were built in 1836 and were originally part of a six-house row. The surviving houses possess the most extensive collection of cast-iron elements in Charlestown. The lots of these houses were carved from the estate of Samuel Dexter, secretary of war in President John Adams's cabinet. The much-altered, cupola-topped Dexter Mansion is still extant on Green St., behind these houses. Dexter Row was built by Shadrach Varney, for many years the manager of the Blacksmith's Department at the Charlestown Navy Yard (see also Site 13). It is possible that Alexander Parris, architect of Boston's Quincy Market and buildings for the Charlestown Navy Yard during the 1830s, designed this handsome group (see Parris Site 13 and T6; Quincy Market p. xxxii and T1).

Dexter Row was also known as "Physicians' Row" during the mid-nineteenth century because of the concentration of doctors living and practicing in these upscale row houses. Above all, Dexter Row is significant as one of a half dozen or so masonry town-house groups built before 1845, documenting Charlestown's transition from a town of wooden dwellings to a city of relatively sophisticated brick residences. Of the original six, the three row houses closest to Green St. were torn down to accommodate a one-story, circa 1940s commercial building.

7. **Charlestown Five Cents Savings Bank**
(1876), **Main St. at 1 Thompson Sq.,**
by Moffette and Tolman

The Charlestown Five Cents Savings Bank Building ranks among the finest Victorian-

Five Cents Saving Bank, Charlestown. *(From Souvenir of the 50th Anniversary of the Dedication of Bunker Hill Monument, Boston: Bunker Hill Times, 1893, p. 83.)*

era commercial blocks in the United States. It is listed on the National Register of Historic Places. Built in 1876 and designed by Moffette and Tolman, this bank, with its polychromatic sandstone surface treatments, arched windows, and heavy mansard roof with slates and copper cheneau intact, is a superb example of the High Victorian Gothic style. This structure currently houses a small commercial mall. The bank's huge original iron vaults are still in evidence on the first floor.

8. **Union Block** (1830s): 112, 114, 116 Main St.

The Union Block, a group of three masonry town houses, is a good example of the type of severely elegant Greek Revival row housing erected in Charlestown during the 1830s. This trio is characterized by planar wall surfaces, crisp lines, granite and brownstone trimmings, classicized entrance enframements, and tall second-floor windows with ornate cast-iron banding. This block and the adjacent street, as already mentioned, were named for the East India ship *Union.* Built in 1837, the Union Block's original owners were the furniture manufacturers Henry Forster, Jacob Forster, Jr., and

Edward Lawrence. By the mid-nineteenth century, the Union Block, like Dexter Row, had become a "Physicians' Row."

Follow Main St. southeasterly away from Thompson Sq. (This is the right fork as you walk toward downtown Boston.) Walking along Main St., one passes masonry and wooden structures dating from the late eighteenth to early nineteenth centuries. Because our focus is the Victorian era, these significant residential and commercial structures will be mentioned only briefly.

No. 121–123 Main St. (ca. 1814), with its distinctive round corner, was built for Captain Joseph Cordis. Standing with its narrow end wall to Main St., the Thompson-Sawyer House, at the corner of Main St. and 9 Thompson St., is a freestanding Federal wood-frame house that dates from about 1805. It was the birthplace of Timothy Thompson Sawyer, Charlestown historian and author of *Old Charlestown* (1902). Next door at 119 Main St. (ca. 1794) is the Timothy Thompson, Sr., House. It was the birthplace of Benjamin Thompson, president of the Warren Institute for Savings, state senator, and U.S. congressman. On the nearby corner of Main and Pleasant Sts., the Warren Tavern (ca. 1780), 2 Pleasant St., is said to be the oldest structure in Charlestown. Named in honor of General Joseph Warren, who died leading American troops at Bunker Hill, it was the meeting place of King Solomon's Lodge, the first Masonic Lodge in Charlestown, organized in 1784 with Paul Revere as its Grand Warden.

Cross Main St. at Pleasant St.

9. **92 Main St.** (1822), Nathaniel Austin, builder

Notice the stone building that was built by General Nathaniel Austin, Middlesex County sheriff and major-general of the Massachusetts Militia. The granite for this building was quarried at Austin's short-lived quarry on Outer Brewster Island in Boston Harbor. No. 92 Main St. contained Charlestown's first successful newspaper, the *Bunker Hill Aurora and Farmers and Mechanics Journal*, published here from 1827 to 1871, well into the Victorian era.

Turn right onto Devens St., which represents the outermost ring of streets in Thomas Graves's 1630 plan of Charlestown streets that centered on and around Harvard Hill. Devens St. was named for the aforementioned General Charles Devens. During the Colonial period, the street was variously called "Crooked Lane" and "Bow Street."

10. **St. John's Episcopal Parish House,** 27 Devens St., second floor by Ware and Van Brunt (ca. 1870); first floor by P. C. Barney (1901)

St. John's Episcopal Parish House started out as a one-story chapel built from designs provided by the prominent Boston architectural firm of Ware and Van Brunt. The Stick-style second floor is the original chapel. It was hoisted on top of a new brick first floor designed by P. C. Barney in 1901. The new first floor originally contained double parlors, a men's meeting room, boys' room, choir room, and a kitchen. The parish house, together with St. John's Church, presents one of Charlestown's most evocative Victorian vignettes (see Van Brunt and Howe T5, T12; Ware and Van Brunt T12).

11. **St. John's Episcopal Church** (1841), 31 Devens St., by Richard Bond

St. John's Episcopal Church is an interesting example of the early Gothic Revival ecclesiastical style in the Boston area. Its main facade is faced with rusticated stone blocks, whereas its side and rear wall are faced with less expensive red brick. The main facade is dominated by a castellated tower reminiscent of that of St. John the Evangelist Church (1831) on Bowdoin St.,[1] Beacon Hill. As early as 1838, a group of gentlemen met in the home of the Navy Yard's chaplain to discuss the founding of this church. St. John's was built in 1841 from designs provided by Boston architect Richard Bond. Bond was the architect of Boston's Lewis Wharf, Salem's City Hall, and the Gore Library (1840; nonextant) at Harvard University. St. John's was the first Episcopal Church in Charlestown.

12. Harvard School (1871–72), 20 Devens St., by Samuel J. F. Thayer

The Harvard School was designed by Samuel J. F. Thayer, the Boston architect responsible for a number of New England city halls including those in Providence, R.I., Brookline, Stoughton, and Methuen. Architecturally, this granite-trimmed brick school is a hybrid of Second Empire center pavilion massing and High Victorian Gothic elements. In recent years it has been adapted for reuse as housing for the elderly.

At the next intersection, bear to the left onto Old Rutherford Ave.; follow this for two blocks. Then turn left on Washington St. and proceed one block to Harvard St.

At the corner of Harvard St. and Harvard Sq. is the old Harvard School of 1847, predecessor to the school at 20 Devens St. Although it has had a cupola added to its roof to call attention to its new status as luxury 1980s condominiums, this building retains a high percentage of its original red brick and granite.

Turning right onto Harvard St., we find an enclave of handsome row houses dating from the early to middle years of the Victorian era.

13. 7–23 Harvard St. (ca. 1835–36), Shadrach Varney, builder

This group of nine town houses is the earliest extensive masonry row in Charlestown. Built on "the old parsonage lands" of the First Parish Church, this late Federal group's architect may have been Alexander Parris. This row's redbrick walls follow the sweeping curve of Harvard St. Enhancing this picturesque streetscape are remnants of a once-continuous band of cast-iron second-floor balconies containing Greek key and Chinese fretwork panels. Among this row's more illustrious mid-nineteenth-century owners was Edward F. Barker, assistant paymaster in the U.S. Navy during the Civil War. Barker, of 13 Harvard St., served under Admiral Farragut at Mobile Bay. Horatio Wellington of 21 Harvard St. was a Charlestown city councillor and alderman as well as the owner of a profitable coal wharf in East Cambridge. Shadrach Varney, builder of this row and a Charlestown Navy Yard blacksmith, was the original occupant of 17 Harvard St.

14. 28 Harvard St. (1858–59)

This Italianate/mansard mansion was built for magazine publishing tycoon Moses Dow (1810–86). Architecturally, this house is significant as an early mansard-roofed house in Charlestown. It is the largest and most elaborately ornamented of the Dow-developed town houses at 18–24 and 36–38 Harvard St., as well as 1–4 Harvard Place, the last on a charming cul-de-sac off Harvard St. Built at a cost of the then-princely sum of $25,000, this house symbolizes Dow's hard-won success as an entrepreneur. Dow's life is a case study in perseverance paying off after innumerable business failures. At the age of forty, he launched the highly successful *Waverley Magazine,* which was published in the Dow-owned Waverley Hotel at City Sq. (nonextant). The construction of Dow's town houses on Harvard St. and Harvard Place is said to have ushered in a new era for Harvard Hill as an upscale residential quarter. The local newspaper praised Dow for "his faith and confidence in Charlestown as an abiding place." At the time of his death, in 1886, his net worth was $893,845.78.

15. The Edward Everett House (1814), 16 Harvard St.

The Edward Everett House represents the most architecturally sophisticated foray into the Federal style in Charlestown. Built in 1814 for wealthy local shipbuilder Matthew Bridge, this house is discussed at length in this tour because of owners who figured prominently on the

Moses A. Dow. (From Souvenir of the 50th Anniversary of the Dedication of Bunker Hill Monument, Boston: Bunker Hill Times, 1893, p. 32.)

national scene during the Victorian era. The most illustrious owner of this house was Edward Everett (1794–1865). He lived here while serving as governor of Massachusetts (1835–39). Everett also served as a congressman (1824–34), minister to Great Britain (1841), and president of Harvard College (late 1840s). He was later appointed secretary of state and was elected to the U.S. Senate. In 1860 Everett was a candidate for vice president on the Conservative Party ticket.

By the 1840s William Carleton, inventor and proprietor of a lamps and gas fixtures manufactory, lived here (see also Site 26). He was the founder of Carleton College in Northfield, Minn. Interestingly, automotive industrialist Henry Ford considered buying this house during the 1910s and moving it to his Greenfield Village Museum in Dearborn, Mich.

16. City Sq.

Continue along Harvard St. to City Sq., an area whose appearance has changed radically at least a half dozen times in the course of its 365-year history. Originally called Market Sq., it was for many years the focus of the town's political, commercial, and social life. A farmer's market was conducted here until well into the nineteenth century. By 1868 the Second Empire style was utilized in the design of the domed Charlestown City Hall and the aforementioned Waverley Hotel, which stood on the southwest side of the square. Characterized by attractive lawns, plantings, sculpture, seating, and other amenities, City Sq.'s latest "new look" dates to the mid-1990s. The park's landscape elements and street furniture were created as part of the Central Artery (Big Dig) transportation project.

The only remnant of City Sq.'s Victorian streetscape is Roughan Hall (ca. 1892), situated at the entrance to Park St. This yellow-brick commercial block exhibits Renaissance Revival characteristics. It was built by Michael Roughan to house offices, a great hall, lodge rooms, and club quarters.

To resume the tour, take Main St., which departs City Sq. along the left side of Roughan Hall.

17. 18–34 Main St. (1828–29)

Originally known as the "Phoenix Build-ings," 18–34 Main St. is actually a single commercial/residential block. This Fed-eral/Greek Revival–style building is charac-terized by granite post-and-lintel construction on the ground floor and upper floors faced with red brick. During the mid-nineteenth century the street-level stores included a tinsmith shop (No. 16), candle factory (No. 28), painting business (No. 32), and glazing concern (No. 34).

18. 55–61 and 69–71 Main St.
(ca. early–mid-1790s)

Standing side by side on Main St. between Winthrop St. and Monument Ave. are two survivors from the rebuilding of Charles-town during the early to mid-1790s. Nos. 55–61 Main St. were built for John Larkin, the man best remembered for lending his horse to Paul Revere for his famous mid-night ride on April 18, 1775. These houses are part of Charlestown's remarkable col-lection of freestanding wooden houses dat-ing from the late eighteenth to the early nineteenth centuries. Both houses are characterized by boxy, hip-roofed late Georgian forms, which were adapted for commercial purposes during the late nine-teenth century. At some point in the 1960s or 1970s, the first floor of the old Larkin House was returned to a more historically appropriate residential appearance. The first-floor plan of Nos. 55–61 was trans-formed into Louis Klous's clothing store beginning about 1875. Klous was literally a rags-to-riches success; members of his fam-ily started out as street peddlers selling rags. An article in the *Charlestown Enterprise* on December 14, 1889, stated, "Louis Klous has gained a wide reputation for garments that for style, fit, workmanship and price are second to none in the City of Boston."

Nos. 69–71 Main St., originally owned by John Hurd, a well-to-do merchant, retain their late-nineteenth-century storefront, complete with stained-glass windows bear-ing the inscription "Donovan and Fallon Drugs." The upper floors retain much of their original late-eighteenth-century sur-face treatments, including clapboards, win-dows with 6/6 wood sash, ornamental quoins at each corner, and a hip roof. The second floor oriel window on the Monu-ment Ave. side is a Victorian-era addition.

After viewing the Larkin and Hurd houses turn right onto Winthrop St. and proceed to Warren St.—or "Back Street," as it was called before the American Revolution.

19. St. Mary's Roman Catholic Church
(1887–96), 55 Warren St.,
by Patrick C. Keely

St. Mary's Roman Catholic Church is the second church by this name in Charles-town. The first St. Mary's was built as early as 1828 on Old Rutherford Ave. (then called Richmond St.) in the Lynde's or Prison Point section of Charlestown. This early St. Mary's was built to serve the Catholic workers of the Charlestown Navy Yard and the East Cambridge glass factories. The present St. Mary's site possesses an interest-ing and ironic history, given its later reli-gious associations. From 1650 until the Revolution, a rum distillery was located on this lot. During the early nineteenth cen-tury, this tract contained the soap and can-dle factory of Francis Hyde of 21 Cordis St. The Roman Catholic Archdiocese of Boston acquired this lot in April 1885 at a cost of $32,000. The cornerstone was laid on Octo-ber 23, 1887. This church was constructed of rock-faced granite with redbrick trimmings and designed in the Gothic Revival Style by the prolific Patrick C. Keely (1816–96), who was based in Brooklyn, N.Y.

St. Mary's architect, Patrick C. Keely,[2] was born in Ireland. He immigrated to the United States in 1841. Keely is reputed to have built at least five hundred Roman Catholic churches and cathedrals in New York State alone, exclusive of New York City. The architect's son C. P. Keely is credited with the supervision of the church's interior design work. The *Charlestown Examiner* at the time of this church's dedication, on October 1, 1892, remarked that its interior was "richly tinted and gilded . . . all of the finish of wainscoting and pews are in oak, highly polished. . . . there are 42 oak chairs for the altar boys in the sanctuary. . . . There are sixteen clusters of gas and electric jets for illuminating purposes." The windows of St. Mary's were made in Munich, Germany. An October 1, 1892, *Enterprise* article explained that "unlike many stained glass windows they do not shut out the light of nature and the church is not made gloomy even on the darkest and gloomiest days." The center window over the high altar was a gift of the bishop of Hartford, brother of the pastor of St. Mary's.

The church's altars were built by Charles E. Hall and Company and were characterized by "the best Vermont statuary and Mexican and Algerian onyx, being highly wrought and carved." It is interesting to note that the original altar of the first St. Mary's was recycled as the altar of the second church's baptistery. Additionally, the church's ceiling is noteworthy for its exposed trusses finished in fine tracery and panel work. Certainly the lavish interior treatments were a major reason for the construction costs of the church reaching an estimated $200,000. (To see the interior of St. Mary's, contact the church office.) Charlestown is fortunate to have two churches that represent early and late phases of Keely's career. In addition to St. Mary's, completed near the end of his life, St. Francis De Sales Church at the top of Bunker Hill on Bunker Hill St. was built in 1859, when Keely was still relatively new to the Boston architectural scene.

20. St. Mary's Roman Catholic Parochial School (1901–2), 49 Warren St., by Keely and Houghton

Across Winthrop St., to the right of St. Mary's Roman Catholic Church, is the former parochial school affiliated with this church. Currently housing senior citizens, St. Mary's Roman Catholic Parochial School was designed by Patrick C. Keely's successor firm of Keely and Houghton. This school's surface treatments are characterized by planar Barrington brick surfaces with gray granite trimmings and arched, corbelled cornices in the Romanesque Revival manner. Essentially rectangular in form, this school measures forty feet along Warren and one hundred feet along Winthrop St. For years prior to this building's construction, the Roman Catholic Archdiocese utilized the Old Training Field School for St. Mary's Parochial School classes. According to a September 28, 1901, article in the *Charlestown Examiner,* the new school "will house nine class rooms. Long corridors will extend the length of the building on the east side with stairways at either end of iron and fire proof materials. . . . The framing of the building will be of hard pine and the interior finish to be of ash and oak. The building will be warmed by steam heat and the illumination electric lights."

Before continuing northward along Winthrop St. to the Old Training Field, note the unusual town house just to the west of St. Mary's at 59 Warren St.

21. **59 Warren St.** (1871), Robert R. Wiley, builder.

Together with St. Mary's Roman Catholic Church and Parochial School to the east, 59 Warren St. forms one of the most memorable and intact Victorian streetscapes in Charlestown. Although this building appears to be the rectory of St. Mary's, it has never been affiliated with this church. This town house is constructed of brick and is characterized by highly unusual form and surface ornamentation. Here, the main facade is treated as a series of three stepped segments: bow front, entrance bay, and side ell. Gothic Revival ornamentation is in evidence on a second-floor corner oriel and the hip-on-mansard roof's dormer treatments. Striking a vaguely Egyptian Revival note is a triangular dormer window. This house might be characterized as "Charles Bulfinch meets Charles Addams." It was built in 1871 by and for local master mason Robert R. Wiley (1828–1903).

By 1885 John E. Maynard, "the Bowdoin Square Livery Man," one of Charlestown's "self-made men" ("Our Self Made Men" 1), owned this property. During the early 1900s, 59 Warren St. was the home of prominent teamster/contractor/real estate developer Patrick O'Riordan. In 1860 O'Riordan left employment at the Charlestown Navy Yard to begin a career as a teamster and contractor. Initially, his business had only one horse to its name but, thanks to his considerable energy and ambition, by the 1870s he was one of the leading contractors in Boston, with stables on Dorchester Ave., South Boston, and Chelsea St., Charlestown. By that time he owned 160 horses. The Dorchester Bay main sewer and the sewers of South Boston and Beacon St. in Boston and Brookline were all constructed by O'Riordan. Interestingly, it was

O'Riordan's workers who put into place the fluted portion of the Civil War *Soldiers' and Sailors' Monument* on the Boston Common—a task thought to be impossible because of the columns' great weight.

22. **Engine House No. 50** (ca. 1915), 32 Winthrop St.

Engine House No. 50 was built as a fire station serving the Old Training Field area and vicinity. A fire station has been located on this lot since the early 1850s. The first firehouse was oriented toward a stable yard adjacent to Soley St., the next street west of Winthrop St. The present fire station is a richly ornamented cast-stone-trimmed redbrick structure that artfully blends elements of the Georgian and Renaissance Revival styles. Its Winthrop St. facade is characterized by a high degree of symmetry and well-executed door and window surrounds, including garage doors set within wide arches accented by console keystones. The second floor exhibits a trio of tall windows flanked by Doric pilasters and surmounted by a pedimented entablature.

23. **34–44 Winthrop St.** (ca. 1860s)

Nos. 34–44 Winthrop St. is a group of five Italianate brownstone-trimmed redbrick row houses that overlook the Old Training Field (Winthrop Sq.). During the late nineteenth century, No. 34 was the home of John Boyle O'Reilly (1844–90), the famous Irish Nationalist, adventurer, balladeer, poet, author, and journalist. He was born at Dowth Castle, County Meath, Ireland, on June 28, 1844. In June 1866 he was arrested in London for anti-British activities and sentenced to twenty years of penal servitude. In October 1867 he was sent to the penal colony of West Australia to serve out his sentence. According to the *Charlestown Enterprise, Special Edition, 50th Anniversary of the Bunker Hill Monument* (June 1893), O'Reilly, "after enduring prison life for about a year, . . . made his escape in an open boat, was picked up at sea by the American whaling barque, 'Gazelle,' and finally reached Philadelphia in November, 1869" (54). In 1870, at age twenty-six, he became editor of the Catholic newspaper the Boston *Pilot*. He retained this position until his death twenty years later. In addition to his editorial work, "he first attracted attention by his original and powerful ballads of Australian life" (54), including "Amber Whale," "Dukite Snake," "Monster Diamond," "King of the Vasse," and others. On the basis of his experiences in British prisons, O'Reilly exposed the tyranny of British rule in books as well as ballads. He was the author of *Songs from the Southern Seas* (1873), *Moondyne* (1879), and *In Bohemia* (1886). He and his wife, Mary S. Murphy, and their four daughters were living at 34 Winthrop St. at the time of his death in 1890 (see O'Reilly T6).

John Boyle O'Reilly, engraving (ca. 1870–90). Among the foremost Catholic leaders was the poet O'Reilly. *(Courtesy of the Boston Athenæum.)*

24. **Old Training Field** (Winthrop Sq.) and the *Soldier's and Sailor's Monument*

Although the Old Training Field was set out around 1640, its present appearance was shaped by relatively recent changes to its landscape made during the Victorian era and World War I. The historical significance of this open space transcends its local importance. Much of the fighting during the Battle of Bunker Hill occurred on or near the Old Training Field. Over its history, the field has served Charlestown's citizens as a grazing land, military parade grounds, schoolyard, platform for political rallies, public ornament, children's playground, and a peaceful retreat within a densely built-up urban environment.

In 1827 the Training Field School was erected at the Common and Winthrop Sts. corner of the Old Training Field. It was moved across the street to its present location at 3 Common St. in 1847 because Charlestown's city fathers deemed this schoolhouse to be "the needless destroyer of the symmetry of the park" (Sawyer 234). The removal of the Training Field School was a harbinger of even greater changes to this park's appearance. By 1852 the once-unbroken expanse of lawn was crisscrossed by paths. In 1868 the integrity of the Training Field's original shape was threatened by plans, proposed by local lawyer and jurist George Washington Warren, to bisect this historic open space with a boulevard that would extend from City Sq. to the *Bunker Hill Monument*. Fortunately for the integrity of the field's historic configuration, this grandiose scheme was never realized, and Park St. was the only part of the boulevard that was ever laid out. In 1872 the last vestiges of the Old Training Field's Colonial era appearance were obliterated with the removal of the old split-rail fence, which was replaced by an elegant cast-iron enclosure. At that time the Old Training Field was renamed Winthrop Sq., but the original name persists among neighborhood people to this day.

In addition, the handsome granite Civil War *Soldier's and Sailor's Monument* (ca. 1870) was installed on the Adams St. side of the park, replacing a three-tier cast-iron fountain (1850s) similar to those in the squares of Boston's South End (see T2). Boston sculptor Martin Milmore (1844–81) received the commission to create this memorial. For most of his career, Milmore worked in partnership with his brother Joseph. Martin conceived the designs and modeled them in clay; Joseph translated them into stone. The Milmores were responsible for some of the earliest Civil

War memorial sculpture in the United States, including works at Forest Hills Cemetery,[3] Roxbury (1865), Claremont, N.H. (1869), the Egyptian Revival Sphinx at Mount Auburn Cemetery[4] (1870s), and the *Soldiers' and Sailors' Monument* (1877) on Flagstaff Hill on the Boston Common (see *Soldiers' and Sailors' Monument,* note 6 T6).

Composed of Hallowell, Maine, granite, the Old Training Field's memorial sculpture consists of a tall cornice-headed plinth with four panels bearing inscriptions. Surmounting the plinth is a low platform that supports three figures. The central, female figure is ten feet high and represents the United States. The figure is depicted crowning two male figures representing the army and the navy with laurel wreaths. The Old Training Field's present paths date from 1919. A drawing featured on the front page of the *Charlestown Enterprise* (dated July 5, 1919) shows this green space as we know it today.

Much of the Old Training Field's charm is dependent on its "frame" of buildings. Actually, the buildings on each side of the park represent a distinct phase in the evolution of Charlestown's built environment.

Common St. side (east) of the Old Training Field (between Adams and Park Sts.)

This section of Common St. recalls the late-eighteenth- and early-nineteenth-century development of Charlestown. Here stand clapboard-clad, hip-roofed wooden houses, including the former **Salem Turnpike Hotel** at 16 Common St./19 Putnam St. Built in two stages in 1795 and 1805, the hotel served as a stopover for Essex County farmers who came to town to sell their produce in Charlestown's Market Sq. (later City Sq.). **No. 14 Common St.,** built in 1806, is a stylish and substantial three-story Federal house. It was built for John Tapley, a master

Soldier's and Sailor's Monument, Old Training Field. *(From M. F. Sweeter,* King's How to See Boston: A Trustworthy Guidebook, *Knights Templar ed., Boston: Moses King, 1895, p. 232.)*

craftsman specializing in ironwork, who did much work at the Charlestown Navy Yard. **No. 25 Common St.** was built around 1800 and is part of Charlestown's interesting collection of gambrel-roofed buildings. It was part of the extensive property holdings of housewright James Gould.

Common St. side (south) of the Old Training Field (between Park and Winthrop Sts.)

At this point, Common St.'s path turns at Park St., running one short block to Winthrop St. This edge of the Old Training Field symbolizes the prosperous antebellum Charlestown of the 1820s and 1830s, fully recovered from the ravages of the Revolution and moving toward its eventual incorporation as a city in 1847. The redbrick **Training Field School** at 3 Common St. was built to serve the educational needs of children of the northeastern section of town. It is the oldest extant grammar school building in Charlestown. As previously noted, it originally stood at the Common/Winthrop St. corner of the Old Training Field and was moved to its present location in 1847. By 1848 the original two-story building had acquired a third floor, although it retains its original gable-roof configuration. This building served as a school for 140 years, starting out as a public school, then serving for a time as a private academy, and finally becoming, by the late nineteenth century, St. Mary's Roman Catholic Parochial School. Next door to the west is **1–2 Common St.**, a wood-frame double Federal house built around 1827 by housewright Richard Shute and bricklayer Jonas Barret.

Winthrop St. Side of the Old Training Field

This side of the Old Training Field reflects a more diverse streetscape in terms of residential building types and styles, with the majority dating to the mid- to late nineteenth century, including the aforementioned 34–44 Winthrop St. (Site 23). Also noteworthy is the **St. Mary's Roman Catholic Church Parrish Hall** (1913–15), at 46–50 Winthrop St. It was designed by the Boston architectural firm of Wells and Dana (active ca. 1910–30).

Adams St. side of the Old Training Field

This side of the Old Training Field, with its unbroken expanse of redbrick row houses, provides an appropriately Victorian backdrop for Milmore's Civil War memorial. Edmund Quincy, a local early-twentieth-century American Impressionist painter, immortalized this Adams St. row in his painting *Farmers Market on Winthrop Square* (ca. 1940) (*Journal and Year Book*). Built in 1828, **9–12 Adams St.** represent the oldest masonry brick row houses built in Charlestown. The town houses in the Adams St. group generally represent examples of the Greek Revival and Italianate styles or hybrids of these two popular mid-nineteenth-century historic architectural styles. **Nos. 2–3 Adams St.** are side-hall-plan, brownstone-trimmed redbrick row houses built around 1850. Local carpenter Porter Cross may have been responsible for part of their construction. **Nos. 4, 5, and 6 Adams St.** were built in 1849 by local builder William Bragdon. Early owners of **7–8 Adams St.** (ca. 1850) included John P. Barnard, stabler (No. 7), and George H. Braman, dry-goods dealer (No. 8). **No. 1 Adams/63 Winthrop St.** is notable for its unusual trapezoidal form. The Adams St. and Winthrop St. walls of this double house fan out like an open book. Built around 1855, 1 Adams St. was originally owned by George Stimpson, "gentleman," and 63 Winthrop St. was first occupied by trader John Mullay.

Returning to Winthrop St., walk north-westward up Breed's Hill to the Bunker Hill Monument.

25. **63, 65,** and **67 Winthrop St.**

No. 63 Winthrop St., together with 65 and 67 Winthrop St., visually constitutes one of the most memorable Victorian streetscapes in Charlestown. Situated on the steep incline of Breed's Hill, these masonry town houses stand close together between Wallace Ct. and Adams St., separated from each other by narrow passageways. Most of Charlestown's memorable streetscapes may be thought of as "walls" of attached masonry row houses. Here, this trio of free-standing town houses with their planar (No. 63) and bowed (Nos. 65 and 67) main facades invites consideration as separate, sculptural forms of considerable charm. Nos. 65 and 67 were built in the mid-1850s. The lots of these town houses were part of a twenty-lot tract purchased by the prominent lawyer and jurist George Washington Warren in 1849 from the John Binney estate.

26. **1–8 Wallace Ct.** (ca. 1850)

Wallace Ct. ranks among Charlestown's most picturesque cul-de-sacs. Bordered by eight two- and three-story masonry Greek Revival/Italianate row houses constructed around 1850, these flat-front dwellings were evidently built by local carpenter William Bragdon. Wallace Ct. was extant as a path as early as 1839. It takes its name from the Wallace family, who lived and farmed in this vicinity during the eighteenth century and whose property was destroyed during the Battle of Bunker Hill. Wallace Ct. was part of George Washington Warren's afore-mentioned tract. This tract is shown in a Suffolk County deed plan dated April 1849 (Plan Book 4A, Plan 38). William Carleton

was an important early property owner on Wallace Ct., owning Nos. 1, 2, and 3 Wallace Ct. by 1850. As a leading Charlestown and Boston manufacturer of lamps, lanterns, gas fixtures, and chandeliers, he became extremely wealthy from patented inventions within the realm of lighting fixtures. During the mid-nineteenth century he resided in the old Edward Everett House (Site 15). He built 3 Wallace Ct. for his daughter and son-in-law, Luther Whitney, who was employed in his father-in-law's lamp manufacturing concern.

27. **70 and 72 Winthrop St.** (ca. 1865–70)

These stylish and substantial Italianate/mansard town houses were built around 1865–70. Situated at the corner of Winthrop St. and Monument Ct., these houses provide an attractive introduction to the elegant Victorian town houses of Monument Sq. Constructed of red brick with brown-stone trimmings, these houses feature flights of heavy granite steps, full-length octagonal bays, and brownstone belt courses, which tie the buildings together into a handsome architectural package. Charles F. Newell purchased these house lots in May 1867 at a cost of $6,000.

Turning right onto Monument Sq. from Winthrop St., continue northward to the two redbrick bowfront mansions at 6 and 7 Monument Sq. at the corner of Chestnut St.

28. **6 and 7 Monument Sq.** (1848).

Constructed in 1848, these buildings are the earliest town houses erected on the square. These late Federal/Greek Revival town houses possess bow fronts, and No. 6 retains its original cupola. These houses possess a fine collection of cast-iron elements, including front-yard fences and lacy, New Orleans–style covered balconies. No. 6 was built for the aforementioned George

father of the Boston architect Gridley J. F. Bryant, developed the first commercial railroad in the United States to transport the enormous twelve-foot blocks to a wharf on the Neponset River, from which they were transported (via barge) to Charlestown (see G. Bryant T1).

The construction of the *Bunker Hill Monument* was plagued by lack of funds. When the project seemed irrevocably stalled in 1840, Sarah Josepha Hale,[5] "America's first woman editor," who ran the Boston-based *Ladies Magazine,* saved the day by rallying hundreds of female followers to the cause. They ultimately contributed $30,035.53 toward the completion of the monument—from bake sales! Dedicated by President John Tyler on June 17, 1843, the granite *Bunker Hill Monument* weighs 6,700 tons and reaches a dizzying height of 210 feet.

From the Old Training Field follow Winthrop St. past its intersections with Adams St. and Wallace Ct. Pause at Winthrop St.'s intersection with High St. to view the Bunker Hill Monument atop Breed's Hill.

Turn right onto Monument Sq., and proceed to climb the stairs to the monument (opposite Monument Sq.'s intersection with Chestnut St.). Facing the monument, turn left and proceed down the stairs by William Wetmore Story's statue (1881) of Colonel William Prescott (see Prescott's grandson, William H. Prescott, T6). At the bottom of the stairs cross High St. and walk straight down the hill on Monument Ave.

30. Monument Ave.

Set out during the mid-1850s over the last vestige of pastureland on the south slope of Breed's Hill, Monument Ave. runs from Warren St. to Monument Sq. Monument Ave. was purposely aligned with the *Bunker Hill Monument* so that this distinctive structure serves as an impressive northern focal point for this thoroughfare. (During the 1850s and 1860s, Boston-area architects and planners were influenced by the French predilection for aligning thoroughfares with distant monuments, fountains, and the like.) Monument Ave. represents the most sophisticated example of Charlestown city planning up to that time. Mayor Frothingham, in the *50th Anniversary of the Bunker Hill Monument,* wrote, "It will be one of the most desirous places of residence in the city. . . . Land situated like this is calculated to invite the erection of a class of buildings both valuable and ornamental."

As you stroll southward on Monument Ave., it is worth viewing a number of town houses from both architectural and historical standpoints.

No. 60 Monument Ave. (1894) is architecturally significant as Charlestown's finest example of a late Victorian town house. A successful blend of the Richardsonian Romanesque and Georgian Revival styles, it was built from designs by Boston architect Charles S. Halstrom. It was built for Jeremiah O' Riordan, son of the prolific Charlestown contractor Patrick O'Riordan (Site 21), who was a leading contractor and real estate speculator in his own right.

Nos. 52–54 and 56 Monument Ave. are masonry, mansion-scale double- and single-family residences designed in the High Victorian Gothic and mansard styles. Built around 1867, No. 52 was owned for many years by Thomas R. B. Edmands, owner of Thomas R. B. Edmands and Company, makers of pottery and drainpipes.

Nos. 47 and 49 Monument Ave. date from 1854–55, the earliest years of Monument Ave.'s development. Designed in the Italianate style, these redbrick houses are essentially intact—with the exception of No. 49's post-1868 mansard roof addition.

Nos. 47 and 49 were built by housewrights Charles and John E. Wilson, who were responsible for a large percentage of the house construction along Monument Ave. The Wilson brothers built numerous residences and several schoolhouses in Charlestown during the mid-nineteenth century. Charles died in 1860, but John, the original owner of No. 49, was active in local building trades from the 1830s to 1890s.

Nos. 15–45 Monument Ave. further attests to the talents of the Wilson brothers. Built in 1855, and containing sixteen attached granite-trimmed redbrick Greek Revival/Italianate houses, this is the most extensive row of identical town houses built in Charlestown. Particularly noteworthy are the cast-iron balconies on most of the second floors.

No. 22 Monument Ave. (ca. 1880) is a late example of the Italianate style and was built on the site of Alfred Carleton's Wood and Coal Company, a prosperous mid-nineteenth-century Charlestown enterprise. The construction of this house swept away the last commercial concern on this street and brought to fruition the Bunker Hill Monument Association's early 1850s vision of Monument Ave. as a residential enclave of upscale homes bordering a memorable, direct approach to the Bunker Hill Monument.

Follow Monument Ave. to its end, and turn right on Main St. for one block. This tour concludes at the historic Warren Tavern (ca. 1780), at the corner of Main and Pleasant Sts.

To return to the subway, follow Main St. for two more blocks and turn left on Austin St. to the Orange Line's Community College T Station.

·T**10**R·

VICTORIAN BOSTON'S
CHOCOLATE VILLAGE

by Anthony M. Sammarco

Tour Location: See Greater Boston Key Map for location of the tour, page xli. See T Stop Diagram for the T stop location, page xl.

About Walking the Tour: Our tour destination, Dorchester Lower Mills and Milton Village, is less than a twenty-five-minute ride on the T from Downtown Crossing. Take the Red Line's Ashmont train to the end of the line. At Ashmont station there's a free transfer to the surface trolley, also part of the Red Line, which goes to Mattapan. Get off the trolley at the third stop, Milton Station. (Along the way you'll pass through Cedar Grove Cemetery. *Ripley's Believe It or Not* once listed this as the only trolley in the world to pass through a cemetery.) Ascend the stairs to Adams St.; the tour begins at the first tall brick building on your left. Refreshments may be found over the nearby bridge on the Dorchester Lower Mills side of the Neponset River.

Thumbnail Sketch of Sights: See Introduction, page xxxvi.

Approximate Walking Time: 1 ½ hours.

T Stop: Ashmont Station, Red Line, and Surface Trolley to Milton Station; about 25 minutes from downtown.

By Car: Drive south along Dorchester Ave. from Boston to Pierce Sq., the junction of Adams and Washington Sts. and Dorchester Ave.

Begin at: The Associates Building on Adams St. (to the left when one reaches the top of the stairs from the Milton T Station) in Milton Village.

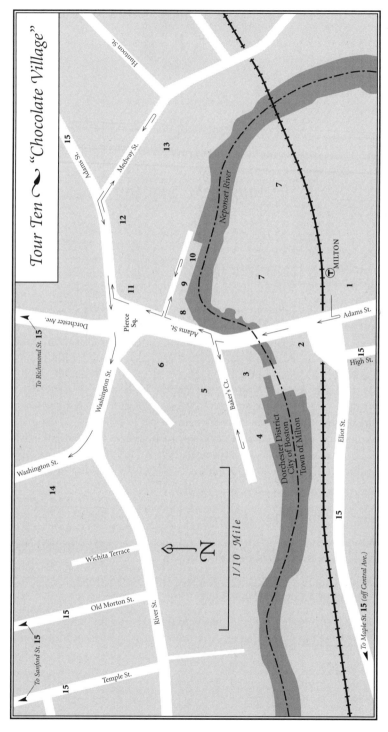

Tour Ten ～ "Chocolate Village"

Huntoon St.

Medway St.

13

15

Adams St.

12

11

Pierce Sq.

Dorchester Ave.

To Richmond St. 15

Washington St.

6

5

Baker's Ct.

Adams St.

8

9

10

7

Neponset River

7

MILTON

1

Adams St.

2

High St.

15

3

4

Dorchester District
City of Boston
Town of Milton

Eliot St.

15

Washington St.

14

Wichita Terrace

N

1/10 Mile

Old Morton St.

15

River St.

Temple St.

15

To Sanford St. 15

To Maple St. 15 (off Central Ave.)

INTRODUCTION

The Lower Mills, known by the Neponset tribe of the Massachusetts Native Americans as "Unquety," meaning, in Algonquin, lower falls, was the site of the first gristmill in New England (1634), the first powder mill in New England (1665), the first iron slitting mill (1710), the first paper mill in New England (1728), the first chocolate mill in America (1765), the first manufacturer of folio and quarto letter paper in New England (1803), and the first producer of power-sawn veneers in the United States (1817). By the Civil War, the Lower Mills, which includes parcels of land beside the Neponset River in the towns of Dorchester and Milton, was made up of commercial manufacturers that once employed over a thousand people.

Chocolate was one of the most prolific, as well as profitable, concerns developed since the introduction of the cacao bean to the colonies in the mid-eighteenth century. Four independent chocolate manufacturers were once located in the Lower Mills, with the Baker (Site 3), Preston (Site 10), Dr. Jonathan Ware (Site 9),

A cacao pod, detail of an undated broadside. *(Courtesy of the Anthony M. Sammarco collection.)*

and Webb and Twombley (Site 2) chocolate companies producing so much chocolate that the pervasive and heady aroma led to the area's being called "Chocolate Village." Though a few of the commercial concerns continued into the twentieth century, the competitive chocolate manufacturers were all to be absorbed by the Baker Chocolate Company by 1881, the oldest manufacturer of chocolate in this country.

The Baker Family and Baker Chocolate

As tradition has it, in 1765 Dr. James Baker (1739–1825) of Dorchester met John Hannon, "a penniless Irish immigrant," crying on the banks of the Neponset River. Inquiring as to his distress, Baker learned that Hannon was destitute, but that he possessed the skill of making chocolate. Because chocolate was not only a delicious commodity but also a fashionable extravagance imported from Europe, Baker financed Hannon in a leased, small wood-framed mill in Milton Village where, for almost fifteen years, "Hannon's Best Chocolate" was manufactured and sold with a guaranteed money-back policy that stated, "If the Chocolate does not prove good, the Money will be returned."

Hannon is said to have sailed to the West Indies in 1779, according to the town history, to purchase cacao beans, but the rumor was that he deserted his wife, Elizabeth Gore Hannon. However, whatever the reason, he never returned, and a year after his departure, after hiring Nathaniel Blake to carry on the business, the "Widow" Hannon, who was remarried in 1782 to William Walker, sold her share of the enterprise to Dr. James Baker, who established the Baker Chocolate Company in 1780.

Edmund Baker[1] (1770–1846) and later Colonel Walter Baker[2] (1792–1852) entered the family business and continued the tradition of manufacturing chocolate that was marketed to be as "absolutely pure as it is soluble," with a money-back guarantee if

Paper wrapper of Hannon's Best Chocolate, used 1765–79. *(Courtesy of The Milton Historical Society.)*

one was not satisfied for any reason with the product. During the early years of the Victorian period, Walter Baker, educated at Harvard College (class of 1818), as had been his father and grandfather before him, entered the family business after having studied law with Judge Tappan Reeve in Litchfield, Conn. Therefore, Baker was able not only to continue the family's production of chocolate, but also to protect its brand name "Baker's" from infringement by his numerous competitors. Walter Baker's success was evident: in 1839 he donated the funds to build Lyceum Hall on Dorchester's Meeting House Hill, declining the honor of having the hall named for him, and in 1852 he donated a spire clock to his church, the Second Church in Dorchester.

Henry L. Pierce and Baker Chocolate (1854–96)

Following the death of Walter Baker in 1852 and the death of his brother-in-law Sidney Williams two years later, Henry Lillie Pierce (1825–96), a step-nephew of Walter Baker, and a $3.00-per-week clerk in the

Baker Chocolate counting house prior to 1854, leased the chocolate mill at Lower Mills, paying the trustees of the Baker estate a substantial sum over the next three decades. Pierce began to plan long-range goals: to expand the physical size of the chocolate mills and to market his product throughout the country.

Pierce was an honest and just man; having worked at Baker's as an employee, he was inclined to treat his employees fairly when he assumed control. During the post–Civil War years, Pierce (Site 8) began to enter his chocolate in various competitive exhibitions, and it received highest awards in 1873 at the Vienna Exhibition in Austria and, in 1876, at the Philadelphia Centennial Exhibition held in honor of the hundredth anniversary of the United States. In 1883 Pierce adopted his trademark, having seen the pastel portrait *Das Schokoladen Mädchen* by Jean-Etienne Liotard at the Dresden Art Gallery in Germany. It portrays Anna Baltauf (ca. 1740–1825), a chocolate server who met her future husband, Prince Dietrichstein, the nephew of the Austrian Empress Maria Theresa, and married him in 1765. Pierce renamed it "La Belle Chocolatière," and the

The Old Stone Mill, photograph ca. 1868. *(Courtesy of The Milton Historical Society.)*

chocolate server became synonymous with the oldest manufacturer of chocolate.

In 1895, nine years after the incorporation of the company and nine years after he was allowed to purchase the company from the Baker Estate, Pierce said, "The die is cast. Walter Baker and Company are now a corporate body. They say that corporations have no soul, but they outlive men, and I have done what I think is best for the business and for everyone" (B. Miller 56).

In the three decades following the Civil War, Pierce created an impressive, profitable, and effective urban mill complex, as well as an architecturally cohesive group of buildings along Adams St. These Victorian commercial buildings, thought to be the finest extant mill complex in the city of Boston, are the architectural highlights of our Lower Mills walking tour. The Lower Mills had, in the years following Pierce's lease of the Baker Chocolate Company, gone from a mill village to an industrial area, and the company, which had increased forty-fold under Pierce's leadership, employed hundreds. The noted Boston architectural firm of Bradlee, Winslow and Wetherell carried out the building of the mill complex. With the use of red brick and consistent architectural detail, the architects successfully created a cohesive group of mills with a unique character.

[*Established* 1780.]

"LA BELLE CHOCOLATIÈRE."
W. BAKER & CO.'S REGISTERED TRADE-MARK.

"La Belle Chocolatière," W. Baker and Company's registered trademark. (*From* Boston: Its Commerce, Finance and Literature, *New York: A. F. Parsons, 1892, p. 111.*)

Baker Chocolate Company during the Forbes Years

Henry L. Pierce died in 1896, and the company was sold the following year to the Forbes Syndicate, which was headed by financier and Milton summer resident J. Murray Forbes (Site 5). Forbes and other Milton residents purchased the ten thousand shares of the company for $4.75 million from the Pierce estate and continued to expand the physical plant. Between 1897 and 1927, the Forbes Syndicate built the Ware Mill (1902; Site 9), the Preston Mill (1903; Site 10), the Power House (1906;  Site 4), the Forbes Mill (1911; Site 5), and the impressive Administration Building (1919; Site 6). Not only was the mill space doubled, but the use of advertising in local and nationwide newspapers and magazines made Walter Baker and Company a household name. The Forbes syndicate began to invest heavily in full-page color advertisements in such nationwide magazines as *Liberty, Collier's, Youth's Companion,* and *St. Nicholas Magazine.*

These beautifully illustrated advertisements touched upon every aspect of society in the United States, from the blond and blue-eyed child asking only for Baker's cocoa and young fraternity men enjoying their cocoa, to World War I doughboys enjoying Baker's cocoa rather than French

DORCHESTER (BOSTON):
WALTER BAKER & CO.

Walter Baker & Company, showing the growth
of the company. (*From M. F. Sweetser,* King's
Handbook of the United States, *Buffalo:
Moses King, 1891, p. 383.*)

away was the annual cookbook. The cookbook grew from a small, twelve-page pamphlet in 1870 to a lavishly illustrated, full-color cookbook by the early years of the twentieth century. These cookbooks not only instructed one in the proper way to melt chocolate, but also offered recipes for elegant desserts such as charlotte russe, chocolate éclairs, and chocolate bombe, as well as favorites such as chocolate cake, brownies, and numerous types of fudge. In 1927 the Forbes Syndicate sold Walter Baker and Company to the Postum Company (now known as General Foods), which continued the production of chocolate on the site until 1966, when the operation was moved to Dover, Del.

Architects of the Baker Chocolate Mill Complex

The Baker Chocolate mill complex was primarily the work of Nathaniel Jeremiah Bradlee (1829–88), Walter Winslow, and George Homans Wetherell, well-known architects whose partnership led to the design of numerous commercial structures in Boston. The firm was known successively as Bradlee and Winslow, Winslow and Wetherell, and Winslow and Bigelow (see N. J. Bradlee T2, T4, T5, T9, T11; N. J. Bradlee and Winslow T4; Winslow and Bigelow T1). It was not until 1919, when Milton architect George F. Shepard, Jr., of the firm of Shepard and Stearns, designed the Administration Building on the site of the former Hotel Milton, that the connection with the initial architectural firm came to an end.

The Victorian Mill Village Today

Today, the Lower Mills offers an important example of a nineteenth-century mill village incorporating commercial buildings within a residential neighborhood. The

wine in a small French inn. In one particularly engaging advertisement, Little Red Riding Hood approaches her grandmother's house with a basket full of chocolates and dainties, all made with Baker's chocolate. These advertisements ensured not only that Baker's chocolate was known and used by the general public, but that the company's undisputed status as the oldest manufacturer of chocolate in the United States was reinforced by its marketing managers.

During this period premiums were offered by the company to loyal customers, who could redeem coupons for bone china chocolate services, complete with a cocoa pot and cups and saucers, all embossed with a profile of "La Belle Chocolatière." These sets were made in England by Shelley, in Germany by Dresden, and in France by Limoges china factories, and they were widely sought by the public. Other premiums included embossed serving trays, silver-plated cocoa spoons, and brooches bearing the image of the company trademark. However, the most sought-after give-

Associates Building (1881), Milton Village, by Rotch and Tilden, site of the Milton Public Library from its founding to 1904. *(Courtesy of The Milton Public Library.)*

mill village includes intact mills, originally with over fifteen acres of floor space, and storehouses as well as mill-manager and mill-worker housing. Here, one can marvel at the mill complex that made chocolate not only a delicious manufacture, but also an immensely profitable one.

We begin beside the Associates Building (to the left of the top of the stairs from Milton T Station). Our walking itinerary follows the arrangement of the buildings and not the chronological date of their construction.

1. **Associates Building** (1881), Adams St., by Rotch and Tilden

This impressive Queen Anne commercial block was a radical change in the concept of a mill village being transformed into an urban area. It is a distinctive building—a combination of commercial space on the first floor, professional offices on the second floor, and an assembly hall on the third floor. With the use of decorative brickwork and terra-cotta details, panels, keystones, and roof

tiles, this sophisticated design by Arthur Rotch (1850–94) and George T. Tilden (1845–1919) made an impact on the growth of the Lower Mills. Rotch and Tilden, both of whom lived in Milton during the summer, successfully incorporated Romanesque arches with Queen Anne details, such as the massive dormers and a projecting oriel, all of which ensure its prominent place in the development of the area.

Return to the Milton T Station stairs; on the opposite side of the street on the right corner is

2. **Webb Mill** (1882), 1 Eliot St., Milton Village, by Bradlee and Winslow

The Webb Mill was built in the Romanesque Revival style using both red brick and rough-hewn brownstone as corner quoining and detail work. The use of large arches for both window surrounds and an entrance drive, from Adams St. to a loading

The Webb Mill, etching, 1887. *(From Reverend Albert K. Teele,* The History of Milton 1640–1887, *Boston: Press of Rockwell and Churchill, 1887, p. 373.)*

dock, makes this mill a dramatic contrast to the Pierce Mill across the river. With a staggered brick cornice and superb cast-iron gates to the entrance drive, the Webb Mill epitomizes the use of the Romanesque in Boston. The mill was named for the Webb Chocolate Company (1843–81), formerly known as the Webb and Twombley Chocolate Company, founded by Josiah Webb and Josiah Twombley. The mill was built by Henry L. Pierce a year after the competitor's company was purchased and subsequently named for the former manufacturer.

Across the river the first building on the left is

3. Baker Mill (1895), 1245 Adams St., Dorchester Lower Mills, by Winslow and Wetherell

The Baker Mill is a classically designed Romanesque Revival mill with massive arches joining four stories. With an arched cornice, the redbrick mill has corner quoining and large windows with brick detailing.[3] Named for Walter Baker and the family that founded the company in 1765 and operated it until 1852, the mill was built on the site of the stone mill (1813) that had been rebuilt after a fire (1848) in fireproof Quincy granite and was often referred to as the "Old Stone Mill." Baker Mill is at present unused.

Walk into the cobblestone street on the left; behind the Baker Mill is

4. Power House (1906), 10 Baker's Ct., by Winslow and Bigelow

This classical redbrick building was built as the electrical power station for the Baker Chocolate complex. Electricity replaced the earlier steam engines and permitted the installation of a refrigeration plant with three boilers and two generators that allowed for the production of chocolate throughout the year. Owing to chocolate's low melting point, production often had been suspended during the summer months prior to the erection of the Power House. A two-hundred-foot smokestack rises high above the house, making it one of the more readily identifiable parts of the mill complex. There is hope that the Power House will be saved and reused as condominiums.

Retrace your steps; on your left is

5. Forbes Mill (1911), 1235 Adams St., Dorchester Lower Mills, by Winslow and Wetherell

The Forbes Mill[4] (now on your left), built two decades after the Baker Mill, is an almost exact replica of the earlier mill. The mill was named for J. Murray Forbes of Milton and Boston's Back Bay, who headed a syndicate of investors which had purchased the Baker Chocolate Company in 1897, after the death of Henry L. Pierce the previous year. Forbes's summer estate was located on Milton Hill, a short walk from the mill complex.

The Forbes estate, a Greek Revival house designed by Isaiah Rogers (1800–69) for Sarah Perkins Forbes, the mother of the successful China trade merchant, has become the **Captain Robert Bennet Forbes House** (1833), 215 Adams St., Milton {www.forbeshousemuseum.org; call (617)-696-1815 for tour schedules}. The Forbes Syndicate operated the chocolate mills until 1927, when the mills were sold to the Postum Company. The Forbes Mill has been converted to luxury condominiums.

The next site is to the left, up the mild incline of Adams St.

6. Administration Building (1919), 1205 Adams St., Dorchester Lower Mills, by George F. Shepard

Milton resident and architect George F.

The Adams Street Mill (left) and the Pierce Mill
(ca. 1910–20), postcard. *(Courtesy of the
Anthony M. Sammarco collection.)*

These two storehouses were built in the late 1880s utilizing both the Queen Anne and Romanesque Revival styles. Simple in form, especially in regard to their intended use, these redbrick storehouses had wood docks that enabled the workmen to load horse-drawn wagons and, later, diesel trucks with wrapped and boxed chocolate that was delivered throughout Boston or shipped by railroad. Today, the use of the storehouses is being debated, and it is hoped that they will become an integral part of the Lower Mills revitalization.

Continue up Adams St.; on the other side you will find

8. Pierce Mill (1872), 1220–1222 Adams St., Dorchester Lower Mills, by Bradlee and Winslow

Named for Henry Lillie Pierce, the Pierce Mill was the first structure built to allow for the expansion of the production of chocolate. Not only did Pierce have his office here (in the projecting wing on the right, overlooking the Neponset River), but also chocolate was produced and wrapped here. The Pierce Mill was built two years after Dorchester was annexed by the City of Boston and is an impressive Second French Empire design that used red brick and arched windows, contrasting window lintels, and a heavily bracketed cornice. The pedimented gables and the brick stringcourses carry one's eye across the facade, and the mansard roof, which retains its cast-iron cresting, as well as its sloping location, gives additional importance to its

Shepard, Jr., of the architectural firm of Shepard and Stearns, designed this classical Georgian Revival building, the first instance of a building in the Baker complex not designed by Bradlee, Winslow and Wetherell or their successors. Built to house the executive offices and a small museum on the history of the Baker Chocolate Company, it has a monumental limestone Ionic portico and a balustrade along the roofline and, with its siting on a knoll overlooking Adams St., can be seen from all the mill buildings. A large neon sign, which illuminated the Lower Mills with "Walter Baker" until 1966, remains in place on the roof. The interior is in an impressive classical style and has a sweeping marble staircase that rises to meet a life-size reproduction of "La Belle Chocolatière" (1920), by Boston artist Henry E. Smith. The Administration Building, converted to artists' lofts and studios, opened in the fall of 2002.

Visible, but set back near the Neponset River, are

7. Storehouses (1888–90), Adams St., to the south of the Pierce Mill, by unknown architect

Washington Warren, a prominent lawyer and jurist, and president of the Bunker Hill Monument Association 1847–75. This organization was responsible for the erection of the *Bunker Hill Monument* and surrounding 115-house-lot development on the summit of Breed's Hill. The organization was a major political force in Charlestown during the nineteenth century. Mr. Warren was a graduate of Harvard College (1830) and served as mayor of Charlestown for the first four years after its incorporation as a city (1847–50). According to Charlestown historian Timothy Thompson Sawyer, "many distinguished visitors to the Monument were entertained by him with liberality and elegance" (412).

Bunker Hill Monument on Charlestown's Old Seal. *(From Souvenir of the 50th Anniversary of the Dedication of Bunker Hill Monument, Boston: Bunker Hill Times, 1893, p. 16.)*

No. 7 Monument Sq. was originally owned by Peter Hubbell, a New Yorker who made a fortune in Charlestown's thriving mid-nineteenth-century ice export industry as well as the profitable Bay State Brick yards in northwest Cambridge. He was president of the Monument Bank and the Charlestown Gas Company and a major patron of St. John's Episcopal Church in Charlestown. Timothy Thompson Sawyer noted that Mr. Hubbell "was a very active man and often jumped from the platform when [train] cars were in motion; but he made one jump too many and lost a leg as a consequence."

Cross the street and climb the stairs to the Bunker Hill Monument.

29. *The Bunker Hill Monument* (1825–43), Monument Sq.

The *Bunker Hill Monument* was built between 1825 and 1843 to mark the site of the Battle of Bunker Hill on June 17, 1775. It is well known that early historical accounts of this battle mistakenly identified the scene of this bloody skirmish as Bunker Hill rather than Breed's Hill. The much higher Bunker Hill is actually the next hill west of Breed's Hill. What is less well known is that in 1794, an earlier monument constructed of wood in the form of an eighteen-foot Tuscan pillar was erected atop Breed's Hill by members of King Solomon's Lodge (Site 8) to honor "Major-General Joseph Warren and Associates."

Between 1818 and 1825 fifteen acres of Russell's pasture were chosen by Dr. John Collins Warren and others as a site for a suitable memorial to a battle that the patriots lost, but at which they nevertheless proved their willingness to stand up to British military might. The Bunker Hill Monument Association chose an Egyptian Revival obelisk for this fabled hilltop and hired Solomon Willard as the supervising architect. The choice of an obelisk reflects the prevailing romantic predilection of the time for references to the ancient world. Egypt was evocative of things enduring and eternal—the Egyptian Revival style was deemed the appropriate architectural mode to commemorate an event that should live on forever in the hearts and minds of the United States.

The project required innovative methods to transport the heavy Quincy granite to the hilltop. Engineer Gridley Bryant, siting. Today, the Pierce Mill has been converted to apartments.

Pass through the entrance to the courtyard.

9. **Ware Mill** (1902), accessible through the courtyard to the rear of the Pierce Mill, by Winslow and Bigelow

The Georgian Revival Ware Mill is an elegant classical redbrick building on the site of Dr. Ware's Chocolate Company. This former competitor was purchased by Henry L. Pierce, who built a classically detailed mill with corner quoining, dentiled cornice, and keystones above the window lintels. The Ware Mill, named after Dr. Jonathan Ware, the former manufacturer and a well-known physician in Milton, now serves as apartments. A codfish weathervane soars high above the building.

Farther on is

10. **Preston Mill** (1903), to the rear of the Forbes Mill, adjacent to the Ware Mill, by Winslow and Bigelow

The Preston Mill uses architectural details similar to those of the Ware Mill, except for a more heavily dentiled cornice. The mill was named for Dr. James Baker's brother-in-law, Edward Preston (1744–1819), who had founded Preston's Chocolate Mill in 1768, three years after Baker's mill commenced the production of chocolate in the Lower Mills. The mill was sold by the Preston heirs in 1859 to Henry D. Chapin, who in turn sold it to Henry L. Pierce a year later. The Preston Mill, like the Pierce and Ware mills, has been converted to apartments.

On your right as you exit the courtyard is

11. **Adams Street Mill** (1888–89), 1200 Adams St., Dorchester Lower Mills, by Winslow and Wetherell

The Adams Street Mill was built in the Romanesque Revival style in red brick, with a gentle curve conforming to Adams St. as it bends to enter the Lower Mills. With arched windows and an arched brick cornice, the mill is one of the least ornamented structures in the mill complex. The arched connector that joins this mill with the Pierce Mill spans the entrance to a cobblestone-paved courtyard that was once a loading area. Here cacao beans would arrive in burlap bags and leave in neatly wrapped bars of Baker's chocolate. Today, the courtyard's entrance leads to the apartments in the Pierce, Ware, and Preston mills. The Adams Street Mill was named for Adams St., the former "Lower Road," which connected Dorchester's Meeting House Hill with the Lower Mills until 1840, when it was renamed in honor of President John Adams.

With Adams Street Mill on your right, walk around the corner to your right and along Adams St. to find on the next corner to the right

12. **Mason Regulator Company** (1888), 1190 Adams St., corner of Adams and Medway Sts., Dorchester; now Standish Village

The Mason Regulator Company once produced regulators for clocks and other mechanisms to mark the passage of time. This mill was built in the Queen Anne style in red brick with an impressive turreted tower on the corner of the building. The turret retains its original weathervane, and its massive windows and lintel details create an attractive building. The mill has been renovated for Standish Village at Lower Mills, an assisted-living facility for the elderly.

Turn into Medway St. to see

13. **Mason House,** 25 Medway St., Dorchester Lower Mills, possibly designed by John A. Fox

Built for the Mason family, who owned the Mason Regulator Company, this large wood-framed house is a fine example of a Stick-style residence of the late nineteenth century. With impressive details such as exterior paneling, interesting mullion window treatments, and an imposing entrance porch, the house offers a rare example in Dorchester of an intact house of this style. The house has been converted to condominiums in recent years.

Retrace your steps now to Pierce Sq., and walk along Washington St., bearing to the right. On your left will be

14. **Henry L. Pierce House** (ca. 1830), 1133 Washington St., Dorchester Lower Mills, by unknown architect

This impressive Greek Revival house with attic lantern windows was built circa 1830 and was purchased in 1849 by Jesse Pierce, an educator at Milton Academy who had recently moved to the Lower Mills with his wife, Elizabeth Vose Lillie, and their two sons. The house was also the residence of Henry Lillie Pierce, president of the Baker Chocolate Company. After Dorchester was annexed to the City of Boston on January 4, 1870, Pierce served as mayor of the city in 1872 and 1877, as well as a member of the Massachusetts House of Representatives in 1861, 1862, and 1866, and as a U.S. congressman between 1873 and 1877. Today, the Pierce House has been converted to commercial office space, but it still represents the domestic quality of the Lower Mills.

Scattered throughout the area (see no. 15 on map) are

15. **Workers' Housing**

Fine examples of workers' row housing can be found along Adams, Richmond, River, Old Morton, Temple, and Sanford Sts. in Dorchester Lower Mills and Eliot, High, and Maple Sts. in Milton—all of which are within walking distance of this tour.

Return to Milton Station.

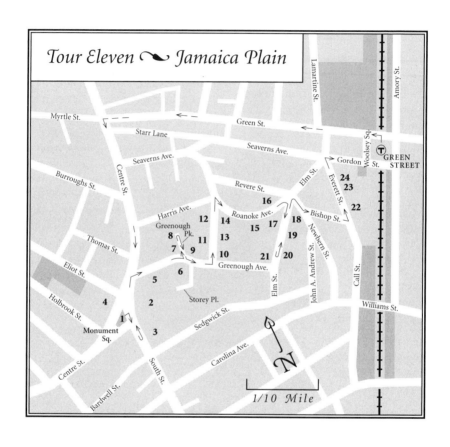

Tour Eleven ~ Jamaica Plain

Myrtle St.

Starr Lane

Green St.

Seaverns Ave.

Seaverns Ave.

Lamartine St.

Amory St.

Woolsey Sq.

Gordon St.

GREEN STREET

Burroughs St.

Centre St.

Seaverns Ave.

Revere St.

Elm St.

Everett St.

24
23

22

Harris Ave.

Roanoke Ave.

16

Bishop St.

Thomas St.

Greenough Pk.

12 14

15 17 18

8 11

13

19

7 9

10

21 20

Greenough Ave.

Newbern St.

John A. Andrew St.

Call St.

Eliot St.

5

6

Holbrook St.

4

2

Storey Pl.

Elm St.

Williams St.

1

Monument Sq.

3

Sedgwick St.

Centre St.

South St.

Carolina Ave.

N

Bardwell St.

1/10 Mile

VICTORIAN JAMAICA PLAIN: MONUMENT SQ. AND SUMNER HILL

by *Edward W. Gordon*

Tour Location: See Greater Boston Key Map for location of the Tour, page xli. See T Stop Diagram for the T stop location, page xl.

 About Walking the Tour: Site 1 is located at the historic Monument (formerly Eliot) Sq. crossroads near Centre St., an unusually vibrant commercial thoroughfare complete with tempting restaurants and interesting shops, our tour takes us through residential neighborhoods, winds its way, over mildly ◢ hilly terrain through the more elevated section of Sumner Hill, and descends southward into the Stony Brook Valley. The tour ends near the Green St. (Orange line) Station.

Thumbnail Sketch of Sights: See Introduction, page xxxvi.

Approximate Walking Time: 1 to 1½ hours.

Alternate T Stop: Green St. T Station, Orange Line; about 15 minutes from downtown Boston. (Upon leaving the station, turn left and walk west on Green St. a little over ⅓ mile, until you come to the end of the street. Turn left on Centre St. and walk four blocks along Centre St. to Monument Sq.)

Alternate T Stop: Monument Sq. Take the T Bus 39, from the back (the Clarendon St. side) of Back Bay/South End Station (shown on map on p. 18) at Copley Sq., directly to Monument Sq.

Begin at: The Civil War Monument, Monument Sq. at the junction of Centre, South, and Eliot Sts., just south of the Jamaica Plain business district.

INTRODUCTION

Historically, the Jamaica Plain neighborhood has always been part of a larger municipal entity. Like the Boston neighborhoods of Allston and Roslindale, "J.P." has never existed on its own as an independent town. Nevertheless, few parts of Boston have developed such a distinctive identity —an identity inextricably bound to exceptional natural beauty, antique housing stock, prominent families, productive industries, and creative residents. During the Colonial and Federal periods, Jamaica Plain's fertile farmlands fell within the central segment of the settlement of Roxbury. At the time of its founding in 1630, Roxbury extended westward from Boston to Dedham. In 1851 the town of West Roxbury was separately established and included what is now Jamaica Plain. Eliot (later Monument) Sq. was considered the social and political center of the community, and in 1868 a town hall, which still stands, was built next door to the Loring-Greenough house. West Roxbury had a short life as an independent town; by 1873 the conventional wisdom no longer viewed independence as a positive state of affairs and the town voted to annex itself to Boston.

The origin of the name Jamaica Plain has never been firmly documented. According to late-nineteenth-century historian Samuel Adams Drake, the local Colonial-era gentry were overly fond of their Jamaican rum. During the Colonial era, this section of Roxbury was sometimes referred to as "Jamaica End" or "Pond Plain." Contrary to the concept of a plain, the neighborhood is flat in only two areas: one bounded by Centre St. and the east side of Jamaica Pond and the other following roughly the Stony Brook Valley.

In the late seventeenth and eighteenth centuries, the village of Jamaica Plain grew up around Monument Sq. (then called Eliot Sq.), with scattered farms along Centre and South Sts. Indeed, Jamaica Plain farms supplied Boston markets with fruits and vegetables. In 1689 John Eliot, pastor of the First Church of Roxbury and a famous evangelist to Native Americans, gave seventy-five acres of land to the town for the support of a school and a schoolmaster. This tract is still the historic center of Jamaica Plain and two buildings, Eliot School (1832) and Eliot Hall (1855), as well as Eliot St. still bear his name. In the second half of the eighteenth century, the scenic qualities of Jamaica Plain led many of Boston's leading citizens, including Governor Francis Bernard and John Hancock, to build summer residences there. In 1769 the third or middle parish of Roxbury was established on the site of the present Unitarian Church.

On the eve of the Revolution, the Tory gentry, including the Lorings, abandoned their Jamaica Plain estates, preferring political exile in Great Britain to living among neighbors who wanted to break free from the monarchy's control. Most of the eighteenth-century estates remained intact until the early Victorian era, when the Boston and Providence Railroad (1834) opened Jamaica Plain to residential subdivisions. Although the financial panic of 1837 temporarily derailed development, residential enclaves like Sumner Hill were alive with the sounds of house construction during the 1840s and 1850s. After the Civil War, Queen Anne, Shingle-style, and Colonial Revival houses were added to the existing housing stock of Greek Revival, Italianate, and mansard dwellings. Houses later prized by late-twentieth-century preservationist homeowners for the beauty of their materials and the high quality of their craftsmanship had been originally home to lawyers, physicians, and provisions dealers as well as captains of Stony Brook Valley industry. Indeed, breweries, carriage factories, rubber mills, tanneries, and a chemical dye works were but short walks from the areas of up-scale housing located near Franklin Park and Jamaica Pond, as well as atop Sumner Hill.

During the last quarter of the nineteenth century, Frederick Law Olmsted's creation of the famous Emerald Necklace park system at the edges of the neighborhood ensured Jamaica Plain's place as one of the most desirable places to live. Today, Jamaica Plain has more open green space, both publicly and privately owned, than any other part of Boston. Over time, innovations related to public transportation provided commuters with alternatives to the Boston and Providence line. Horsecar railroad tracks extended to Jamaica Plain's Centre St. by 1857, were thrust out along Washington St. in 1864, and reached West Roxbury by the 1870s. The Washington and Centre St. lines were electrified in 1890 and 1891, respectively.

SUMNER HILL

Sumner Hill encompasses the hilly, rugged terrain between Centre and South Sts. (west) and the old Boston and Providence Railroad tracks (east). Extending northward from Sedgwick to Green St., its building stock, with the exception of undistinguished commercial buildings bordering Centre St., is overwhelmingly residential and dates from 1845 to 1895. In general, Sumner Hill is characterized by substantial, well-crafted frame houses situated on ample, tree-shaded, and pudding stone wall–enclosed lots.

The nucleus of the Sumner Hill residential area is the Loring-Greenough estate at 12 South St. The "Mansion House," with its adjoining carriage house and gardens, is the last of numerous country houses of its period in Jamaica Plain. Built in 1760 for naval officer Joshua Loring, the substantial Georgian Loring house was used as a hospital at the beginning of the American Revolution. Now open to the public as a house museum, the Loring-Greenough house's interior contains interesting eighteenth- and nineteenth-century woodwork, wallpapers, and furnishings.

In 1830 Sumner Hill was still devoid of cross streets, and its few structures were spread out along the southeastern side of Centre St. Sumner Hill was part of the estate of David Stoddard Greenough, whose widow, Maria Foster Greenough, upon her death in 1843 left her property to her second husband, William Hyslop Sumner (1780–1861). William H. Sumner, the son of Governor Increase Sumner, was the developer of East Boston in the 1830s. Sumner's Greek Revival/Regency residence at 10 Roanoke Ave. was reportedly well-stocked with Madeira and decorated with European and American paintings, as he was a connoisseur of both vintage spirits and fine art. Twenty years after his death, St. John's Episcopal Church was built across the street from Sumner's mansion on land that had been left to the church in his will. Designed in the English Country Gothic style from designs provided by Harris M. Stephenson, the church stands at the southern crest of Sumner Hill.

Beginning around 1845, Sumner set out a curvilinear street system whose paths followed contours predicated by the elevated terrain; it was one of the earliest commuter suburban enclaves in the country. Sumner Hill's street names refer to places in Virginia and the Carolinas, including New Bern (spelled in Sumner Hill as "Newbern"),

Roanoke, and Virginia (now Revere St.). Sumner Hill represents an early example of the custom of choosing street names on the basis of a particular theme. Surveyors of the distinctive, meandering roads of the early commuter suburbs were undoubtedly influenced by the systems of paths in the rural garden cemeteries of the 1830s: Mount Auburn in Cambridge, Mass. (see Mt. Auburn Cemetery T12), Laurel Hill in Philadelphia, Greenwood in Brooklyn, and Forest Hills Cemetery[1] (1847), approximately a mile away.

Among the noteworthy subdivisions within the larger Sumner Hill development was Alveston St., named in honor of Anna Greenough Burgyn's estate in North Carolina, set out in 1859 and dubbed "the street of the Civil War colonels" because several of its original homeowners held that rank. The segment of Alveston between Greenough and Roanoke Aves. was built up with generously proportioned, ornate Italianate mansard houses between the early 1860s and the early 1870s. During the 1870s commercial development adjacent to the Jamaica Plain depot at Woolsey Sq. was paralleled by residential construction activity along nearby Elm, Bishop, and Newbern Sts. The work of local architect/builder John D. Webster is represented in the mansard-stick houses at 9, 11, and 15 Bishop St. (1870s) as well as at the mansion of his father, H. B. Webster, at 73 Elm St.

Striking an oddly urban note within this leafy suburban setting are groups of three and four masonry row houses, including 22, 24, and 26 Greenough Ave. and 60–64 Elm St. Built just before the real estate market collapsed during the financial panic of 1873, these houses suggest that their developers thought that a trend toward lucrative row-house construction might ensue on the heels of the rows' completion. This was not the case. The subdivision of the row houses' lots represents a third generation of subdivision within the Colonial-era Loring estate.

During the 1880s and 1890s the construction of architecturally sophisticated Queen Anne and Colonial Revival residences reinforced Sumner Hill's status as a fashionable suburban enclave. Greenough Ave.'s cul-de-sac offshoots, such as Greenough Park and Storey Place, provided intimate, picturesque settings for clapboard and wood shingle–clad residences designed primarily by the noted architect William Ralph Emerson (1833–1917). Emerson is perhaps best known for the Queen Anne design of the former Boston Art Club at Newbury and Dartmouth Sts. in the Back Bay; his residential work frequently incorporated his signature motif: a carved, stylized pine tree typically placed at the apex of a gable.

Unlike surrounding neighborhoods, Sumner Hill was never developed with three-deckers. The nearest evidence of three-deckers, one of Boston's signature house types of the period 1885–1930, is along Green St. at the eastern edge of the area. Since the 1970s, Sumner Hill houses have been purchased and restored by successive waves of preservationists, whose impact is evident in the repairs to original fabric as well as in the appropriate paint colors.

We begin at the Civil War monument, at the junction of Centre, South, and Eliot Sts., just south of the Jamaica Plain business district. Originally the focus of Jamaica Plain's Colonial-era agricultural community, over time the historic Centre and South Sts.' intersection is bordered by important local institutions, including the Loring-Greenough House Museum, Curtis Hall (the old West Roxbury Town Hall, 1868), as well as the Unitarian Church (1853).

Monument Sq., Jamaica Plain, *West Roxbury Soldiers' Monument* and First Church in Jamaica Plain (1853), by N. J. Bradlee. *(Courtesy of the Boston Athenæum.)*

1. **Civil War Monument** (*West Roxbury Soldiers' Monument*, 1871), **Monument Sq.,** by W. W. Lummis

The distinctive Victorian Gothic Civil War monument, designed by W. W. Lummis of Lynn, marks the triangular park at Monument Sq. The monument's land was the site of the first schoolhouse in Jamaica Plain (1676). Composed of granite, complete with pointed arches on each side and topped by a full-length sculpture of a Union soldier, the monument's interior vault contains a pillar of Italian marble on which are inscribed the names of fallen West Roxbury soldiers. On the north side of the monument is a slate slab, a Colonial-era milestone. Bearing the inscription "5 Miles Boston Townhouse P. Dudley Esq. 1735," this marker is five miles from the Boston Townhouse (now known as the Old State House[2]).

    Cross busy South St. to

2. **The Loring-Greenough House** (1760), **12 South St.** {Open on scheduled tour days and by appointment; www.lghouse.org; (617)-524-3158}

The Loring-Greenough House is the last well-preserved example of a pre–Revolutionary War mansion in Jamaica Plain. Built for Commodore Joshua Loring of the British Royal Navy, the Loring House, with its high-style Georgian ornamentation, including a Chinese Chippendale balustrade atop the substantial hip roof, makes a sophisticated design statement for its place and time. The Lorings abandoned their sizable estate, since their Tory politics were not in tune with those of their patriotic farmer neighbors. General Washington used the former Loring residence as a hospital in 1775–76. From 1786 until 1924, David Stoddard Greenough and his descendants owned this house. Slated for the wrecker's ball, the mansion was saved by a women's group called the Jamaica Plain Tuesday Club in 1924.

The Loring-Greenough House. *(From Justin Winsor, ed.,* The Memorial History of Boston, *vol. 2, Boston: James R. Osgood and Company, 1881, p. 345.)*

Interior of the Loring-Greenough House, with dog beside fireplace (1894). Photograph by Annie Hazen Thwing. *(Courtesy of the Boston Athenæum.)*

3. **Curtis Hall** (1868), by George Ropes, Jr.; formerly West Roxbury Town Hall

Situated next door to the Loring-Greenough House, Curtis Hall, now the Municipal Building, served briefly as West Roxbury's town hall from its completion in 1868 until 1874—the year West Roxbury/J.P. was officially annexed to Boston. This building was named for Nathaniel Curtis, a wealthy Boston merchant and West Roxbury landowner; the land was purchased from David S. Greenough. The Norfolk County deed documenting this sale stipulates "the said town shall suitably fence the said lot and keep the fences in repair."

Designed in the French Second Empire style by Boston architect George Ropes, Jr., the building possesses the massing typical of the style, with a center pavilion flanked by wings. From 1876 until 1908 the building served as the first branch of the Boston Public Library to purchase books with public funds. The second floor's interior and the original mansard roof were destroyed by fire in 1908. In 1912 a handsome granite Doric entrance porch was added to the main facade. Known as the Municipal Building since the library's relocation to the Craftsman-style building next door, the structure has served in recent years as a Little City Hall and youth recreation center. *Across the street is*

4. **First Church in Jamaica Plain** (1853), 6 Eliot St., by Nathaniel J. Bradlee; the site of the First Meetinghouse (1769); now the First Church in Jamaica Plain Unitarian Universalist

Dominating the north side of the square at the corner of Eliot and Centre Sts. is the Unitarian church, the site of the First Meetinghouse. At the rear of the church is an eighteenth-century burying ground and the John Eliot School. A noted missionary to Boston-area Native Americans during the late seventeenth century, John Eliot produced an American Indian translation of the Bible. In his will, Eliot bequeathed land in Jamaica Plain for the purposes of accommodating a meetinghouse, school, and burying ground. The Unitarian church was designed by the noted Boston architect Nathaniel J. Bradlee. Orginal Bradlee plans for the church are in the collection of the Boston Athenæum.[3] Essentially, this granite church is a late example of the type of towered Gothic Revival church introduced to Boston during the late 1820s at Old Trinity Church (nonextant) on Summer St. in downtown Boston (see Bradlee T2, T4, T5, T10).

Walk back to the Loring-Greenough House and continue past it on Centre St. to the corner of the Loring-Greenough property. Turn right onto Greenough Ave., a pleasant street of primarily large Queen Anne houses designed by William Ralph Emerson and others. Most of these houses were built on lots carved from the Greenough estate during the 1880s and 1890s.

5. 7 Greenough Ave. (1893), by Blackall and Newton

Blending asymmetrical Queen Anne form with Georgian Revival ornamentation, this dignified residence provides a fine introduction to the architectural treasures of Greenough Ave. Designed by Boston architects Blackall and Newton in 1893 for a member of the Greenough family, this house is particularly noteworthy for the turned and carved elements of the entrance porch. Both of the residence's architects received prestigious Rotch Fellowships, which funded architectural studies in Europe. Born in Chicago, Clarence Blackall[4] was a talented theater architect who was responsible for the designs of the Colonial and Wilbur Theatres[5] in Boston's Theater District (see Blackall T6).

6. 15 Greenough Ave. (1880), by William Ralph Emerson

Providing a memorable glimpse of late Victorian-era Jamaica Plain, this handsome residence is the centerpiece of a streetscape of Queen Anne houses designed during the 1880s. Clad with clapboards and wood shingles, this rambling residence overlooks an ample front lawn and a driveway whose semicircular configuration survives from the late nineteenth century. Ornamenting the apex of the main facade's highest gable is Emerson's signature motif: an abstract pine tree characterized by a trunk with extended, wavy limbs.

No. 15 was presented in a French publication as cutting-edge American design for its day. César Daly selected 15 Greenough Ave. as one of three buildings by Emerson to be included in his *L'Architecture Américaine* (1885). No. 15's original owner was Joseph Hardon, a partner in a Sumner St.,

Boston, millinery firm (see William Ralph Emerson T2, T4, T5, and note 11 T12).

7. 18 Greenough Ave. (1885), attributed to William Ralph Emerson

Probably designed by William Ralph Emerson, this Queen Anne residence is particularly noteworthy for its lovely stained-glass windows and Medieval Revival characteristics, such as the second-story overhang and half-timbered gables. It marks the entrance to the picturesque Greenough Park cul-de-sac. No. 18's original owner was Cyrus White, a Centre St., Jamaica Plain, dealer in "Home furnishings, Hardware, Plumbing, Furnaces, Ranges, Stoves, Drain Pipe Gas Fittings." White invented the "Tropic" Furnace, which according to an 1888 advertisement "not only supplies an abundant amount of heat with a small expenditure of coal, but has also made it very 'warm' for its competitors."

Much of the Greenough Ave. area's charm is tied to the presence of two cul-de-sacs, Greenough Park and Storey Place, located opposite each other just to the west of the avenue's intersection with Alveston St. Turn left onto Greenough Park and proceed to the last house on the left.

8. 1 and 2 Greenough Park (1856); Queen Anne ell (1880s) by R. W. Emerson

Originally half its present size, this house evolved from an 1856 Italianate dwelling that was enlarged by the addition of a Queen Anne rear ell during the 1880s, characterized by a nearly seamless blending of side-hall plan end-gable house with a Queen Anne rear ell. The house is enlivened by porches and a dormer oriel. The original mid-1850s component was among the first houses built on the Greenoughs' initial subdivision of their estate. The original owner was Levi Champion, expressman. In 1872 the Greenough Park cul-de-sac was set out by Jamaica Plain grocer David Keezer, who owned a number of properties in the area.

Resume your exploration of Greenough Ave.

9. **22, 24, 26 Greenough Ave.** (1875)

This trio of redbrick, polygonal-bayed row houses were built for F. B. Beaumont, a former Union Army officer who settled on Sumner Hill during the late 1860s. Beaumont may have thought he was starting a trend toward the development of the neighborhood as a quarter for masonry town houses, but instead his town-house trio is a delightful anomaly within a neighborhood of overwhelmingly wooden suburban buildings.

Turning left from Greenough Ave. to Alveston St., one enters the picturesque realm of substantial, mansard-roofed suburban residences noteworthy for ornamentation that includes quoining at corners, elaborate window enframements, porches with arched bracing, and dormers with arched roofs. Many of the basements are constructed of ledge stone probably quarried on site. Set out in 1859, with most of the houses dating from the early 1860s until the economic downturn of 1873, Alveston St. was referred to as "the street of the Civil War colonels."

10. **40 Alveston St.** (ca. 1860s); addition (1891)

According to local lore, this house achieved its present appearance in 1891, when a circa 1860s Italianate house was connected to an 1891 structural component characterized by a distinctive medieval sensibility. Exhibiting rough wooden shingles, a multiplicity of gables, and massive brick and stone chimneys, this house ranks among the more substantial residences in the area. Thomas L. Livermore, the original owner, was an officer of the Lockwood Manufacturing Company, builders of "steam ships, tow boats, steam yachts, Lighters, Engines and Heavy machinery."

11. **31 Alveston St.** (1871–72)

This stylish and substantial house provides evidence of original owner David Keezer's success as a local grocer. Scattered about Jamaica Plain are a half dozen or more Second Empire residences that adhere to the formula evident at 31 Alveston St. Here a flush-board–sheathed, quoin-edged center pavilion is flanked by bay "wings" exhibiting windows with elaborate Italianate surrounds. This boxy, rectangular residence is surmounted by a bell-cast mansard roof sheathed with slate shingles.

12. **23 Alveston St.** (ca. 1870)

Enclosed by a mansard roof that is concave rather than convex, the main facade is stepped out in a pleasing manner. Exhibiting windows set off by surrounds displaying incised linear Neo-Grec motifs, this house was built around 1870 for Colonel F. B. Beaumont. He numbered among the former Union officers of that rank who settled on Sumner Hill after the Civil War. After the return of peace to the nation in 1865, Beaumont found work as a clerk on Court St. in Boston and moved from Arlington to Jamaica Plain in 1866.

13. **28 Alveston St.** (1863)

Shaded by mature trees, this house ranks among the most pleasing of Alveston's Second Empire residences by virtue of its proportions and design details. Here the main block is offered up for inspection on a high ledge-stone foundation. The center entrance is sheltered by a type of porch enlivened by curvilinear bracing that is typical of Jamaica Plain houses of this style. The house was built for Benjamin W. Putnam. His occupation is listed in *Boston Business Directories* of the early 1860s as "insurance agent and teacher of drawing." Perhaps Putnam's draftsmanship is evident in the delicate leaf detail in the lintels of the second-story windows.

14. 20 Alveston St. (1863–64)

Memorably anchoring the corner of Alveston St. and Roanoke Ave., this Second Empire residence at 20 Alveston St. was built by housewright Stephen Heath for insurance agent John Bumstead of Dedham. Heath had purchased the lot from brothers John E. and George Williams, harness makers of Green St., who stipulated in a Norfolk County deed that no building was to be erected within twenty feet of Alveston St., and that no public stables, distillery, or workshop was to be built on the premises for twenty years.

At Alveston's intersection with Roanoke Ave., follow Roanoke's meandering path over the top of Sumner Hill and descend into the Stony Brook Valley. Sumner Hill's street pattern was conceived during the 1840s, when the winding pathways of the early rural romantic cemeteries were beginning to influence the street patterns of the early commuter suburbs just outside Boston and other U.S. cities.

The creator of Sumner Hill's street pattern has not been documented, but David Stoddard Greenough's daughter, Anna

William H. Sumner (1780–1861).
(Courtesy of the Boston Athenæum.)

Greenough Burgyn, or Greenough family friend and Forest Hills Cemetery founder General Nathan Dearborn, or both, may have had a hand in the design system of meandering streets. Mrs. Burgyn was married to a gentleman from Tidewater country in the Carolinas and is said to have chosen street names in the development such as Roanoke, Newbern, Carolina, and Virginia (later Revere).

15. 10, 11, and 14 Roanoke Ave.

The imposing Greek Revival/Italianate 10 Roanoke Ave. was the "country mansion" of General William Hyslop Sumner (1780–1861), lawyer, legislator, adjutant general, art collector, and philanthropist, as well as the developer of East Boston and the man for whom the Sumner tunnel was named. Built in 1852, No. 10 is a mansion-scale residence featuring unusually formal treatments, such as a narrow, pedimented pavilion, wide corner pilasters, and a handsome Doric entrance porch at its north elevation. During the 1840s Sumner purchased a significant amount of acreage from the Greenoughs.

No. 10 represents the nucleus of the neighborhood that evolved from former Greenough lands during the early years of Sumner ownership. Born in 1780 to Massachusetts Governor Increase Sumner and his wife, Elizabeth Hyslop, William H. Sumner was educated at Phillips Andover Academy and Harvard, where he studied law. The author of *The History of East Boston* (1858), Sumner was by all accounts an avid art collector; he had several examples of the work of Washington Allston, his friend and Harvard classmate, hanging in his Roanoke Ave. retreat. Upon his death in 1861, he bequeathed to his wife, according to Norfolk County probate records, "my wearing apparel, four wheeled carriages, booby hut,[6] sleigh, horses, tools and implements of agriculture, also my hay and other articles in the barn, and my domestic animals, the provisions, vegetables, wines and liquors in my house and cellar."

Located directly across the street from Sumner's mansion, the house at 11 **Roanoke Ave.** (1885–86) is one of the finest examples of a Queen Anne–style residence in Jamaica Plain. The stucco-parged residence at 14 **Roanoke Ave.** was for many years the home of the Dole family that became synonymous with the pineapple industry in the Hawaiian Islands during the late nineteenth and early twentieth centuries {see street plaque}.

Continuing southward on Roanoke Ave., stop at the crest of the hill to experience an extraordinary Victorian-era landscape, complete with distant views of Franklin Park's hills, while in the middle ground are the remaining industrial buildings of the Stony Brook Valley. On the east side of the street, overlooking lawns that sweep down to Elm St., is the ledge stone–constructed St. John's Episcopal Church (Site 16). To the west is the pudding stone wall–enclosed grounds of the well-preserved cupola-topped Ridell House at 6 Roanoke Ave. (Site 17). Directly ahead is the diminutive form of another ledge stone–constructed, chapel-scale house of worship originally known as the Jamaica Plain Methodist Church (Site 18).

16. St. John's Episcopal Church (early 1880s), 1 Roanoke Ave., by Harrison M. Stephenson

In his will, William H. Sumner provided funding for an Episcopal church that began to rise on a lot across the street from his house during the early 1880s. Rendered in the manner of an English Country Gothic church, St. John's Episcopal Church is constructed of ledge stone and contains a fine collection of stained-glass windows. The church's architect was Harrison M. Stephenson (1845–1909), a resident of Jamaica Plain who was initially employed during the early 1860s by the noted Boston firm of Nathaniel J. Bradlee and by 1870 was in partnership with Daniel Appleton.

17. 6 Roanoke Ave. (1873), William P. Faulkner and Daniel Chipman, builders

Like St. John's, this Second Empire residence at 6 Roanoke Ave. is perched at the crest of a hill and presides over lawns that sweep down to high ledge-stone retaining walls bordering Roanoke Ave. and Elm St. This cupola-topped house was built for Boston merchant Samuel Ridell, by local contractors William P. Faulkner and Daniel Chipman. Bristling with bays and porches, this building's main block and rear ell are surmounted by substantial slate shingle–sheathed mansard roofs. Much of the south side of Sumner Hill's vintage character is dependent on the presence of this residence, restored in recent years.

Opposite the end of Roanoke Ave., the former Jamaica Plain Methodist Church stands at the corner of Elm and Newbern Sts. Looking southwestward, Elm St. is an atypically urban masonry streetscape of modestly scaled town houses and a large high school.

18. Jamaica Plain Methodist Church (1871), 40 Elm St. (Elm and Newbern Sts.)

The origin of the Jamaica Plain Methodist Church presents something of a mystery. It was constructed of Roxbury pudding stone, but little is known about its founding religious society or the identity of its architect. The chapel-scale building is of interest for its distinctive shape, with its rectangular form enclosed by an extremely narrow, steeply pitched gable room. The building is a key component in the middle ground of the memorable view of the Stony Brook Valley that unfolds from atop the southern slopes of Sumner Hill.

19. 60, 62, 64 Elm St. (1870s)

This redbrick row house trio is an essential element of a streetscape that includes the Tudor Revival Jamaica Plain High School. Built as an investment property for Boston merchant and Roanoke Ave. resident Samuel S. Ridell, **60 Elm St.** was designed by Arthur Vinal, architect for the city of Boston during the 1880s. Vinal's public buildings include the fire station at Boylston and Hereford Sts. in the Back Bay, as well as the Municipal Waterworks Building at Chestnut Hill and numerous residences in the Back Bay and Dorchester. **Nos. 62 and 64 Elm St.** were built by contractors William P. Faulkner and Daniel Chipman.

20. Jamaica Plain High School (1901), 76 Elm St., by Andrews, Jaques and Rantoul; north wing (late 1920s); now "Sumner Hill House"

The former Jamaica Plain High School was designed in the Tudor Revival style by the Boston architectural firm of Andrews, Jaques[7] and Rantoul and constructed of red brick, Indiana limestone, terra-cotta, and steel. A redbrick north wing was erected

during the late 1920s. With flooring composed of steel beams with terra-cotta arches between them and partitions composed of terra-cotta blocks, the 1901 segment was one of the first fireproof school buildings in the city of Boston. This "marvel of fire proofing" also had an iron staircase enclosed in a brick shaft, which provided a second means of exit from all parts of the addition in case of fire. The construction of the 1901 segment was difficult because of the difference of about forty feet in the grade between Elm St. and John A. Andrew St. at the rear of the building. Incidentally, John A. Andrew St. was named to honor the governor of Massachusetts during the Civil War, who was largely responsible for convincing President Lincoln to allow African Americans to serve in the Union Army (see also 54th Regiment T6, T7).

Although the row houses and high school can be readily viewed from Roanoke Ave., a brief detour is recommended to view the H. D. Webster House at 73 Elm St., corner of Greenough Ave.

21. J. D. Webster House (1876), 73 Elm St., by John D. Webster

This house apparently represents the masterpiece of its obscure architect, John D. Webster, whose work seems to be confined to Jamaica Plain. Here the front yard is enclosed by a massive pudding-stone retaining wall, and a pair of ancient copper beech trees flanks the front walk. Characterized by an amalgam of Italianate, Stick-style, and mansardic elements, this substantial house is dominated by a center, towered component, which is crowned by a polychromatic slate roof. The house presents a romantic, pleasingly gloomy countenance, which has been described by a walking-tour participant as reminiscent of Charles Addams's drawings for the *New Yorker*.

Going back to the old Methodist church and rounding the corner, proceed eastward along Bishop St., which branches off Newbern St. to the left. Bishop St. is a delightful thoroughfare bordered by Italianate houses built and designed between 1877 and 1888 by John D. Webster. Noteworthy for the individuality of their designs are 9, 13, and 15 Bishop St.

Turn left onto Everett St. to view a collection of ornate Queen Anne houses whose backyards terminate at the bluff above the Amtrak/ Orange Line railroad tracks (formerly the Boston and Providence Railroad).

22. **22 Everett St.** (ca. 1884–90)

Situated opposite Everett St.'s intersection with Bishop St., this house was built for tailor John M. Call, Jr., and ranks among the finest examples of the Queen Anne style in the city of Boston. Call's father lived in an even more substantial house once located on the undeveloped lot between 8 and 22 Everett St. During the 1870s the Calls were major landowners in the area, owning the entire tract bounded by Everett St., Gordon St., the railroad tracks, and a point opposite Bishop St.'s intersection with Everett St. (Prior to the early 1870s, Everett St. was known as Starr St.)

Characterized by asymmetrical facades, No. 22 exhibits all manner of projecting and recessed components, including porches, bays, and a corner tower; it is crowned by a multigable roof. One of the first San Francisco–style "Painted Ladies" in the Boston area, this house was among the early spectacular restorations in the Sumner Hill area during the 1970s.

Advertisement for Sturtevant Blowers (1880s). Benjamin F. Sturtevant was a leading Boston area industrialist who had a sizable factory complex in the Stony Brook Valley. *(From* The Boston Directory, Containing the City Record, Directory of the Citizens and Business Directory, *1888, p. 1698.)*

23. **8 Everett St.** (1882–83)

Another very fine example of the Queen Anne style in Boston, this house possesses significant historical associations with the noted Boston industrialist Benjamin F. Sturtevant. An engine manufacturer by trade, Sturtevant was the inventor of the "Sturtevant Blower," a type of fan used to cool overheated machinery. *The Boston Directory* advertisements note that he manufactured "Exhausting fans, steam fans Hot Blast Apparatus, steam heaters, counter shafts and blast gates." Sturtevant's factories were located at various points along the Boston and Providence Railroad in the Stony Brook Valley. His showrooms were located on Purchase St. in Boston. During the first decades of the twentieth century, State St. attorney Henry D. Hyde owned this property.

24. 6 Everett St. (1880)

Exhibiting design similarities to 8 and 22 Everett St., this artfully rendered Queen Anne residence was built in 1880 for tea and tobacco dealer Russell F. Hyde. Undoubtedly related to next-door neighbor Henry D. Hyde of 8 Everett St., Russell F. Hyde was presumably one of the neighborhood's railroad commuters, for he commuted to a store located on Commercial St. just steps from the Boston Harbor waterfront. By 1890 the electric trolley provided Jamaica Plain residents with an alternative to the train for getting to jobs in downtown Boston.

The tour ends at 6 Everett St. To access the nearby Green St. T Station (Orange line), turn right at Gordon St., and turn left at the bottom of Gordon St. into the street named Woolsey Sq. You will see the Green St. Station.

To return to the Jamaica Plain business district, turn left onto either Seaverns Ave. or Green St., then left again onto Centre St. to the starting point at Monument Sq.

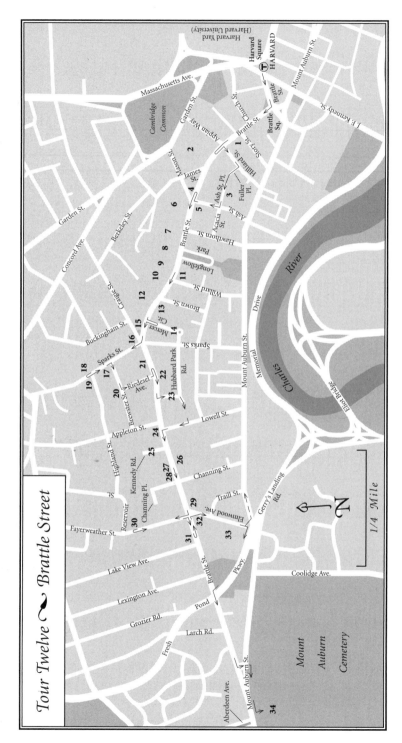

Tour Twelve ∿ Brattle Street

A VICTORIAN BOULEVARD PRESERVED: CAMBRIDGE'S BRATTLE STREET

by Charles Bahne

Tour Location: See Greater Boston Key Map for location of the Tour, page xli. See T Stop Diagram for the T stop location, page xl.

About Walking the Tour: The tour through a level residential neighborhood begins at the intersection of Story and Brattle Sts. and travels along stately Brattle St. and its nearby side streets. It concludes at James Russell Lowell's home, "Elmwood," but provides for the possibility of a concluding visit to the historic landscaped Mount Auburn Cemetery. Return transportation to Harvard Sq. is available by the T bus on Mount Auburn St., from either ending site.

Thumbnail Sketch of Sights: See Introduction, page xxxvi.

Approximate walking time: 1¼ hours (with a ¾-hour return walk from Mount Auburn Cemetery to Harvard Sq. via Mount Auburn St.—a Harvard Sq. T bus on Mount Auburn St. is available.)

T Stop: Harvard Station, Red Line; about 10 minutes from downtown Boston.

By Car: Paid parking garages are located on Eliot and Bennett Sts., between Harvard Sq. and the Charles River. On-street parking in the Harvard Sq. business district is limited, and resident permit parking rules in adjacent neighborhoods are routinely enforced, although they are not in effect on Sunday.

Begin at: The Blacksmith House, 56 Brattle St., near the corner of Brattle and Story Sts. (Leave the Harvard Sq. T station by the main exit. Cross the street toward the store called the Coop; then bear left, past the newsstand on the corner. Follow Brattle St. away from Harvard Sq. The expansive sidewalk will begin to curve steadily to the right beside a series of storefronts. Round the curve until you reach Church St. on the right. Cross to the opposite (left) side of Brattle St.

to the nearby Story St. corner. The Blacksmith House will be ahead on the left, behind an outdoor café in the courtyard.)

INTRODUCTION

"No gentleman in Cambridge walks— except upon Brattle Street." So wrote Denman Ross (Site 15) a century ago, affirming that this was the one street in the city where a proper person could embark on a pleasure stroll without incurring the disapproval of his neighbors. Or, as a satirical newspaper columnist wrote in 1894 in *The Town Crier,* "The Brattle-street life is an ideal state. . . . Like heaven, it is not so much a locality as a condition" (2).

For more than 240 years, this has been one of the most elegant residential thoroughfares in America. Brattle St. today is a rare survivor of the grand boulevards that once graced nearly every U.S. city, having escaped (from Ash St. to Lowell Park) both commercial development and apartment houses. It is a museum of American domestic architecture, featuring houses from the mid-eighteenth century to the late twentieth century. Virtually all remain single-family residences today.

Brattle St. became an exclusive residential district around 1760, when several wealthy supporters of the Crown purchased or built estates along the road to Watertown. All seven of these Colonial-era mansions remain today, giving the street its nickname, "Tory Row"; yet these eighteenth-century estate houses are far outnumbered by dwellings that were built on Brattle and adjoining streets during the Victorian era. Although many of these later houses are in the Colonial Revival style—inspired, no doubt, by their authentic Georgian neighbors—most other styles of the nineteenth century are also represented here.

Development of the neighborhood began in earnest after 1856, when New England's first street railway line began operation along Brattle St. But when metropolitan Boston's horse-drawn streetcars were electrified beginning in 1889, the influential residents of Brattle St. refused to allow overhead wires to be strung here. The electric trolleys were instead routed along parallel streets, and the horsecar rails on Brattle St. were taken up in 1894.

The Brattle St. area has also long been known for its illustrious residents. Victorian-era notables include the poets Henry Wadsworth Longfellow and James Russell Lowell, as well as others who were active in literature, science, politics, and industry. Especial treats to the spring walker are the large number of flowering shrubs and trees that have been planted all along the street. Notable among these are a profusion of lilac bushes, many of which were planted by the Longfellow family during the nineteenth century.

At the corner of Brattle and Story Sts., just west of the Story St. intersection, a stone marker on the side of a block of stores commemorates the site where the "spreading chestnut-tree" of Longfellow's poem "The Village Blacksmith" once stood:

Under a spreading chestnut-tree
The village smithy stands;
The smith, a mighty man is he,
With large and sinewy hands;
And the muscles of his brawny arms
Are strong as iron bands.

Thirty yards west of the marker is a yellow Federal-style house, still affectionately known as the Blacksmith House.

Dexter Pratt's smithy, showing the chestnut tree, watercolor by Vautin, ca. 1845. *(Courtesy of the National Park Service, Longfellow National Historic Site.)*

1. Blacksmith House (1808), 56 Brattle St.; the Dexter Pratt residence {Plaque}

This was erected in 1808 for blacksmith Torrey Hancock. Hancock subsequently built his shop, or smithy, at the Story St. corner. In 1827 the house and smithy were purchased by Hancock's apprentice, Dexter Pratt, who would later become the hero of Longfellow's poem. Pratt lived and worked here until his death in 1847. "The Village Blacksmith" was published in 1841. Although the famous opening stanza is an accurate depiction of Pratt and his smithy, Longfellow took much poetic license in his portrayal of Pratt's family situation.

When Brattle St. was widened in 1870, efforts were made to preserve the famed chestnut tree: it was left standing in the middle of the street, several feet beyond the new curb, but it succumbed a few years later. A chair made from its wood and carved by the poet's nephew, William Pitt Preble Longfellow, was donated to Longfellow by the schoolchildren of Cambridge; it can be seen inside the poet's house (Site 8). W. P. P. Longfellow's architectural work will be seen later (Site 18) in this tour.

Blacksmith House is now owned by the Cambridge Center for Adult Education.[1] A modern sculpture (1989) commemorating the chestnut tree is mounted on the courtyard's east wall, opposite the front door of the Blacksmith House. Incorporated into the sculpture are the tools and anvil that blacksmith Dimitri Gerakaris used to forge the artwork.

On the opposite side of Brattle St., beyond Appian Way, is

2. Radcliffe Yard (1885–1931)

Nearby Harvard College, when it was established in 1636, was the first college in British America—but it was exclusively for men. In December 1878 Arthur Gilman, a historian, wrote to Harvard President Charles Eliot proposing a plan to "afford to women opportunities for carrying their studies systematically forward further than it is possible for them now to do in this country" (Gilman 177). Gilman's plan envisioned Harvard professors giving separate women's classes in a parallel course of instruction. Two months later a program of "Private Collegiate Instruction for Women" was advertised, and the first classes were held in September 1879 in rented rooms at 6 Appian Way.

The school was incorporated three years later as "The Society for the Collegiate Instruction of Women," although it was commonly known as "Harvard Annex" or simply "the Annex." The name was changed to Radcliffe College in 1894, in honor of Lady Ann (Radcliffe) Moulson, an Englishwoman who had donated Harvard's first scholarship fund in 1643. The policy of separate classes for men and women lasted until World War II, when a shortage of male

students led to the inauguration of coeducational classes. Harvard subsequently assumed an increasingly greater share of the responsibility for educating women students.[2]

Acquisition of land in this city block was begun in 1885 and was substantially complete by 1917. The first building purchased was the **Fay House** (1807) on the far left-hand corner at Garden and Mason Sts. This Federal-style mansion was enlarged and remodeled by A. W. Longfellow in 1890. Other Radcliffe Yard buildings of architectural note include the **Hemenway Gymnasium** (1898), by McKim, Mead and White; several Colonial Revival buildings by A. W. Longfellow; and two earlier houses facing Brattle St., **69 Brattle St.** (1838) and **77 Brattle St.** (1821).

To reach the next site, retrace your steps back to Hilliard St. (opposite Appian Way) and turn right. Turn right again onto Fuller Place, which is behind the Loeb Drama Center. At the end of this alley, follow the pathway that leads to Ash Street Place.

3. James A. Hunnewell Residence
   (1848), **6 Ash Street Place,** Oliver Hastings, builder

Ash Street Place, a cul-de-sac off nearby Ash St., was laid out about 1836. Although the north side of the alley is now dominated by the Cronkhite Graduate Center, the south side retains its nineteenth-century character. Among the small mid-nineteenth-century houses is this Carpenter Gothic gem. The original owner, James A. Hunnewell, was a jeweler and watchmaker with a shop in Harvard Sq. Oliver Hastings was a prolific local builder; several

The James A. Hunnewell House (ca. 1860), 6 Ash Street Place. *(Mrs. Ruth P. Gray collection, courtesy of the collections of the Cambridge Historical Commission.)*

other examples of his work will be seen on this tour. The house has been restored to its original appearance, copied from a Civil War–era photograph.

Turn right at the corner of Ash St. and walk one block to Brattle St.[3] The next tour site is directly opposite, at the corner of Brattle and Mason Sts.

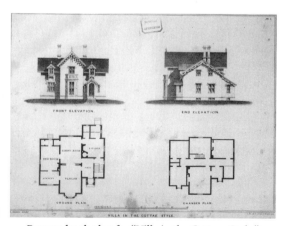

Pattern-book plan for "Villa in the Cottage Style," 85 Brattle St. *(Courtesy of the Boston Athenæum.)*

4. 85 Brattle St. (1847), Michael Norton, builder

This unusual Gothic cottage was copied from a pattern book—Chester Hills's *The Builder's Guide* (1847)—that was published in New Haven, Conn., in the same year that the house was built. The plate portraying this house, entitled "Villa in the Cottage Style," was credited to Henry Austin. The irregular massing and plan are well suited to the acute corner lot. The exterior features flush board siding scored to imitate ashlar stone; sand may have been mixed into the original paint to enhance the effect. Of special note is the trefoil window in the gable.

Continue to the left up Brattle St., away from Harvard Sq.

5. Stoughton House (1882), **90 Brattle St.,** by H. H. Richardson; additions 1900, Shepley, Rutan and Coolidge; further alterations, 1925 and 1989; the Mary Fiske (Mrs. Edwin) Stoughton residence

One of the few private residences designed by Richardson, the Stoughton House has earned an international reputation as one of the first and finest examples of the Shingle style. A contemporary critic, George William Sheldon, described the house as follows:

> The architect has used on the external walls, as well as on the roofs, cypress shingles of a size somewhat larger than usual, and has caused them to be painted a deep olive-green. . . . When Mr. Richardson built this house, he set the style, so to speak, for many other country houses; and since its erection, the use of shingles instead of clapboards has greatly increased, while the entire absence of all frivolous ornamentation of scroll-work, and other souvenirs of the "Vernacular" architecture of former years, set hundreds of architects thinking[4] [quoted in Scully 95–96].

Stud construction techniques, which were invented in the 1840s, gave architects the flexibility to mold the form of a wooden house in three dimensions, instead of being restricted to a simple rectangular box. But it was not until about 1880 that designers began to take full advantage of these new possibilities. Here Richardson has placed the stairway in a great rounded bay to the left of the entrance, and the second floor overhangs the first in a manner reminiscent of seventeenth-century New England frame houses. The entire form was then enveloped in a shingled skin, which flows over the projections and into the recesses, much like the surface of a balloon. The L-shaped plan and the low horizontal massing are also typical of Shingle-style houses.

Stoughton House (ca. 1885), 90 Brattle St., by H. H. Richardson, before alterations and construction of a high fence. *(Courtesy of the Society of the Preservation of New England Antiquities.)*

Richardson disliked working on private houses, preferring instead to design buildings for corporations and institutions. Because the architect's fee was a percentage of the construction cost, the commission for designing a house would be less than for a larger building. At the same time, Richardson found that a homeowner would often demand more individual attention from the architect himself than would a corporate client. This house was an extreme case: After receiving a series of letters from an ungrateful Mrs. Stoughton, Richardson withdrew from the project before the interior design could be completed (see Richardson T4, T5).[5]

Stoughton House has been altered several times over the years, and construction of a high brick wall in 1900 has made the house difficult to see from the street. A 1900 addition to accommodate the large library owned by Mrs. Stoughton's son extended the right part of the facade forward by several feet; and a porch over the entrance was enclosed by placing glass in the three arched openings. Later changes include the addition of a garage door and a false chimney to disguise an elevator shaft. The original roof shingles have also been replaced with smaller ones.

*Two doors up the street, at **94 Brattle St.**, is the Henry Vassall House (ca. 1746), one of the seven loyalist mansions that stood along this street in the years just prior to American independence. The nineteenth-century concrete-block fence in front of this house was erected when the street was widened in 1870; it represents one of the earliest-known uses of concrete as a construction material in this country. (A similar fence, in poorer condition, survives from the same street-widening project at 133 Brattle St. and 24–26 Craigie St.)*

On the other side of Brattle St. is the

6. **Episcopal Theological School;** now known as the Episcopal Divinity School. *Looking from right to left:* **St. John's Chapel** (1868), by Ware and Van Brunt; west end entrance (1967); **Quadrangle– Lawrence Hall, Reed Hall, Burnham Hall** (1872–80), by Ware and Van Brunt; **Winthrop Hall** (1892), by Longfellow, Alden and Harlow

The Episcopal Theological School was founded in 1867, the same year that a group of bishops put forth a declaration condemning the influence that the Church of England still had on the Episcopal Church in the United States. Benjamin Tyler Reed, the school's founder, desired the school to be in sympathy with American institutions and to uphold the truths of the Reformation "against all attempts at ritualism and sacerdotalism" (quoted in Hodges 255). He purposely located the school in Cambridge on account of the advantages to be had from proximity to Harvard. "E.T.S.," as the school was affectionately called in Cambridge, played an important role in the development of the Episcopal Church in Massachusetts and in the United States during the last third of the nineteenth century.

The school's earliest buildings were the work of Ware and Van Brunt, the architects who at the same time created Harvard's Memorial Hall in 1870 (see Van Brunt Site 28). Ironically, St. John's Chapel (1868), at the corner of Brattle and Mason Sts., is modeled after an English parish church. The entrance was originally at the side, but a new end entry was added in the 1960s. Behind the chapel is the Quadrangle, built in phases during the 1870s, and inspired by the cloisters of a Flemish village. A bell tower, lost in a hurricane, originally surmounted the quadrangle's center building. Farther still to the rear, Winthrop Hall

(1892) follows the Ruskinian Gothic theme. The latter building, a dormitory, was designed by A. W. Longfellow (Site 10).

The original buildings are all of pudding stone with trim of red brick and white Pictou (Nova Scotia) sandstone. Pudding stone, a locally popular material during the late-nineteenth-century Gothic Revival, gets its name from an English pudding—perhaps more like an American fruitcake—in which the fruits and nuts are embedded inside the dessert, only to be revealed when it is cut open. The conglomerate stone similarly contains smaller pebbles of various colors, embedded in a matrix that was deposited by the glaciers. Pudding stone is found throughout the Roxbury area; it was quarried from a site near the present Brigham Circle in Boston.

7. 101 Brattle St.

(1844), the Oliver Hastings residence, Oliver Hastings, builder

This broad-pilastered Greek Revival house shows an English Regency influence. Notable features include the curved central entrance bay, wrought-iron balconies and trellises, and a monitor roof. Oliver Hastings was a prominent local builder who designed most of the houses he built. His own residence here was erected on land that had formerly been part of the Craigie estate

Henry W. Longfellow with his daughter Edith in front of the Craigie-Longfellow House.
(Courtesy of the National Park Service, Longfellow National Historic Site.)

(Site 8). Perhaps the finest surviving example of Hastings's work, it was also a demonstration of his skill to potential customers. In 1888 Hastings's house was sold to the Reverend William Lawrence, who later served as dean of the adjacent theological school and then as the Episcopal bishop of Massachusetts. In 1924 it was acquired by the Episcopal Theological School; it is now a student residence.

8. Vassall-Craigie-Longfellow House (1759), 105 Brattle St., possibly designed by Peter Harrison; enlarged 1793; carriage house (1845), designed by Henry Wadsworth Longfellow {Tours seasonally; www.nps.gov/long; (617)-876-4491}

This Georgian mansion is nationally significant for its connection with the golden age of American letters, as well as for its Revolutionary War associations. It was erected in 1759 for John Vassall, Jr. Like the other wealthy loyalists in Cambridge—many of whom were also his relatives [6]—Vassall fled Cambridge for the safety of Boston early in 1775. General George Washington chose Vassall's vacant mansion as his headquarters soon after he arrived to take command of the Continental Army in July 1775. Washington lived here for nine months, until April 1776, with his wife, Martha, joining him in December 1775. Real estate speculator Andrew Craigie purchased the eighty-seven-acre estate and added the side piazzas in 1793. Craigie died virtually bankrupt in 1819. For the next twenty-two years his widow, Elizabeth, sold off parts of the estate grounds (which Craigie had enlarged to 140 acres) and rented out rooms in the mansion in order to eke out a living.

Henry Wadsworth Longfellow (1807–82) arrived in Cambridge in December 1836, having been appointed the Smith Professor of Modern Languages at Harvard College. The following summer, the thirty-year-old linguist—then better known for his scholarly work than for his poetry—rented a room from Mrs. Craigie. The landlady was at first unwilling to rent to the young-looking, "unbearded" teacher, who reputedly protested, "But Madam, I am no student. I am a professor in the University" (quoted in H. Hawthorne 106).

Longfellow had met and courted Fanny Appleton while on a tour of Europe. Unsuccessful at first, the poet eventually won his love's heart, and the two were wed in Fanny's home at 39 Beacon St., Boston (see p. 104 and F. Appleton T6). At the time of Longfellow's marriage[7] to Fanny Appleton in 1843, the poet's lodgings in Cambridge were coincidentally on the market to settle the estate of Elizabeth Craigie, who had passed away two years earlier. Nathan Appleton[8]—considered to be the wealthiest man in Massachusetts—purchased Craigie House and five acres of land as a wedding gift for his daughter,[9] and the mansion was Longfellow's residence until his death in 1882.

In his later life, Longfellow became wealthy in his own right from royalties earned on his many best-selling books of poetry, such as *The Song of Hiawatha* and *Evangeline*. His descendants lived in the house until 1974, keeping the ground floor open as a museum for many years. The poet's furnishings have been preserved in situ, and the house is now open to the public as a property of the National Park Service. The carriage house and garden behind the mansion were reputedly designed by Longfellow himself (see Longfellow Introduction, T3, T6),

Opposite the poet's house is Longfellow Park, donated to the city by the author's descendants in 1913. At the far end of the park, facing Mount Auburn St., is the *Henry Wadsworth Longfellow Memorial,* sculpted in 1914 by Daniel Chester French. It pays tribute also to several of the classic figures he created in his poetry, among them Miles Standish, the Village Blacksmith, the Spanish Student, Evangeline, and Hiawatha.

9. **113 Brattle St**. (1887), by Andrews and Jaques; the Edith Longfellow Dana residence

Adjacent to the Longfellow house we find a pair of dwellings built for two of the poet's daughters shortly after his death. (A third daughter—"grave Alice," as the poet called her in "The Children's Hour"—continued to live in the family homestead.) This symmetrical, twin-gabled Queen Anne house was erected for "Edith with golden hair," who had married Richard Henry Dana III, the son of her father's close friend and fellow author. Restored to its original wine color, the house is one of the few Brattle St. homes that are no longer private residences (see Sites 14, 21; and Andrews, Jaques and Rantoul T11).

Across the street at 108 Brattle St. (1870) stands another Longfellow family home, built for the poet's son Ernest, an artist. Early in the twentieth century Ernest's house was

stuccoed, and most of the original Stick-style trim was removed. The house is today hidden behind a tall concrete wall.

10. **115 Brattle St.** (1887), by Longfellow and Harlow; the Annie Longfellow Thorp residence

Colonial Revival designs became fashionable for American domestic architecture in the 1880s and 1890s after the 1876 centenary of the American Revolution sparked renewed interest in our nation's heritage. The Colonial Revival style was especially popular here on Brattle St., where the "new" designs made a natural fit with the seven "real" Georgian mansions (and two early Federal estates) located along the street.

Annie Longfellow—"laughing Allegra" in "The Children's Hour"—commissioned her cousin, Alexander Wadsworth Longfellow, Jr., to design this house for her in 1887. It is a textbook example of the early Colonial Revival, stylistically derived from the authentic Georgian house that stands just two doors away. In this case, both the architect and the client were intimately familiar with the eighteenth-century model from childhood. Noted architectural historian Bainbridge Bunting has called it "a perfect example of Queen Anne–gone–Colonial" (Bunting n.p.). Among the features of the Annie Longfellow house that can be used to distinguish the revival from the true Georgian are the large picture windows, the high gambrel roof (with room beneath it for a full story and an attic), the carriage entrance or porte cochere at the right end, the leaded-glass tracery of the sidelights flanking the entrance, and the fine detail of the "carved woodwork" (actually molded mastic) on the curved entrance porch.

Alexander Wadsworth Longfellow, Jr., the poet's nephew, studied in Paris at the Ecole des Beaux-Arts and then returned to New England. "Waddie" Longfellow, as he was called, was a senior draftsman in the office of H. H. Richardson, but he left Richardson's employ to form his own firm shortly before the master's death in 1886. A. W. Longfellow is known both for his Romanesque designs and for his work in the Colonial Revival (Sites 2, 19).

11. **112 Brattle St.** (1846), S. D. Brown, builder

This late example of a Greek Revival "cottage" is unusual for having its entrance and main facade facing the side street, whereas the columned porch is on the shady side facing Brattle St. This was one of the earliest houses to be built on the less desirable south side of the street, and the unorthodox site plan is probably a response to the lot location. Of particular note is the fine entrance doorway on Willard St.

12. **121 Brattle St.** (1844), the Joseph Worcester residence

Like his neighbor Longfellow, lexicographer Joseph Worcester (1784–1865) had been a tenant of Mrs. Craigie, having taken rooms from her just a few months before Professor Longfellow arrived at Craigie House in 1837. When the Craigie property was sold in 1843, Worcester purchased a large parcel west of the estate house. This house, built the following year, is a gable-fronted, wide-pilastered Greek Revival house whose broad cornice projection anticipates the Italianate style. In the right front corner of the lawn, an area of low ground marks the site of "Worcester's Pond." This was a favorite play spot of the neighborhood children, including Longfellow's progeny, who swam in the pond in the summer and skated on it in the winter.

In his own day, men and women of letters considered Worcester's dictionaries to

be far superior to those of his rival, Noah Webster. Oliver Wendell Holmes, in *The Poet at the Breakfast-Table* (1872), claimed facetiously that "the literary men of this metropolis are by special statute allowed to be sworn [on Mr. Worcester's dictionary] in place of the Bible" (Holmes, 3:8). It was felt by many that the utilitarian Webster had removed much of the elegance and fullness from the language. These errors were rectified by Noah Webster's son, who was also responsible for the marketing effort that made *Webster's Dictionary* a household term.

On the other side of the street are

13. **126 Brattle St.** (1890), by Cram and Wentworth; and **128 Brattle St.** (1892), by Cram, Wentworth and Goodhue

These two houses were designed by Ralph Adams Cram, who later gained fame as a distinguished scholar of the medieval era and a passionate medievalist. Cram, who was not yet thirty years old when he drew up plans for these houses, eventually became one of the most important religious architects in America. His firm designed more than fifty churches in forty states and overseas. His specialty was the Gothic Revival, but he also did work in several other styles. Cram was also dean of architecture at the Massachusetts Institute of Technology (MIT). Here his medieval interests are demonstrated by the half-timbering, leaded glass, steeply pitched roofs, and massive chimneys of these early works.

Turn left at the next corner to see

14. **Mercer Circle,** street plan (1885) by E. F. Bowker
    1, 3, 4, 6, and 8 Mercer Circle (1885), by Francis R. Allen (Allen and Kenway); **5 and 9 Mercer Circle** (1886–87), by Andrews and Jaques; **2 Mercer Circle**

(1894), by James T. Kelley; **7 Mercer Circle** (1922), architect unknown

Mercer Circle was laid out on the grounds of the Gardiner Greene Hubbard estate (Site 22) after Hubbard had removed to Washington, D.C. Developed at the same time as Hubbard Park (Site 23), Mercer Circle was not quite so exclusive. Hubbard named the street after his mother-in-law, Gertrude Mercer McCurdy. In response to a *Cambridge Tribune* reporter's query, Hubbard remarked:

> While I don't pose as a philanthropist, I really did intend to open a street which should afford some of the best and most desirable homes in the city. It cost me something like $3000 to macadamize and grade the street. I filled in the lot and then I planned for nine houses, all of which should be unique in architecture, handsome and convenient in design, thorough in construction and absolutely perfect in sanitary arrangements. The houses thus far built fulfill this description exactly, and the four that are yet to come will not be less desirable. It is my intention to rent the houses for the present (though I should not refuse to sell), and at some future day, when the right sort of people occupy them, to sell them on such terms as will enable the tenants to pay for them very gradually [quoted in "Comprehensive Plan" 1].

Most of the houses remained in Hubbard's ownership until after his death in 1897. Taken as a whole, Mercer Circle demonstrates the excellent quality and stylistic variety of Queen Anne architecture. Although the majority of the houses were designed by just one architect, that is not apparent to the casual observer. The street itself, with gently curving contours and a circular island, still retains much of the appearance of a pre-motorcar carriageway.

Return to Brattle St. and turn left. Cross the street by the traffic island, then turn right on Craigie St.

15. 26 Craigie St. (1868), by James R. Richards; the Denman W. Ross residence

This Second Empire mansard house takes full advantage of its prominent corner site, with three formal facades, each visible from the street. Each facade in turn features tripartite symmetry, which was an important element in early mansard designs. This was the lifelong home of Denman Waldo Ross, who was a pioneering scholar in the Arts and Crafts movement. Ross taught an influential course in Principles of Design at Harvard Summer School. He was also an artist, a collector, and a major benefactor of Boston's Museum of Fine Arts. This house was built for his parents, and the Ross family remained residents here until the late 1960s.

The broad intersection of Brattle, Craigie, and Sparks Sts. was known informally as "Wash Tub Square" at the turn of the century, on account of a large circular watering trough that was placed in the middle of the street for the convenience of horses and other draft animals.

Across Craigie St. is

16. 27 Craigie St. (1854), by Henry Greenough; the Eben N. Horsford residence

This Italianate villa was for many years the home of Eben N. Horsford, a Harvard chemistry professor and amateur archaeologist. Baking powder, which was invented by Horsford, is still sold under the "Rumford" brand name that he established— Horsford was Harvard's Rumford Professor of the Application of Science to the Useful Arts. After his retirement, Horsford developed and promoted a theory that the Charles River valley was the "Vineland" discovered by Leif Eriksson and the Vikings in the year 1000 (see *Leif Eriksson commissioned by Horsford* T8). One of the chief arguments of this theory, which has since been thoroughly refuted, was that the Native American name *Norumbega*—which refers to a site on the Charles River in present-day Newton—was a corruption of the word "Norwegian."

Horsford's house was designed by Henry Greenough, an "artistic dilettante" and amateur architect who designed several buildings in Cambridge. Greenough's father had been a local real estate dealer and builder, and his first designs were supplied for the family business. As a young man, he traveled extensively in Europe with his brother Horatio, later to become a well-known sculptor in Boston. The design features a symmetric facade with rounded windows inspired by the Italianate style. The flush board siding is scored to imitate ashlar masonry; the gray paint scheme further reinforces the illusion of stone. An unusual feature is that the main entrance is on the right side, facing the carriageway.

Craigie St. was laid out in 1852 on land owned by Professor Worcester, formerly part of the Craigie estate (Sites 8 and 12). The street was quickly built up with fine residences. Adjacent to Professor Horsford's house is 25 Craigie St. (1856), a wide-pilastered, center-gable Greek Revival house built by K. W. Baker in 1856. Beyond Buckingham St. is 23 Craigie St. (1855), by Oliver Hastings, an Italianate mansion whose mansard roof may have been added later.

Return to the intersection of Brattle and Craigie Sts.; turn right onto Sparks St. alongside the large Armenian Orthodox Church, built in 1960.

17. "Brewster Block" (1875), 61–67 Sparks St.

This panel brick row of four houses is unusual for this neighborhood, both because of its brick construction and because the area is dominated by detached houses. Although brick making was an important industry in Cambridge from the 1840s until the 1960s, the city's residents have always had a distinct preference for wooden dwellings—a preference that extended even to the wealthiest families in the city. Virtually the only detached residences of brick were those that were erected for the brickyard owners and their families, and even many row houses were built of wood. This block was built as rental property for William Brewster (Sites 20 and 21). The trim is of Nova Scotia sandstone.

18. 70 Sparks St. (1878), by Longfellow and Clark; the Edward Dodge residence

This is an early example of Queen Anne architecture, with half-timber work and other medieval details that are derived from the early British work of Norman Shaw. Built for the son of the family that lived next door, the house was deliberately set far from the street to provide privacy from the adjacent dwellings. As a result, it has a picturesque setting in a hollow behind an ample front yard.

William Pitt Preble Longfellow, the architect of this house, was professor of architecture at MIT and, after 1881, editor of the influential *American Architect and Building News.* He was also a nephew of the poet, and an older cousin of A. W. Longfellow, whose Colonial Revival work also appears throughout this neighborhood (Sites 2, 10, 19).

Directly across Sparks St. is

19. 1 Highland St. (1894), by Longfellow and Alden; garden and gazebo (1896) by Charles Eliot, landscape architect; the J. A. Noyes residence

This corner house is an outstanding example of the Colonial Revival, designed by A. W. Longfellow. The gardens on its west side were designed by Charles Eliot, whose father, Charles W. Eliot, was president of Harvard University from 1869 to 1909. The younger Eliot served as an apprentice to Frederick Law Olmsted and later was a partner in the Olmsted firm (see Olmsted T3, T9, T11). A visionary who is considered to be the founder of greater Boston's metropolitan parks system, Eliot resigned private practice to become the first commissioner of the Metropolitan Park Commission. He was responsible for the creation of the nation's first public beach at Revere Beach, and he also helped plan Cambridge's park system.

Retrace your steps along Sparks St. for one block, and turn right on Brewster St.

20. Brewster St. tenant houses 17–19 and **23–25 Brewster St.** (1885) and **29–35 Brewster St.** (1884)

Brewster St. is dominated by these wooden Queen Anne row houses built for the Brewster family, who rented them to junior faculty of Harvard College. Among the many unusual details in the woodwork are carved shell motifs above the first-floor windows and the latticework on the porch of Nos. 23–25. The house at No. 35 was the seasonal home of the poet Robert Frost (1894–1963) for the last twenty years of his life.

Turn left on Riedesel Ave., and return to Brattle St. The next site is two houses to the left on Brattle St.

21. 145 Brattle St. (1887), by Andrews and Jaques; the William Brewster residence

This Colonial Revival house has brick end walls, a feature copied from many authentic Georgian houses. It was built for William Brewster, a noted ornithologist and author of *Birds of the Cambridge Region;* Brewster's study and classroom were in a brick building that survives behind the main house.

This was the original site of the Lechmere-Sewall-Riedesel House, a true Georgian of 1761, which underwent much remodeling at the hands of the Victorian Brewsters. In 1869 it was jacked up and had a new first story built underneath it; in 1886 it was moved to its present site at 149 Brattle St., and its original top floor was removed.

William Brewster and his father, John, were instrumental in the development of the streets behind their house. But whereas most other neighborhood property owners sold off lots for construction of large single-family houses, the Brewsters erected smaller rental houses, as we have already seen (Sites 17 and 20).

22. 146 Brattle St. (1850), nonextant; the Gardiner Greene Hubbard residence

Two immense copper beech trees, probably planted about 1850, mark the site of the Italianate mansion of Gardiner Greene Hubbard. A prominent Boston attorney, Hubbard purchased a large parcel on the south side of Brattle St. in 1849. He laid out sixty-seven house lots in the portion nearest the Charles River; but he reserved six acres facing Brattle St. for himself, where he built his mansion the following year.

Hubbard was responsible for construction of the Boston area's first street railway, which opened on March 26, 1856, and which conveniently linked his Brattle St. home with his Boston law office. Described as "the prime mover in almost every project at that time for the practical benefit of the city" (Cox 396), Hubbard also organized private companies to provide running water and piped-in gas to local residents.

Hubbard's contributions to modern society resumed a few years later. His daughter, Mabel, was deaf as a result of a childhood bout with scarlet fever. In 1873 fifteen-year-old Mabel Hubbard enrolled in a special class at Boston University, taught by a young Scottish professor named Alexander Graham Bell—who was at that time acknowledged as a leading expert on the education of the deaf.

Romance soon blossomed between Mabel Hubbard and her tutor, and Professor Bell's experiments with telegraphy also attracted the interest of Mabel's father, who had long opposed the monopoly held by the Western Union Company. Both efforts were successful: The Hubbard mansion, with its acres of formal gardens, was the site of the 1877 wedding—as well as of some of Bell's early experiments on the telephone (see Bell T2). As the primary investor behind his son-in-law's invention, Gardiner Hubbard also became the first president of the Bell Telephone Company.

Hubbard and his family moved to Washington, D.C., in 1879, after which Hubbard subdivided this property into Hubbard Park and Mercer Circle (Sites 14 and 23). While in Washington, Hubbard also founded the National Geographic Society. His Brattle St. mansion was taken down in 1939.

Continue up Brattle St.; then turn left on Hubbard Park Rd.

23. Hubbard Park, original street plan (1885) by E. F. Bowker; revised 1907

Like Mercer Circle (Site 14), Hubbard Park was laid out on the grounds of the Gar-

diner Greene Hubbard estate. Unlike the speculative development in Mercer Circle, however, the houses in Hubbard Park were built to the plans of individual owners. The street plan of Hubbard Park was also considerably revised in the early twentieth century, in contrast to the near-original appearance of its sibling development.

48 Hubbard Park Rd. (1887), by Cabot and Chandler

Note especially the quadrant-shaped veranda at 48 Hubbard Park Rd., also known as the rear of 152 Brattle St., which closely followed the curve of the original carriageway. This house was specially designed for Mrs. Richard Henry Dana, Jr., who was confined to a wheelchair. One of her great pleasures was to be wheeled out to the far end of the porch, where she could look down the road. Mrs. Dana was the widow of the author of *Two Years before the Mast* (1840), and the mother-in-law of Edith Longfellow Dana (Site 9) (see Dana T6).

Between 26 and 32 Hubbard Park Rd., a walkway leads out to Lowell St. Turn right on Lowell to return to Brattle St.

24. **157 Brattle St.** (1895), by William G. Rantoul

This massive Medieval Revival (or "Tudor Revival") house features such neo-Tudor details as leaded-glass windows with stained-glass coats of arms, a first floor of random ashlar boulders, and an unusual Tudor-arched entrance door (see also Andrews, Jaques and Rantoul T11).

Next door at 159 Brattle St. is the Hooper-Lee-

Nichols House (ca. 1685; ca. 1746), home of the Cambridge Historical Society. {Tours on selected days or by appointment; www.cambridgehistory.org; (617)-547-4252} The house has been sequentially altered, enlarged, "modernized," and "antiqued," according to the fashion of the day, in order for it to appear its "proper age."

25. **Kennedy Rd.** (1863)

This cul-de-sac was the carriage entrance to the estate of Frank A. Kennedy, a local cracker manufacturer (and no relation to Boston's famous political clan). Like his father, Frank Kennedy was a pioneer in the machine-aided mass production of cookies and crackers for distribution to retail outlets. The Kennedy Biscuit Works[10] was founded in Cambridgeport in 1839. Fifty years later it was the largest bakery enterprise in the United States. Kennedy's firm named its products after local cities and towns, including such treats as Cambridge Salts, Boston Common Crackers, the Melrose, the Shrewsbury, the Waverly, and the Newton. The last was a fruit-filled cookie that came in several varieties, most notably fig. In 1889 the Kennedy firm was sold to

The Kennedy Biscuit Works (ca. 1880s), Green St., Cambridgeport, drawing. *(From Arthur Gilman, ed.,* The Cambridge of Eighteen Hundred and Ninety-Six, *Cambridge, Mass.: Riverside Press, 1896, facing p. 378.) (Courtesy of Charles Bahne.)*

A Kennedy's Biscuit box. (© Mark Vassar, photographer, courtesy of the Cambridge Historical Society.)

the New York Biscuit Company, which later became part of the National Biscuit Company (Nabisco).

26. 168 Brattle St. (1888), by Arthur Little; the Joseph Thorp residence

New England's grandest houses were historically built on the north side of the street, to allow the front rooms to receive light and heat from the sun. Lots on the south side of the street were considered less desirable. The architect of this Colonial Revival house found a unique solution to this problem: he pointed the main facade away from the street, so that it looked south over a two-acre meadow. As a result, the house turns its back on the street, presenting a somewhat unusual appearance to the public.

Joseph Thorp, for whom this house was built, was the father-in-law of Annie Longfellow, whose house was seen earlier (Site 10). Architect Arthur Little wrote one of the earliest architectural books on Colonial design, *Early New England Interiors* (1878). He was also an early practitioner in the Shingle style, designing several large houses in that style on Boston's North Shore in the early 1880s. The Thorp house draws inspiration from both styles, with details taken

from the Colonial Revival but massing adapted from the free-flowing Shingle style.

*The house next door at 170 **Brattle St.** is an 1852 design by Oliver Hastings, which originally stood on the grounds of the Episcopal Theological School (Site 6). It was moved here in 1965.*

27. 165 Brattle St. (1873); the John Bartlett residence.

This Stick-style mansard was built for John Bartlett (1820–1905), a Harvard Sq. bookseller. Bartlett made his store a center for literary gossip. Professors and students learned to "ask John Bartlett" when they sought quotations to use in their research. For years Bartlett kept a voluminous memoranda book in his store, which eventually begat *Bartlett's Familiar Quotations,* first published in 1855.

28. 167 Brattle St. (1883), by Henry Van Brunt; the Henry Van Brunt residence

Architect Henry Van Brunt designed this house as his own residence. A fine example of Queen Anne style, it features irregular fenestration and a wraparound porch; the latter is formed by an extension of the sweeping roofline. A Harvard graduate, Van Brunt trained in architecture with Richard Morris Hunt, who had established an informal studio in New York City in the 1850s. Returning to Boston, Van Brunt formed a partnership with another of Hunt's students, William R. Ware. The venture of Ware and Van Brunt was responsible for the designs of Harvard's Memorial Hall (1870), the Episcopal Theological School (Site 6), and the First Church in Boston (1867), among other buildings in and around Boston (see Ware and Van Brunt T9).

Ware served as the first dean of architecture at MIT until 1881, when he took a simi-

lar position at Columbia University. Following Ware's departure for New York City, Van Brunt established a new partnership with Frank A. Howe; this duo collaborated on Cambridge's new public library in 1888 (see Van Brunt and Howe T5, T9). Van Brunt subsequently moved to Kansas City and built a second architectural career in the Midwest.

29. **174 Brattle St**. (1885); the William E. Russell residence

William Eustis Russell, known as the "Little Giant" of Massachusetts, was a reformer who was active in Democratic Party politics at the city, state, and national level in the 1880s and 1890s. Russell was known as the "Boy Mayor" during his four terms at the helm of Cambridge. He was then elected governor of the Commonwealth when he was just thirty-three years old, making him the youngest man to hold that position. He served three distinguished terms before retiring to private law practice.

At 175 Brattle St. is another Georgian mansion, built in 1764 for George Ruggles, a "planter late of Jamaica," and sold in 1774 to Thomas Fayerweather.

Turn right on Fayerweather St. to view the next site.

30. **28 Fayerweather St.** (1882), by Sturgis and Brigham; the A. A. Carey residence

This gambrel-roofed residence was one of the earliest fully developed Colonial Revival houses built in America. Although the massing lacks the symmetry of later Colonial Revivals—and of the authentic Georgian houses that inspired the style—the individual details of this pioneering effort are all based on eighteenth-century sources. Notable features include the Palladian window, the alternating triangular and segmental pedimented dormers, and a balcony

with a broken pediment over the second-floor door (see Sturgis and Brigham T5, T6). The latter two details are similar to those of the John Hancock mansion of 1737, which formerly stood near the State House on Beacon Hill in Boston.

The 1863 demolition of Hancock's historic home sparked great controversy, which eventually led to the establishment of the historic preservation movement in New England. Before the Hancock house was taken down, measured drawings[11] of it were made by John H. Sturgis, who had also studied Georgian architecture during his years of residence in England. Nearly twenty years later, Sturgis designed this house.

Across the street at 27 Fayerweather St. (1886) is an early work by Timothy F. Walsh. The design combines features of the Shingle style and the Medieval Revival, with expressed half-timbering in the gable that is reminiscent of the Stick style. With his partner, Joseph Maginnis, architect Walsh was later responsible for the Gothic buildings at Boston College's Chestnut Hill campus and for many Catholic churches and related buildings in the Boston area.

Retrace your steps back to Brattle St. and turn right. Proceed to the second house on the right.

31. **195 Brattle St.** (1895), by H. Langford Warren; the George Pierce Baker residence

This Medieval Revival house has an appropriate Elizabethan appearance, because it was built for the Shakespearean scholar George Pierce Baker (1866–1935). The first-floor treatment is an early example of the use of stucco, which was far more popular after the turn of the century. Note also the elaborate brickwork of the two chimneys. This house was erected for Baker when he was twenty-nine years old, in the same year as his appointment to an assistant professorship at Harvard. Baker later established the university's department of criticism and dramatic writing; he left Cambridge in 1924 to teach at Yale.

To view the final two sites, go back to the intersection of Fayerweather St., and turn right onto Elmwood Ave.

32. **182 Brattle St.** (1895), by William Ralph Emerson

At the "point" of Brattle St. and Elmwood Ave. is this shingle-clad house by William Ralph Emerson,[12] who was a cousin of Ralph Waldo Emerson. Architect Emerson was known for his Queen Anne work in the 1870s. He was also an early practitioner of the Shingle style, who designed country estates in Massachusetts and seaside houses in Maine. This later design, with its hip roof, was also influenced by the bungalow style of the American West, as were many of its neighbors along Elmwood Ave. and Traill St. (see William Ralph Emerson T2, T4, T5, T11).

33. **"Elmwood"** (1767), 33 Elmwood Ave., also called the Oliver-Gerry-Lowell house

This Georgian mansion was built for Thomas Oliver, a British loyalist who fled Cambridge in 1774. Following the Revolution, the estate became the home of Elbridge Gerry,[13] who later served as governor of Massachusetts and as vice president of the United States. After Gerry's death in 1814, the mansion was purchased by the Reverend Charles Lowell. It was the birthplace and lifelong home of author and abolitionist James Russell Lowell (1819–91), who christened the house "Elmwood" on account of the many elm trees on the estate grounds.

The founding editor of the *Atlantic Monthly,* James Russell Lowell[14] later edited the *North American Review* with his friend Charles Eliot Norton. In 1855 he succeeded Henry Wadsworth Longfellow as the Smith Professor of Modern Languages at Harvard, a post that he held until 1876. Lowell also served as U.S. ambassador to Spain and to England. His cousin, poet Amy Lowell[15] (1874–1925), was a frequent childhood visitor to this house. Since 1963 Elmwood has belonged to Harvard University, which now uses the mansion as the official residence of the university's president.

Although it is somewhat beyond the scope of this tour, walkers may wish to explore Mount Auburn Cemetery while they are in the vicinity. (A large grocery store is opposite the cemetery if you are looking for refreshment or other amenities.)

Mount Auburn Cemetery is about four-tenths of a mile up Mount Auburn St., which continues on the far side of busy Fresh Pond Parkway. The convergence of roads here presents a difficult crossing for pedestrians; for a better route turn right at the end of Elmwood Ave., and follow the sidewalk next to the parkway and Lowell Park. Turn left at the traffic light onto Brattle St., and follow Brattle for one long block until it merges with Mount Auburn St. At this point there is a crosswalk to the cemetery, and another at the next traffic light, at Aberdeen Ave.

34. **Mount Auburn Cemetery** (1831), 580 Mount Auburn St. {Maps, brochures available on racks behind entrance gate, parking available; audio tours offered, walking tours; wwwmountauburn.org; (617)-547-7105, programs ext. 821}

Mount Auburn, with its main gate at the Watertown end of Brattle St., was the nation's first landscaped garden cemetery, inspired by the Cimitière du Père Lachaise in Paris. Many Brattle St. denizens, includ-

Main gate of Mount Auburn Cemetery
(ca. 1859), with horse-drawn streetcar in front.
(Collection of Bradley H. Clarke.)

ing Longfellow and his wife, are buried here. It was said that proper Bostonian families had a share at the Boston Athenæum, a pew at Trinity Church, and a plot at Mount Auburn.[16]

Whether you choose to end your tour on Elmwood Ave. or to visit Mount Auburn

Cemetery, T buses are available on Mount Auburn St. (frequent on weekdays and Saturdays, about every 35 minutes on Sundays) for the return trip to Harvard Sq.

Elmwood Ave. T Bus Stop: From the end of Elmwood Ave., Mount Auburn St. is accessible by foot to your immediate left. Turn left on Mount Auburn St., and then cross the street to the bus stop. Mount Auburn Cemetery T Bus Stop is located outside the cemetery gate.

If you prefer to walk back to Harvard Sq., other streets in the neighborhood that are worthy of exploration include Lexington Ave., Lake View Ave., Appleton St., Buckingham St., and Berkeley St.

NOTES

Notes to the Introduction

1   The future King Edward VII was mounted on "Black Prince" during a military review on the Common. The sculptor Thomas Ball used the same horse, belonging to Col. T. Bigelow Lawrence, as his model for George Washington's charger in his statue (see T6 and T8) for the Public Garden (M. Howe, *Boston Common* 51).

2   Phebe A. Hanaford, a Reading, Mass., resident and member of the Essex Institute, wrote that Prince Arthur's demeanor and presence at Peabody's funeral (Portland, Maine) "reflected credit upon the mother [Queen Victoria] whom England and America delight to honor" (268).

3   George Peabody had given magnificently on both sides of the Atlantic. His aid to London's disadvantaged and his gifts to museums, libraries, music conservatories, lecture halls, and universities (among them the Peabody Institute, Danvers; the Peabody Institute, Peabody; the Peabody Museum and Essex Institute, Salem; and the Peabody Museum at Harvard) are lasting tributes to a man of foresight, who has been called "the most effective advocate of British-American friendship in the history of the two countries" (Hoyt 141).

4   The miniature of Queen Victoria is so large that "a furnace [was] specially built to manage so large a piece of porcelain" (Hoyt 141). Queen Victoria is dressed in "black silk, with a dark velvet train, both of which were trimmed in ermine. Her head-dress was a favorite Mary-Stuart cap, surmounted with a demi-crown" (qtd. from a Boston newspaper by Hanaford 147).

5   Queen Victoria's letter to Peabody reads: "The Queen would not, however, have been satisfied without giving Mr. Peabody some public mark of her sense of his munificence; and she would have gladly conferred upon him either a baronetcy or the Grand Cross of the Order of Bath, but that she understands Mr. Peabody to feel himself debarred from accepting such distinctions" (Hanaford 144).

6   See H. Adams (T6).

7   "Little Boston" appears in O. W. Holmes's *Professor at the Breakfast Table* (1860).

8   With its stylized Victorian botanical border, its title banner, and its incorporation of the seals of the City of Boston and of the State of Massachusetts, the 1975 cover was a skillful modification of the frontispiece of *King's Handbook of Boston,* whose central engraving in the ninth edition of 1889, as well as others, had been a depiction of the New England Mutual Life Insurance Company (1874, building nonextant). To highlight the new, successful drive for adaptive preservation of landmark architecture, the Old City Hall engraving, page 73 in *King's,* was adroitly substituted (see Old City Hall T4).

9   The lovely Linley Sambourne House, previously administered by the Victorian

Society for the Royal Borough of Kensington and Chelsea, is located at 18 Stafford Terrace, London, W8 (close to Kensington High St.). It is an outstanding Victorian town house (1868–74) that formerly belonged to the illustrator and *Punch* cartoonist Edward Linley Sambourne (1844–1910) (http://www.rbkc.gov.uk/linleysambournehouse; telephone (from U.S.A.): 011-44-207-602-3316, ext. 305).

10 Quotation from Edwin Arlington Robinson's "Isaac and Archibald" (lines 318–19).

Notes to Preface: Touring Boston's Topography

1 The Shawmut peninsula was described in 1896 as follows: "The surface was very abrupt, irregular, hilly, and undulating, deeply indented by coves, and surrounded by salt marshes left oozy by the ebbing tides, and separating the shores from the river channels. The peninsula contained less than 1000 acres, and the narrow neck which joined it to the main, was often swept by spray and water" (*Encylcopædia Britannica* 73).

2 To determine whether locations in Boston are on or off landfill, consult *Gaining Ground: A History of Landmaking in Boston* (2003) by Nancy S. Seasholes; the unusual multicolor frontispiece "Boston Old and New," in *The Memorial History of Boston*, vol. I (1880), edited by Justin Winsor; and the classic *Boston: A Topographical History*, by Walter Muir Whitehill.

Notes to Tour 1. Boston's Nineteenth-Century Waterfront

1 [See Thomas Ball's statue (1878) of Josiah Quincy, T4, T6. *Editor*]

2 [The granite eagle over the main entrance at the crest of the head house is eight feet high and weighs eight tons. Passengers hurrying to take one of the approximately 750 trains that arrived and departed daily in 1901 were kept abreast of the time by the twelve-foot dial of the clock face under the eagle (Tewksbury 153–54). *Editor*]

Notes to Tour 2. Boston's South End

1 *Cyclorama of the Battle of Gettysburg* is now displayed in its own building at the Gettysburg National Military Park, Gettysburg, Pa.

2 [See Pierce T5. *Editor*]

3 [Also spelled Keeley. *Editor*]

Notes to Tour 3. Ethnic Diversity in the Victorian North End

1 [See Edwin Munroe Bacon (1844–1916) T6. *Editor*]

2 [The words "JULIUS ROTTENBERG, BANKER" are carved near the top of the stone facade, but are now covered over by a blank panel. *Editor*]

Notes to Tour 4. The Commercial District: With Charles Street Jail

1 [*King's Handbook of Boston* (1889) described the Great Fire of 1872 this way: "On November 9, this year [1872] at 7:15 o'clock in the evening, the Great Boston Fire broke out. The flames started at the corner of Summer and Kingston Sts., and spread with terrible speed. In spite of the efforts of the firemen [the epizoötic epidemic rendering almost all the horses useless], the flames spread north-east and north into the very heart of the substantial business district of the city,

where a great proportion of the buildings were of solid granite, and used for wholesale business. Aid was summoned from the suburban and even from distant cities; and special trains bearing fire-engines came hastening into the panic-stricken city from all sides. Buildings were blown up in the hope that the gaps thus left would not be bridged by the furious on-sweeping flames, and the gas was cut off, leaving the city almost in darkness. The militia went on duty to aid the police in preventing the wholesale lawlessness that threatened to add to the terrors of the time. When the fire finally stopped, it had spread over 65 acres, and destroyed about $80,000,000 [in 1872 dollars] worth of property and many lives, leaving the entire district bounded by Summer, Washington, Milk, and Broad Sts. a smoking chaos of ruins. Boston recovered with almost incredible elasticity and pluck from this terrible blow; and the 'burnt district' is to-day a section of imposing and substantial business warehouses, its appearance greatly improved, and the wealth and convenience of this part of the city thereby increased" (18). Editor]

2   [While the Ames Building was under construction, the city fathers established a height limit of 125 feet on all subsequent buildings, thus ensuring that the Ames Building would be the city's tallest for over two decades (until the Custom House tower was erected). Editor]

3   [Oliver Ames and Sons shovel-making company (nearly two million spades and shovels were made a year) was located in North Easton, Mass. H. H. Richardson designed North Easton's railroad station, Oakes Ames Memorial Hall, and Ames Free Library. Editor]

4   [Its dedication was announced in a newspaper article in 1874. Bryant had designed an almost identical, but smaller, Transcript Building on the same site, dedicated in February 1872, just nine months before the Great Fire devastated the area. Editor]

5   [Boston in the 1890s was described by the Encyclopædia Britannica of 1896 as the second city in "commerce, wealth, banking capital and valuation in the United States" (72). It is the prosperity of post–Civil War commerce that enabled Boston business not only to recover from the Great Fire of 1872, but also to continue funding the ongoing Back Bay fill at the same time. Editor]

6   [All of the Wigglesworth Building's original 1873 storefronts, with cast-iron posts, survive. Editor]

7   [Triglyphs are vertically grooved blocks with metopes (the panels between them) in a Doric frieze. A guilloche is a decorative band or running ornament forming a pattern of circles, intertwining lines, or loops. Editor]

Notes to Tour 5. Back Bay: Boylston, Dartmouth Streets, Copley Square

1   [According to the Boston Directory (1861), John D. Bates was a merchant whose Bates and Company was located 55 Commerical Wharf (see T1). During the same year his son, John Bates, Jr., lived here and had the same work address. Sarah Choate Sears (1858–1935), a friend of Isabella Stewart Gardner (see Gardner Introduction and T6, T8), was an artist and art collector. Editor]

2   [Margaret Henderson Floyd purposefully included Victorian buildings that have been demolished to act, as she said, like "'ghosts' of Back Bay architecture." Editor]

3 [*The Triumph of Time* (unveiled 1901), on the ceiling of the Elliott Room, was painted in Rome by Julia Ward Howe's son-in-law, John Elliott (1858–1925). *Editor*]

4 [Near the corner of Newbury and Dartmouth Sts. is the large trompe l'oeil *Café DuBarry Newbury Street Mural* (1991), by Joshua Winer (1956–). A depiction of Henry Hobson Richardson may be seen just to the right of the Café DuBarry entrance stairs. H. H. Richardson is the second figure to the right; a portrayal of Isabella Stewart Gardner (see Introduction, T6, T8) stands nearby. *Editor*]

5 [Darth Vader is a *Star Wars* arch-villain, more machine than man, hence lacking humanity. The inference is that the building lacks human scale. The structure is placed (on Boylston St. on the north side of Copley Sq.) without recognition of its architectural context, and its appearance and composition are foreign (other-worldly) in contrast with the buildings and building materials of its Back Bay neighbors. *Editor*]

Notes to Tour 6. Boston's Victorian Authors

1 It is worth planning a trip to Concord around the limited visiting days and open hours of the Ralph Waldo Emerson House, a National Historic Landmark, at 28 Cambridge Turnpike, Concord (close to the Concord Museum); (978)-369-2236.

2 Dickens's room (338) was located at the corner of School St. and Chapman Place (Spring 182). The Parker House was by William Washburn and G. J. F. Bryant.

3 Before the Parker House expanded (1885) to fill this corner, it was the site of Edward Everett Hale's (1822–1909) childhood home, which was in turn succeeded by T. O. H. P. Burnhams's "Antique Bookstore," packed with old books.

4 Headquarters of the Boston Preservation Alliance, an advocate for historic preservation in the city; www.bostonpreservation.org; (617)-367-2458; and PreservatiONMASS, a statewide nonprofit organization dedicated to preserving the Commonwealth's historic and cultural heritage, www.historicmass.org; (617)-723-3383. Also headquarters of WalkBoston, a pedestrian advocate organization that promotes walking for transportation, health, recreation, and safety; tours, www.walkboston.org; (617)-367-9255.

In new City Hall (T4), the Boston Landmarks Commission (1 City Hall Plaza, www.cityofboston.gov/environment/landmarks, (617)-635-3850), acts with local historic district commissions to protect Boston's historic buildings through Landmark and district designations, administering demolition delays, and providing information.

Historic Boston Inc., at nearby 3 School Street (www.historicboston.org, (617)-227-4679), is devoted to the preservation of key endangered historic sites in Boston. Historic Boston (1960) bought and restored the Old Corner Book Store (Site 9).

See also heritage and preservation groups (note 14), and T4 (between Sites 1 and 2, and 5 and 6). The Boston Society of Architects (Historic Resources Committee, http://committees.architects.org/hrc/index.htm) features preservation and restoration; the Society of Architectural Historians/New England Chapter promotes research, education, cultural heritage, and preservation; www.sah. org.

5 Phillis Wheatley (1754–84), our first published African American poet, wor-

shiped in the church here. On display is an early copy of her *Poems on Various Subjects* (1773) (see *Boston Women's Memorial* T8).

6   Although it is not a stop on our trek today, on the base of the Common's Civil War *Soldiers' and Sailors' Monument* (1877), by Martin Milmore (1844–81) (see M. Milmore T9), one may discover Henry Wadsworth Longfellow depicted on the steps of the State House (in the "Departure for War" relief). And among the figures mentioned in our tour in the "Sanitary Commission" relief are Edward Everett Hale, George Ticknor, and James Russell Lowell.

7   During the last year of Robert Browning's life, Sarah W. Whitman (Site 40) gave a talk to the society entitled "Robert Browning in His Relation to the Art of Painting." A Boston Browning Society Web site is under construction. For information e-mail mpetronella@bentley.edu or vincent.petronella@ umb.edu.

8   Braithwaite was the editor of *Yearbook of American Poetry* (1913–39) and *Anthology of Massachusetts Poets* (1922).

9   Walkers may remember Robinson's poems "Richard Cory" and "Miniver Cheevy" or his volume *The Man against the Sky* (1916). His three Pulitzer prizes were for *Collected Poems* (1921), *The Man Who Died Twice* (1924), and *Tristram* (1927).

10 Democratic morality is exemplified in the Shaw family's choice of the form of the monument. Saint-Gaudens's sketch of a solitary horseman, similar to Thomas Ball's equestrian statue of George Washington (1869) in the Public Garden (Site 78), was considered to be a glorification of Shaw and was rejected. In his second depiction Shaw is placed in the company of members of the 54th Regiment; Augustus Saint-Gaudens took particular care to individualize each face.

11 In the 1940s play *The Male Animal,* James Thurber and Elliot Nugent used the Sacco-Vanzetti prison letters to focus on freedom of speech.

12 The present Hotel Bellevue (1899), at 21 Beacon St., replaced the Bellevue Hotel at 17 Beacon St., in which Alcott often stayed. In the 1899 Hotel Bellevue, John Fitzgerald Kennedy announced his run for the U.S. Senate during the residence of his maternal grandparents, "Honey Fitz" and Josie Fitzgerald (see T3). The author of *Profiles in Courage* (1956) and a frequenter of the nearby Boston Athenæum, Kennedy took pains to honor literature not only at his own inauguration as president but also at the dedication of the Robert Frost Library at Amherst College. "When power narrows the areas of a man's concern," he declared, "poetry reminds him of the richness and diversity of his existence."

13 Thought to be the basis of Santayana's Mr. Nathaniel Alden (McIntyre 21), George Francis Parkman (1823–1908) bequeathed Parkman House to Boston. He was the reclusive son of the murdered Dr. George Parkman (see Site 32).

14 The Massachusetts Historical Society, a National Historic Landmark, is located at 1154 Boylston St., Boston; www.masshist.org; (617)-536-1608.

15 Mrs. Harrison Gray Otis wrote *The Barclays of Boston* (1854) while she was living at 41 Mt. Vernon (nonextant), at the corner of Joy St. (Carruth 30). This corner is now home to Beacon Press.

16 If you travel to the Berkshires, visit "Arrowhead" in its lovely pastoral setting, 780 Holmes Rd., Pittsfield, Mass.; www.mobydick.org; (413)-442-1793. Dr. Oliver Wendell Holmes lived nearby on the road named for him and was Melville's physician for a time.

17 Two of Whittier's houses are preserved as house museums. Each home brings to life a very different period of Whittier's lifetime. The country setting of the John Greenleaf Whittier Birthplace, 305 Whittier Rd., Haverhill, Mass., is located on Route 110 (Amesbury Rd.), 3.3 miles east of downtown Haverhill; www.john-greenleafwhittier.com; (978)-373-3979. The John Greenleaf Whittier Home is located in a quiet residential setting at 86 Friend St., Amesbury, Mass.; www.johngreenleafwhittier.com/aboutmuseum.html; (978)-388-1337.

18 The Greek Revival entrance of No. 59 was depicted in a line drawing for the title page of Ferris Greenslet's biography, *Life of Thomas Bailey Aldrich* (1908), and in a photogravure chosen by Lilian Woodman Aldrich for the frontispiece of her intimate memoir, *Crowding Memories* (1920).

19 One may visit the Nutter House (the Thomas Bailey Aldrich Memorial) on Court St. in Portsmouth, N.H., now part of Strawbery Banke Museum. The T. B. Aldrich Memorial is one of the earliest (1907) period-preserved homes in the country (Mark Twain attended its dedication). Aldrich lived at Nutter House 1849–52 with his grandfather Bailey and made vivid the memories of his Portsmouth childhood in *The Story of a Bad Boy* (1869), an inspiration for Twain's *Adventures of Tom Sawyer* (1876).

20 The Crispus Attucks Memorial monument was placed on the Boston Common in 1889. Crispus Attucks is buried in the old Granary Burying Ground (Site 4).

21 Although not on the Hill, Silas Lapham's expensive waterside town house, destroyed by fire in fiction, has a verifiable physical site at 302 Beacon St., Howells's former home, which has been replaced by another town house. In an 1884 letter to Henry James, Howells expressed the hope that *The Rise of Silas Lapham* would pay for 302 Beacon St. Howells subsequently moved to New York, leaving the city he once depicted as "death-in-life" (quoted in Brooks, *Howells* 191).

22 In a fascinating enumeration of the location of diverse sites in Boston fiction, Carruth (pseudonym for Frances Carruth Prindle) explains that Howells's inspiration for the Coreys' home was actually the former home of one of Howells's friends and was located on the same side but below Mrs. Harrison Gray Otis's house. The vintage photograph in Carruth's 1902 text does not at all resemble today's No. 48 or Howells's description of the exterior entrance of the Corey residence, but Carruth's text gives us an additional clue. In 1902, 48 Mt. Vernon was the Curtis Hotel.

Delving into our vintage guides of Victorian Boston, we find that the Curtis Hotel was located at 43, 45, and 47 Mt. Vernon. This address would place the Corey residence back on the odd-numbered side, in fact at the crest of Mt. Vernon, and technically "below" the corner Otis House. Yes, we at last have found the address, 45 Mt. Vernon, that matches Carruth's vintage photograph. No. "48" was, as it turns out, a misleading typo.

Carruth, evidently familiar with the interior of No. 45, indicates that the entrance and part of the interior corresponded to Howells's description (30). Because Howells described the Corey entrance as being similar to well-known, tasteful doorway entrances of houses by the same architect opposite the Common on Beacon St., we have quite a selection of famous architects from which to choose: Asher Benjamin (54–55; 70–75 Beacon); Cornelius Coolidge (33–34 Beacon); Alexander Parris (39, 40, and 42 Beacon); Charles Bulfinch (45 Beacon; 9 Park); and Ephraim Marsh (56–57; 63–64 Beacon) (McIntyre 116–18).

Furthermore, several Mt. Vernon entrances suit the spirit of Howells's architectural detail and sustain our premise that a composite house may have been an inspiration as well. In fact, Howells's architectural terms are our ultimate textual evidence for a "composite solution." Among the numerous nearby addresses whose entries might be portrayed in part are 73 Mt. Vernon St., nearly across the street from our location; No. 32, the Howes's home (Site 33); and No. 59, the Thomas Bailey Aldrich home (Site 37) (see p. 108; note 18). Each is suggestive of Howells's appreciation of classic architecture.

23 Grant's residential life resembles that of John T. Wheelwright's Mr. Sewell in *Child of the Century* (1887); his "life had been spent on that part of the Earth's surface which is contained in a circle with a radius of five miles . . . with the tarnished gilt dome of the State House as a center" (quoted in Carruth 67). Wheelwright himself lived for a time at 99 Mt. Vernon St.

24 Sampling Dickinson's home in Amherst allows us the rare opportunity to share the flavor of an unusual household. The Dickinson Homestead, 280 Main St., Amherst, Mass.; www.dickinsonhomestead.org; (413)-542-8161.

25 At 87 Pinckney, just below, lived for a time the Harvard professor and literary critic F. O. Matthiessen (1902–50). Born at the close of the Victorian Era, Matthiessen wrote *American Renaissance: Art and Expression in the Age of Emerson and Whitman* (1941), which explored the tension growing out of the conflict between nineteenth-century democratic idealism and aesthetic complexity as a source of the best writing; it became a leading college textbook. This text—although it virtually ignores the work of Emily Dickinson, Harriet Beecher Stowe, and Edgar Allan Poe—remains a good introduction to the intellectual richness of the mid-nineteenth century.

26 Miss Pride's home is sometimes mistakenly given a Louisburg Sq. address rather than a Pinckney St. address. (Jean Stafford married Robert Lowell.)

27 To tour a home in which the Hawthornes lived, visit The Wayside (see also note 28). The Alcotts lived at The Wayside, as did Margaret Sidney (Harriett Mulford Lothrop; 1844–1924), author of *Five Little Peppers and How They Grew* (1882). Lothrop was instrumental in the preservation of the house. It is now a National Historic Landmark, 455 Lexington Rd., Concord, Mass.; www.nps.gov/mima/wayside/Home1.htm; (978)-369-6975.

28 The atmospheric Old Manse (now a National Historic Landmark), in which the Hawthornes and Emerson lived at different times, is located at 269 Monument St., Concord, Mass.; www.thetrustees.org/pages/346_old_manse.cfm; (978)-369-3909. Look for the writing scratched on a windowpane by Sophia Peabody Hawthorne with her diamond wedding ring (see also notes 1 and 27).

29 At one time Edwin Bacon was also editor of the *Boston Advertiser* and the *Boston Post*. Dexter's *Cyclopedia of Boston and Vicinity* (1886) lists ten women journalists (two used male pseudonyms) as members of the Boston Press (ca. 1886). Two are cited in this walk: Lilian Whiting, author of *Boston Days* (1902), who wrote for the *Traveller*, and Lucy Stone, for the *Women's Journal*. Two wrote for the *Globe*,

Miss Hatch and Mrs. Washburn, two for the *Herald,* Mrs. A. M. B. Ellis ("Max Eliot") and Mrs. Jenkins ("Jay"). The others deserve attention also. They are Sallie Joy White, *Advertiser;* Susie Vogl, *Woman's Journal;* Miss Soper, *Journal;* Miss Aldrich, *Home Journal* (247).

30 Louisa May Alcott's Orchard House, a National Historic Landmark, is located at 399 Lexington Rd., Concord, Mass.; www.louisamayalcott.org; (978)-369-4118 (see also note 27).

31 Longfellow's magnificent home may be visited at 105 Brattle St., Cambridge, Mass.; www.nps.gov/long/pphtml/facilities.html; (617)-876-4491 (see T12 for more detailed directions).

32 Jewett's Maine residence, the Sarah Orne Jewett House (1774,) is worth a special visit. One of the historic properties cared for by SPNEA, it is located at 5 Portland St., South Berwick, Me.; SPNEA, www.spnea.org; (207)-384-2454 (see SPNEA headquarters T4).

33 Many of Fields's literary treasures have safely found their way into Boston area museums and libraries.

34 The site of Holmes's 164 Charles St. home is the parking lot on the river side of Charles St., just as you reach Charles Circle. Holmes's residence at 296 Beacon St. has been replaced, but the adjoining 294 Beacon (to the right), which contained his famous library, remains.

35 In the twentieth century, Langston Hughes, heckled on Boston Common as a communist, gave readings in the Afro-American Culture Center at the Charles Street Meeting House.

36 Henry James, Jr., William James, and Alice James are also buried in Cambridge Cemetery, as are William Dean Howells and Thomas Wentworth Higginson.

37 T. S. Eliot lived in Cambridge for a time while teaching at Harvard (see note 3 T12).

38 At the turn of the twentieth century, Boston's literary historians spoke of the Back Bay location of Hester Prynne's isolated cottage (R. Wilson 186; Wolfe 95). When Hawthorne lived and married in Boston, earlier in the nineteenth century, relatively recent landfill had been added adjacent to the Charles St. border of the Common that created a new man-made shoreline at what is now Arlington St.

39 To learn more about four centuries of Greater Boston writers, from those living in the seventeenth century to the those living in the twenty-first (and those of Cambridge and Concord), you may wish to continue your adventures with the Boston History Collaborative's twenty-mile "Literary Trail of Greater Boston" (www.lit-trail.org). The Collaborative offers theme tours of the city, as does Boston by Foot (www.bostonbyfoot.com; ⟨617)-367-2345).

Notes to Tour 7. Black Heritage Trail®

1 [See John Hancock house T12, and note 11, T12. *Editor*]
2 [See Massachusetts Historical Society, note 14, T6. *Editor*]
3 [See Child T6, T8. *Editor*]
4 [Both of these streets were destroyed for the Government Center urban renewal project in the 1960s. *Editor*]
5 [See Cornhill location T4. *Editor*]

Notes to Tour 8. Walking with Women in Victorian Boston

1 [Fifteen years later, in 1880, the number of women workers (above fifteen and below sixty years of age) was 38,881 of a Boston working force of 149,164. Of the 38,881 women workers, 1,329 worked as teachers; 1,883 worked in hotels and boardinghouses; 1,435 were laundresses; 3,013 tailors; 5,511 dressmakers; 2,077 accountants; 15,996 domestics (Sweetser, *Alphabetical Guide* 130–31). *Editor*]

2 [The commemorative memorial, by Sheila Levrant de Bretteville and Susan Sellers, entitled *Hear Us,* was dedicated in October 1999, "honoring the contributions of women to public life in Massachusetts." In 1995 the Massachusetts State Senate, in an attempt to make the art on display in the State House "more inclusive," asked an advisory committee to choose a woman who either had made a "major contribution" to Massachusetts or "represented a group of women who had made such a contribution." The committee instead recommended that six women be chosen: Dorothea Dix (1802–87), Lucy Stone (1818–93), Sarah Parker Remond (1824–94), Josephine St. Pierre Ruffin (1842–1924), Mary Kenney O'Sullivan (1864–1943), and Florence Luscomb (1887–1985) (Rothman "Hear Us"). Hence, at the close of the twentieth century a half dozen women who lived or were born during the Victorian era were represented in the State House by a bronze portrait gallery of head-and-shoulders bust-medallions. Each is set in a marble panel accompanied by two of her quotations. *Editor*]

3 In 1977, another brave woman, Lucille Longview, introduced a resolution to study the role religion plays in the lives of women. One result of that study was a new songbook with gender-inclusive language.

4 [The Hillards also lived at 54 Pinckney St. See Hillard T6. *Editor*]

5 Whitney used a woman model for Eriksson, which offended some because the hips are not anatomically accurate. [Also spelled Erickson, Ericson, or Ericksson, the Viking ship is represented at the base of the pedestal. The statue of Eriksson was commissioned by Eben N. Horsford. Anne Whitney also did a marble bust of Horsford (see Leif Eriksson; Horsford T12). *Editor*]

6 [Whitney's *Charles Sumner* would have been destined for the Public Garden (see Sumner T7). *Editor*]

7 [The *Harriet Tubman "Step on Board" Memorial* is an eye-catching ten-foot bronze statue portraying Tubman leading five fugitive slaves to freedom. Cunningham used her father's face as a model for one of the runaway slaves. It is located in Harriet Tubman Sq., on the corner of Columbus Ave. and Pembroke St. in the South End, along with *Emancipation* (1913; recast), a statue by the African American Victorian-born sculptor Meta Vaux Warrick Fuller (1877–1968). It represents the nascent freedom of a man and woman emerging from bondage as symbolized by the confines of a tree trunk. *Editor*]

Harriet Tubman Sq. may be reached on T2 (between Sites 29 and 30, near Columbus Ave., West Canton, and Appleton Sts.), or from the Boston Public Library in Copley Sq. at the end of this tour by following these directions:

Face the Boston Public Library; turn left and walk to the corner. Turn right and walk along Huntington Ave./Avenue of the Arts. On your right pass Exeter St. and Ring Sts. Pass the Prudential Center complex. When you come to West Newton St., turn left to cross Huntington Ave. Walk along West Newton two or three blocks. At the intersection of West Newton and Columbus Ave., turn left and walk one block to Pembroke St. to find the triangular park called Harriett Tubman Sq. *Editor*].

8   [Check opening hours and days in advance for the Isabella Stewart Gardner Museum, 280 The Fenway, Boston, Mass.; www.gardnermuseum.org; (617)-566-1401. To reach the museum by T, take the Green line E-train to the Museum stop. Cross Huntington Ave. (toward the gasoline station) to Louis Prang St. Pass a small park, Evans Way, on your left, and pass the street on the other side of the park that runs alongside the museum. *Editor*]

9   [See Wheatley, note 5, T6. *Editor*]

10 [32 Eliot St., Jamaica Plain, a private residence; not open to the public. See location of Eliot St. T11. *Editor*]

11 [The mural *Notable Women of Boston* (1980) by Ellen Lanyon (1926–), installed in the Boston Public Library's Johnson Addition lobby (on loan from Simmons College), recognizes the accomplishments of nine Boston women; seven of whom were Victorian or Victorian-born: Sister Ann Alexis (1805–75); Lucy Stone (1818–93); Mary Baker Eddy (1821–1910); Ellen Richards (1842–1911); Mary Morton Kehew (1859–1918); Anne Sullivan (1866–1936); and Melnea Cass (1896–1978). *Editor*]

12 For more information about women in Boston, write to Patricia C. Morris, 17 Whitney St., Chestnut Hill, MA 02267.

Notes to Tour 9. Charlestown in the Victorian Era

1   [See location of Bowdoin St. near Site 23 on map, p. 85. *Editor*]

2   [Also spelled Keeley. *Editor*]

3   [Daniel Chester French's *Milmore Memorial* (1891), "The Angel of Death Staying the Hand of the Sculptor," in Forest Hills Cemetery, was created for Martin Milmore and his brother Joseph (1842–86) (see directions to Forest Hills Cemetery, note 1, T11). *Editor*]

4   [See Mount Auburn Cemetery T12. *Editor*]

5   [Sarah Josepha Hale (1788–1879) edited *Ladies Magazine* (1828–37) in Boston and later *Godey's Lady's Book* (1837–77) in Philadelphia. See S. J. Hale T8. *Editor*]

Notes to Tour 10. Victorian Boston's Chocolate Village

1   Edmund Baker was the son of Dr. James and Lydia Bowman Baker.

2   Colonel Walter Baker was the son of Edmund and Sarah Howe Baker.

3   Note the highly decorative lions' heads.

4   Large terra-cotta circular medallions above the windows distinguish the Forbes Mill.

Notes to Tour 11. Victorian Jamaica Plain: Monument Square and Sumner Hill

1   [To reach Forest Hills Cemetery from Boston, take the Orange Line to Forest Hills Station. Open daily, 8:30 A.M. to dusk; www.foresthillstrust.org; (617)-524-0128. *Editor*]

2   [For location see Old State House T4. *Editor*]

3   [See Boston Athenæum T6. *Editor*]

4   [Blackall is at times spelled Blackhall. *Editor*]
5   [The Colonial Theater, 106 Boylston St., is near Site 15, T4, and the Wilbur Theater, 246 Tremont St., is near Site 17, T4. *Editor*]
6   [According to the Victorian *Century Dictionary* (1889), a "booby-hut" is a kind of hooded sleigh. A booby is also a type of bird. *Editor*]
7   [Jaques is at times spelled Jacques. *Editor*]

Notes to Tour 12. Cambridge's Brattle Street

1   42 Brattle St., now the Cambridge Center for Adult Education, briefly was the home (1832) of Margaret Fuller (see Fuller T6, T8).
2   Radcliffe College was formally merged into Harvard University in 1999, when it became the Radcliffe Institute for Advanced Studies. [See also Society to Encourage Studies at Home T6; E. C. Agassiz T5, T6; Girls High School, woman's education T8. *Editor*]
3   Readers who are interested in modern architecture should note the house at 9 Ash St. (at the corner of Acacia St., immediately opposite Ash Street Place), which was architect Philip Johnson's first completed project, built in 1941 (see Johnson T5). No. 14–16 Ash St. {plaque} was briefly the home of poet T. S. Eliot (1888–1965).
4   The influence that this house had on other designers may perhaps have been exaggerated, as a number of shingle-clad houses had been built earlier in New England by less famous architects. Nevertheless, the Stoughton House received much contemporary coverage in the architectural press.
5   Richardson's letter to Mrs. Stoughton is quoted in O'Gorman 128.
6   Vassall's uncle Henry lived across the street at No. 94. Between 1760 and 1768, four of John Vassall's relatives by marriage also bought or built estates along the Watertown road. These are presently located at 149 Brattle St. (near Site 21), 159 Brattle St. (adjacent to Site 24), 175 Brattle St. (opposite Site 29), and 33 Elmwood Ave. (Site 33).
7   It was the second marriage for Longfellow, whose first wife died during the couple's European visit. (Longfellow had succeeded George Ticknor as Smith Professor of Modern Languages at Harvard.)
8   Nathan Appleton had been the founding partner (with Francis Cabot Lowell) of America's first integrated textile mill, located in Waltham, Mass., in 1815. After F. C. Lowell's death, Appleton invested in mills in Lowell, Manchester, and other cities.
9   Sadly, Fanny Longfellow burned to death in this house in 1861, when her gown caught fire from drops of hot sealing wax. She rushed to her husband's arms with a wild cry and never said another word. Longfellow's long white beard, so familiar in portraits of the poet, was grown because scars from the burns on his neck made shaving impractical.
10 The bakery factory, located on Green St. just outside Central Sq., Cambridge, has been converted to apartments and offices.
11 [A replica (1925) of the John Hancock House, home of the Ticonderoga, N.Y., Historical Society (THS), was built from "blueprints" based on "drawings of the exterior and interior" made by John Hubbard Sturgis (1834–88) and "used

through the kindness of R. Clipston Sturgis (1860–1951), a nephew" (William G. Dolback, "The Story behind Ticonderoga's Hancock House," in *Patches and Patterns Extended*, Ticonderoga Historical Society, vol. 1, no. 1, January 1990). According to Dolback, vice president of THS, the "main house exterior and the hall way and two east side rooms on the main floor follow the original floor plan." Hancock House, given by Horace A. Moses (of Strathmore Paper Company) to the New York State Historical Association "to perpetuate American Traditions in History and the Fine Arts," is a museum, research library, and "depository for historical materials and replicas" (www.thehancockhouse.org).

[The preservation of the crucial measurements by two leading Victorian Boston architects, J. H. Sturgis and R. C. Sturgis, certainly provides inspiration for the future possibility of also reconstructing John Hancock House in Boston (see R. Clipston Sturgis, east and west wings of the State House, Site 22, T6). The site of the demolished J. Hancock mansion (plaque on fence) is near the west wing of the State House. J. H. Sturgis's measured drawings are in SPNEA's archives. *Editor*]

12 William Ralph Emerson, architect, and Ralph Waldo Emerson, theologian, philosopher, and poet (see T6), were third cousins once removed. William Ralph Emerson (1833–1917), the designer of this house and a resident of Milton, should not be confused with William Emerson (1874–1957), who was also an architect. The latter was dean of Architecture at MIT and a Brattle St. resident (Zaitzevsky, *Architecture* 28–29).

13 In 1812, while Gerry was governor of Massachusetts, the Commonwealth's General Court (legislature) passed an act to redistrict itself, which Gerry signed into law. Members of the opposing party felt that the district lines were unfairly drawn; a wag commented that one particularly malformed district wanted only wings to resemble some fabled monster of antiquity. An artist drew wings, claws, and a beak on a map of the district, and christened it a "salamander"—a mythical beast supposed to be able to survive fire. Another observer asked "Why not call it a 'gerrymander'?" The caricature was published in the *Boston Gazette*, and thus was born the infamous political creature.

14 [See James Russell Lowell; *Atlantic Monthly; North American Reveiw* T6. *Editor*]

15 [See Amy Lowell T6. *Editor*]

16 [Among the prominent Bostonians mentioned in our tours, who lived or died during the Victorian era and are buried at Mount Auburn are Oliver Wendell Holmes, Isabella Stewart Gardner, Julia Ward Howe, Samuel Gridley Howe, Dorothea Dix, Mary Baker Eddy, Fannie Farmer, Thomas Bailey Aldrich, Louis Agassiz, James T. Fields, Annie Fields, James Russell Lowell, Francis Parkman, Josiah Quincy, Nathaniel P. Willis, Josephine St. Pierre Ruffin, Harriet A. Jacobs, Charles Sumner, Charles Bulfinch, Horatio Greenough, William E. Channing, Phillip Brooks, and Amy Lowell. *Editor*]

BIBLIOGRAPHY

❧

Adams, Henry. *The Education of Henry Adams: An Autobiography.* New York: Random House, Modern Library, 1931.

———. *The Life of George Cabot Lodge.* Boston: Houghton Mifflin, 1911.

"Adams, Henry H." Introduction to *The Late George Apley* by John Marquand. New York: Washington Square Press, 1963.

Agger, Lee. *Women of New England.* Vol 1. Portland, Me.: Gannett Books, 1986.

Alcott, Louisa May. *Little Women.* 1868–69. Reprint, Boston: Little, Brown, 1994.

Aldrich, Mrs. Thomas Bailey (Lilian). *Crowding Memories.* Boston: Houghton Mifflin, 1920.

Allston, Margaret [Anna Farquhar]. *Her Boston Experiences.* Boston: L. C. Page, 1900.

Amory, Cleveland. *The Proper Bostonians.* New York: E. P. Dutton, 1947.

Antin, Mary. *The Promised Land.* Boston: Houghton Mifflin, 1969.

Atlas of the City of Boston: Boston Proper and Back Bay. Philadelphia: G. M. Hopkins, 1890, 1898, 1908, 1922, 1928.

Atlas of the County of Suffolk, Massachusetts: Vol. 1st, Including Boston Proper. Philadelphia: G. M. Hopkins, 1874.

Bacon, Edwin M. *The Book of Boston: Fifty Years' Recollections of the New England Metropolis.* Boston: Book of Boston, 1916.

———. *Boston: A Guide Book.* Boston: Ginn, 1903.

———. *King's Dictionary of Boston.* Cambridge, Mass.: Moses King, 1883.

———. *Literary Pilgrimages in New England: To the Homes of Famous Makers of American Literature and Among Their Haunts and Scenes of Their Writings.* New York: Silver, Burdett, 1902.

Bates, Arlo. *Love in a Cloud: A Comedy in Filigree.* Boston: Houghton Mifflin, 1900.

———. *The Puritans.* Boston: Houghton Mifflin, 1898.

Bearse, Austin. *Reminiscences of Fugitive-Slave Law Days in Boston.* Boston: Warren Richardson, 1880.

Beatty, Noelle Blackmer. *Literary Byways of Boston and Cambridge.* Washington, D.C.: Starrhill Press, 1991.

Bell, Millicent. *Marquand: An American Life.* Boston: Little, Brown, 1979.

Bellamy, Edward. *Looking Backward: 2000–1887.* 1888. Reprint, New York: Random House, Modern Library, 1951.

Birmingham, Stephen. *The Late John Marquand: A Biography.* Philadelphia: J. B. Lippincott, 1972.

Blumenson, John J. G. *Identifying American Architecture: A Pictorial Guide to Styles and Terms, 1600–1945*. Nashville, Tenn.: American Association of State & Local History, 1977.

Boston City Council. *Exercises at the Dedication of the Monument to Colonel Robert Gould Shaw and the Fifty-fourth Regiment of Massachusetts Infantry, May 31, 1897*. Boston: Municipal Printing Office, 1887.

Boston City Planning Board. *The North End: A Survey and a Comprehensive Plan*. Boston: Author, 1919.

The Boston Directory, Containing the City Record, a General Directory of the Citizens, Business Directory, and Street Directions. Boston: Sampson, Murdoch and Co., 1875–1920.

The Boston Directory, Embracing the City Record, a General Directory of the Citizens and a Business Directory. Boston: Adams, Sampson, and Co., 1861.

Boston Landmarks Commission Inventory Files.

Boston 200. *Boston: The Official Bicentennial Guidebook*. Boston: E. P. Dutton, 1975.

Braithwaite, William Stanley. "In the Public Garden." In *The House of Falling Leaves with Other Poems*. Boston: John W. Luce, 1908.

Bromley, George W., and Walter Bromley. *Atlas of the City of Boston and Charlestown, Mass.*: 1868, 1875, 1892, 1901, 1911, 1917, 1922.

Brooks, Van Wyck. *The Flowering of New England, 1815–1865*. 1936. Reprint, Boston: Houghton Mifflin, 1981.

———. *Howells, His Life and World*. New York: E. P. Dutton, 1959.

———. *New England: Indian Summer 1865–1915*. Cleveland: World Publishing, 1940.

Buchanan, Paul, and Anthony Mitchell Sammarco. *Milton*. Dover, N.H.: Arcadia Press, 1996.

Bunting, Bainbridge. *Houses of Boston's Back Bay*. Cambridge, Mass.: Belknap Press of Harvard University Press, 1967.

———. Survey Notes (unpublished manuscript, circa 1970. Cambridge Historical Commission files).

Bunting, Bainbridge, and Robert H. Nylander. *Survey of Architectural History in Cambridge. Report Four: Old Cambridge*. Cambridge, Mass.: Cambridge Historical Commission, 1973.

Bunting, W. H. *Portrait of a Port: Boston: 1852–1914*. Cambridge, Mass.: Belknap Press of Harvard University Press, 1974.

Butcher, Philip, ed. *The William Stanley Braithwaite Reader*. Ann Arbor: University of Michigan Press, 1972.

Cambridge Historical Society. *Cambridge on the Cutting Edge: Innovators and Innovations*. Cambridge, Mass.: Author, 1996.

Campbell, Robert, and Peter Vanderwarker. *Cityscapes of Boston: An American City through Time*. Boston: Houghton Mifflin, 1992.

Carlock, Marty. *A Guide to Public Art in Greater Boston*. Boston: Harvard Common Press, 1993.

Carruth, Frances Weston [Prindle, Francis Carruth]. *Fictional Rambles in and about Boston*. New York: McClure, Phillips, 1902.

Cather, Willa. *Not under Forty*. New York: Alfred A. Knopf, 1936.

Charlestown Enterprise. December 14, 1889, July 5, 1919, issues; see also *Souvenir of the 50th Anniversary of the Dedication of the Bunker Hill Monument,* June 1893.

Cheney, Ednah. *Life, Letters and Journals of Louisa May Alcott.* Boston: Little, Brown, 1928.

"A Comprehensive Plan for the Development of Brattle-Street Real Estate." *Cambridge Tribune,* 14 August 1886, 1.

Constitution of the Victorian Club. Boston: Victorian Club, 1903.

Conwell, Col. Russell H. *History of the Great Fire: Boston, November 9–10, 1872.* Boston: Quaker City Publishing House, 1873.

Cox, George Howland. "Financial and Manufacturing." In Arthur Gilman, ed., *The Cambridge of Eighteen Hundred and Ninety-Six.* Cambridge, Mass.: Riverside Press, 1896.

Crawford, F. Marion. *The American Politician.* New York: Macmillan, 1906.

Crawford, Mary Caroline. *Romantic Days in Old Boston: The Story of the City and of Its People during the Nineteenth Century.* Boston: Little, Brown, 1910.

Cullen, James Bernard. *The Story of the Irish in Boston.* Boston: James B. Cullen, 1889.

Cushing, George M., and Ross Urquhart. *Great Buildings of Boston.* New York: Dover, 1982.

Damrell, Charles S. *A Half Century of Boston's Buildings.* Boston: Lewis Hager, 1895.

Delamar, Gloria T. *Louisa May Alcott and "Little Women."* Jefferson, N.C.: McFarland, 1990.

DeMarco, William M. *Ethnics and Enclaves: Boston's Italian North End.* Ann Arbor, Mich.: UMI Research Press, 1981.

Dickinson, Emily. *Selected Letters.* Thomas H. Johnson, ed. Cambridge, Mass.: Belknap Press of Harvard University Press, 1996.

Directors of the North End Union. "The North End Union" (pamphlet). May 1893.

Drake, Samuel Adams. *Historic Mansions and Highways around Boston.* Rev. ed. 1906. Reprint, Rutland, Vt.: Charles E. Tuttle, 1971.

———. *Old Landmarks and Historic Personages of Boston.* Rutland, Vt.: Charles E. Tuttle, 1872.

———. *Old Landmarks and Historic Personages of Boston.* Rev. ed. Boston: Little, Brown, 1900.

Edel, Matthew, Elliott D. Sclar, and Daniel Luria. *Shaky Palaces: Homeownership and Social Mobility in Boston's Suburbanization.* New York: Columbia University Press, 1984.

Edgerly, Lois. *Give Her This Day.* Gardiner, Me.: Tilbury House, 1990.

Ehrlich, Eugene, and Gorton Carruth. "Boston." In *The Oxford Illustrated Literary Guide to the United States.* New York: Oxford University Press, 1982.

Elliott, Maud Howe. *Lord Byron's Helmet.* Boston: Houghton Mifflin, 1927.

———. *Three Generations.* Boston: Little, Brown, 1923.

Emerson, Ralph Waldo. "Boston." In *The Compete Works of Ralph Waldo Emerson.* Vol. 12. Boston: Houghton Mifflin, 1890.

———. "Conversations in Boston." In *Memoirs of Margaret Ossoli.* Boston: Phillips, Sampson, 1851.

Encyclopædia Britannica: A Dictionary of Arts, Sciences and General Literature with New Maps and Original American Articles by Eminent Writers. Vol. 4. Chicago: Werner Company, 1896.

Federal Highway Administration and Massachusetts Department of Public Works. *Third Harbor Tunnel Project, Interstate 90 Draft Environmental Impact Statement/Report Historic Resources Survey.* Boston: Federal Highway Administration and Massachusetts Department of Public Works, 1982.

———. *Third Harbor Tunnel Project, Interstate 90/Central Artery, Interstate 93 Final Environmental Impact Statement and Final Section 4(f) Evaluation.* Boston: Federal Highway Administration and Massachusetts Department of Public Works, 1986.

Feldman, Steven, and the Staff of Genesis 2. *Guide to Jewish Boston and New England.* Boston: Combined Jewish Philanthropies of Greater Boston, 1986.

Fields, Annie. *Authors and Friends.* Boston: Houghton Mifflin, 1897.

———. *Memories of a Hostess: A Chronicle of Eminent Friendships Drawn Chiefly from the Diaries of Mrs. James T. Fields.* M. A. DeWolfe Howe, ed. Boston: Atlantic Monthly Press, 1922.

Fields, James. *Yesterdays with Authors.* Boston: Houghton Mifflin, 1888.

Flagg, Mildred B. *Boston Authors: Now and Then.* Cambridge, Mass.: Dresser, Chapman & Grimes, 1966.

Flexner, Eleanor. *Century of Struggle: The Women's Rights Movement in the United States.* Cambridge, Mass.: Belknap Press of Harvard University Press, 1975.

Floyd, Margaret Henderson. *Architectural Education and Boston: Centennial Publication of the Boston Architectural Center.* Boston: Boston Architectural Center, 1989.

———. *Henry Hobson Richardson: A Genius for Architecture.* New York: Monacelli Press, 1997.

———. "A Terra-Cotta Cornerstone for Copley Square: Museum of Fine Arts, Boston, by Sturgis and Brigham (1870–1876)." *Journal of the Society of Architectural Historians* 32 (May 1973): 83–103.

———. "W. G. Preston (1842–1910) at Narragansett Pier." In *Buildings on Paper: Rhode Island Architectural Drawings, 1825–1945,* William H. Jordy and Christopher Monkhouse, eds., 142–46, 230–31. Providence, R.I.: Bell Gallery, List Art Center, Brown University, 1982.

Forbes, Allan, and Ralph M. Eastman. *Some Statues of Boston.* Boston: State Street Trust, 1946.

Freely, John. *Boston and Cambridge (Blue Guide).* New York: W. W. Norton, 1994.

Gilman, Arthur, ed. *The Cambridge of Eighteen Hundred and Ninety-Six.* Cambridge, Mass.: Riverside Press, 1896.

Goodman, Phebe S. *The Garden Squares of Boston.* Hanover, N.H.: University Press of New England, 2003.

Gordon, Edward W. *Final Report: Historic Resource Survey of Charlestown, MA,* prepared for the Boston Landmarks Commission (1985–1987).

Grant, Robert. *The Chippendales.* New York: Charles Scribner's Sons, 1909.

Greenslet, Ferris. *The Life of Thomas Bailey Aldrich*. Boston: Houghton Mifflin, 1908.

Grimké, Archibald H. "Anti-Slavery Boston," *New England Magazine*. December 1890 (new series, III).

Hale, Edward Everett. *Historic Boston and Its Neighborhood: An Historical Pilgrimage Personally Conducted by Edward Everett Hale Arranged for Seven Days*. New York: D. Appleton, 1898.

———. *Man without a Country and Other Tales*. Boston: Roberts Brothers, 1895.

Hall, Florence Howe. *Memories Grave and Gay*. New York: Harper Brothers, 1918.

Hamilton, Edward Pierce. *A History of Milton*. Milton, Mass.: Milton Historical Society, 1957.

Hanaford, Phebe A. *The Life of George Peabody: Containing a Record of Those Princely Acts of Destitute, Both in America, the Land of His Birth and in England, the Place of His Death*. Boston: B. B. Russell, 1870.

Handlin, Oscar. *Boston's Immigrants: A Study in Acculturation*. Rev. ed. Cambridge, Mass.: Belknap Press of Harvard University Press, 1959.

Harrell, Pauline Chase, and Margaret Supplee Smith. *Victorian Boston Today*. Boston: New England Chapter of the Victorian Society in America, 1975.

Harris, Cyril M., ed. *Historic Architecture Sourcebook*. New York: McGraw-Hill, 1977.

Harris, John. *The Boston Globe Historic Walks in Cambridge*. Chester, Conn.: Globe Pequot Press, 1986.

———. *The Boston Globe Historic Walks in Old Boston*. Chester, Conn.: Globe Pequot Press, 1982.

———. *The Boston Globe Historic Walks in Old Boston*. 2d ed. Chester, Conn.: Globe Pequot Press, 1989.

Hawthorne, Hildegarde. *The Poet of Craigie House: The Story of Henry Wadsworth Longfellow*. New York: D. Appleton–Century, 1936.

Hawthorne, Nathaniel. "My Kinsman Major Molineaux." In *Nathaniel Hawthorne's Tales*. James MacIntosh, ed. New York: W. W. Norton, 1987.

———. *Passages from the American Notebooks*. Boston: Houghton Mifflin, 1900.

———. *The Scarlet Letter*. Seymour Gross, ed. New York: W. W. Norton, 1988.

Hayden, Dolores. *The Grand Domestic Revolution*. Cambridge, Mass.: MIT Press, 1981.

Hays, Elinor Rice. *Morning Star: A Biography of Lucy Stone*. New York: Harcourt, Brace & World, 1961.

Herndon, Richard, comp. *Boston of Today*. Boston: Post Publishing, 1892.

Higginson, Thomas Wentworth. *Army Life in a Black Regiment and Other Writings*. 1869. Reprint, New York: Penguin Books, 1997.

———. *Carlyle's Laugh*. Boston, Houghton Mifflin, 1909.

———. *Cheerful Yesterdays*. Boston: Houghton Mifflin, 1898.

———. *Contemporaries*. Boston: Houghton and Mifflin, 1899.

The History Project. *Improper Bostonians*. Boston: Beacon Press, 1998.

Hodges, Rev. George. "The Episcopal Theological School." In *The Cambridge of Eighteen Hundred and Ninety-Six*. Arthur Gilman, ed. Cambridge, Mass.: Riverside Press, 1896.

Hogarth, Paul. *Walking Tours of Old Boston.* New York: E. P. Dutton, 1978.

Holleran, Michael. *Boston's "Changeful Times": Origins of Preservation and Planning in America.* Baltimore: Johns Hopkins University Press, 1998.

Holmes, Oliver Wendell. *The Autocrat of the Breakfast-Table.* 1859. Reprint, Boston: Houghton Mifflin, 1891.

———. *The Poet at the Breakfast-Table.* In *The Works of Oliver Wendell Holmes in Thirteen Volumes.* Vol. 3. Boston: Houghton Mifflin, 1893.

———. *The Poetical Works of Oliver Wendell Holmes.* 1852. Reprint, Boston: Houghton Mifflin, 1890.

———. *The Professor at the Breakfast Table.* In *The Works of Oliver Wendell Holmes in Thirteen Volumes.* Vol. 2. Boston: Houghton Mifflin, 1892.

Howe, Daniel Walker. *Victorian America.* Philadelphia: University of Pennsylvania Press, 1976.

Howe, Helen. *The Gentle Americans: Biography of a Breed.* New York: Harper & Row, 1965.

Howe, Julia Ward. *Reminiscences: 1819–1899.* Boston: Houghton Mifflin, 1900.

Howe, M. A. DeWolfe. *Boston Common: Scenes from Four Centuries.* Boston: Houghton Mifflin, 1921.

———. *Boston, the Place and the People.* New York: Macmillan, 1903.

Howells, William Dean. *Imaginary Interviews.* New York: Harper & Brothers, 1910.

———. *Literary Friends and Acquaintance.* New York: Harper & Brothers, 1900.

———. *A Modern Instance.* 1882. Reprint, New York: Penguin Books, 1984.

———. *My Mark Twain.* New York: Harper & Brothers, 1910.

———. *The Rise of Silas Lapham.* 1884. Reprint, New York: W. W. Norton, 1982.

Hoyt, Edwin P. *The Peabody Influence: How a Great New England Family Helped Build America.* New York: Dodd, Mead, 1968.

Hunnewell, James F. *A Century of Town Life.* Boston: Little, Brown, 1888.

James, Henry. *The American Scene.* 1907. Reprint, New York: Charles Scribner's Sons, 1946.

———. *The Bostonians.* 1886. Reprint, New York: Random House, Modern Library, 1956.

———. *Charles W. Eliot: President of Harvard University 1869–1909.* Boston: Houghton Mifflin, 1930.

———. "A New England Winter." In *The American Novels and Stories of Henry James.* F. O. Matthiessen, ed. New York: Alfred A. Knopf, 1951.

Jewett, Sarah Orne. *A Country Doctor.* Boston: Houghton Mifflin, 1884.

Johnson, Deidre. "Jacob Abbott." Available at www.readseries.com/auth-a/ab-bio.html (last accessed June 24, 2003).

Jordy, William H. "The Beaux Arts Renaissance: Charles McKim's Boston Public Library." In *American Buildings and Their Architects, IV: Progressive and Academic Ideals at the Turn of the 20th Century.* New York: Oxford University Press, 1972, 314–75.

Journal and Year Book for the 104th Annual Fair. St. John's Episcopal Church, Charlestown, November 3 and 4, 1943.

Kaplan, Justin. *Mr. Clemens and Mark Twain.* New York: Simon and Schuster, 1966.

Karcher, Carolyn L., ed. *Lydia Maria Child's An Appeal in Favor of That Class of Americans Called Africans.* Amherst: University of Massachusetts Press, 1996.

Kaufman, P., P. Morris, and J. Stevens. *The Boston Women's Heritage Trail.* Boston: Women's Heritage Trail, 1991.

Kay, Jane Holtz. *Lost Boston.* 2d ed. New York: Houghton Mifflin, 1999.

Kilham, Walter H. *Boston after Bulfinch.* Cambridge, Mass.: Harvard University Press, 1946.

King, Moses. *King's Hand Book of Boston.* Boston: Moses King, 1878.

———. *King's Hand-Book of Boston.* 9th ed. Boston: Moses King, 1889.

Knowles, Jane S. "Changing Images of the Boston Athenaeum." In *Change and Continuity: A Pictorial.* Boston: Boston Athenæum, 1976.

Kohl, Nancy L., ed. *Abigail May Alcott's Receipts and Simple Remedies: Best Way of Doing Difficult Things All Tried and Proved.* Concord, Mass.: Nancy L. Kohl and the Louisa May Alcott Memorial Association, 1980.

Lawrence, Robert Means. *Old Park Street and Its Vicinity.* Boston: Houghton Mifflin, 1922.

Lerner, G., ed. *Black Women in White America.* New York: Vintage Books, 1973.

Lewis, Lloyd, and Henry J. Smith. "Oscar Wilde Visits the Hub." In *State of Mind: A Boston Reader.* Robert N. Linscott, ed. New York: Farrar, Straus, 1948.

Lewis, R. W. B. *The Jameses: A Family Narrative.* New York: Farrar, Straus & Giroux, 1991.

Linden-Ward, Blanche. *Silent City on a Hill: Landscapes of Memory and Boston's Mount Auburn Cemetery.* Columbus: Ohio State University Press, 1989.

Lingner, Richard. "Ralph Curtis: Artist, Playboy and Confidant." Lecture given at Isabella Stewart Gardner Museum, December 28, 2002.

Lodge, Henry Cabot. "Senator Lodge Was Once a Boy." Excerpted from *Early Memories* in *State of Mind: A Boston Reader,* Robert N. Linscott, ed. New York: Farrar, Straus, 1948.

Longfellow, Fanny Appleton. *Mrs. Longfellow: Selected Letters and Journals of Fanny Appleton Longfellow.* Edward Wagenknecht, ed. New York: Longmans, Green, 1956.

Longfellow, Henry Wadsworth. *The Complete Poetical Works of Henry Wadsworth Longfellow.* Boston: Houghton Mifflin, 1894.

Lowell, James Russell. *Complete Poetical Works of James Russell Lowell.* Boston: Houghton Mifflin, 1897.

Lowell, Robert. *For the Union Dead.* New York: Farrar, Straus & Giroux, 1965.

———. *Life Studies.* New York: Farrar, Straus & Cudahy, 1959.

Lyndon, Donlyn. *The City Observed: Boston—A Guide to the Architecture of the Hub.* New York: Vintage Books, 1982.

MacDonald, E. Edward. *Old Copp's Hill and Burial Ground with Historical Sketches.* 12th ed. Boston, 1891.

Mallory, R. P. *Panoramic View of Charlestown from Bunker Hill Monument* (engraving). 1848.

Marquand, John P. *The Late George Apley*. Boston: Little, Brown, 1937.

Marsh, Vincent. "North End Planning Study for Boston, Massachusetts." Unpublished Master's thesis. Cornell University, Ithaca, N.Y., 1981.

Massachusetts Historical Commission Inventory Files and National Register Registration Forms.

Maycock, Susan. "Hartwell and Richardson: An Introduction to Their Work." *Journal of the Society of Architectural Historians* 32 (May 1973): 132–45.

Maynard, Mary, and Mary-Lou Maynard Dow. *Hassle-Free Boston*. Lexington, Mass.: Stephen Green Press, 1984.

McAlester, Virginia, and Lee McAlester. *A Field Guide to American Houses*. New York: Alfred A. Knopf, 1984.

McIntire Map of Boston and Vicinity, 1852. (State Library, Massachusetts State House, Boston, Mass.)

McIntyre, A. McVoy. *Beacon Hill: A Walking Tour*. Boston: Little, Brown, 1975.

Mead, Edwin. "Boston Memories of Fifty Years." *Fifty Years of Boston: A Memorial Volume Issued in Commemoration of the Tercentenary of 1930*. Boston Tercentenary Committee, ed. Boston: Subcommittee of Memorial History of the Boston Tercentenary Committee, 1932.

———. Foreword to Edward Everett Hale, *A New England Boyhood*. New York: Grosset & Dunlap, 1927.

Meigs, Cornelia. *Invincible Louisa*. Boston: Little, Brown, 1939.

Meyerson, Joel, and Daniel Shealy. Introduction to *The Inheritance* by Louisa May Alcott. New York: Penguin Books, 1998.

Meyerson, Joel, and Daniel Shealy, eds. *The Journals of Louisa May Alcott*. Boston: Little, Brown, 1989.

———. *Selected Letters of Louisa May Alcott*. Boston: Little, Brown, 1987.

Middlesex County Deeds. Middlesex County Court House, Cambridge, Mass.

Miller, Bruce, ed. "A Calendar of Walter Baker & Company, Inc., and Its Times (1765–1940)." New York: General Foods, 1940.

Miller, Edwin Haviland. *Salem Is My Dwelling Place: A Life of Nathaniel Hawthorne*. Iowa City: University of Iowa Press, 1991.

Miller, Naomi, and Keith Morgan. *Boston Architecture 1972–1990*. Munich: Prestel, 1990.

Morison, Samuel Eliot. *One Boy's Boston*. 1962. Reprint. Boston: Northeastern University Press, 1983.

Morse, John T., Jr. *Life and Letters of Oliver Wendell Holmes*. Boston: Houghton, Mifflin, 1896.

Moss, Roger W., and Gail Caskey Winkler. *Victorian Exterior Decoration: How to Paint Your Nineteenth-Century House Historically*. New York: Henry Holt, 1987.

Nell, William Cooper. *The Colored Patriots of the American Revolution*. Boston: Robert F. Wallcut, 1855.

Norfolk County Probate Records. Norfolk County Court House, Dedham, Mass.

Norfolk County Registry of Deeds. Norfolk County Court House, Dedham, Mass.

O'Connell, Sean. *Imagining Boston*. Boston: Beacon Press, 1990.

O'Connor, Thomas H. *The Boston Irish: A Political History.* Boston: Northeastern University Press, 1995.

———. *Fitzpatrick's Boston: 1846–1866.* Boston: Northeastern University Press, 1984.

———. *The Hub: Boston Past and Present.* Boston: Northeastern University Press, 2001.

O'Gorman, James F. *Living Architecture: A Biography of H. H. Richardson.* New York: Simon & Schuster, 1997.

Orcutt, William Dana. *Good Old Dorchester.* 1893. Reprint. Norwood, Mass.: Plimpton Press, 1916.

O'Reilly, John Boyle. "Crispus Attucks." Exercises at Faneuil Hall. *A Memorial of Crispus Attucks, Samuel Maverick, James Caldwell, Samuel Gray and Patrick Carr from the City of Boston .* Boston: Boston City Council, 1889.

Otis, [Mrs.] Harrison Gray. *The Barclays of Boston.* Boston: Ticknor, Reed and Fields, 1854.

"Our Self Made Men." *Charlestown Enterprise.* September 3, 1887, 1.

Palmer, Foster M. "Horse Car, Trolley, and Subway." in *Proceedings of the Cambridge Historical Society,* 39 (1961–63): 78–107.

Parsons, A. F. *Boston: Its Commerce, Finance and Literature.* New York: A. F. Parsons, 1892.

Peabody, Elizabeth Palmer. *Letters of Elizabeth Peabody.* Bruce A. Ronda, ed. Middletown, Conn.: Wesleyan University Press, 1984.

Perry, Bliss. *Park Street Papers.* Boston: Houghton Mifflin, 1908.

Pollan, Rosalind. *Jamaica Plain Project Completion Report,* Part I. Boston: Boston Landmarks Commission, 1983.

———. *North End Project Completion Report.* Boston: Boston Landmarks Commission, 1990.

Portfolio Club. *The Architectural Sketch-Book.* 4 vols. Boston: J. R. Osgood, 1873–76.

"Prisons." In *Built in the USA.* Diane Maddex, ed. Washington, D.C.: Preservation Press, 1985.

Quincy, Josiah. *History of the Boston Athenæum.* Cambridge: Metcalfe, 1851.

Rettig, Robert Bell. *Guide to Cambridge Architecture: Ten Walking Tours.* Cambridge, Mass.: MIT Press, 1969.

Richards, Laura E., and Maud Howe Elliott. *Julia Ward Howe: 1819–1910.* 2 vols. Boston: Houghton Mifflin, 1916.

Richardson, Marilyn. *Maria W. Stewart: America's First Black Woman Political Writer.* Bloomington: Indiana University Press, 1987.

Robinson, Edwin Arlington. "Isaac and Archibald." In *Collected Poems.* New York: Macmillan, 1921.

Rodgers, Patricia H., Charles M. Sullivan, and the Staff of the Cambridge Historical Commission. *A Photographic History of Cambridge.* Cambridge, Mass.: MIT Press, 1984.

Roman, Judith A. *Annie Adams Fields: The Spirit of Charles Street.* Bloomington: Indiana University Press, 1990.

Ross, Marjorie Drake. *The Book of Boston: The Victorian Period, 1837–1901.* New York: Hastings House, 1964.

Rothman, Ellen K, and Peter O'Connell. "Hear Us: Honoring the Contributions of Women to Public Life in Massachusetts." Brochure. Northampton, Mass.: Massachusetts Foundation for the Humanities, 1999.

Ryan, Dennis P. *Beyond the Ballot Box: A Social History of the Boston Irish, 1845–1917.* Rutherford, N.J.: Fairleigh Dickinson University Press, 1983.

———. *The Irish in Boston.* Boston: United Boston Irish, 1975.

Sammarco, Anthony Mitchell. *Dorchester.* Vol. 1 Dover, N.H.: Arcadia Press, 1995.

———. *Dorchester.* Vol. 2. Dover, N.H.: Arcadia Press, 2000.

———. "Dorchester Lower Mills: From Unquety to Birthplace of the Industrial Revolution." *Dorchester (Mass.) Community News,* January 20, 1995, 8.

———. *Images of America, Charlestown.* Dover, N.H.: Arcadia Press, 1996.

———. *Images of America, Jamaica Plain.* Dover, N.H.: Arcadia Publishing, 1997.

———. "Industrial Development along the Neponset River." *Milton (Mass.) Record Transcript,* November 17, 1989, 1.

———. "Lower Mills Square Named after Chocolate Company Owner, Mayor." *Dorchester (Mass.) Community News,* April 20, 1990, 6.

Sammarco, Anthony Mitchell, and Paul Buchanan. *Milton Architecture.* Dover, N.H.: Arcadia Press, 2000.

Santayana, George. *The Last Puritan: A Memoir in the Form of a Novel.* 1935. Reprint, New York: Charles Scribner's Sons, 1964.

Sawyer, Timothy Thompson. *Old Charlestown.* Boston: Little, Brown, 1902.

Schindler, Solomon. *Israelites in Boston.* Boston: Author, 1889.

Schlesinger, Arthur M. *The Age of Jackson.* Boston: Little, Brown, 1953.

Scully, Vincent J., Jr. *The Shingle Style and the Stick Style: Architectural Theory and Design from Downing to the Origins of Wright.* Rev. ed. New Haven, Conn.: Yale University Press, 1971.

Seaburg, Carl. *Boston Observed.* Boston: Beacon Press, 1971.

Seasholes, Nancy S. *Gaining Ground: A History of Landmaking in Boston.* Cambridge, Mass.: MIT Press, 2003.

Shackleton, Robert. *The Book of Boston.* Philadelphia: Penn Publishing, 1920.

Shand-Tucci, Douglass. *The Art of Scandal: The Life and Times of Isabella Stewart Gardner.* New York: HarperCollins, 1997.

———. *Built in Boston: City and Suburb, 1800–2000.* Amherst: University of Massachusetts Press, 1997.

Shurtleff, N. B. *A Topographical and Historical Description of Boston.* Boston: Alfred Mudge and Son, 1871.

Sicherman, B., and C. Green. *Notable American Women.* 3 vols. Cambridge, Mass.: Harvard University Press, 1971.

Sketches of Boston, 1848–1929. Boston: L. P. Hollander, 1929.

Slautterback, Catharina. *Designing the Boston Athenæum: 10½ at 150.* Boston: Boston Athenæum, 1999.

Smith, Betty S. "Whitman, Sarah de Prix Wyman." *American National Biography.*

John A. Garraty and Mark C. Carnes, eds. Vol. 23. New York: Oxford University Press, 1999.

Smith, Dexter, *Cyclopedia of Boston and Vicinity.* Boston: Cashin & Smith, 1886.

Smith, Margaret Supplee. *Between City and Suburb: Architecture and Planning in Boston's South End.* Ann Arbor, Mich.: Xerox University Microfilms, 1977.

———. "The Custom House Controversy," *Nineteenth Century* 3 (Summer 1977): 99–105.

Smith, Margaret Supplee, and John Morehouse. "Architecture and the Housing Market: Nineteenth Century Rowhouses in Boston's South End." *Journal of the Society of Architectural Historians* 52, no. 2 (June 1993).

Somerset Club. *A Brief History of the Somerset Club of Boston: With a List of Past and Present Members, 1852–1913.* Boston: Privately printed, 1913.

South End House, Residents and Associates of. *Americans in Process: A Settlement Study.* Robert A. Woods, ed. Boston: Houghton Mifflin, 1902.

Southworth, Susan, and Michael Southworth. *Boston Society of Architects A.I.A. Guide to Boston.* Chester, Conn.: Globe Pequot Press, 1984.

———. *The Boston Society of Architects' AIA Guide to Boston.* 2d ed. Chester, Conn.: Globe Pequot Press, 1992.

Souvenir of the 50th Anniversary of the Dedication of Bunker Hill Monument, 1843–1893. Charlestown, Mass.: Bunker Hill Times, 1893.

Spring, James W. *Boston and the Parker House.* Boston: J. R. Whipple, 1927.

Stanwood, Edward. *Boston Illustrated.* Boston: J. R. Osgood & Company, 1872.

———. *Boston Illustrated.* Boston: J. R. Osgood & Company, 1875.

State Street Trust Company. *Boston's Growth: A Bird's Eye View of Boston's Increase in Territory and Population from Its Beginning to Present.* Boston: Author, 1901.

Stott, Peter. *A Guide to the Industrial Archeology of Boston Proper.* Cambridge, Mass.: MIT Press, 1984.

Strachey, Lytton. *Eminent Victorians.* Garden City, N.Y.: Garden City Publishing, 1918.

Strouse, Jean. *Alice James: A Biography.* Boston: Houghton Mifflin, 1980.

Suffolk County Deeds, Suffolk County Court House, Boston, Mass.

Sutton, S. B. *Cambridge Reconsidered: 3½ Centuries on the Charles.* Cambridge, Mass.: MIT Press, 1976.

Sweetser, M. F. *King's How to See Boston: A Trustworthy Guidebook.* Knights Templar ed. Boston: Moses King, 1895.

Sweetser, M. F., and Moses King. *An Alphabetical Guide to Boston.* Boston: Macullar Parker, 1883.

Swift, Lindsay. *Literary Landmarks of Boston: A Visitor's Guide to Points of Literary Interest in and about Boston.* Boston: Houghton Mifflin, 1903.

[Tewksbury, J. H.] *Historic Boston: Sight-Seeing Tours around the Hub.* [Boston]: Young Men's Christian Associations, 1901.

Tharp, Louise Hall. *Mrs. Jack.* Boston: Little, Brown, 1965.

Thoreau, Henry David. *Familiar Letters of Henry David Thoreau.* F. B. Sanborn, ed. Boston: Houghton Mifflin, 1894.

Thwing, Annie Haven. *The Crooked and Narrow Streets of the Town of Boston.* Boston: Marshall Jones, 1920.

Todisco, Paula J. *Boston's First Neighborhood: The North End.* Boston: Boston Public Library, 1976.

"The Town Crier." *Cambridge Tribune,* August 18, 1894, 2.

Tryon, W. S. *Parnassus Corner: A Life of James T. Fields, Publisher to the Victorians.* Boston: Houghton Mifflin, 1963.

Tufts, Peter. *Map of Charlestown,* 1818.

Turner, Arlin. *Nathaniel Hawthorne: A Biography.* New York: Oxford University Press, 1980.

Valenti, Patricia Dunlavy. *To Myself a Stranger: A Biography of Rose Hawthorne Lathrop.* Baton Rouge: Louisiana State University Press, 1991.

Wagenknecht, Edward, ed. *Mrs. Longfellow: Selected Letters and Journals of Fanny Appleton Longfellow.* New York: Longmans, Green, 1956.

Waite, Helen Elmira. *Make A Joyful Sound: The Romance of Mabel Hubbard and Alexander Graham Bell.* Philadelphia: Macrae Smith, 1961.

Weinberg, Helene Barbara. "John LaFarge and the Decoration of Trinity Church, Boston." *Journal of the Society of Architectural Historians* 33 (December 1974): 323–53.

Wharton, Edith. "The Lamp of Psyche." In *The Collected Stories of Edith Wharton.* R. W. B. Lewis, ed. New York: Charles Scribner's Sons, 1968.

Whitehill, Walter Muir. *Boston: A Topograpical History.* Cambridge, Mass.: Belknap Press of Harvard University Press, 1959.

———. *Boston: A Topographical History.* 2d ed. Cambridge, Mass.: Belknap Press of Harvard University Press, 1968.

———. *Boston: A Topographical History.* 3d ed. Cambridge, Mass.: Belknap Press of Harvard University Press, 2000.

———. *Boston Public Library: A Centennial History.* Cambridge, Mass.: Harvard University Press, 1956.

Whiting, Lilian. *Boston Days.* Boston: Little, Brown, 1902.

Whitman, Walt. *Specimen Days in America.* 1882. Reprint, New York: E. P. Dutton, 1906.

Whittier, John Greenleaf. *The Complete Works of John Greenleaf Whittier.* Boston: Houghton Mifflin, 1895.

Wieder, Arnold A. *The Early Jewish Community of Boston's North End.* Waltham, Mass.: Brandeis University, 1962.

Williams, Alexander W. *A Social History of Greater Boston Clubs.* Barre, Mass.: Barre Publishers, 1970.

Wilson, Rufus Rockwell. *New England in Letters.* New York: A. Wessels, 1904.

Wilson, Susan. *Boston Sites and Insights.* Boston: Beacon Press, 1994.

———. *The Literary Trail of Greater Boston.* Boston: Houghton Mifflin, 2000.

Winslow, Helen M. *Literary Boston of Today.* Boston: L. C. Page, 1903.

Winsor, Justin, ed. *The Memorial History of Boston, Including Suffolk County, Massachusetts, 1630–1880.* Vol 3. Boston: J. R. Osgood, 1881.

———. *The Memorial History of Boston, Including Suffolk County, Massachusetts, 1630–1880.* 4 vols. Boston: J. R. Osgood, 1881–1883.

Wolfe, Theodore F. *Literary Shrines: The Haunts of Some Famous American Authors.* Philadelphia: J. B. Lippincott, 1895.

.Woods, Robert A., ed. *The City Wilderness.* Cambridge, Mass.: Riverside Press, 1898.

Works Progress Administration. *WPA Guide to Massachusetts: The Federal Writers' Project Guide to 1930s Massachusetts.* 1937. Reprint, New York: Pantheon Books, 1983.

Zaitzevsky, Cynthia. *The Architecture of William Ralph Emerson, 1833–1917.* Cambridge, Mass.: Fogg Art Museum, 1969.

———. *Frederick Law Olmsted and the Boston Park System.* Cambridge, Mass.: Belknap Press of Harvard University Press, 1982.

———. "A New Richardson Building." *Journal of the Society of Architectural Historians* 32, no. 2 (May 1973).

———. "Victorian Jamaica Plain." In *Victorian Boston Today: Ten Walking Tours.* Pauline Chase Harrell and Margaret Supplee Smith, eds. Boston: New England Chapter of the Victorian Society in America, 1975.

ABOUT THE CONTRIBUTORS

Charles Bahne

Charles Bahne is an urban historian specializing in the Boston area and the founder and owner of Newtowne Publishing, a publisher and distributor of tourist guides and other books about Boston. He graduated from the Massachusetts Institute of Technology with a B.S. in Urban Studies and Planning. He is the author of the perennially popular *Complete Guide to Boston's Freedom Trail* (1985). Bahne is also an associate editor of *Rollsign*, the magazine of New England transit history, published by the Boston Street Railway Association. He was editor for three editions of *Car-Free in Boston* and for a time for the Association for Public Transportation's newsletter *Mass. Transit*. He has been a contributing editor for the travel magazine *Getting There*. Among his other publications are travel and historical articles in *Passenger Train Journal* and the *Boston Globe*.

Bahne worked for four seasons as a park ranger with the Boston National Historical Park, a unit of the U.S. National Park Service. He has also worked as a museum guide at the Old State House in Boston and in the education department of the Museum of Transportation in Brookline. A former president of the New England Chapter of the Victorian Society in America, he teaches courses in Boston history and architecture at the Cambridge Center for Adult Education and regularly gives talks about Boston and Cambridge to clubs and historical societies. Charles Bahne designed the first-rate series of maps for *Victorian Boston Today*.

Richard O. Card

Richard O. Card, a resident of the South End since 1963, founded the South End Historical Society in 1966, was its first president, and was for many years its historian, assembling the nucleus of the society's photograph collection. He has written many articles, collected hundreds of South End photographs and documents, and is currently working with the Washington Main Streets project toward the creation of a series of historical kiosks along the new MBTA Silver Line. Also active in a number of other groups, he is a member of the board of the New England Chapter of the Victorian Society in America, an advisory trustee of Maine Maritime Museum, historian of the Bath (Maine) United Methodist Church, and a former chairman of the board of Boston Center for the Arts. Now retired after thirty-three years with Bank of Boston, Card was a vice president in Systems Development.

Pauline Chase-Harrell

Pauline Chase-Harrell is a social and architectural historian who has combined consulting in historic preservation with teaching, writing, and lecturing. President of the consulting firm of Boston Affiliates, Inc., she has also taught courses at Tufts, Northeastern, and Boston Universities, and the University of Massachusetts–Boston. She chaired the Boston Landmarks Commission for its first twelve years and was a founding board member of the National Alliance of Preservation Commissions. Her books include *Historic Maritime Resources: Planning for Preservation,* with Marcia Myers (1990); *Arrowhead Farm: Three Hundred Years of New England Husbandry and Cooking* (1983); and *Preserving New England,* with Jane Holtz Kay (1986). She has also written numerous articles for *Glamour, Nineteenth Century, Boston Magazine,* and other periodicals. A former Victorian Society in America board member and a founding board member of the VSA New England Chapter, she was coeditor, with Margaret Supplee Smith, of *Victorian Boston Today* (1975).

Margaret Henderson Floyd {*In Memoriam*}

Margaret Henderson Floyd studied art and architectural history with Bainbridge Bunting and received an M.A. degree in Art History in 1957 for her research on Spanish churches built on former Toltec holy sites in Cholula, Mexico. She was professor of art and architectural history at Tufts University (1977–97).

Floyd, interested in historic preservation, developed the architectural inventory system for the Commonwealth of Massachusetts. She was a founder of the VSA New England Chapter. Her publications focused on the history of architecture and its associated decorative arts and explored questions about the design of the Museum of Fine Arts (1870–76), the first major U.S. public building to be constructed of architectural terra-cotta. Her research on the architects Sturgis and Brigham led to an exploration of the picturesque English design aesthetic that established the character of the Back Bay and of New England architecture.

Floyd studied Boston's contribution to architectural education and the city's influence on the development of American architectural theory and education from the founding of the United States' first school of architecture at MIT in 1866 to the arrival of modernism with Walter Gropius at Harvard's School of Design (1936–52). In *Harvard: An Architectural History* (1983), edited by Floyd, and in *Architectural Education and Boston* (1989), she explored facets of the educational matrix from which New England regionalism, the career of H. H. Richardson, and modern architecture developed, many of which have reemerged with the rise of postmodernism. In *Architecture after Richardson: Regionalism before Modernism—Longfellow, Alden and Harlow in Boston and Pittsburgh* (1994), Floyd related the persistence of a New England tradition on a national level and connected it with the modern movement in America. In her most recent book, *Henry Hobson Richardson: A Genius for Architecture* (1998),

Floyd placed Richardson's buildings within the architectural ambience of nineteenth-century England and New England.

It is with the generous assistance of the late William B. Floyd that "Touring through Time to the Heart of Back Bay: Boylston and Dartmouth Streets with Copley Square," the work of his Boston-conversant wife, the late Margaret Henderson Floyd, appears in this edition.

Edward W. Gordon

Edward W. Gordon has been president of the New England Chapter of the Victorian Society in America since 1991. He is the former executive director of the Gibson House Museum (1990–2001). Since 1993, he has been a board member of the National Victorian Society in America and serves on its Preservation and Symposia committees. He is currently the site administrator of the Old Schwamb Mill in Arlington, Mass. For twenty years he has worked as a historic preservation consultant preparing nominations of buildings and districts to the National Register of Historic Places. Additionally, Gordon works as a consultant on Massachusetts Historical Commission Comprehensive Historic Resource Surveys. Gordon is also a seasonal Boston area tour guide for various destination management companies and has taught Boston architectural history at the Boston Center for Adult Education since 1977. In January 1998 he was appointed to the Massachusetts State House Senate Arts Committee by Senator Thomas Birmingham and in 1999 was presented the John F. Ayer Award for outstanding contributions to the field of Massachusetts history by the Bay State Historical League. Gordon is a member of the National Trust for Historic Preservation, the Society of Architectural Historians, the South End Historical Society, and the Greater Boston Tour Guide Association; he is also co-editor of *The Beacon* newsletter of the Victorian Society in America, New England Chapter.

Wilfred E. Holton

Will Holton is associate professor of sociology at Northeastern University. He graduated from Vanderbilt University in 1964, majoring in sociology with a minor in history, and then earned two degrees in sociology at Boston University, an M.S. in 1966 and a Ph.D. in 1972. He joined the faculty at Northeastern University in 1973, where his teaching and research focus on neighborhood change, group relations, poverty, and political issues in Boston. Since 1975 he has taught the popular "Sociology of Boston" course, for which he has prepared a text, "Discovering Boston: A Social Perspective on the City." From 1984 to 2000 he operated "Discovering Boston Walking Tours." In 1986 Holton delivered a series of N.E.H. lectures titled "The Social History of the South End" at the South End Branch of the Boston Public Library. His current major research focuses on the motivations for the massive project that filled the 850-acre Back Bay marsh in Boston in the nineteenth century. Holton is president of The Partnership of the Historic Bostons, a nonprofit organization that educates the public about its historical legacy from the town of Boston, England.

Eugenia Kaledin

Eugenia Kaledin is an independent scholar with a Ph.D. in American and New England Studies from Boston University and a B.A. and M.A. from Harvard. After teaching at Northeastern University's Burlington branch for many years, and also at the University of Pennsylvania on a Mellon Fellowship, she taught courses at Yale, Wellesley, and Harvard. In 1985 she became a Fulbright professor at the University of Beijing in China, and in 1991 she taught in Czechoslovakia on a similar grant. She has recently worked on a community oral history film about a local arrest during the Vietnam War. Her available books are *The Education of Mrs. Henry Adams* (1981; 1994), *Mothers and More: American Women in the 1950s* (1984), and *Daily Life in the United States, 1940–1959: Shifting Worlds* (2000). Kaledin's "Literary Boston: A Writer's Thinking Tour," in the VSA/NE's 1975 edition, covered multiple centuries and unearthed several sites that have now become traditional ones in subsequent literary explorations of Boston.

Robert B. MacKay

Robert B. MacKay was a Boston University graduate student when the first version of his downtown tour was published in *Victorian Boston Today* (1975). He is now the director of the Society for the Preservation of Long Island Antiquities and chairman of the New York State Board for Historic Preservation.

After completing studies at Milton Academy, Boston University's undergraduate school and Harvard's graduate school, MacKay received his doctorate in American Studies in 1980 from Boston University, having written his dissertation on Boston's Charles Street Jail. As a graduate student in the 1970s, he did extensive research on the commercial architecture of Boston's central business district, both before and after the Great Fire of 1872. A recipient of several fellowships, he continues to serve on panels and committees and as a trustee for numerous associations in the New York area. Among his publications are articles in periodicals and collections such as *Antiques, Arts and Antiques,* and the *Macmillan Encyclopedia of Architects.* He has edited *Between Ocean and Empire: An Illustrated History of Long Island* (1985), *A.I.A. Architectural Guide to Nassau and Suffolk Counties, Long Island* (1992), and *Long Island Country Houses and Their Architects, 1860–1940* (1994).

J. Marcus Mitchell and Gaunzetta L. Mitchell

J. Marcus Mitchell, artist, community historian, and advocate of the Metropolitan Council for Educational Opportunity (METCO), was curator and director of the American Museum of Negro History (later the Museum of Afro-American History) when it was first established in the Charles Street Meeting House.

He was a founder of the Boston Negro Artist Association (1965; now Boston African American Artists) and worked to design a trail in Boston that celebrated black art and history for the 1963 centennial of the Emancipation Proclamation.

J. Marcus Mitchell refined an earlier version of Black Heritage Trail® with his wife, Gaunzetta L. Mitchell. The Mitchells' vision was to focus the trail on the vitally important sites on Beacon Hill. He and Gaunzetta typed the first draft of the 1968 booklet that evolved into the Black Heritage Trail® (see also Byron Rushing, the Staff of the Museum of Afro-American History, and Sue Bailey Thurman) (S. Wilson, *Boston Sites and Insights* 208–10).

Patricia C. Morris

Patricia Morris has recently retired from the Boston Public Schools, in which she started teaching in 1966. Since that time she continued to be concerned about the need for change in urban schools; her Ed.D. dissertation was entitled "The Urban Elementary School Teacher: A Feminist Analysis" (University of Massachusetts–Amherst, 1990). Her most recent work has been in curriculum development, with a focus on gender equity, and in teacher training. Morris was the first director of the Boston Women's Heritage Trail.

Morris served on the Boston Landmarks Commission of Public Art to honor women. She has worked with the Women's Educational and Industrial Union and has served on the Education Advisory Board of the Bostonian Society. She received recognition for outstanding achievement in 1993 by the Boston City Council and was named "Woman of the Year" by the College Club of Boston in 1990. Among her publications are "The Boston Women's Heritage Trail" and "Remembering Her Story." Currently, Morris is an instructor and on the board of the Learning Enrichment Program at the University of Massachusetts–Boston. She is a frequent lecturer and member of the Advisory Board of the Theological Opportunities Program at Harvard Divinity School. At present, Morris is working with members of the Women's International League for Peace and Freedom to publish research on Cape Cod women.

Mary Melvin Petronella

Mary Melvin Petronella, editor of *Victorian Boston Today* (2004), looks forward to the time when Boston establishes a "Victorian Heritage Trail" and hopes that this VSA/NE series of tours will serve as a pilot for that purpose.

Petronella, who serves as president of the Boston Browning Society (est. 1885), is a longtime adjunct assistant professor of English at Bentley College. She began teaching English literature at Northeastern University before joining the Student Affairs staff at Bentley College as its first international student advisor. She established the college's International Student Office and its services while working part-time and then commenced teaching at Bentley. While she was developing a course on W. D. Howells's novel *The Rise of Silas Lapham*, Petronella's interest in Victorian Boston and its milieu, the fine arts, world cultures, and Isabella Stewart Gardner led to her research and her courses on Victorian Bostonians, Gardner and her museum, and American authors abroad.

A frequent lecturer on Mrs. Jack and Victorian residents of the Back Bay, Petronella has spoken at the Harvard Club, the Isabella Stewart Gardner Museum, Mystic Seaport, the Boston Athenæum, King's Chapel, Wellesley College Club, the William Hickling Prescott House, and the National Arts Club (Gramercy Park, N.Y.). For several summers, she coordinated the talents of VSA/NE board members for the Bentley College Elderhostel's "Victorian Boston Week." At present she teaches communication courses at Bentley.

Formerly a board member of the Gibson House Museum and a vice president of Boston University Women's Council, Petronella serves as a corporator of the Louisa May Alcott Memorial Association and is a longtime board member of the VSA/NE. She is currently writing a book on Boston life and literature.

Byron Rushing

From 1972 to 1985 State Representative Byron Rushing was president of the Museum of Afro-American History. Under his direction, the Museum of Afro-American History purchased and began the restoration of the African Meeting House. In 1979 Rushing oversaw the lobbying effort in Congress to establish the Boston African American National Historical Site, a component of the National Park Service. The Black Heritage Trail concept began with "Negro Freedom Trails of Boston," conceived by Sue Bailey Thurman and developed by J. Marcus and Gaunzetta L. Mitchell. Henry Hampton invented the title "Black Heritage Trail." Rushing researched and wrote this version of the trail in 1976 and revised it in 1981 and 1983; it was edited by the Staff of the Museum. As a legislator Rushing sponsored the creation of Roxbury Heritage State Park and serves on its Advisory Committee. He occasionally leads walking tours of African American and working-class neighborhoods in Boston and Roxbury and is president of the Roxbury Historical Society. (See also J. Marcus and Gaunzetta L. Mitchell, the Staff of the Museum of Afro-American History, and Sue Bailey Thurman.)

Anthony Mitchell Sammarco

Anthony M. Sammarco is a noted Boston historian who has authored over thirty books on the history and development of his native city and its many neighborhoods. Among his best-selling books are the *Great Boston Fire of 1872, Boston: A Century of Progress, Boston's Back Bay, Boston's South End, Boston's West End, Cambridge,* and *Boston's Harbor Islands.*

A respected and perennially popular lecturer, he often presents lectures before historical societies, clubs, and neighborhood associations on the rich history and traditions of an ever-evolving city. Treasurer of Bonney's Express, Inc., a Boston-based transportation company, he also teaches Boston history courses at the Urban College of Boston and is president of the Bay State Historical League.

Margaret Supplee Smith

Margaret Supplee Smith is professor and chair of the Art Department at Wake Forest University, Winston-Salem, N.C. After receiving her Ph.D. from Brown University, Smith taught at Boston University, where she was the founding director of the Graduate Program in Historic Preservation. She has taught art and architectural history at Wake Forest since 1979 and helped to establish the college's Women's Studies Program. She coordinated the North Carolina Women's History Project for the N.C. Museum of History and curated the exhibition that opened the museum's new building in 1994. Smith co-authored, with Emily Herring Wilson, *North Carolina Women Making History* (1999) and is currently writing a book on the architecture of American ski resorts. She was coeditor with Pauline Chase-Harrell of the 1975 edition of *Victorian Boston Today.*

The Staff of the Museum of Afro-American History

The staff of the Museum of Afro-American History edited the Black Heritage Trail.® The Museum of Afro-American History's mission is to preserve and interpret the contributions of people of African descent and those who have found common cause with them in the struggle for liberty and justice for all Americans. Through educational workshops, youth camps, exhibits, special events, and unique partnerships, it places the African American experience in an accurate social, cultural, and historical perspective. Incorporated in 1967, the museum is nationally and internationally known for the African Meeting House and Abiel Smith School on Boston's Beacon Hill, the African Meeting House on Nantucket, and Black Heritage Trails® in Boston and Nantucket. For additional information, please visit the museum's Web site at http://www.afro ammuseum.org or call (617)-725–0022.

Sue Bailey Thurman

Sue Bailey Thurman (1903–96) helped found the American Negro Museum of History (1964) in Boston and the Negro Freedom Trails of Boston, from which today's Museum of Afro-American History and the Black Heritage Trail® have evolved. The Black Heritage Trail® began its evolution from a concept devised by Thurman. She and her daughter, Ann Chiarenza, published a large map whose title was "Negro Freedom Trails of Boston." It featured sites on Beacon Hill as well as in Cambridge and Roxbury (see also J. Marcus and Gaunzetta L. Mitchell, Byron Rushing, and the Staff of the Museum of Afro-American History). Thurman was an important Gandhi-inspired voice for civil rights in the United States, as was her husband, Dr. Howard Thurman (1899–1981), the dean of Marsh Chapel and professor of spiritual resources and disciplines at Boston University, who promoted a nonviolent philosophy and was himself an inspiration to Martin Luther King, Jr. (S. Wilson, *Boston Sites and Insights* 208–10). Both Sue Bailey Thurman and Howard Thurman interviewed Gandhi in India.eIndex

INDEX

sketch, xxxiii; Tremont St., 30; Tremont St. Methodist Church, 31; Union Park, 21–22; Washington St., 23–24; West Newton St., 25; Worcester Sq., 27; Zion German Lutheran Church, 22

South Station, 15–16, 234n.2 (T1)

Sparks St. (Cambridge), 226

spinning contests, 144

Spiritualism, 81

Spiritualist Temple, 80–81

Spruce St., 105

Stafford, Jean, 114

Stahl-Bennett, 52, 76–77

stained-glass windows, 37, 64, 127, 179, 180, 207, 210

Standish Village (Dorchester), 198

Stanton, Elizabeth Cady, 163, *163*

Stanton, Henry, 163

State House, xliv, *xlv*, 99–100, 146, 153–56, *154*, 241n.2

State Prison (Charlestown), 172

State Street Block, 10

statues: Back Bay Tour (T5), 65; Charlestown Tour (T9), 187; Commercial District Tour (T4), 54; Victorian Authors Tour (T6), 91, 99–100, 123, 129, 233n.1; Walking with Women Tour (T8), 144, 146, 159, 162, 164–65, 233n.1, 241–42n.7, 241n.5

steamships, *xxxii,* 5, 8, 9, 11

stenciling, 71, 72

Stephenson, Harrison M., 210

Stern, Robert A. M., xxxiv, 67

Stewart, James W., 157

Stewart, Maria W., xxxv, 157

Stick style, 199, 211, 223

Stimpson, George, 184

Stone, Lucy: Victorian Authors Tour (T6), 95, 239n.29; Walking with Women Tour (T8), 152–53, 161, 163, 164, 166, 241n.2, 242n.8

Stony Brook Valley, 211

storehouses, 197

Story of a Bad Boy, The (Aldrich), 120, 238n.19

Story of Experience, A (Alcott), 114

Story, William Wetmore, 95, 187

Stoughton House, 219–20, 243n.4

Stoughton, Mary Fiske, 219–20

Stowe, Calvin, 86

Stowe, Harriet Beecher, 43, 84, 91, 111, 114, 119, 136, 161

Strachey, Lytton, xxxii–xxxiii

Strangers and Wayfarers (Jewett), 111

Strauss, Johann, Jr., 25

street design: xxxv; Back Bay Tour (T5), 63, 70, 80; Brattle Street Tour (T12), 227; Charlestown Tour (T9), 170; Jamaica Plain Tour (T11), 209; 19th-Century Waterfront Tour (T1), 5, 6; South End Tour (T2), 24; Victorian Authors Tour (T6), 108. *See also* streetscape

"Street, The" (Lowell), 128

Streeter, Sebastian, 39

streetscape, xxxv, xxxvi, 35, 45, 63, 65, 66, 70, 79, 80, 81, 110, 119, 177, 178, 181, 184, 185, 207, 210, 211. *See also* street design

Strickland and Blodgett, 64

Stubbins, Hugh, 74

stucco, 210, 230

Study of Hawthorne, A (G. P. Lathrop), 106

Sturgis and Brigham, 67, 69, 77–78, 80, 126, 230

Sturgis, John Hubbard, 78, 79, 80, 230, 243–44n.11

Sturgis, R. Clipston, 99, 243–44n.11

Sturtevant, Benjamin F., 212

Sturtevant Blowers, 212, *212*

subway. *See* first subway; MBTA

subway kiosks: Copley Sq., 82; Park St., 84

Sudbury, Richard, 115

Suffolk County Court House, 52

Suffolk County Jail, 51–52

Suffolk St., 22

suffrage movement, 145, 149, 153–54, 160–61, 165

Sullivan, Anne, 242n.8

Sullivan, Louis, 76

Sullivan, Robert, 106

Sullivan Sq. (Charlestown), 171

Summer St., 58–60

Summer Street Bridge, 15

Sumner, Charles, 41, 135, 139, 159–60, 244n.16

Sumner Hill (Jamaica Plain), 203–4, 207–13

Sumner, Increase, 209

Sumner, William Hyslop, 209–10

Sun Court, 42

Swedenborgianism, 81

Swift, Lindsay, 127

synagogues, 23, 46

T. *See* first subway; MBTA

T. O. H. P. Burnham's "Antique Bookstore," 236n.3 (T6)

T Wharf, 9, *9*

Tamerlane and Other Poems (Poe), 92

Tapley, John, 183–84

Taylor, ("Father") Edward Thompson, xxxiv, 41–42

teamsters, 181

Teddy Bear (Shure), 68

telephone, 227

temperance movement, 162

Temple Ohabei Shalom, 23

tenements, 39, 138. *See also* housing

Tennyson, Alfred, Lord, 91

terra-cotta, 58, 70, 75–76, 78, 79, 211, 242n.4 (T10)

Thacher Street, 47

Thackeray, William Makepeace, 91, 104, 105

Thaxter, Celia, 96, 111

Thaxter, Levi, 96

Thayer (S. V. R.) House, 79

Thayer, Samuel J. F., 21, 177

Theater District, 207

"thinking centre," Boston as, xxvii, xxxiv–xxxv, 125

Third Baptist Church, 126, 135

Thompson, Benjamin, 176

Thompson, Helen, 106

Thompson-Sawyer House, 176

Thompson Sq. (Charlestown), 172

Thompson, Timothy, Sr., 176

Thoreau, Henry David, 90, 91, 94, 96, 118, 146

Thorp, Annie Longfellow, 223

Thorp, Joseph, 229

Thurber, James, 237n.11

Thurman, Sue Bailey, xxxv, 131

Ticknor and Fields, 88, 91, 115, 116, 117

Ticknor, Anna Eliot, 97–98

Ticknor, George, 96–97, 237n.6, 243n.7

Ticknor, William D., 117

women's education, 27, 38, 97–98, 150, 217
Women's Educational and Industrial Union, 165
Women's Era, 126
Women's Era Club, 163–64
Women's Home Missionary Society, 37
Women's International League, 107, 158
Women's Jail, 155
women's organizations, 163–64
women's rights, 145, 152, 157, 163
Women's Rights Convention (1848), 163
Wood and Coal Company, 188
Woodville, Richard Caton, 6
Worcester, Joseph, 223–24, 225
Worcester Sq., 27
Worcester's Pond (Cambridge), 223
workers' housing, 199. *See also* housing
World Religions (Sargent), 73

World Trade Center, 15
World War I, xxviii, 158
World War II, 158, 172

Yearbook of American Poetry, 237n.8
Young, Ammi Burnham, 10
Young, Victor, 36

Zaboglio, Francesco, 42
Zakrzewska, Marie, 150, 152
Zion German Lutheran Church, 22